FACING WEST

FACING WEST

Americans and the
Opening of the Pacific

JOHN CURTIS PERRY

PRAEGER

Westport, Connecticut
London

Library of Congress Cataloging-in-Publication Data

Perry, John Curtis.
    Facing West : Americans and the opening of the Pacific / John
Curtis Perry.
        p. cm.
    Includes bibliographical references and index.
        ISBN 0–275–94920–6 (alk. paper).—ISBN 0–275–94965–6 (pbk. :
alk. paper)
        1. United States—Commerce—Pacific Area—History.   2. Pacific
Area—Commerce—United States—History.   3. Merchant marine—United
States—History.   4. United States—Foreign economic relations—
Pacific Area.   5. Pacific Area—Foreign economic relations—United
States.   I. Title.
    HF3043.P48   1994
    382'.097309—dc20   94–11302

British Library Cataloguing in Publication Data is available.

Library of Congress Catalog Card Number: 94–11302
ISBN: 0–275–94920–6
        0-275-94965-6 (pbk.)

First published in 1994

Praeger Publishers, 88 Post Road West, Westport, Connecticut 06881
An imprint of Greenwood Publishing Group, Inc.

Printed in the United States of America

∞™

The paper used in this book complies with the
Permanent Paper Standard issued by the National
Information Standards Organization (Z39.48–1984).

10 9 8 7 6 5 4 3 2 1

In Memoriam
R.G.A.
E.O.R.
C.Y.

Facing West from California's shores,
Inquiring, tireless, seeking what is yet unfound,
I, a child, very old, over waves, towards the house of maternity,
    the land of migrations, look afar,
Look off the shores of my Western sea, the circle almost circled;
For starting westward from Hindustan, from the vales of
    Kashmere,
From Asia, from the north, from the God, the sage, and the hero,
From the south, from the flowery peninsulas and the spice islands,
Long having wander'd since, round the earth having wander'd,
Now I face home again, very pleas'd and joyous,
(But where is what I started for so long ago?
And why is it yet unfound?)

Walt Whitman
Facing West from California's Shores
(1891–92)

Contents

Part IV   Girdling the Earth, 1869–1914

Part V   Conquering the Skies, 1914–1941

Part VI   War, the North Pacific, and "The New American Frontier," 1941–1945

Part VII   America, the New Global Hub?

Illustrations

Acknowledgments

Many people helped me with this book. I thank the following Fletcher students (and others) for their talent and enthusiasm for digging out often-obscure materials, photocopying, and other research chores: Allison Avery, Lisbeth Bernstein, Mark Davidson, John Doyle, Paul Eckert, Augusta Pipkin Heywood, Jeon Jae Ook, Charles Lee, Rob McKeon, John Moran, Theresa Moran, Lyman Perry, Jan Presser, Amy Rauenhorst, Frances Seeds, Nicholas Stevens, Richard Wilbur, Rob Williams, and Zhao Xin. To Deborah Chaba, I owe special thanks for resourcefulness, zest, and persistence applied to the tedious task of checking notes. For advice and assistance of various kinds, I am most grateful to Paul Brooks, Malcolm Wilde Browne, Liwa Chiu, Kathleen Clair, Terrence Cole, James Cox, Mark Dawson, R. E. G. Davies, Hollis S. French, David R. Godine, Masato Kimura, Jill Kneerim, Elizabeth Perry, Mark A. Stroup, Keiko Thayer, Pamela Trippe, Rhonda Vitanye, and Peter Booth Wiley. Sally B. Cutler took her sharp pencil to my punctuation; Henry P. Coolidge read and commented on an early draft of the manuscript, as did other friends whose wisdom I plundered: John P. Roche, John J. Stephan, James C. Thomson, Jr., and Kevin Starr. I am uncommonly grateful to my neighbor David Herbert Donald for his close, critical, and yet encouraging reading of the entire manuscript in an earlier version. Sarah Hollis Perry, my beloved wife, sacrificed much of a vacation to a ruthlessly honest reading of the work. All of the above people have made this book better than it otherwise would have been.

Here also I express my gratitude to the late Chang Hi Lee, corporate statesman of the new Korea, and to the Japan Economic Foundation for financial support of the lengthy research and writing process that this book required.

None of the above bears any responsibility for deficiencies in the final product, unseen by them.

Preface

In the North Pacific today, the world's most populous nation, the world's largest nation, the world's leading manufacturer, and the world's greatest military power meet. China, Russia, Japan, and the United States face one another across the North Pacific. Their individual and collective global importance is unquestionable; the region where they meet thus forms a fulcrum, a crucial balance point of international interaction.

Now, as the twentieth century ends, a North Pacific center of wealth and power has emerged, generated by manufacturing and nourished by commerce. In the late 1970s, trade flowing across the Pacific began to exceed the trade across the Atlantic; the margin is now ballooning. The North Atlantic, former global center, recedes in importance as statistics reveal the greatest and most sudden shift in the geographical distribution of industrial production and wealth in world history.

Although the British journal *Economist* (July 21, 1984, p. 13) noted that "pundits have been forecasting the dawn of the Pacific age for so long that most people have turned over and gone back to sleep," even Europeans have begun to wake to the region's new importance. Americans have done more than any other people to link the North Pacific region together—diplomatically, technologically, and commercially. Americans were the first to anticipate a Pacific era in world affairs.

Philosopher George Berkeley, with his popular verses on "westward the course of empire," first pushed American thinking in the direction of the Pacific by suggesting a natural progression of history that had carried the core of world culture from the Mediterranean to North Europe. He predicted that this progression would ultimately take cultural centrality across the Atlantic to America. Americans like John Quincy Adams enthusiastically endorsed the Berkeleian idea that the United

States would embody the "noblest empire of time" and saw the nation as eventually extending to the Pacific.

American interest and ambition did not stop at the shoreline, however. Both commercially and culturally, the Pacific loomed as a huge new maritime world lying beyond the new continent, seeming to promise opportunities for Americans not to be had in the European-dominated Atlantic. Whales and the China trade provided powerful early inducements for Americans to sail the Great Ocean. The Pacific, Herman Melville's "tide-beating heart of the earth," summoned forth the adventurous American spirit because it offered both an intrinsic source of wealth and a way to acquire it and because it provided a huge hunting ground and promised a pathway to the coveted commerce of Asia, a strategic key to the legendary wealth of the Orient.

Some Americans (and people in other lands) perceived the Pacific as a frontier. This was more metaphor than reality. The true frontier was to be found not at sea but on its shores, along the oceanic rimlands encompassing both the North American Pacific and the North Asian Pacific, the latter beckoning to Americans as a new and promising "Far West" that embraced the maritime fringes of China, Japan, Korea, and Siberia. The outward movement of Americans is part of an even larger theme in world history, the expansion of Europe, that included both the maritime push of Western Europe and the continental thrust of Russia. All of these forces—American, European, and Russian—would meet uneasily in the North Pacific, provoking tumult and encouraging change throughout the region.

On the Asian side of the North Pacific, scarcely more than 150 years ago, a ring of new coastal cities arose that were prodded into life by foreign diplomats and foreign merchants, sojourners from the North Atlantic world who were joined by local entrepreneurs eager to take part in new international commercial networks. These seaports and entrepôts were distinguished for their economic vitality and cosmopolitan flavor; among them, to mention only a few, were Yokohama, Tianjin (Tientsin), and, largest of all, Shanghai.

The rising Asian Pacific urban centers complemented equally new cities of the American Pacific, like San Francisco, Seattle, and Vancouver, which, with their Chinatowns, offered their own international cultural exoticism. All of these new cities, nourished by oceanic traffic, functioned as both instruments for cultural segregation and places for the playing out of intramural cultural contentions, in what historian David J. Weber (*The Spanish Frontier in North America*, p. 13) defines as varying processes of accommodation, assimilation, synthesis, or resistance.

The ocean, even in warfare, does not provide an environment for this kind of richly textured human encounter. Maritime space does not function like the continental space that Frederick Jackson Turner talked about so eloquently in his argument for the importance of the frontier in American history. For humankind much of the ocean remains a watery desert broken only by the wake of an occasional ship rippling the surface or the contrail of a solitary airplane dappling the sky above.

Gradually the Pacific yielded its vastness to the will and abilities of those who wanted to create pathways across it for the movement of people, goods, and ideas. The prime oceanic trade routes stretch across the North Pacific; they form the setting for this book. American entrepreneurs were paramount among these builders, and this book is their story. These imaginative and intrepid individuals were the first to bind together for commercial purposes all four great nations of the North Pacific: China, Russia, Japan, and the United States. The American successes show what individual initiative, talent, and audacity can do. American activity was largely private, not governmental; individual, not collective; and sporadic, not systematic.

In this book I am therefore concerned with people, not policy. The United States had no policy for bridging the Pacific. The events sprawl untidily across the following pages, seeming to unfold almost at random. Yet a great dream did prod and shape them from behind, and this dream gives coherence and continuity to the narrative.

Individual Americans were drawn to cross the North Pacific, the shortest route to Asia, because of a powerful and persisting perception that fused myth with reality; they had an image of the wealth of Asia, of "the Orient," a place that came increasingly to be identified with China. As the nineteenth century wore on, Americans increasingly despised the condition of China, but, paradoxically, they were, at least in a commercial sense, prepared to accept the Chinese myth that China, the Middle Kingdom, formed the center of the world. Americans believed that to command the trade of the Orient, potentially the world's most lucrative commerce, would be to capture global economic primacy. In the oceanic world the United States lay between Asia and Europe, and Americans hoped to exploit this geography of position to that purpose. The dream would have the United States emerge as the world's vital center.

Other nations wanted their own commercial networks, however. Rivalries, at various times with the Russians, the British, and ultimately the Japanese, gave a sharp adversarial edge to the American thrust across the Pacific. Japan, America's chief current commercial rival, differs from the historical experience of the Iberian powers, Holland, France, Britain, or Russia because Japanese strategic aspirations have always been regional, not global. Japan has not, except during the years leading up to and including World War II, sought to command the intercontinental trade routes; it prefers only to use them to its best commercial advantage.

The American effort is only part of a larger international competition over the past five centuries to link the continents and dominate the trade routes. The two capes, the African Good Hope and South American Horn; the Arctic sea passages, northwest and northeast, American and Asian; the two canals, Suez and Panama; and the three transcontinental railroad systems, the Eurasian and the two North American—they were all part of an intensely competitive, dynamic, evolutionary commercial and strategic process that continues today.

The goal of each contending nation has been to achieve the position of global hub of communications and transport and thus to make itself the commercial center of the world. Throughout most of the contest, Great Britain and the United States were chief competitors and successive claimants to the victor's crown. Throughout the struggle, Americans sought to use the North Pacific as their means to win.

Few people have seen this great global commercial and strategic struggle holistically or written about it comprehensively. This book looks directly only at the American experience but puts it within a context of that whole.

Dreamers as well as doers, some famous, some obscure, contributed to the chronicle of the American reach for the Orient. The Pacific excited the American imagination, inspiring novelists and poets to dream of what this new world might offer to Americans. The builders of systems of transport were businessmen and wanted to make money, but personal power and pride of nation often seemed as important to them as financial profit. Trade, which many Americans saw as a potential unifier of the world, was of more than a commercial or strategic concern to them; they invested it also with moral worth. Material success connoted moral superiority, to which everyone should aspire.

Pioneering American transport entrepreneurs repeatedly put old technologies to stunning new uses across the North Pacific, where the routes to Asia were shortest, establishing new tempos and opening new dimensions for travel. The clipper ship, the paddle-wheel steamer, and the seaplane all found startling success in the Pacific at a time when such modes of transport were giving way elsewhere to newer ones. The means of transport proved of more than intrinsic importance; ships and planes were often interpreted as symbols of American courage, American power, and American ingenuity.

Builders shared with dreamers an expansive confidence in the superiority of the United States, as well as a fierce optimism about the future global role, however vaguely defined, that American civilization was destined to play. In a Pacific era that would be inevitably dominated by the United States, a dominion to which their energies and their abilities would largely contribute, dreamers and builders alike saw a world subscribing enthusiastically to superior American values of freedom, democracy, Christianity, and industrial progress.

Harsh realities accompanied these high ideals. The history of the American push across the Pacific is also one of exploitation: a savage despoiling of the environment and a brutal treatment of the powerless, be it the indigenous Aleut or the immigrant Chinese. Racism injected violence into American behavior toward other peoples and other cultures. Asia was not immune to its own racism. And Asian nationalisms fought the imposition of American values when Asia, beginning with Japan, began to shake off its long passivity.

Thus the American reach for the Orient becomes part of a far greater drama, the reemergence of East Asia into world prominence. Americans must ask what place this macrohistorical event will leave for us in a new North Pacific world, one we did so much to help create yet is now so characterized by an increasingly active and rich East Asia.

The story begins long ago, even before the birth of the thirteen colonies, with humanity's first recorded struggles to cope with the terrifying immensities of the world's largest ocean.

FACING WEST

PART ONE

THE CRUEL PACIFIC: A PROLOGUE

CHAPTER ONE

Opening the Great Ocean

By protracting every voyage, the vast reaches of the Pacific placed extraordinary demands on human endurance. The Pacific formed the greatest and most persisting blank on the global map. Its cruel size—twice that of the Atlantic, one-third the globe's surface, nearly 10 percent more than the earth's entire surface land mass—was daunting. Its remoteness from Europe, home to the early global oceanic explorers, discouraged even the bravest of navigators. Yet for these people of the Atlantic world, the Pacific exercised the magnetic power of a great frontier, a place of enormous unknown possibilities, perhaps even an El Dorado and a source of fabulous riches.

Vasco de Balboa, not the "discoverer of the Pacific" but the first European to see the great ocean from the American side, in 1513 named it the "South Sea" and, wading into its waters, claimed it all for his royal master, the king of Spain. Europeans from at least the time of Marco Polo in the thirteenth century had known the Asian fringes of the great ocean. Seven years after Balboa, Ferdinand Magellan, a Portuguese commander in Spanish employ, opened a southwest passage from Europe to Asia. Working his way down toward the unknown tip of South America, Magellan sighted the straits that now bear his name. After a thirty-eight-day struggle with tidal rips, reefs, and furious winds, he found himself in such tranquil, wide-open waters that he named them the "Pacific."

Magellan's is the first recorded trans-Pacific crossing, and one of his ships was the first to sail around the world, although Magellan himself died in the Philippines. Far to the north, the indigenous people moved easily and frequently across the narrow seas separating Asia from America. The rest of the world would not know about this for a long time.

Both names, *Pacific* and *South Sea*, Magellan's and Balboa's, retained currency for four hundred years. Not only were the names of the ocean

European, but so too was the very concept. The Pacific had hitherto been known and thought of only in parts, not as a whole.[1]

From the Atlantic to the Pacific, from one end of Eurasia to the other, segmented trade or trade by region had flourished at least since the dawn of the Christian era, conducted by local merchants working through intermediaries.[2] Some of the trade was overland; more of it went by sea. Camel caravans could compete successfully with shipping in the carriage of luxury goods between China and West Asia, but land traffic was more vulnerable to unfriendly interference, and water provided the only economical medium for carrying items that were heavy or fragile. Bulk trade tended to be local; only luxury goods could be economically transported great distances.

The Mediterranean, the Indian Ocean, and the China Sea, each with its coastal fringes, formed its own independent maritime world, interacting only with immediate neighbors. On the eve of the Columbian era and Europe's first great wave of expansion, China was the world's most advanced nation in wealth, domestic commerce, urban life, technology, and statecraft. China at its peak achieved a superb maritime technology. Its capacious multimasted vessels with their watertight compartments, sternpost rudders, and magnetic compasses were technologically without rival. But the technology was not linked to any persisting sense of adventure. Had the Chinese wished to do so, they could have gone to Europe long before Europe came to them.

Along the Asian rim of the Pacific, especially the China coast south of the Yangzi River (Chang Jiang), merchants had long vigorously pursued commerce, but by and large their ships cautiously hugged the shore, and their captains never willingly ventured out into the uncharted oceanic space of the Pacific. Luzon in the Philippines, to the east, was about as far as they went. And, secure in their sense of self-sufficiency, the Chinese were satisfied to allow Arab, Persian, and Indian merchants to carry on much of their foreign trade.

Circumstance reinforced attitudes. Prevailing winds and currents flow toward the Asian mainland, making egress difficult, whereas the monsoon in its predictable north-south seasonal rhythm encouraged maritime China to look to the south along the coast toward Southeast Asia and not to the east and open sea.

Island Japan looked west to China and the continent, not east into the unknown ocean. East Asians may have been blown inadvertently out into the Pacific from time to time but did not choose to explore it.

The Polynesians were skillful and courageous long-distance Pacific sailors, but they failed to link themselves to any other maritime world. Their own oceanic sphere remained isolated and unknown intercontinentally until the Europeans came.

Portugal's brilliant late-fifteenth-century discovery of the global wind system enabled its intrepid sailors to stitch together the hitherto separate regional maritime worlds into a new, integrated, global whole. The Portuguese began by mastering the art of sailing in the North Atlantic, one of the world's roughest and most challenging seas. They made the oceans of the world one medium, and one increasingly dominated by Europeans. Well satisfied with the Indian Ocean route to South and Southeast Asia and its lucrative spice trade that was their chief objective, the Portuguese left the wide Pacific to their Iberian rivals.

The Spaniards, seizing leadership in their early exploration, boasted that the Pacific was a "Spanish Lake." At least for its southern portions, they were correct. Much of the north, though, remained completely unknown. Local peoples knew parts; no one knew the whole. Across the "lake," Spaniards laid down the first trans-Pacific transportation route, tying Europe via Mexico and the New World to the Philippine archipelago and beyond. China was the real goal, and Manila Bay, facing the Asian mainland, already formed a commercial and cultural crossroads, offering access to south China ports. Thus America, South and Central, formed a key link between Asia and Europe. North Americans would ultimately dream of dominating this tricontinental route.

Seeking silk, not spices, the Spaniards hoped to use the Philippines as a base from which they could even conquer China, toppling that great state, as they had the empires of the Incas and the Aztecs, with a handful of men but ample resolve and abundant confidence that God would bless such a noble undertaking. The problem of enduring great distance, however, remained acute.

All these sailors faced the problem of how to preserve food for an extended trip. On any voyage, the diet tended to deteriorate progressively and could be improved only by stopovers to enable the revictualing of perishables. Scurvy, a loathsome and particularly painful disease, posed the chief threat. Its causes and its cure long baffled everyone. Sailors knew only that if they stayed too long at sea, they were certain to fall victim to it.

"This disease," writes the Reverend Richard Walter, an early long-distance maritime traveler,

so particularly destructive to us, is surely the most singular and unaccountable of any that affects the human body. For its symptoms are inconstant and innumerable, and its progress and effects extremely irregular, . . . yet there are some symptoms which are more general than the rest. . . . [Their] common appearances are large discoloured spots, dispersed upon the whole surface of the body, swelled legs, putrid gums, and above all, an extraordinary lassitude of the whole body, especially after any exercise, however inconsiderable; and this lassitude at last degenerates into a proneness to swoon, and even die, on the least exertion of strength, or even on the least motion.

This disease is likewise attended with a strange dejection of the spirits, and with shiverings, tremblings, and a disposition to be seized with the most dreadful terrors on the slightest accident.

But it is not easy to compleat the long roll of the various concomitants of this disease; for it often produced putrid fevers, pleurisies, the jaundice, and violent rheumatick pains, and sometimes it occasioned an obstinative costiveness, which was generally attended with a difficulty of breathing; and this was esteemed the most deadly of all the scorbutick symptoms: At other times the whole body, but more especially the legs, were subject to ulcers of the worst kind, attended with rotten bones, and such a luxuriancy of fungus flesh, as yielded no remedy. But a most extraordinary circumstance, and what would be scarcely credible upon any single evidence, is, that the scars of wounds which had been for many years healed, were forced open again by this virulent distemper.[3]

The Reverend Mr. Walter knew what he was talking about, for he had served as chaplain aboard the flagship *Centurion* during Commodore George Anson's circumnavigation (1740–44). On this expedition more than half the seamen who left England died during the voyage, most of them from scurvy; of the six warships in the squadron *Centurion* was the sole survivor.[4]

Scurvy was only one of the punishments exacted by vitamin deficiencies in the sailor's diet. Nowhere was he more vulnerable than in traversing the Pacific. The Spanish galleon route between Acapulco and Manila especially challenged its users because it was so long and provided no stopovers. The Spaniards had Guam, in the Marianas, but that island was too close to Asia to break the trip effectively, and apparently they never found Hawaii, the Polynesian paradise. Thus, they missed the chance to establish a strategic mid-Pacific base, affording food and refreshment to weary and ill trans-Pacific voyagers.

Glistening with salt crystals, dark as mahogany, shrunken, and so hard as to be almost impossible to chew, the staple meat, beef or pork, might better have been given over to the hand of a "magician than a cook to make it edible," one traveler complained.[5] And rough weather often kept the ship's ovens unlit and the passengers restricted to cold food and drink. Oddly enough, sailors seldom seemed to fish. Instead, when the supply of salt meat ran low, they resorted to the ubiquitous rat. The rat population of a ship might be as much as five times the human population.[6]

Rat feces and rat fleas bred disease; paradoxically, the eating of rat flesh helped prevent it.[7] Skinned, grilled rat was probably not as unappetizing in the consumption as in the anticipation. The shipboard rat, after all, fattened on a diet of biscuit crumbs and, if fortunate, bits of cheese. The rat is a synthesizer of vitamin C; its flesh, if not overly cooked, serves as an antiscorbutic and was probably healthier to eat than the planned menu. At least it was fresh.

Drinking water was stored in wooden casks, and would begin to breed a rich biological life of its own after several months. Sailors preferred wine, beer, or rum, seeking consolation in quantities consumed. Ship's biscuit provided the staple food, baked in advance of the trip. With its coarse whole-wheat flour, biscuit was high in fiber and calories. It served as a good filler. Yet it too failed to age gracefully, becoming musty, sour, and weevily. "Walking" biscuits were best eaten after dark when they could not be seen. But the smell as well as the sight could be distressing. Pigafetta, Magellan's chronicler, says, "We ate old biscuit turned into a powder, swarming with worms and stinking with the urine of rats."[8] Patagonian wild celery that was harvested en route, its vitamins staving off scurvy, probably saved Magellan's expedition from extinction.

Poor nutrition wracks brain as well as body. Vitamin B deficiency exacts severe neurological consequences. Loss of the ability to concentrate, night blindness, faulty judgment, and propensity to irrational anger due to lack of adequate diet were surely a cause of some of the tragic losses wrought by the sea.[9]

For a quarter of a millennium (1565–1815), until Mexico established its independence, one or two Spanish ships sailed every year from Manila to Acapulco and back again in the world's longest continuous voyage.[10] At first these ships were small; ultimately they were huge galleons, round-stemmed, ungainly but commodious and castle-like, their broadness of beam balancing their towering top-heavy poops and forecastles. Spanish government fiat cramped commerce by imposing many restrictions: the tonnage of ships, their number (ultimately only one a year), the value of the cargo, and the ports the ships could use.

Seville silk merchants lobbied for restrictions, fearing Chinese competition, and no one liked the idea of silver leaving the country. The rules were often breached, but their very existence was inhibiting and consequential. The Philippines were less Hispanicized than they would have been had lines of communication with Spanish America been shorter and stronger. And if the Spaniards had permitted themselves to develop a stopover, a haven and place to trade in Alta California, that province would have been bound more tightly to Mexico, less likely to gain ultimate independence.[11]

The eastward and westward tracks of the galleons, dictated by the pattern of the winds, were separated north and south by more than twenty degrees of latitude. Thanks to the tradewinds, Acapulco to Manila proved an easy run of eight to ten weeks, but the eastward passage was a different story.

Departing Manila and heading northeast, up off Japan, sailing into the great arc of the North Pacific, the galleon could catch the prevailing westerlies blowing above latitude thirty, which could propel her eastward, running free, all canvas filled, to the California coast and down to Mexico. But to gain this path, the ship had to navigate the perils of San Bernardino Straits and the eastern shores of Luzon with their fearsome shoals, erratic currents, and heavy swells. Sudden squalls and typhoons could severely damage or even destroy the ship, but even delay carried terrible consequences to all aboard; hunger and thirst, disease and death. Calms could be as vexatious and dangerous as storms. Over the 250 years of the "Manila galleon," thousands of lives and countless treasure were lost and much suffering incurred in this journey across the Pacific.

The Spaniards built these galleons in Manila, on European design smartly turned out in teak by accomplished Chinese carpenters.[12] But poor maintenance and incompetent seamanship made the ships vulnerable to disaster. They carried too many people and too much freight, particularly heading east, heavy with the luxury goods of China. Aboard rode priests and padres, soldiers and civil officials, traveling to and from the Philippines. The great ship furnished a major means for moving information as well as people, since long-distance communications were still coincident with transport. The capital may have controlled the colony, but distance diluted authority; news and orders traveled at an *adagio* tempo. Three years were required for an exchange of information between Madrid and Manila conveyed via Mexico.

Passengers riding the galleons complained that they were virtual prisoners aboard, confined to close quarters, enduring stupefying inactivity, and experiencing oppressive boredom. Cockfights, theatricals, and gambling helped pass the time. Passenger baggage was limited to "two leather-covered chests or trunks, three and a half feet long, seventeen inches wide and fifteen inches deep, a mattress, a pair of bottle-cases for wine, writing materials, and ten China jars, in which to carry chocolate, caramels, sweets, biscuits, or anything else, so long as they may be kept underneath the bed."[13] The stringency of these regulations was perhaps somewhat eased by the fact that each passenger was allowed to bring along two personal servants.

The voyage usually lasted some five months, but it could be protracted to seven, with starvation rations and scurvy looming grimly and inevitably at the end. A passenger wrote, "The voyge [sic] from the *Phillipine* [sic] islands to *America* may be call'd the longest, and most dreadful of any in the world . . . enough to destroy a man of steel, much more flesh and blood."[14] One of the galleons remained at sea so long that she lost her entire crew to disease; eventually she was spotted drifting silently down the coast south of Acapulco, bearing a cargo of silk and a company of corpses.

Neither the ships, nor the routes, nor the duration of the trip changed much over the centuries of the Manila galleon. In maritime matters, the era was not one of rapid technological change, and the Spaniards participating were not innovators. They were engaged in the business of trade, not the adventure of exploration. Orders forbade captains taking any unnecessary deviation from the appointed routes.

Eastward the galleons bore silks, fine cottons, heavily embroidered vestments, and richly worked tapestries, as well as exotic bibelots and bric-a-brac of Chinese manufacture. Persian carpets perhaps, or spices and aromatics, filled out the cargo, although Spanish hope of diverting the global flow of spices—pepper, cinnamon, mace—from the Indian Ocean and Portuguese hands to the Pacific and their own came to nothing. To the Philippines, the Spaniards brought Peruvian silver, cacao, wines, and oil, for local sale and reexport. We cannot be certain, but this was a likely route for the first entry of New World crops—the sweet potato, the Irish potato, maize, and the peanut—to China, thereby enormously increasing food production and population there.[15] Ultimately the peanut may have been more important to China than any quantity of silver.

Long before the Spaniards came across the Pacific, Chinese junks had frequented Philippine harbors, and Chinese merchants remained essential to the commercial life of the islands. Japanese also traded there, and some of their goods passed into Spanish hands. Manila was terminus for the galleons but just a way station for the China traffic in which the Spaniards served as mere intermediaries, taking advantage of preexisting patterns established by the Chinese that linked China to the Philippines and hence to Europe in a new way. After winning their independence, the Latin Americans would not follow this Spanish trade pattern. Latin America exhibited no independent interest in China, and China showed no interest in Latin America.

At its core, the Spanish trans-Pacific trade was silk for silver. These two items were by far the most important in the inventory.[16] In America, silver was plentiful and cheap. The Spanish dollar, coined in Mexico, became a standard medium of exchange throughout the international commercial world of the Pacific well into the nineteenth century. And perhaps one-third of the silver mined in the New World ended up in the hands of the Chinese, who displayed a voracious appetite for it.[17]

Spain's monopoly of this lucrative trans-Pacific trade, its access to the fabled wealth of Asia, and its obsessive secretiveness inflamed the imagination, excited the jealousy, and provoked the fury of its rivals. When Christopher Marlowe reminded his Elizabethan audiences that "the trade of Asia is the foundation of commerce," he was merely echoing a European belief held since the time of the Romans and encouraging his countrymen to exploit the opportunity presented.[18]

Francis Drake, the first Englishman to venture into the Pacific and the first commander to complete a global circumnavigation (1577–80), came looking for Spanish treasure and found it. The crown's share alone of the booty he seized was enough to liquidate Queen Elizabeth's foreign debt.[19] Drake visited California, naming it "New Albion," but he did not find the Northwest Passage he wanted, that northern oceanic shortcut to Asia for which Englishmen had been searching on the Atlantic side since John Cabot began the hunt in 1497.

The trans-Pacific world at its widest reach remained only partially known for a long time; its only voyagers were the Spaniards, crisscrossing in familiar thin and lonely tracks. They were interested in the Pacific, it seems, simply as a pathway, as a route between New Spain in America and its far western extension, the Philippines, and to China beyond. The galleon traffic in the long run amounted to very little. It failed to grow because of the prejudice of the Spanish government against trade, manufacturing, capitalism, and a market economy. These attitudes were probably far more damaging to the continuing health of the Spanish empire than was political or military overstretch.

The other great European maritime powers—by the eighteenth century, principally Britain and France—continued to engage in consuming struggles and fierce rivalries elsewhere, and the human costs of navigating the Pacific inhibited them. Disease exercised an even greater menace to survival than the terrors of the sea or the threat of the enemy. But Russian energies, long entirely continental, or perhaps we should say riverine, began to spill over into the far North Pacific in the early 1700s.

A century before, the Russians had begun to move across the great Siberian land mass, leaping from one river system to the next, with periodic forays north to the shores of the Arctic. In 1648 an illiterate cossack named Semen Ivanovich Dezhnev sailing from the Arctic reached the mouth of the Anadyr River flowing into the Pacific. Dezhnev's report, written by a subordinate, mouldered, forgotten in the provincial archives, and so Vitus Bering, a Dane, one of many foreigners then in tsarist employ, could rediscover the straits separating Asia from America where Dezhnev had aleady sailed.[20] Bering is immortalized by the well-known straits; Dezhnev gets only an obscure cape.

Bering landed on the coast of Alaska and became the first European to encounter the native peoples of the region. Subsequently shipwrecked on one of the Komandorskie islands off Kamchatka, he died probably of hypothermia or gangrene, brought on by hunger, thirst, and despair. But his men brought back news of his geographical discoveries and of an abundance there of "soft gold"—furs of sea mammals like the otter and the seal, as well as plentiful skins of the familiar fox, beaver, and ermine. Desire for furs propelled the Russians to further discovery as they moved down across the great tusk of the Aleutian Islands onto the coasts of the Alaskan mainland.

At Kodiak Island, in 1784, under the leadership of Grigorii Shelikhov, the Russians established their first permanent North American settlement, a base for the introduction of Russian civilization—its writing, religion, architecture, and cuisine—into the New World. Shelikhov dreamed of towns, not trading posts, of a vast Russian state in North America, with cities and cathedrals, a thriving commerce, and a prosperous manufacture. He saw Russian America as a potential world economic center, with the North Pacific serving as connective tissue with the mother country.[21]

Spain still claimed the entire American Pacific coast. Nonetheless, the Spanish empire was centered far to the south, and its expansive energies worldwide were atrophying by the late 1700s. Spain explored the Pacific littoral widely but not in any sustained or systematic fashion. Nor did the Spaniards choose readily to share what knowledge they gained. The heroic glory of their discoveries all too often remained unknown, knowledge confined to the dust of the archives.

To the other powers, therefore, Spanish territorial claims often appeared bizarre and irrational. Even at its peak, the Spanish presence north of San Francisco Bay, although solidified on that particular shore in 1776, never amounted to much. Spanish interest in North Pacific America was defensive; Spain wanted a buffer, not a zone for expansion. Mexico did not have a surplus population, and its people had no incentive to move to a cold north. Furs, fish, and timber did not lure Spanish sojourners. Potential seaports—the future sites of Seattle, Victoria, and Vancouver—were left nameless and unpopulated.

St. Petersburg, as would Washington and London, saw the virtues and the possibilities of this area; Madrid and Mexico City did not. Spain lost out in the North Pacific by default, ultimately to the greater benefit of the United States than anyone else.[22] "In the end," writes Henry Adams, "far more than half the territory of the United States was the spoil of Spanish empire, rarely acquired with perfect propriety. To sum up the story in a single word, Spain had immense influence over the United States; but it was the influence of the whale over its captors,—the charm of a huge, helpless, and profitable victim."[23]

For Great Britain, the Pacific seemed to provide two promising possibilities: one was to tap rich as-yet-unfound lands, perhaps even an unknown continent. The *Terra Australis Incognita* was an ancient and persisting European geographical fantasy, perceived as a possible global counterweight to the Northern Hemisphere, a continent so large as to be necessarily rich in precious metals. Mastery of its commerce would yield a glittering prize in the European global rivalry for wealth and power.[24]

Opening a new avenue of transport between Europe and Asia, perhaps the northwest passage across America, seemed to offer a second potential opportunity in the Pacific whereby Englishmen could break the monopoly enjoyed for so long by the Manila galleon and build a grand oceanic strategy for dominating world trade.

The British already knew three global maritime routes to Asia. Two meant traveling far to the south, either east or west, and rounding Africa or America at either of the two continental capes, Good Hope or the Horn. Both were long distances, remote from the center of British power; both were vulnerable to attack en route. A third way was the shortest, traversing the narrow waist of the Americas, which linked by land the central and western Pacific with the Caribbean and Atlantic. But this route lay firmly in Spanish hands, and the Spaniards were already exploiting it via Panama and Mexico.

The awkwardness of the transshipment required to get goods across land imposed a real problem. The galleon trade worked smoothly for silk and silver because both, having exceptionally high value for their weight, could be economically carried on muleback across Mexico or Panama. But more cumbersome commodities like furniture, or fragile ones like porcelain, could not be so easily handled. Bulk goods demanded all-water routes.

In order to investigate the possibilities of new intercontinental oceanic seaways, as well as to advance human knowledge in general, Captain James Cook, Britain's greatest maritime explorer, was dispatched on a series of three Pacific voyages, beginning in 1768, that would form the climax of European Pacific discovery and make possible the American Pacific experience.

CHAPTER TWO

Captain Cook and the American Corporal, John Ledyard

James Cook, a Yorkshire farm laborer's son, chose the sea over the land; he began as a simple seaman and ended a world-renowned scientist. The range of his interests constantly grew, including seamanship and navigation, mapmaking, and astronomy; in the course of his experience, he taught himself. Cook and his associates became anthropologists and ethnographers, collecting voluminous amounts of information and vast stores of material objects, writing and sketching, and compiling a huge inventory of materials for later rumination and analysis by the international scientific community.

By his first two expeditions, Cook settled once and for all the question of the supposed great habitable southern continent. Magellan had discovered the enormous width of the Pacific. Cook surveyed its breadth, sailing from the coasts of Antarctica to the edge of the Arctic Ocean, farther to the south and farther to the north than any man before him—at least who lived to tell of it. In the process of these prodigious discoveries, Cook demonstrated that a number of men could live years at sea and survive. Cook is important to this story because he removed some of the terror of trans-Pacific travel.[1]

Samuel Pepys remarks that "Englishmen and more especially seamen, love their bellies above everything else."[2] Cook seems to have taken the adage to heart. He was consistently anxious that his men be well nourished and healthy, and he was fully prepared to force them to eat what he thought best.[3] In the fleet Cook was notorious for his insistence on fresh foods, no matter how exotic, or distasteful to the conservative palate of the seaman, be it walrus, penguin, "or the haunch of a Tahitian dog baked in the island way."[4] Cook himself admits that "few men have introduced into their Ships more novelties in the way of victuals and drink than I have done.[5]

The average sailor of Cook's time had lived an impoverished and un-healthy life even before going to sea. Aboard ship he was thrust into an unheated, poorly ventilated, crowded space, inadequately clad in cloth-ing that was frequently damp or wet and infrequently clean. He was exposed to all weathers, all climates, and all manner of diseases. Below deck he slept and ate in an atmosphere reeking with the stench of the bilges and unwashed bodies. Yet the sailor's life demanded mental alert-ness and physical fitness, quick response and high expenditure of energy.

Cook sought to recruit healthy men and to keep them so. His concern for their well being led him to establish a three-watch schedule instead of the conventional two. This meant that every man served four hours on duty followed by eight hours off, instead of four on and four off. His men cheered. Furthermore, like it or not, and many did grumble, Cook's men were obliged to change their clothing, air their bedding, and fu-migate their quarters regularly; they scrubbed the bulkheads with vin-egar and scoured the decks with dry sand and holystones (blocks of pumice shaped like Bibles). Cook wanted a clean ship and a dry ship.

As a young man, Cook had suffered from the horrors of scurvy. By his maturity, the disease was generally understood to be dietary. Sailors knew through experience that fresh food could prevent or cure scurvy. Cook's ideas therefore were not original. Nor were they all correct. Cook attributed freedom from scurvy to sauerkraut and malt while discount-ing the value of lemon juice.[6] But ruthless persistence made his technique peerless, and his crews remained healthy whereas those of other com-manders sickened and died.

Imposing in height yet plain in manner, Cook attracted admiring at-tention. His face was described as full of expression, his brown eyes quick and penetrating. Sir Hugh Palliser, a captain under whom Cook served, writes of him: "Cool and deliberate in judging; sagacious in de-termining; active in executing; steady and persevering in enterprising . . . unsubdued by labour difficulties, and disappointments." Here was no ordinary commander, and many of his contemporaries recognized his quality.[7]

During his third and last Pacific voyage, this noble man faltered. He seemed to have suffered a personality change, becoming increasingly morose and withdrawn and yet subject to violent, unpredictable spasms of temper. His leadership suffered from his weakening memory, poor judgment, and uncharacteristic indecisiveness at critical moments. All this may not simply be due to extreme fatigue, although Cook was an exhausted man. In retrospect, it seems likely that earlier, when in the tropics, Cook had contracted intestinal parasites that now impeded the absorption of vitamins of the B group, thiamine and niacin, into his system.[8] Cook's malaise would lead to his premature death. He would never see England again.

On this third voyage, "instead of the looming haystack of a southern continent," Cook was searching for "the slim needle of a Northwest Passage" from the Pacific side.[9] Everyone knew by now that Hudson's Bay was not a route to the west but a huge cul-de-sac; any passageway from the Atlantic to the Pacific must lie farther to the north, along the shores of the Arctic Ocean. But perhaps ingress might be easier from the Pacific than from the Atlantic.

Discovery of the route might yield rich return to a Britain more and more deeply concerned with Asia. In Cook's time, the geographical shape and the center of economic gravity of British dominion were beginning to change profoundly, shifting from the Atlantic to the Indian Ocean and the "Far East." Clive's triumph at Plassey (1757) cemented the British presence in India and created a firm base for future expansion to the east beyond. On the other side of the world, the Declaration of Independence made by the thirteen American colonies, eight days before Cook put out of Plymouth, and the overripening of the West Indies sugar-based economy were signs that any imperial future for Britain would necessarily lie outside the Atlantic and Caribbean.

Among Cook's men aboard the *Resolution* served a young American corporal of marines named John Ledyard. His presence there, his participation in the great voyage, would inspire the first American dreams of direct access to China across the North Pacific.

John Ledyard is probably better known today among the members of the Dartmouth College Canoe Club than he is anywhere else. Every spring an expedition down the Connecticut River—from Hanover, New Hampshire, to Saybrook, Connecticut—takes place in memory of a celebrated exploit of this former Dartmouth student and intrepid explorer. But canoeing down the Connecticut was only the beginning for Ledyard.

John Ledyard is the first American from the Atlantic world known to have traveled in the Pacific, to visit the Sandwich Islands (Hawaii), Russian America, and eastern Siberia.[10] Born in 1751 and growing up in Groton, Connecticut, hard by the lively seaport of New London, Ledyard was infected by the rhythm and romance of foreign trade, which provided, after all, the chief source of wealth for the American colonies, more important for Americans then than ever after. Ledyard's father died young, leaving the family in poverty. The youth tried to read for the law. But as his early biographer, Jared Sparks, put it, "neither the profound wisdom, the abstruse learning, nor the golden promises of the law, had any charms for him."[11]

John was then taken in hand by the Reverend Eleazar Wheelock, a friend of his grandfather and founder of the new Dartmouth College, located deep in the forests lining the banks of the northern reaches of the Connecticut River. There Dr. Wheelock trained future clergy to minister to the Native American, and there John Ledyard was invited to study. Thus, this youth was exposed early on to the Christian missionary movement, the impulse that began with the attempt to convert "the red man" and ultimately would form a powerful and persisting part of the American interest in Asia and the Pacific.

The young Ledyard had more than Christian piety in mind. He was possessed of a decided taste for drama and a strong sense of self-advertisement. He arrived at college in horse and sulky, no small achievement considering the state of the roads and the modesty of his purse. The back of the carriage was stuffed with bolts of cloth for cutting and sewing into costumes, and Ledyard regaled his classmates with plays that he staged, produced, and in which he starred. Jared Sparks observes, "He did not intend time should pass on heavy wings at Dartmouth."[12]

The discipline of regular class attendance, preparation, and prayer proved too much for Ledyard. One of his classmates later recalled that "as a scholar . . . [Ledyard] was respectable, tho he did not excel—He was gentlemanly and had an independent singularity in his manner, his dress, & appearance that commanded the particular notice & attention of his fellow students."[13] With the endorsement of the Reverend Dr. Wheelock, Ledyard organized a winter camping expedition so that students could learn to live like Indians. "All of us, unless it might be Ledyard [were] well satisfied not to take such another jaunt," remembered one of the participants.[14]

Soon after, Ledyard left campus, without notice, to spend an extended time traveling and living alone among the Indians whose ways he found so fascinating. As his uncle, Thomas Seymour, later recalled, the young John "acquired a tincture of the language & manners of the Natives of the forest."[15] Ledyard became more interested in learning about the Indians than in converting them; he was more shaped by them than shaper of them. Here again he stands as a paradigm of the later experience of many Americans in Pacific Asia, of missionaries in China, for example.

The last Dartmouth College saw of John Ledyard was in the spring of 1774 when, having got the help of some classmates in felling a tall pine tree, he hacked out a dugout canoe fifty feet long and three feet wide. Stocking it with dried venison, a bearskin rug, a copy of Ovid, and a Greek Testament, he blithely pushed off the riverbank bound for Hartford, 140 miles downstream through a largely unpopulated, undeveloped area.

Immediately north of Bellows Falls and certain disaster, Ledyard, hearing the rush of water ahead, put down his book just in time to propel the canoe safely to shore. Kind and helpful farmers lent him a team of oxen to make a portage around the falls. He reached Hartford safely and had the satisfaction of astonishing his Uncle Thomas and other family members by his unexpected arrival.

Not until some time later did Ledyard finally relinquish the hope of pursuing theological studies. No clergyman proved willing to endorse the untrained youth's candidacy for the ministry, nor did Ledyard want any more formal study. For lack of other employment and remembering his childhood attraction to the sea, he signed up and shipped out of New London as an able-bodied seaman, sailing to Gibraltar and on to the Barbary coast. Eventually fetching up in England, Ledyard had the good fortune to be signed on by the celebrated Cook.

In Jared Sparks's admiring judgment, Ledyard exercised "great power in recommending himself to the favor of others, whenever he chose to put it in action. His manly form, mild but animated and expressive eye, perfect self-possession, a boldness not obtrusive, but showing a consciousness of his proper dignity, an independent spirit, and a glow of enthusiasm giving life to his conversation and his whole deportment— these were traits which could not escape so discriminating eye as that of Cook."[16] If Cook did indeed personally select Ledyard, it was likely a simple matter of seeing before him a healthy and energetic young man, eager to join up. There were never too many of these, particularly for the challenges of the unknown Pacific.

Ledyard's real education would be with Cook and aboard the *Resolution* (1776–80). Sailing from Plymouth on July 12, 1776, knowing nothing yet of the momentous American Declaration of Independence (this big news took forty-four days to reach Britain),[17] Cook and company headed south around the Cape of Good Hope to New Zealand and on to the far northeast reaches of the Pacific. En route from the Society Islands to North America, Cook discovered Hawaii, which he would subsequently name for his patron, the First Lord of the Admiralty, the Earl of Sandwich, and to which he would ultimately return to a tragic and violent death on the beach at Kealakekua Bay. In his last diary entry, Cook writes of the strategic value of Hawaii, "so excellent a situation," and probably the most valuable discovery made by Europeans in the Pacific Ocean.[18]

The expedition touched North America first at Nootka Sound on the western shore of what is today known as Vancouver Island. The officers aboard the *Resolution* celebrated the event by dining on fricassee of rat.[19]

Densely forested with towering stands of spruce, hemlock, cedar, and the majestic Douglas fir growing virtually to the shoreline, hills ranging behind in series, backed by snowcapped mountains, Nootka provided not a particularly good anchorage, but it offered ample firewood and good drinking water, plus raw materials in abundance for masts and spars to refit Cook's two ships, both of which needed such attention desperately. The timber resources of this whole rain-drenched coastal region formed one of the largest forests of the world, and they would, in the end, provide the region's greatest source of wealth.

But neither the climate nor the native peoples of Pacific North America proved as benign as those Polynesia provided.[20] Mooring their ships off rocky ledges instead of sandy beaches, Cook's men went about their chores in chilly fog and drizzle instead of warm sun and balmy air. Cook kept everyone busy repairing the ships, cutting wood, drawing water, and brewing the spruce beer that no one liked very much but the captain thought healthy. Indeed it was both a good laxative and a supposed cure for gonorrhea, a common complaint of seamen.

The local people supplied the sailors with wild garlic and bracken fern, which Cook prized for its scurvy-fighting properties. But the indigenes did not grow vegetables; they lived principally off the bounty of the sea, and they lived well. Far more skillful fishermen than the British, the Indians supplied their visitors with delicious fish.

"It was the first time," Ledyard writes, "that I had been so near the shores of that continent which gave me birth from the time I at first left it; and though more than two thousand miles distant from the nearest part of New-England I felt myself plainly affected." To his pleasure, the natives he met there were "the same kind of people that inhabit the opposite side of the continent," those with whom he had got acquainted earlier in the forests around Hanover.[21]

Cook and his men only dimly perceived the range of the material culture enjoyed by these North Pacific peoples—their tools, weapons, boats, and clothing—failing to grasp any of the power and subtlety of their spiritual culture. Because the natives did not practice agriculture or build towns, they were readily dismissed as "savages."

Cook found people at Nootka more desirous of iron than of anything else, but metal of any kind would do. They "came on board the Ships and mixed with our people with the greatest freedom" and stole anything iron they could; "they would cut a hook from a tackle or any other piece of iron from a rope, the instant our backs was turned." They stripped the small boats clean; "one fellow would amuse the boat keeper at one end of the boat while another was pulling her to pieces at the other."[22] But the Indians were willing to trade as well as eager to steal, and the visitors found them to be accomplished bargainers.

What was most astonishing about Nootka was, as Ledyard observes, "the variety of its animals, and the richness of their furr." Cook's party traded for furs simply for their own use as clothing, not intending any kind of business speculation. "Neither did we purchase a quarter part of the beaver and other furr skins we might have done, and most certainly should have done had we known," Ledyard writes, "of meeting the opportunity of disposing of them to such an astonishing profit . . .

skins which did not cost the purchaser sixpence sterling sold in China for 100 dollars."[23] The Chinese prized fur which they used as a badge of rank and a mark of wealth. And in the penetrating cold of the Peking winter, furs provided welcome warmth to members of the imperial court and other privileged persons.

Ledyard met his first Russians at Unalaska Island on the eastern end of the Aleutian chain. Unfortunately members of the Cook expedition and the Russians had no language in common and could not exchange much information, but Cook seized the opportunity to send dispatches home to the admiralty via the Russian communication network across Siberia.[24]

After Cook's death, Ledyard returned to England with the expedition, traveling by way of the China coast, where the furs were sold. His book, written hurriedly in Hartford during the winter of 1783 and sold outright to a local printer, was the first account of the great adventure to be published. Ledyard quarried a large chunk of his book, without attribution, from the journal of John Rickman, second lieutenant on the *Discovery*.[25] For Ledyard it was both twenty guineas easily earned and a chance for fame because he was able to put himself before the public in a stronger light than the facts of the expedition's history might have warranted.

In June 1784, Cook's own version of the great events appeared posthumously in three handsomely illustrated volumes, edited and completed by his associates. In three days an avid public bought out the first printing.[26] Cook's discoveries were therein documented and thereby disseminated, with the commercial opportunities freely laid open to anyone who cared to learn of them.

In the meantime Ledyard was attempting to persuade American merchants to seize advantage from the marvelous new entrepreneurial opening he perceived, expressing the hope that his *Journal* would be "useful to America in general but particularly to the northern States by opening a most valuable trade across the north pacific Ocean to China and the east Indies."[27] In Philadelphia and in New York Ledyard tried in vain to interest skeptical merchants in his services as business agent aboard (supercargo as it was called) for a trading voyage to Asia via Cape Horn and Pacific North America.

The risk capital essential for any such new venture was none too abundant in the United States at the time, and John Ledyard's persuasive powers failed to pry any cash loose from the cautious businessmen to whom he talked. Robert Morris, the great Philadelphia financier, at first said he would help substantially, but his enthusiasm cooled and the ship he ended up sponsoring, *Empress of China*, sailed from New York directly to Canton in February 1784, via the old familiar Portuguese route around the Cape of Good Hope, not by way of Nootka. John Ledyard was not on board.[28]

The proposed new route via Cape Horn seemed too risky. One of the major investors in *Empress*, William Duer, intending to make the voyage himself, objected strenuously to any suggestion of sailing around the Horn. "The state of my affairs and that of a young family will not justify me in adding a dangerous experiment in navigation to one of commerce."[29] No American ship would leave for the North American Pacific until the *Columbia* and *Lady Washington* put out of Boston in September 1787.

Ledyard gave up hope that he would find any backing in the United States. He expressed his sadness to his mother in June 1784, just before leaving New London for Europe: "You have no doubt heard of my very great disappointment at New York. For a moment, all the fortitude that ten years misfortune had taught me could hardly support me."[30]

Yet the young man was still buoyed by his desire for fame, "my passage to glory," as he put it.[31] In Europe his thoughts began to turn from commerce to discovery, from profit to pure adventure. In Paris, Thomas Jefferson, the resident American minister, offered Ledyard both moral encouragement and material help. Both men were fascinated by the apparent relationship between the native peoples of North America and Eurasia, speculating that the similarity "renders it possible that ours are descended from theirs or theirs from ours."

Jefferson later wrote that finding Ledyard "of a roaming, restless character, I suggested to him the enterprise of exploring the Western part of our continent, by passing thro St. Petersburg to Kamschatka [*sic*], and procuring a passage then in some of the Russian vessels to Nootka Sound, whence he might make his way across the continent to America [*sic*]; and I undertook to have the permission of the Empress of Russia solicited."[32]

Ledyard leaped at the opportunity Jefferson suggested. But the great Catherine declined to endorse his plan, dismissing the trip as "chimaerical" and probably suspecting the American's motives.[33] Ledyard went without Russian endorsement. Jefferson writes, "He had but two shirts, and yet more shirts than shillings. Still he was determined to obtain the palm of being the first circum-ambulator of the earth."[34] Jefferson liked that image, but Ledyard intended to walk only where he had no alternative.

Making his way across Russia by stagecoach, the *kibitka*, scarcely luxurious in harsh Siberian winter but better than walking, Ledyard found his nation widely known to Russians, even in remote places. "At Irkutsk the name of Adams has found its way."[35] He was hospitably treated by Russian officials and assisted along the way until the long arm of the tsarist police finally found him in Yakutsk in December 1787. Tsarina

Catherine ordered him arrested, deported, and banned from ever again setting foot on Russian soil. Ledyard seems to have been the first American to be thrown out of Russia as a suspected spy.[36]

Ledyard's enthusiasms turned elsewhere, but at age thirty-nine, in Cairo, he was seized by a sudden and fatal disorder while preparing to explore Africa. Frustration and failure had scarred Ledyard's life. As Jefferson put it, Ledyard was a man of "too much imagination."[37] The voice of the great Cook carried far more consequence than that of his young corporal of marines. But the medium would be incidental, the message what ultimately mattered. Here Cook and Ledyard spoke the same: a new source of wealth for the bold and ambitious lay in the North American Pacific.

Ledyard dead was more potent than Ledyard alive.[38] Jared Sparks's admiring popular biography (1828) would create a legendary hero for Americans attracted by the audacity and exuberance of this first American to have looked at China as the Far West, not the Far East. One of Ledyard's admirers was William S. Clark, popular teacher in Japan (1877–78), potent shaper of Japanese ideas about Americans, and himself a legend, but to the Japanese. Clark says of Ledyard: "His is the character for me, bold and spirited, persevering and sure of success. Though baffled in every undertaking he was never disheartened. Though wretchedly poor his motto was 'ahead.' ... Without money and without friends except such as he made where he chanced to be, he travelled through the whole length and breadth of Europe and Asia, mostly on foot.[39]

Ledyard sought to open the nascent North Pacific fur trade to a vast new American-dominated international triangle, with its three points resting at New England, Nootka, and Canton. This new pattern of commerce offered a lucrative opportunity to dispose of three profitable cargoes at each of the three points of the triangle. A fourth salient reached out to embrace Hawaii, for Cook's Sandwich Islands provided a blissful haven for the weary, half-sick, and sex-starved seafarer.

Twenty years after Ledyard, Meriwether Lewis and William Clark, under President Jefferson's instigation, would do in North America what Ledyard originally proposed, but in the reverse direction and in organized expeditionary fashion. Yet despite the achievement of those two, America's initial leap to the shores of the Pacific would be accomplished not by land but by sea; not by foot or on horseback, or even by covered wagon. A transcontinental highway existed as yet only in the imagination.[40] The first vehicle of expansion would be the tiny sailing ship, for which Ledyard had looked, battling its way around Cape Horn, heading to the Oregon country, and then on across the Pacific to China.[41]

From where we stand, John Ledyard seems more myth than reality, a quixotic and theatrical figure, both admirable and absurd, a man whose acts were less significant for their substance than for their spirit, but a man whose story fired the imagination of those future Americans who would turn their eyes westward toward the far Pacific.

PART TWO

"TO GLORY ARISE!" 1784–1844

CHAPTER THREE

The Pacific: Key to New American Wealth?

Hail Land of light and joy! thy power shall grow
Far as the seas, which round thy regions flow;
Through earth's wide realms thy glory shall extend,
And savage nations at thy scepter bend.
Around the frozen shores thy sons shall sail,
Or stretch their canvas to the ASIAN gale.

Timothy Dwight, America[1]

These prophetic lines reflect the restless energies, the exuberant self-confidence, and the sense of mission that would ultimately propel Americans across the Pacific, but practical matters came first in American thinking. Having gained political independence, Americans were determined that their new nation would not remain a commercial colony.[2] Before 1783 their British masters forbade any American to carry on trade east of the Cape of Good Hope. Asia was closed. After 1783, Americans hoped to find in a new world of the Asian Pacific a key to commercial independence.

Maritime industries lay very much on the American mind. Long before independence, John Adams had foreseen an enormous potential for commercial wealth in the American colonies because of their seemingly unlimited supplies of timber and naval stores (pitch, tar, and resinous substances). America had all the material requisites for shipbuilding, coupled with a burgeoning, increasingly prosperous population.

The Revolutionary War may have been long and costly, but war, and the peace that followed, opened fresh opportunities in finance, commerce, and manufacturing for exploitation by ambitious Americans. John Ledyard may have been a commercial failure; others were not.

The Treaty of Paris (1783) made the United States of America a sovereign nation, with the Mississippi River its official western boundary. The new country's size was more than twice that of France plus Spain, or nearly one-quarter of all Europe, including European Russia. But not many people had yet ventured west of the forbidding line of the Appalachian/Allegheny mountain chain. The fewer than 4 million people who called themselves Americans were for the most part thinly strung along the Atlantic coast, struggling to wrest a living from the earth or to harvest it from the waters.[3]

The poor quality of most New England soil encouraged Yankees to look out to their seaward frontier, where better opportunities appeared to lie. That is not to say that most Yankees were occupied with the sea. Ninety percent were not. But those who were tended to be the people who propelled the rhythms and wove the predominating patterns of New England life. The sea shaped the character of much of New England, and New England would dominate the early years of the American maritime experience.[4] Boston would become America's first North Pacific city.

International trade and the seafarer's life offered the chance for lucre and excitement, beckoning the adventurous as it had John Ledyard. But at war's end, the familiar Atlantic suddenly offered only dismal prospects because the peace treaty excluded Americans from the British trading network. Until the war, about 90 percent of American trade was with England and its West Indian colonies.[5] To compensate, areas hitherto locked away from the American commercial grasp were now flung open to Yankee exploration and exploitation. One such place was the fabled Orient. Adam Smith had recently (1776) reinforced the message of Marco Polo, declaring that "China has been long one of the richest, that is, one of the most fertile, best cultivated, most industrious, and most populous countries in the world. . . . China is a much richer country than any part of Europe."[6]

To Americans at the time of independence, the Pacific world was so remote as to be little thought of. And China, which only a handful of Americans had ever seen, imposed its own remoteness on the outsider. The Chinese did not relish commerce with merchants from the North Atlantic world and thus far had opened only the port of Canton (Guangzhou) to them.

Americans at the time of independence may have known nothing firsthand of China and its culture, but rich people were drinking Chinese teas and wearing Chinese silks brought back by British traders.[7] These attractive commodities commanded a good and potential growth market, and now Americans were free to go to China themselves and trade on their own account. The American merchant captain went to China to buy, not to sell. His problem was what he could sell in order to buy. What did the Chinese want?

The United States, overwhelmingly an agricultural nation, had little to offer to such sophisticated customers. Certainly the Chinese evinced little interest in barrel staves or dried codfish. Americans knew that the Chinese craved silver, but Philadelphia, New York, and Boston had little of that to spare. The history of the early American China trade is that of an often circuitous search for specialty items to appeal to the discriminating Chinese. This search would ultimately propel Americans across the Pacific. Americans rapidly learned of the immensity of China's domestic trade. What was frustrating was their inability to stimulate a Chinese taste for a wide range of foreign goods that they might be able to supply.

Ginseng was one such specialty item seized upon by American traders. Robert Morris's *Empress of China*, 360 tons, described as "handsome, commodious and elegant," flying the Stars and Stripes, American built, American manned, and American owned, carried into Canton in August 1784 a cargo of thirty tons of ginseng.[8] Samuel Shaw of Boston, her supercargo, held high hopes of Chinese demand for this "otherwise useless produce of . . . [American] mountains and forests."[9] Ginseng, a root of vaguely phallic shape, is even today greatly esteemed throughout East Asia for its medicinal properties.

At the time of the first American shipment, the root was touted as the means to

soothe nerve irritation, improve the workings of the brain, and cure either high blood pressure or low. It lengthened life, aided the diabetic, strengthened the blood, and cleaned up boils, pimples, or rashes. Appetites were promoted by its ingestion and digestive complaints cured . . . [it] remedied anemia, dysentery, malaria, cancer, sciatica, lumbago. . . . [It was also a means to] stop dizziness and relieve headache, to restore serenity, retard senility, and stimulate sexual passion.[10]

In short, ginseng was good for practically any ailment, but probably the last item in this impressive catalog was the most attractive to the customer.

Samuel Shaw, wondering if perhaps ginseng should be cultivated systematically, wrote hopefully that "it is probable that there will always be a sufficient demand for the [American] article to make it equally valuable [to the Asian]."[11] In fact, American ginseng proved to be of lower quality than that to be found in Manchuria or Korea, and American exporters would suffer from its fluctuating and limited market at Canton. Ginseng would hardly suffice to pay for all that Americans wanted from

China. To complicate the problem, the American market for Chinese goods could also fluctuate. A Philadelphia China merchant complained bitterly in 1810 that tea, the leading import from China, was unsaleable, silk and porcelain then being the only Chinese goods that "command a market here."[12]

Boston merchants meanwhile were reading Cook enthusiastically and thinking about selling furs to to the Chinese, thereby filling Yankee pockets. In 1787 a small group of eager investors, including America's leading architect Charles Bulfinch, were prompted to pool the not inconsiderable sum of $50,000 to outfit a North Pacific expedition comprising two ships, the *Columbia Rediviva* (later shortened to *Columbia*), a full-rigged ship of 212 tons, and the *Lady Washington*, a 90-ton sloop designed to act as her tender.

Captain Robert Gray took command of the smaller vessel, John Kendrick the larger. The purpose of their trip was to sail to the North American Pacific coast, obtain the maximum number of sea otter pelts at minimal cost, take them to Canton, and sell them for tea. They would do exactly what John Ledyard had proposed several years before. These ships were the first from New England to sail to the North Pacific Ocean.[13] And *Columbia* would be the first ship to fly the Stars and Stripes in a global circumnavigation.

For American merchants henceforth, the Pacific would take on a new meaning as a potential pathway linking America directly to Asia, an alternate to the old route around Africa, a way of circumventing Europe, perhaps even a means for wresting mastery of the coveted commerce of the Orient from the Europeans. But sailing to Asia across the Pacific required rounding the Horn. Other navigators had done so—Englishmen, Spaniards, Frenchmen, and the Hollanders who named the promontory after the small Dutch town of Hoorn. No one ever looked forward to sailing the Horn, the "Cape of all Terrors."[14]

Soviet cosmonaut Georgy Grechko, on viewing the earth from space, found Cape Horn beautiful but "gloomy and forbidding—it gave me a sense of danger. I thought, if Cape Horn looks like this from space, how much more dangerous it must seem on earth, and how very brave a man must be to round it in a ship!"[15] Particularly in a tiny sailing ship, he might have added.

For passage to Asia, the seaman would always, if he could, choose the da Gama route around the Cape of Good Hope. Sailing from the North Atlantic to the Pacific coasts of East Asia is even shorter, as well as pleasanter, via this Portuguese path.[16] Cape Horn is as far from the equator as is the southern shore of Hudson's Bay; the Cape of Good Hope is as close as southern Spain.[17] Capetown provided predictably temperate weather and afforded good hospitality. Cape Horn offered neither.[18]

At Cape Colony the hard-working Dutch coaxed the land to yield lav-
ishly, with fruits and vegetables "most of which, either from the equality
of the seasons or the peculiarity of the soil, are more delicious in their
kind than can be met with elsewhere; so that by these, and by the excellent water which abounds there, this settlement is the best provided
of any in the known world for the refreshment of seamen after long
voyages."[19] Many a passing seaman would heartily echo this American
judgment.

The American mariner found that politics did not interfere with his
enjoyment of Capetown. If the British, increasingly masters of the
world's sea-lanes and stopping places, proved haughty or even hostile
to Americans, the Dutch were invariably cordial. The United States was
generally politically neutral but, in any event, purse always took precedence over politics for the practical Dutch. Furthermore, Capetown was
healthy, unlike many other ports of call.[20]

But the Horn passage nonetheless sometimes loomed a grim inevitability. For a trip to the North Pacific fur country or to South Pacific
whaling grounds, either Cape Horn or the neighboring Strait of Magellan
provided the only reasonable way to go. Only the knowledge that, mid-
point in the Pacific, Hawaii lay waiting, an oasis in the watery wastes,
a place for fresh food and delicious dalliance, gave some encouragement
to the mariner contemplating the horrors of the South American route
to Asia.

Clawing around the Horn, a ship was exposed to an intensity of interacting, unpredictable, even treacherous currents, winds, and weather
systems in the meeting place of three oceans. Sailors declared that the
Horn was the stormiest spot on the known earth. Sometimes the struggle
might prove mercifully swift, a matter of only a few days before the
weather yielded passage. Sometimes it might extend to a perilous three
months, the ship wracked by dreadful squalls, laboring through mountainous foamy swells, shaking from stem to stern when hit by heavy
seas, men suffering harsh and piercing cold, blinding hail and sleet, and
enduring perpetually sodden clothing. Rain was even worse than snow,
they said, because it wet a man to the skin, and wet clothes could not
be dried until a ship hit fair weather. Too often the Horn wrought a
chronicle of terror of splitting sails, breaking masts, and shattering spars.
The experience tested seamanship and shipbuilder's art alike. Some inevitably failed.

Few ships sailed within sight of land. If they did, they found it much
as Grechko describes: sterile, rugged, and inhabited not by the legendary
Patagonian giants but by a primitive, impoverished, and unfriendly people wrapped in misery. Sensible mariners gave wide berth to these rocky
shores, passing well to the south through wide open seas.

Herman Melville declared that Richard Henry Dana's description of a voyage round the Horn in 1836 was "written by an icicle." Dana experienced the trip in July, the worst month in the depth of winter, when "the sun rises at nine and sets at three, giving eighteen hours night, and there is [sic] snow and rain, gales and high seas, in abundance."[21] In winter one would travel through perilously ice-choked waters, with bergs and floes that could rip out a ship's bottom almost instantly. The rocking and wallowing bergs, Dana said, cannot be adequately described by pictures because their true and fearsome majesty derives from "their slow, stately motion, the whirling of the snow about their summits, and the fearful groaning and cracking of their parts."[22]

Throughout the age of sail, the Horn remained a challenge for even the boldest and most capable captains:

They never venture in the latitude of it until each has prepared his vessel for the rough weather to be expected in rounding it; for this no precaution is omitted.

Men of war strike part of their armament into the hold; get their anchors between decks; send up stump masts; bend the storm sails; and secure their spars with preventer rigging, as they get near the tempestuous regions."[23]

These are the words of an expert, famed maritime compiler, Matthew Fontaine Maury, who studied the route, sailed it, and later (1834) wrote about it. Sailors took Maury's words as gospel.

The records of the pioneering American vessel *Lady Washington* note of her passage that she "had the Wind violent from the SE accompaneyed with frost and so high a sea that our vessell was allmost Continualy under water and our people wett and uncomfortable . . . the weather excessive coald."[24] *Lady Washington* and *Columbia* lost each other en route, to reunite only at Nootka in August 1788.

Both crews by that time were suffering from scurvy. The natives brought out fresh berries and boiled crab, for which the Americans gladly traded from the large store of objects they had brought along: tools and trinkets; bronze and pewter coins, and medals struck for the occasion; necklaces, combs, looking glasses, and snuff.

But the Americans had come for fur, not food. Above all else they wanted sea otter pelts. The sea otter, which is found only along the great arc of the North Pacific coast, from the Kurils to California, grows probably the finest of all furs. Certainly it is more beautiful than that of any other marine animal. The consistency of the coat is dense, fine, and soft. At its roots, to be glimpsed when the hairs are ruffled, the pelt is silvery white, but the surface color ranges from a lustrous dark reddish-brown to a deep glossy black, depending on the age of the animal and its home. When cured, the skins stretch generously to a size several feet bigger than the animal. To trader William Sturgis, "excepting a beautiful woman and a lovely infant," a sea otter pelt was one of the most exquisite objects nature provides.[25] Sturgis neglects to mention that fleas are also extremely fond of the sea otter, infesting the ships carrying the furs across the Pacific to their Chinese customers.

At Nootka, Captains Gray and Kendrick exchanged ships for the next stage of their journey. Gray took *Columbia* into fame on her global circumnavigation, sailing from the North American coast to Hawaii. There he lay for three weeks, loading fresh fruits, vegetables, and five large casks of salted pork, as well as a number of live hogs to be slaughtered on board to provide fresh meat for added sustenance during a nine-week crossing to Canton.

From the China coast Gray went around the Cape of Good Hope and back to Boston for a grand welcome in August 1790. The ship, "on coming to her moorings in the harbour fired a federal salute—which a great concourse of citizens assembled on the several wharfs, returned with three huzzas, and a hearty welcome."[26] Captain Gray led the parade up State Street with a young Hawaiian chief on his arm, the latter stunning the crowd with his regal bearing, exotic cloak, and headdress of yellow and scarlet feathers.

On a second voyage aboard *Columbia*, Gray ran the terrifying breakers at the mouth of the great river he would name for his ship. His visit there would provide a major basis for the later U.S. claim to the as-yet ill-defined Oregon territory. Despite an earlier Spanish sighting and naming of the river, the American choice of name and the American bid for sovereignty would ultimately stick.

The British claim to Oregon was stronger than the American. More than one thousand miles of unknown country separated the American Mississippi frontier from the Pacific, whereas the British had been aggressive about pushing their continental presence from the Atlantic all the way across. In 1793, Alexander Mackenzie, British pioneer explorer, had shown at least the possibility of traveling from the Atlantic to the Pacific almost entirely by water, as the Russians were doing, he points out, on *their* continent. Mackenzie saw the Columbia River as key to "the entire command of the fur trade of North America."[27] "To this," he said, with grand geopolitical sweep, "may be added the fishery in both seas, and the markets of the four quarters of the globe."[28]

The North American Pacific was emerging as an arena for tense and anxious encounters among the British, the Spaniards, the Russians, and the Americans, all jockeying in a complexity of competing individuals, competing commercial companies, and competing countries. Each party particularly coveted a stretch of coastline with a good harbor; most people were less interested in the hinterlands because the ocean with its perceptible trade routes was deemed much more important than the still largely unknown continental spaces of North America. Trade took precedence over territory. Before the expedition of Lewis and Clark (1804–6), even Americans did not focus much attention on the contiguous Far West. Lewis and Clark found that towering mountains instead of easy portages separated the major river system of the continent's northern center, the Missouri, from any river flowing into the Pacific. Alexander Mackenzie's judgments concerning the ease of moving across North America proved overly optimistic.

For trade with Asia from the Atlantic world, wagon tracks could not compete with oceanic routes. The Rockies and the Cascades barred the possibility of any American "silk road." Nothing like that ancient and lucrative Eurasian transcontinental caravan route threading its way across the arid steppes seemed possible for North America.

Yet the belief that the North American continent was destined to become the commercial intermediary between Europe and East Asia grew into a powerful myth. Thomas Jefferson cultivated it, although never in specific terms. He talked about America and the trade of Asia with John Ledyard, George Clark, and Meriwether Lewis. The dream would grow and flourish in the American consciousness, and give impetus to the efforts of commercial entrepreneurs to build new networks of transport.[29]

Despite John Ledyard's importuning of his fellow Americans, the British had responded even before Bulfinch and his Boston friends to the news of the wealth to be got from the North Pacific. Trader James Hanna brought his brig, appropriately named *Sea Otter*, from Macao eastward across the Pacific to collect a cargo of furs, arriving at Nootka in early August 1785.[30] When Gray and Kendrick came, they found British competitors. Cook had, after all, established a British territorial claim there. And in 1790 the British effectively eliminated Spain from the northern Pacific coast by means of the Nootka Convention, forcing the Spaniards to yield claim to any territory north of San Francisco.

Spain could still boast being the largest West European imperial state, but it had become the weakest. Americans, with a hearty Protestant prejudice, despised the Spaniards for their "indolence and imbecility" and were quick to push them at every opportunity.[31] France may have had pretensions to power in the Pacific, hoping to find a place in this new maritime world, but the fires of revolution deflected Gallic expansive energies from the North Pacific to the continent of Europe.[32] Only the Russians, the Americans, and the British remained as real competitors in the North Pacific race.

Whereas New England began to prosper in what the Yankees called the "North west trade" and the United States protected itself by imposing heavy taxes on foreign ships wanting to bring goods into U.S. ports, England suffered because of the vast geographical monopolies enjoyed by its own great trading companies. The new transoceanic North Pacific trade could not be slotted into old geographical patterns. The South Sea Company asserted its domain over the entire American Pacific coast, north and south, and some distance out into the ocean as well. The East India Company's writ prevented any British subject from trading east of the Cape of Good Hope.

The two British companies thereby split the Pacific world. One historian puts it neatly: "The sea-otter, which was *the* animal of the maritime fur-trade, was only obtainable within the limits of the one [the South Sea Company], and only salable to advantage in China within the monopoly area of the other [the East India Company]."[33] Even if the British merchant secured a license to buy otter pelts from, say, the Tlingits, he could not use any proceeds of the sale of these skins in Canton to buy Chinese goods to sell in England.

Americans were free of all such regulation. They could exercise their commercial wits and concentrate their resources as they wished, and as a result they captured an overwhelming share of the fur trade and amassed some tidy fortunes.

Americans were particularly jealous and proud of their newly won sovereignty; international commerce sharpened feelings of national rivalry. A New York newspaper reported on May 12, 1785, the day after the *Empress of China* returned, that "it presages a future happy period in our being able to disperse with that burdensome and unnecessary traffick, which hitherto we have carried on with Europe—to the great prejudice of our rising empire, and future happy prospects of solid greatness."[34] Captain Green had carried instructions to remind him that he would probably be the first to display the American flag along the China coast and therefore should comport himself with appropriate honor and dignity.[35]

In the Northwest trade, the Russians were handicapped by remoteness from their centers of power and economic activity, which lay well to the west of the Urals. The treaty of Nerchinsk (1689) with Qing (Ch'ing) China had forced Russia to relinquish any claims to the Amur valley with its fertile plain and relatively mild winters for which the Russians had yearned. The Amur region offered both a potential breadbasket and a means of access to the sea. Russian expansive energies were therefore deflected to the Siberian north and east, toward North America. They reflected the same expansive pattern as the earlier eastward movement via portage from river system to river system across Siberia to the Sea of Okhotsk.[36]

But the leap across the Pacific to America required adaptation to the sea. That process was understandably lengthy and continued into the nineteenth century, peaking in the career of Aleksandr A. Baranov, first chief administrator (1799–1817) of the Russian American Company, which was the de facto Russian colonial government in North America.[37] One high Russian official commented,

If we lost Baranov we would be deprived of the means to realize the sweeping plans for which his work has paved the way. The name of this distinguished elder is known in the United States of America, but unfortunately it has not yet reached the same status among his own countrymen; while he receives praise from other nations he drinks from the cup of bitterness of his own people. And Oh God! He accomplishes everything with such successful management![38]

The vigorous Baranov endeavored to bring substance to the grand imperial vision of Grigorii Shelikhov to forge a mighty Russian land-sea empire, feeding on the commerce of China, and anchored in Alaska, California, Hawaii, and, of course, Siberia. The settlements of Sitka, Fort Ross, Kauai, and Okhotsk would serve as nodal points for this putative North Pacific commercial empire. But of all these places, only Okhotsk would become permanently Russian.

By 1795 the Americans had begun to crowd out the British from North Pacific international commerce and to become chief rivals to the Russians. Between 1796 and 1812 virtually the whole maritime fur trade between North America and China passed into American hands.[39] In 1809, a German immigrant, John Jacob Astor, born in the Rhineland town of Waldorf, a man who "by the scope of his mind and the weight of his character" (in Thomas Jefferson's words) "had raised himself to high consideration with the government," obtained a charter from the state of New York to establish a "Pacific Fur Company."[40] Astoria resulted, a trading post built near the mouth of the Columbia River and supplied by sea around the Horn and by the overland route charted by Lewis and Clark. Astoria, the first American settlement on the Pacific coast, was lost to the British in the War of 1812, but the tiny outpost proved important in validating ultimate American claims to the whole of Oregon—"the germ of an empire," as Jefferson phrased it.[41]

In their rivalry with the Yankees, the British were hurt not only by their own monopolistic practices but also by the distractions of the Napoleonic Wars and Yankee readiness to pay high prices for otter skins. Because China goods commanded such a high price in the United States, American traders could both outbid the British and the Russians in acquiring furs and undersell them in dealing with the Chinese.

The Russians were annoyed by losing access to furs they regarded as their own, their very *raison d'être* in North America, and by the American readiness, despite Russian entreaty, to sell guns and powder to the North American indigenes. Firearms in native hands threatened an already precarious Russian authority over the indigenes.

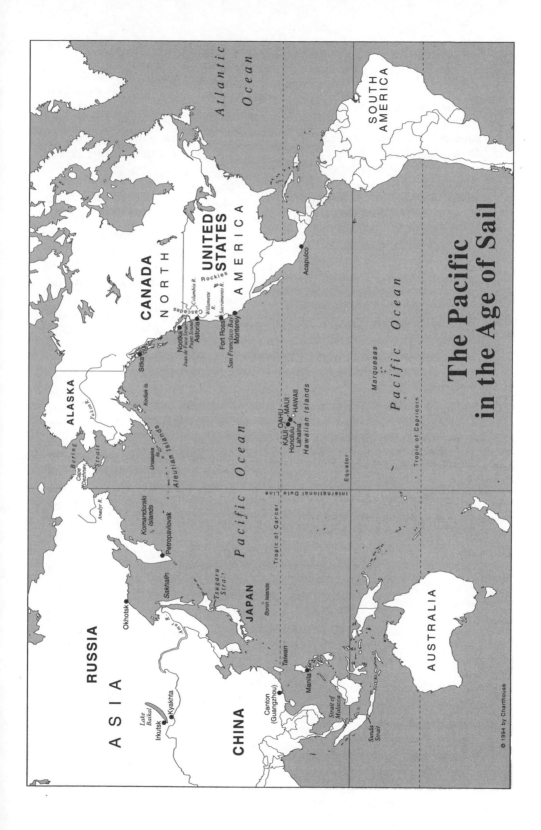

The Pacific
in the Age of Sail

© 1994 by Charthouse

The great land mass of Siberia, despite its sprawling rivers and short portages, was not as easily crossed as were the saltwater spaces exploited by the Yankees. Sitka and Kodiak were closer in both distance and time to the American Atlantic coast than they were to St. Petersburg. Seven months was about the best time for a trip from the Russian capital to Russian America. Boston to Sitka, depending on weather off the Horn, could be done in as little as four months.

Distance slackened the Russian strategic grasp on both coasts of the North Pacific. As a result of the long and uncertain lines of communication with European Russia and the almost total lack of development of Pacific Siberia, the Russians in North America were perennially and often desperately short of everything they needed: food, tools, skilled hands. The sea yielded ample fish, but the land was poor and the climate severe. Even Edenic northern California, where the Russians built and maintained a small colony around Fort Ross (1812–41) some one hundred miles north of San Francisco, proved disappointing. The company lacked practical knowledge of agriculture, and too few people were available to work the land.

Russian desire for what the Yankees might be able to provide—rum, sugar, and hardtack; tools and talent; carpenters, blacksmiths, and ship-wrights—tempered their fear and dislike of Yankee competition. The Russians might have heartily wished the Americans out of the North Pacific, but they needed them there. The Americans in turn were delighted to peddle goods and provide services. Boston could nourish Russian America more cheaply and efficiently than St. Petersburg could.[42]

An American merchant adventurer, Captain Jonathan Winship, sailed from Boston on the ship *O'Cain* in October 1805, traveling 173 days without stop to Hawaii. He boasted that he arrived without a man on the sicklist. At Oahu, Winship took on food, water, and a few burly "Kanakas" (as South Sea islanders were commonly called by American mariners) to flesh out his crew. These Hawaiians were proving themselves superb seamen. Arriving at New Archangel (Sitka), in Captain Winship's words, "We experience the extreme felicity of thanking the Almighty for protecting us in perfect safety, without meeting any accidents since leaving our native country."[43]

Governor Baranov greeted Winship warmly, sending out to the *O'Cain* a daily supply of preserved fish and fresh game. Pressing his hospitality on the Americans caused one of them to write: "All this pleasant intercourse was not without some drawbacks as the Russian idea of sociability is not to break up a party until all the company are drunk."[44] The Americans marveled at the Russian thirst and the Russian capacity for alcohol.

The Russians could not bring furs into China by sea. Canton was closed to them; treaty restricted Russian traders to using a lengthy land route via Kyakhta, a town south of Lake Baikal on the Mongolian frontier. Because getting furs to Canton by sea was so much faster and cheaper, the Russians were eager to cut a deal with the Americans to handle their skins.

As part of the arrangement, Baranov recruited skilled Aleuts, a people who knew the art of hunting the sea otter better than anyone else, and lent them to the Americans. Because of their dependence on the ocean and marine animals, the Aleuts were highly nomadic, traveling in their tiny craft from island to island, sometimes over vast distances. The Aleut territory stretched over twenty-nine degrees of longitude. The Aleuts needed not only long distance but also fast transport. Speed and stealth as well as endurance were essential to their success in the hunt.

They came to be known worldwide for the extraordinary quality and use of their *qajaqs* (kayaks), called *baidarka* by the Russians. These narrow boats with split bows were constructed of flexible wooden skeletons covered with the transparent skins of animals, often sea lion. In Aleut hands the *qajaq* could achieve and sustain an astonishingly high rate of speed, perhaps as great as ten knots, at a time when the average speed of a ship under sail was five knots. The materials used to make these boats not only enhanced the efficiency but also diminished the sound of moving through the water, with enormous advantage to the hunter. James Billings, English navigator and early visitor to the Aleutians, describes his "amazement beyond expression" with these boats: "If perfect symmetry, smoothness, and proportion constitute beauty, they are beautiful beyond anything that I ever beheld."[45]

The Aleuts suffered greatly under the Russian yoke: their numbers shrank by 80 to 90 percent, their abilities were mercilessly exploited, and many of them were obliged to live as virtual slaves.[46] Winship took aboard some 150 of these intrepid hunters, their women, their canoes, and three Russian supervisors on a three-month cruise along the California coast, despite Spanish strictures against such intrusions. The Russians also sent their own hunting expeditions to California, and there was little the Spaniards could do to stop them.

On the long voyage back home to the north, the Aleuts whiled away the time by dancing and singing, which, Winship noted, kept the performers good-humored and the crew entertained. No wormy hardtack or tired salt beef for the Aleuts; they enjoyed their own tasty dried fish and well-seasoned whale oil, supplemented by an occasional seal or sea elephant, depending on the luck of the catch. "Strong feed," the Americans thought, holding their noses over the rancid oil, but the Aleuts thrived on it.[47]

Along the American Pacific coast, merchant mariners from Boston did best, trading with the local people as well as with the Russians; Boston energies animated the whole enterprise. As William Sturgis, one of the most successful of these mariner merchants, would later say, "The Indians had the impression that Boston was our whole country. Had anyone spoken to them of *American* ships, or *American* people, he would not have been understood. We were only known as *Boston* ships, and *Boston* people."[48] For a city of barely twenty-five thousand people, the achievement was extraordinary.

CHAPTER FOUR

Searching for Something to Sell

A perception of new commercial opportunities stimulated the emergence of shipbuilding as one of America's earliest and most successful industries. Shipowning also proved to be a highly lucrative business. America's first notable great fortune, that of Salem tycoon Elias H. Derby, sprang from shipping as the American Revolution drew to a close. Not only was the Pacific newly open, but the subsequent wars of the French Revolution and Napoleon also brought other fresh opportunities to Americans by convulsing the politics of the European continent and disrupting old patterns of trade everywhere. The British blockaded the French; the French harassed the British; the Americans could profit by leaping into the resulting entrepreneurial opening.

Shipbuilding in the age of sail was not simply a matter of carpentry and canvas; it spurred the arts of metalworking because ships needed anchors, chain, brasswork, and iron fittings—objects requiring the skilled hands of the smith and the mechanic. But working with wood was preeminent and timber the prime requisite for ships. The rocky soil of New England may have yielded poor food crops, but it nourished a rich harvest of timber. Americans could exploit a virgin natural resource and use it prodigally. Supplies of both white and live oak, the most favored species for shipbuilding, sufficed for all the needs of American yards throughout the era of wooden shipbuilding. Even using British imports of "cordage, nails, and stores," the Americans could build ships at least 30 percent cheaper than the British could.[1]

As for the British, white oak flourished in the rich clay soils and generous rainfall of southeastern England, and the shipwright seized upon it greedily. But by the 1840s demand came to outrun supply; new growth took much too long. British builders therefore had to reach farther and farther for their prime raw materials, enduring steadily increasing costs.[2]

Furthermore timber became a matter of national security concerns because the defense of the nation depended on the wooden walls of the
Royal Navy. Britain's timber crisis proved a powerful incentive which
Americans lacked, to develop a new technology of constructing iron
ships. If timber had to be imported, iron plates did not. They could be
fabricated in England from materials available in England. And iron was
lighter and stronger than wood, as well as being resistant to worm and
rot.[3]

Americans continued to cut their virgin oak and pine: oak for a ship's
frame and decks, pine for its mast and spars. Oak cut and seasoned
properly offered the advantages of strength and durability, but it carried
the disadvantage of weight. Pine provided a sinuous flexibility, with less
weight than oak. For tophamper, the shipwright found that white pine
served best. For wooden ships, he wanted trees of size and maturity;
second growth usually lacked adequate girth and height. And the
builder required timbers of specific shapes to accommodate the "turn of
a bilge" or the "flare of a bow."[4] Some of these pieces could be extremely
heavy; a ninety-foot mainmast might weigh in at seven tons. Easy water
carriage between forest and yard was essential, and yards were necessarily widely dispersed in order to take advantage of the best access to
timber.

Boston emerged as a center for shipbuilding, part of the reason for its
North Pacific reputation, but its shipyards were scattered north and
south of the town, tending to gravitate toward nearby places where land
was still cheap and labor as well as timber readily available. Some of the
best ships were laid down along the narrow sheltered serpentine banks
of the Mystic River where the tides surging over a bottom clear of rocks
and shoals brought adequate depth of water to float a ship of up to
twenty-five hundred tons, at the time very large indeed.

Here at the village of Medford, Thatcher Magoun, designer and master
builder of ships for the Pacific China trade, a man born while the guns
were thundering nearby at the battle of Bunker Hill (June 17, 1775), chose
to establish his own yard in 1802.[5] Local merchants did not have the
capital to buy big ships or to hire large crews, but the new Pacific commerce in sea otter pelts was reaching its peak, and the demand surged
for cheap, small, sturdy, and fast ships to carry them.

By 1804 the Middlesex Canal opened for direct traffic from the Mer-
rimack valley to Medford and on to Boston. Medford men were important in the early planning of the canal, and its primary cargo was timber
and timber products. As the groves of oak from nearby Winchester came
to be depleted, logs from New Hamsphire could be rafted down by river
and canal with relative ease.[6]

The first American oceangoing ship, a thirty-ton bark, was built in
Medford long before, in 1631.[7] Thatcher Magoun was only the first to

lay out a shipyard there. By the 1830s, some ten of these sprawled on the banks of the Mystic within the distance of a mile. Amid a cacophony of hewing, sawing, and pounding, the builders could keep an appraising eye on one another and perhaps swap ideas on design or technique. The results were superb. "Medford-built" came to be synonymous with the best, and Medford ships came to be known the world around.

By 1845 "one quarter of all the shipwrights in Massachusetts were employed in Medford, and 9660 tons of shipping were launched from its building yards."[8] Magoun sheltered his slipway from the rigors of New England weather with a huge shed, one hundred feet high. Like other successful builders of the time, he worked right alongside his carpenters, joiners, and caulkers. A day at the yard stretched out to twelve hours, from sunrise until dusk or later, but the labor was lightened by grog breaks at eleven and again at four. A quart of rum, they said, was consumed for every ton of ship constructed.[9]

The grog was local. As well as its fast ships, Medford touted its fine rum—the best, they claimed, in the United States, rich and full bodied, made using the highest quality of molasses. Perhaps the sweetness of the spring water also had something to do with the excellence of the product.[10] Although the formula was regarded as a trade secret and closely kept, the makers were generous to the public. A barrel on the street, at the door of the distillery, bore a tin dipper for use of any passerby wanting a sample. In Medford yards a bottle of rum was ritually smashed over the bow of a ship at launching, unless temperance sentiments prevailed. In such a case the shipbuilder was obliged to resort to water.

Launchings were the grandest days in Medford. Schoolchildren would get a half-day holiday so that they could watch and swell the crowd. James Hervey remembers:

How beautiful the brightly painted ship, with her graceful outlines, appeared to me, and with what a thrill I saw the last block knocked away, and the slowly increasing movement of the mighty mass! I can still see the hundred stalwart men on the shore manning the great hawsers, checking and guiding the vessel as she swings into the stream on her way to the wharves of Boston.[11]

Many of these ships would sail to the Pacific. *Niles' Weekly Register*, a journal for American merchants, commented in 1816 that "the English betray much jealousy of the Americans in the China trade. Our well built ships, say they, make quicker voyages than theirs, and sell Chinese produce much cheaper in the European market."[12] A fortunate American China captain might earn for his ship's owner a return of 400 to 500 percent on a single voyage, and in such a case he too would profit handsomely because of the space he was allotted for himself. Even the lowly seaman might be given opportunity to carry cargo on his own account, be it tea, silk, or fine porcelains. These last were ingeniously packed in sealed tubs that were filled with water and sprouting beans whose growth would cushion the delicate dishes against breakage. But tea received first priority; porcelain was originally used chiefly for ballast, packed around the tea to keep it dry. Tea dominated the American China trade until the later nineteenth century.

Most of the American China traders, particularly those from Salem, took the Portuguese route around Africa. Boston used the Horn. For the ship traveling to China via Pacific America, an average investment of about $17,000 would buy the requisite outgoing cargo, which would be bartered, in exchange for furs, to the indigenous peoples along the coast: tin and ironware, brass kettles, wire, beads, knives, nails, looking glasses, bar iron, hatchets, flints, firearms, powder, and cloth, the same sort of goods peddled so successfully by the *Columbia* and *Lady Washington*.[13] Some variety of these items was highly desirable, local tastes being notoriously fickle. Rum and molasses were staples; the latter, sold by the bucket, was sometimes mixed in liberal proportion with seawater. The rum was subject to similar adulteration.

From its beginnings, violence characterized the maritime fur commerce. The usual Yankee trader on the North Pacific coast did not expect to make more than one or two trips and was not much interested in building customer loyalty. The frequently abusive and exploitative treatment accorded the local people generated a predictable response, and the red man retaliated against the white with his own brutality.[14]

Like William Sturgis, Richard J. Cleveland was one of the first Boston men in the "Northwest trade." Cleveland began his mercantile career sitting on the high stool of a counting house clerk, subsequently taking ship in the employ of Elias H. Derby. Derby was well served by his captains, whom he called his "boys," some of them indeed less than twenty years old. Youth was common among American mariners at the time. William Sturgis went to sea at fourteen, became a first mate when he was seventeen, a captain at nineteen. Boys though they may have been in age, they were certainly men in the responsibilities they assumed.

Cleveland, described as "a small, slender man, with a dark complexion; quiet and unobtrusive in his manners, rather taciturn . . . yet quick as steel and flint," broke away from Derby to go on his own, buying in China a fifty-ton cutter he named *Caroline*, manning her with five officers and sixteen crew and sailing from Canton to the American North Pacific.[15]

Cleveland had to scratch for that crew at Whampoa; to recruit it was "only to be done by taking the disorderly and discontented men, who had deserted from the European ships then lying there."[16] Cleveland confides that their "appearance made it difficult to believe that most of them had not been familiar with crime."[17] Violence begets violence. The behavior of the merchant sailor often simply reflected the harsh treatment he had received from his superiors.

Cleveland's crew was large for the size of the vessel not only because of the intensive labor required to sail the ship the rugged route Cleveland wanted to go, but also because of the need for protection against the truculence of the North American indigenes. Lacking even a chart, *Caroline* beat her way closely up the treacherous China coast so as to weather the northern tip of Taiwan during the peak of the northeast monsoon, a passage "looked upon as madness" by the Canton foreign merchant community.[18]

Time was crucial. Cleveland wanted to reach the fur grounds of North America before any potential competitors could. If other bidders for pelts were there, prices would soar, sometimes to amounts higher than even the Chinese would pay. That figure could fluctuate widely also.

The *Caroline* was scarcely larger than the canoes of the North American natives, and this smallness carried one great advantage: a shallow draft that permitted sailing into remote places where few traders before had been able to penetrate. Cleveland therefore expected to get a large number of sea otter skins. And he did, paying two yards of blue broadcloth for each. He was lucky. Despite the perils of the sea, the uncertainties of the market, *Caroline's* refractory crew, and the difficulties of dealing with the local people, the commercial endeavor proved highly successful. Cleveland made his round-trip from Canton in about eight months, realizing a handsome $60,000 or so on an investment of $9000.

The way in which Cleveland operated was not only typical of early American trans-Pacific commerce but also characteristic of international trade in general at that time. Ships went where they could find and sell cargoes; the process was ad hoc. Turning over goods two or three times could double or triple profits with little or no increase in costs. The enterprise resembled that of the tramp freighter of a later day. Cleveland's venture was private, it was isolated, and it was conducted with a highly specific purpose. The profits were high, but so were the risks.

A ship becalmed at sea or riding at anchor offshore was vulnerable to attack by pirates, and pirates abounded along the South China coast. William Sturgis again made himself famous by his "masterly and desperate" defense against an attack by sixteen pirate junks upon his ship *Atahualpa* lying at Macao Roads.[19] "Captain Sturgis had sworn off smoking, but when the fight began, he lit a cigar and informed the crew that he would toss it in the powder barrel rather than yield the ship to the pirates. A passenger, who was 'yellow as a sunflower' with the jaundice, was completely cured by the excitement of the battle."[20] *Atahualpa* would have made a splendid prize; she was carrying aboard a substantial sum in silver, some said as much as 400,000 Spanish dollars.

Seal skins supplemented sea otter pelts as something the Chinese would buy that were available to be picked up on the Pacific route, and while the supply lasted, the money was certainly good. Historian Tyler Dennett estimates that throughout its historic span, the entire American fur trade with China (chiefly otters and seals) earned some $15 million to $20 million, a significant sum to a young, capital-poor nation.[21]

Edmund Fanning of Stonington, Connecticut, wrote a book about his experiences and became one of the best-known sealers. He first sailed in search of seal skins in 1792. Fanning would make many voyages to the Pacific and around the world during the subsequent twenty-five years. Anyone chasing fur seals needed no trading finesse to acquire what he wanted, no diplomatic skills to exercise upon recalcitrant indigenous peoples. Nor was any hunting prowess required. It was a simple, bloody business of cornering the seal ashore and giving it a smart tap on the nose. Kill and skin. As James Fenimore Cooper comments, it was almost as easy as picking up cash on a beach. No species could long sustain such slaughter.

The sea otter too almost disappeared, to enjoy a precarious revival only under the legal protection measures of modern times. Once more on North Pacific shores one can see this shy, cunning, and playful animal, swimming and diving in the kelp beds where it finds mollusks, its favorite food. Yet today's oil spills may ultimately accomplish what the gun and the harpoon failed to do.

A boom in sandalwood roughly coincided with the life span of the American North Pacific fur trade. Sandalwood lured Yankees and other traders farther into the Pacific, to Hawaii and to the south and west beyond. India was the only known source of this finely grained, heavy, sweetly odoriferous wood until the late eighteenth century when Europeans discovered it growing in the mountainous islands of the Central and South Pacific. The Chinese are particularly fond of sandalwood, using it as incense and in fine cabinetry. The wood retains its fragrance for many years, and its chips can be pressed to extract oil, used in perfumes, cosmetics, and medicines.

Almost immediately after Cook, visitors to Hawaii discovered that the sandalwood tree grew there in abundance. The Hawaiians regarded and treated it as if it were nothing special. Two Boston captains found the tree there in 1813 and pointed out its value. As a result, within twenty-five years the forests were completely cleared; the trees were felled, shaved of their bark, sawed into four-foot lengths, and taken to the Canton market. Although the U.S. Congress said, "We must teach the natives how to grow it," that did not happen. As with the fur animals, the greed of the taker exceeded the rate at which their prey could reproduce.[22]

The sandalwood trade lasted long enough to establish Hawaii as the crossroads of the Pacific. The islands had already taken on a new intrinsic interest to Yankee missionaries and Yankee whalers. For mariners, Hawaii served as a ready source of fruits and vegetables, hogs, firewood, salt, and fresh water. Honolulu emerges as the first capital of America's Pacific frontier, an entrepôt for a small but significant flow of goods between the North Atlantic, the North American Pacific coast, and elsewhere in the Pacific world. Honolulu's Pacific primacy would last until the California gold rush of 1849.[23] The rapid development of California following this event eclipsed the international commercial allure of both Hawaii and the Oregon territory. California became a state in 1850; Washington did not until 1899.

Yet by mid-century, the importance of the islands to the United States was clearly established. James Jackson Jarves writes, "If the ports of this group were closed to neutral commerce, many thousand miles of ocean would have to be traversed before havens possessing the requisite conveniences for recruiting or repairing shipping, could be reached . . . should any one of the great nations seize upon them, it might be considered as holding the key of the North Pacific."[24] The favored American position in Hawaii encouraged the American dream of capturing "the commerce of the Orient."

Yankee mariners meanwhile fanned out over vast distances, combining the scattered islands of the South Pacific for other products attractive to the Chinese taste. They found one to be the swiftlet, native to the Pacific. This bird glues its nest to high cliffs and rocky ledges with its own spittle, and it produces that secretion in quantities sufficient to construct the entire nest. For that purpose the swiftlet needs no twigs or any other foreign matter. Yankee sailors learned that the Chinese gourmet prizes both the flavor and the medicinal properties of the gelatinous soup that can be made from these nests and the Americans began to harvest them for sale. But like ginseng or even sandalwood, both the supply and the market were limited.

Demand was also finite for other items gathered in the scattered islands of the Pacific for the Chinese customer: tortoise shell and nacre, for example, to be fashioned into ornaments or used as inlays in fine furniture, or the *beche de mer*; a slug known from its shape as the sea cucumber. This gift of the sea proved to be a labor-intensive product that required collecting, cleaning, and drying over a wood fire. It is a high-protein food much relished by the Chinese epicure for its ability to absorb and enhance the flavor of foods cooked with it, and the Chinese were willing to pay well for it.

Imaginative Yankees found something right at home to sell to the Chinese, and that was ice, cheaply bought, cut from local ponds, and packed in sawdust for the long voyage out around the Horn. In 1842, the Medford-built *Paul Jones* carried the first cargo to American ice out to Canton, despite the crew's fear that the cargo would melt en route and swamp the ship.[25]

Opium is the most publicized nineteenth-century export to China. Americans got involved in the opium traffic only after 1804 or so. The Chinese government endeavored to keep the drug out, but Chinese policy was probably less inhibiting to the American trader than the difficulty of obtaining a supply to sell. The British controlled the source of the best quality, "Bengal"; Americans had to satisfy themselves with the inferior "Turkey" variety. Although opium was certainly part of the commercial landscape, it remained relatively small in the inventory of American exports to China, and it was not carried across the Pacific.[26]

After the sandalwood boom collapsed, the American China trade began moving almost entirely around the Cape of Good Hope and across the Indian Ocean. Only the availability of special cargoes to gather on the way and the desire to establish a route that would cut out the British had made the China trade a trans-Pacific trip for Americans.

The trade began to change in its character. At Canton, which until 1842 remained China's only open port, American companies began to establish resident representatives. The merchant who was buyer, seller, and shipper of goods, as well as banker and insurer, gave way to the specialized businessman. The number of firms in the China trade shrank, but their size grew. In number of ships, Boston dropped below New York. Salem, which had sent many ships to China but via the Indian Ocean route, its harbor now silted, virtually disappears in the statistics. In overall volume, the trade remained static, although hopes remained high.

European and American demand for Chinese porcelain and Chinese handwoven cottons began to decline, coincident with the rise of ability in the North Atlantic world to manufacture these items. Silk was subject to the vagaries of ladies' fashions and the tyranny of the hemline, and therefore was a fluctuating market. Cotton overall became America's chief export within a decade of Eli Whitney's cotton gin (1793), America's first great invention.[27] Raw cotton went to Europe, and cotton cloth became something to sell to, rather than buy from, the Chinese. Here the British held a cost advantage over the Americans. Americans may have been growing their own cotton, but in the manufacture of cloth, as with iron plate and machinery. Britain set the pace for the whole world.

Yet the strategic importance of the marine fur phenomenon had been enormous. The exchanges of metals from the Atlantic world, furs from Pacific North America, and tea and silk from China wove a new pattern of world commerce embracing the wide Pacific as John Ledyard had foreseen. The commerce may have been ephemeral; its results were not.

Fur propelled Americans across the Pacific, thereby opening a prospect of the North Pacific to a people still oriented to the North Atlantic.

For the British, the biggest Canton traders, the path to China always ran around Africa and across the Indian Ocean, the route made familiar by the Portuguese pioneers and by the Dutch who followed them. Americans who came along in turn tended to look toward East Asia through European eyes. Samuel Shaw could therefore speak of China as lying at "the eastern extremity of the globe."[28] But at the same time, naval officer David Porter was voicing a different view.

James Fenimore Cooper describes Porter as "a man of bold and masculine conception, of great resources, and of a high degree of moral courage."[29] During the War of 1812, Porter's frigate, *Essex*, became the first American man-of-war to enter the eastern Pacific.[30] Porter promised his men both "booty and beauty," announcing to them that "the unprotected British commerce, on the coast of Chili, Peru, and Mexico, will give you an abundant supply of wealth; and the girls of the Sandwich Islands, shall reward you for your sufferings during the passage around Cape Horn."[31]

Porter could be of no help whatsoever to the Canton-bound Philadelphia or New York China trader working her way up from Java Head. *Essex* cruised principally off the South American coast, operating alone, ten thousand miles away from home, with only one miserable chart to work with but doing substantial damage to the British whaling fleet before succumbing to tremendous odds under the guns of the Royal Navy. British whaling never recovered from the blow, and the British never were able to challenge American primacy in whale fishing. Missouri senator Thomas Hart Benton later used Porter's experience as an argument for the United States to own a port on the Pacific, to occupy and fortify the mouth of the Columbia, and not yield it to the British, "the most formidable and domineering naval power which the world ever saw."[32]

Porter was all for American expansion in the Pacific. In 1813 he attempted to annex Nukuhiva (the site of Melville's *Typee*) in the Marquesas, renamed by him "Madison's Island." This would have been America's first overseas colony. Porter argued that "our rights to this island being founded on priority of discovery, conquest, and possession, cannot be disputed" and he claimed that the native people had "requested to be admitted into the great American family."[33] Washington ignored Porter's action, but his wartime experience roused his curiosity about the implications of a wider ocean and America's place within it. Porter had a sense of geopolitics. At the end of October 1815 he pointed out to the secretary of the navy, "We, Sir, are a great and rising nation. ... We border on Russia, on Japan, on China."[34] Porter's imagination carried the Stars and Stripes in a great leap westward across the Pacific.

Captain David Porter (Courtesy, National Archives)

CHAPTER FIVE

Science and Shipping

A lthough the United States had become one of the world's leading international maritime traders by the 1820s, Americans were still not contributing to maritime knowledge, and they knew it. Thousands of American vessels cleared American ports yearly, "yet not one of these were [sic] sailed a mile by a chart made by us."[1]

Two great eighteenth-century inventions, the sextant and the chronometer, were making it possible to determine longitude with some precision. Nonetheless, American merchant houses were notoriously reluctant to spend their money on expensive nautical instruments. Bryant & Sturgis severely reprimanded one of their captains for buying a $250 chronometer. Had they known beforehand, "we would have sett fire to the Ship rather than have sent her to sea."[2]

American sailors for the most part stubbornly kept to well-worn ways, using compass, taffrail log, and the sounding lead, and relying principally on dead reckoning. American sailors were superb at seamanship, weak in navigation. And this reflects a general American lag in science and technology in the early nineteenth century.

During the War of 1812, British men-of-war showed that they knew the intimacies of the American coast, its rocks and shoals, its tides and currents, better than their American adversaries did.[3] Jeremiah Reynolds, a popular lecturer, declared in a report to the Congress (1828) that

we are dependent on other nations for all our nautical instruments, as well as charts ... [yet we] have more shipping and commerce than all the nations of Europe had together when Columbus discovered this continent ... we stand a solitary instance among those who are considered commercial, as never having put forth a particle of strength, or expended a dollar of our money to add to the accumulated stock of commercial and geographical knowledge, except in partially exploring our own territory."[4]

Reynolds echoed David Porter who had urged a government-sponsored voyage of discovery to the Pacific Ocean, because "every nation has successively contributed in this way but us; we have proffitted [*sic*] by their labours; we have made no efforts of our own," even though "we possess a country whose shores are washed by the Atlantic and Pacific—a country on which the Sun shines the greater part of his round."[5] Reynolds asserted that the waters of the Pacific, as yet so imperfectly known, were "truly our field of fame."[6]

The Congress talked of the desirability of military posts on the North Pacific coast, David Trimble of Kentucky arguing that by building forts at the mouth of the Oregon (Columbia) and at St. John de Fuco (the Strait of Juan de Fuca), "we may command the trade of China, Japan, and East Indies and the North Pacific. That ocean is the richest sea in the world, and is as yet without a master."[7]

Edmund Fanning, relentless hunter of the fur seal, joined the chorus, pointing out the practical benefits of navigational and geographical knowledge. Fanning argued that the government had an obligation to explore and discover "new places and sources" for the support of Pacific fisheries.[8]

With the strong encouragement of President John Quincy Adams, the Congress in 1828 passed a resolution authorizing an expedition to explore the Pacific. Nothing happened for ten years. The idea seemed both to spawn controversy and to promote paralysis; arguments abounded over the choice of commander, the number of ships, the number and background of the accompanying scientists. In 1837 an exasperated Adams, who ended his career by serving as a congressman from Massachusetts until his death in 1848, said that all he then wanted to hear about the expedition was that it had sailed.[9]

In 1838 navy lieutenant Charles Wilkes took command of the six vessels assigned to the great task. His experienced flagship, *Vincennes*, had been the first American warship to circumnavigate the globe, and the squadron, which put out from Hampton Roads on August 18, represented the largest exploring expedition any nation had hitherto sent to sea.

Wilkes had a stormy personality. His naval career spanned half a century, and although he knew how to give orders he did not know how to obey them. He was a man of large conceit and immense and constant indignation, generous with blame, frugal with praise. His seamen hated him for never sparing the lash. But Wilkes drove himself as hard as he drove his men. He was a man of high ambition and remarkable talents, blessed with extraordinary energy and possessing the tenacity of a bulldog.

Wilkes brought with him nine artists and scientists, called collectively the "scientifics"—or, behind their backs, the "bug catchers" and "clam

Captain Charles Wilkes (Courtesy, National Archives)

diggers"—who cluttered the decks with their apparatus and, worse, their smelly specimens of exotic flora and fauna. These gentlemen were not ordinary men; their number included James Dwight Dana, the most influential American geologist of the nineteenth century.

All were obliged to tear themselves away from home for a protracted period; nearly half of the ship's company stayed the entire four demanding and dangerous years. The painter Titian Ramsay Peale (son of the famous portraitist, Charles Willson Peale), aboard as "naturalist," wrote to his young daughters that the water was barely drinkable but "as we do not come on board ship to be comfortable we content ourselves with anything we can get."[10] Peale and his colleagues worked hard.

Yet Wilkes and company received no popular acclaim and little thanks when they returned. James Fenimore Cooper, who found Wilkes's reports a wonderful source of background material for his fiction, would refer to Wilkes as "the most industrious and least rewarded of all the navigators who have ever worked for the human race."[11] But the authorities were generally indifferent, and the expedition failed to capture the imagination of the public.[12]

Wilkes's purpose was discovery, not conquest; map making, not map coloring. His ardent desire was to enhance the prestige of the U.S. Navy; next to that, his wish was to expand the horizons of science. The expedition accomplished both. Cartography, hydrography, and navigation all benefited, and this redounded to the prestige of the young United States, for which the expedition served as a "declaration of scientific independence."[13] America showed in substantive fashion that its interests spanned the Pacific. And Wilkes inspired others; his would be the first of fourteen American naval scientific expeditions carried out before the Civil War.

Going out by way of Cape Horn and returning via the Cape of Good Hope, Wilkes's circumnavigation served as a means of gathering much information about many Pacific places and peoples hitherto little known to the outside world. Wilkes's visits occurred sixty years after Cook had made the first encounters for Europeans with some of the native peoples of the Central and South Pacific. The Europeans had introduced new tools, new weapons, new diseases, new gods, and new ways of looking at the world. The Wilkes expedition could observe the impact, and that opportunity both stimulated the nascent science of anthropology and raised some uncomfortable questions about what the white man was bringing to the peoples of the Pacific.

Midshipman William Reynolds confided to his diary, "I could not help thinking, how much better it would be to let them [the indigenes] go their own way, but No, No! We must have all the world like us, if we can."[14] And common seaman John Erskine later wrote of the Fiji Islands that "perhaps I may be pardoned for thinking it would have been better if the islands had never been discovered by Europeans; not that Christianity is a failure, but that our civilization is."[15]

The expedition collected more than four thousand zoological specimens, including two thousand new species, and some fifty thousand plant specimens of some ten thousand different species. This huge collection was probably the largest ever assembled under sail. Many items were lost on the trip or after being brought home; the volume of material was simply too large. As historian William Goetzmann remarks, "The results of the expedition . . . far outran the intellectual resources of the country."[16]

As if the collecting were not enough, surveying and charting hundreds of Pacific islands, pushing through the icy fringes of the Antarctic coast, Wilkes and his associates were among the first to identify the seventh continent, where they explored fifteen hundred miles of coastline, their fragile ships in constant risk of being crushed by the mammoth icebergs.[17] "Wilkesland" immortalizes this pioneering Antarctic cruise.

The corpus of data brought home by the expedition led to the publishing of nineteen volumes of reports and atlases. The secretary of the navy declared in 1843 that the charts of the Pacific Ocean alone were worth the costs of the expedition.[18] And they would be of continuing value. Wilkes's chart of Tarawa, for example, the only one available, was used by the U.S. Navy during the bloody invasion of that island in World War II.

Most important of all from the geostrategic aspect, Wilkes took the shadowy shores of the North American Pacific and "clothed them in reality."[19] Hitherto, ignorance of Oregon had caused many Americans to consider it of little value; even expansionists like the redoubtable Thomas Hart Benton had pronounced the Rockies to be the natural western boundary of the United States.[20] Like Jefferson, Benton then thought that a Pacific America would be an independent political entity.

Wilkes charted some eight hundred miles of North American coastline, and he sent some of his men inland to explore and map the Pacific periphery, from Oregon to San Francisco Bay. The United States may then have had no interest in taking lands overseas, but increasingly such reluctance did not extend to settling in contiguous territory such as Oregon, still under dispute with the British.

A rough experience crossing the terrifying bar at the mouth of the Columbia, when Wilkes lost one of his ships and many of his specimens, fueled the argument that the United States needed a longer Pacific boundary so that a safe harbor might be had. Once inside the mouth of the Columbia, the shelter was tolerable, but the entrance was not. Robert Gray had tried for nine days before he could make a safe anchorage.[21]

Puget Sound was one attractive possibility; another was San Francisco, which John C. Calhoun declared the future "New York of the Pacific."[22]

Calhoun's judgment was reaffirmed by Richard Henry Dana who wrote that "if California ever becomes a prosperous country, this bay will be the centre of its prosperity. The abundance of wood and water; the extreme fertility of its shores; the excellence of its climate, which is as near to being perfect as any in the world; and its facilities for navigation, affording the best anchoring-grounds in the whole western coast of America—all fit it for a place of great importance."[23] Until war and settlement with Mexico, Americans feared that Great Britain or France might first secure both California and Oregon, shutting Americans off from their passage to the Orient.

More important than the goods it provided, the early China trade gave a boost to shipbuilding as well as shipping and it schooled American traders in banking and insurance. American China merchants realized that if they were to survive, they must think globally, to gain a sense of the market not only at home and in China but in Britain, Europe, and elsewhere. Above all, the China trade generated for Americans a pool of capital for Boston and New York to invest wherever they wished. Much of this capital would go into the new American railroads, and in Boston, commerce ceded its primacy to finance.[24]

For Americans, the China trade was a symbol of daring and pioneering spirit, of the maritime frontiersman triumphing over physical danger and commercial risk. The rewards appeared great, for the China trade provided spectacle above all. Its goods were exotic and beautiful; its monuments, the great houses and public buildings erected by merchants, were conspicuous for their richness and luxurious appointments. The opulence of the imagery made it easy to embrace the myth that China held staggering future promise for America.[25] Any man walking down the streets of Salem would certainly think so.

But the trade overall remained always a disappointment. Reality never reached the level of expectation, even after Caleb Cushing negotiated the first treaty between China and the United States in 1844. America's foreign trade began an accelerating growth, but the share with China and Asia remained a small part of the whole. And Americans began to shift their perceptions and expectations of China from being a source of luxury goods to being a market for staples—a place to sell goods rather than as a place to buy them.

The American China trade was still not a trans-Pacific phenomenon, although Americans dreamed that it would become so. In the rhetoric of Senator Benton and others in the Congress, the commerce of China as well as that of all Asia should ineluctably move across the Pacific and into American hands. Benton came to see Oregon as the crucial point of linkage. Oregon would provide Americans "the lever by which to overturn the world of British commercial [supremacy]. . . . Then the inhabitants of the great Mississippi Valley, who have in their possession the garden of the world and the granary of the universe, will stretch out one hand to the East Indies through the Pacific chain, the other to Europe through the Atlantic channel, grasping the trade of the civilized earth."[26]

Jefferson's idea of a separate sister Pacific republic faded and died while John Quincy Adams thundered in 1823 that "the finger of Nature" commanded American territorial possession of the eastern shores of the Pacific.[27] Simultaneously with the development of the idea that the natural political reach of the United States should extend from the Atlantic to the Pacific, arose the vaguely defined notion of an American Pacific lying beyond those shores, a new world for the taking, a commercial spin-off of the maritime energies that had first broken open the Pacific for Americans.[28]

The building of canals and turnpikes, the adaptation of steam power to riverine transport, and the coming of the railroad caused "all considerations of mere distance ... [to cease] confound[ing] either the Statesman or the political economist."[29] Americans knew they could move around as they never had before. The prairie schooner by land and the clipper ship by sea, two forms of transport originating in America and peculiarly identified with America, would serve as both symbol and tool for expansion as America began to look westward by land and by sea.

PART THREE

WHITENING THE SEAS, 1844–1869

You've often heard—I pledge my
   word, of what they call *Japan*, boys
But where it lies, why blast my eyes
   I'll let them tell who *can*, boys
I've been that way, but still can say,
   I've only formed the notion
Japan is found, somewhere around
   The North Pacific Ocean

Anonymous sailor, 1831
[New Bedford Whaling Museum]

CHAPTER SIX

Pushing Out Pacific Frontiers

In 1844, special envoy Caleb Cushing negotiated a treaty opening more ports in China to American merchants. In 1869 Americans completed the first North American transcontinental railroad. The interval proved immensely significant both for establishing the United States upon the shores of the North Pacific and for building a variety of new political, strategic, and commercial relationships across the great ocean with China, Japan, and Russia. Americans rose to their historic peak of commercial maritime power.

For total tonnage of commercial shipping, the United States was nudging Great Britain. In ship design, quality of construction, and efficiency of operation, Americans were simply the best. "No other nation shared so largely in the most desirable and profitable commerce of the world."[1] Americans were carrying much of Europe's trade.

In the period 1830–60 tonnage of American vessels quintupled, and the value of foreign trade soared.[2] The trade boom both encouraged and benefited from larger ships and larger and competing seaports with constantly improving wharfage, abilities to handle cargo, and navigational aids. As Edward Towle says, "American oceanic commerce was peripheral only geographically to the core of American economic growth,"[3] and it seemed that Alexis de Tocqueville's prophecy of American global maritime supremacy would come true. "They are born to rule the seas as the Romans were to conquer the world," the Frenchman declared.[4]

The United States, following upon the heels of the British, opened a new trading relationship with China. Americans led in the Atlantic effort to reopen Japan to international life in the Pacific. Americans saw new opportunities in the development of Pacific Siberia. Russia withdrew from North America, selling Alaska in 1867. And that same year when

Russia gave up its only overseas colony, the United States gained its first, the Midway Islands.

Following the example of Charles Wilkes, the American government undertook a major oceanic reconnaissance effort, sponsoring more than a dozen expeditions for practical purposes of hydrographic research or for loftier geopolitical reasons. Americans dominated the world's whale fisheries, a global industry that increasingly focused on the North Pacific, a commercial undertaking that enriched the American economy and broadened American geographical horizons. In the western reaches of the North Pacific, the activities of naval officers Matthew Perry and John Rodgers suggested new routes to Asia for American merchants and missionaries who would be proselytizers not simply of Christianity but of American civilization. A growing sense of mission encouraged the American dream of enrichment through trade with Asia.

To speed travel, Americans built across the waist of Panama the first transcontinental railroad (1850–55), with steamship lines linking both the east and west coasts of the United States to the isthmus. The isthmian railroad was a vast improvement over riding muleback over the mountains and sitting in a dugout canoe along the Chagres River, swatting the ubiquitous and aggressive mosquito and sandfly, and fighting malaria or yellow fever. From the beginning of the great migration to California in 1849 until the completion of the Union Pacific–Central Pacific railroads, the most desirable route from the Atlantic coast was that via Panama. It offered less danger or discomfort and provided a shorter time than either of the alternatives: wagon across the plains and the Rockies or ship around the Horn.

The Panama Railroad was the first large American direct investment abroad. Its single track length was only forty-seven miles, but hot sun, heavy rainfall, thick jungle, and disease made construction difficult, protracted the project to five years, and swelled the cost to $8 million. The investment proved to be highly lucrative. In 1868 alone, the profits were a tidy $2.3 million.[5] Woodburning locomotives pulled passengers from one ocean to the other in four hours. Bulk cargo continued to travel around the Horn, but from the Gold Rush to the opening of the North American transcontinental railroad, the Panama route was a key American artery, the best for passengers, mail (until the brief run of the Pony Express in the early 1860s), newspapers, express cargo, and specie. About $750,000 in gold was shipped from California via Panama, in the tradition of the Spaniards' transporting the silver of Peru back to Europe.[6] The builder of the railroad, shipping magnate William H. Aspinwall, had a keen sense of the potential benefits to be derived by linking the Atlantic to the Pacific with the most modern technology available.

The American mariner perceived the ocean as a global pathway, an avenue for commerce that was fiercely competitive yet, in the ideal, peaceful. American sailors coursed freely around the globe, from seaport to seaport. As the Connecticut captain Alex Palmer said of his older brother Nathaniel: "My home is here in Stonington, but Nat's home is the world."[7] The ocean furnished its travelers a means to achieve, if not an urbane and cosmopolitan sense of cultural relativity, at least a city-based exposure to other nations and peoples, quite unlike, say, the experience of the prairie-bound frontiersman back home.

Whether cosmopolitanism truly took hold with many seamen is questionable, but many were at least aware of the challenge. Naval officer John Reynolds wrote in 1855 that "there is now a fundamental principle in commerce and that is, a thorough and extended knowledge of the dispositions, habits, and necessities of the people, and of the natural capacities and resources of the country where we have commercial intercourse."[8] His particular concern was China, but his observation was applicable anywhere.

Oceanic routes integrated the world economy as never before. Famine in Ireland and revolution in Germany provoked a flood of refugees across the Atlantic and stimulated the demand for shipping. Rapid growth and revolutionary change in transportation and communications increased the output and trading of goods and abetted the transfer of technologies. Shifting patterns of international politics across the North Pacific further stimulated commerce.

America began to experience a great burst of national energy in the 1840s, fueled by unquenchable optimism and self-confidence, drawing deeply from what de Tocqueville would call an ultimate current in the lives of states and societies, a mysterious vital flame. And God, it seemed, had ordained that the United States should increase and prosper.

James Knox Polk inaugurated this extraordinary expansive era. The astounding, and to some, dismaying, news of Polk's triumph at the Democratic National Convention, as America's first dark horse candidate, would appropriately come from Baltimore to Washington by means of the revolutionary new American invention, the electric telegraph. The *London Times* declared Polk's election to be "the triumph of every thing that is worst over every thing that is best in the United States of America." And the venerable John Quincy Adams grimly wrote that "only the interposition of Omnipotence can save the nation."[9]

Polk may not appear on many people's short lists of great American presidents, but he knew what he wanted to do as president, announced his intentions, and carried them out successfully. His chief interest was foreign affairs, and his ruthlessness in pursuit of the national interest as he perceived it would certainly put him on the short list of the most decisive and bellicose of presidents.

Small and frail, seized by the need to emulate his idol Andrew Jackson,

"Old Hickory," and be "strong," Polk, the "Young Hickory," was a risk taker who may have preferred peace but never shrank from the prospect of war—even the possibility of fighting two nations, Great Britain and Mexico, at the same time.[10] Polk made America a power on the Pacific, acquiring some thirteen hundred miles of shorefront and annexing almost as much territory as Thomas Jefferson, getting most of it not with cash but with gunpowder or the threat of it. With the British, he negotiated.[11] But with the Mexicans he used force.

Businessmen in what historian Norman Graebner calls "the trading empire of Boston and New York" had been eyeing Pacific harbors for some time.[12] The United States already possessed millions of acres of undeveloped land and scarcely needed more. Seaports inviting international trade seemed more important.

The Oregon coast, America's only undisputed Pacific frontage, offered not one good deep-water harbor. The Columbia River, northern boundary of the American claim, no longer seemed of particular interest to seamen because of the imposing bar at its mouth, experienced so painfully by Charles Wilkes. William Sturgis was one of many to point out the merits of the Strait of Juan de Fuca, Admiralty Inlet, and the Hood Canal. Puget Sound, it seemed, could furnish a natural link between the grain surpluses of the Mississippi Valley and the huge potential markets of East Asia.

American willingness to relinquish any claim to Vancouver Island made compromise with the British over the entire Oregon region possible. By commanding the Strait of Juan de Fuca, the United States could thwart potential British commercial superiority in the Pacific. But the prospect of California and its harbors began to lessen American interest in Oregon. San Francisco or even San Diego appeared to be more relevant to future commerce across the Pacific, Puget Sound too far north and seemingly out of the way. Polk told Senator Thomas Hart Benton that the "fine Bay of San Francisco" was at all hazards to be kept out of the hands of the British.[13] And the confidential agent of the American government in Monterey was instructed that "the interests of our commerce and of our whale fisheries on the Pacific Ocean demand that you should exert the greatest vigilance in discovering and defeating any attempts which may be made by foreign governments to acquire control over that country."[14]

Polk got the Pacific waterfront, but his frontier stopped at water's edge. He lacked the Yankee eye for international seaborne commerce. And so, although he failed to become president, William Henry Seward, not James Knox Polk, looms as the central figure of nineteenth-century American expansionism. Seward was not as bellicose as Polk, but he became chief exponent of America's manifest destiny, to expand both on the continent and overseas.

Secretary of State William H. Seward (Courtesy, National Archives)

Polk died within months of leaving the presidency, worn out, they said, by the burdens of office. His career was short; Seward's was not. That Seward's mental horizons were global in scope is a surprising perspective for a man born and raised in rural upstate New York.[15] Seward's career dazzles: governor when still in his thirties (1839–43), then U.S. senator (1849–60), twice presidential hopeful, and finally, for most of the last decade of his life, secretary of state, first serving Abraham Lincoln and then Andrew Johnson. Seward's ideas and his way of expressing them showed up early in his career. He matured young and changed little. Unlike some—Lincoln, for example—Seward did not grow in office.

Like Polk, Seward was small and frail, yet people took notice of him. His strong profile and aquiline nose would become the cartoonist's delight. Early on, young Henry escaped a domineering and penny-pinching father and established his independence. He nourished "a great passion to be brilliant, original and dashing; ordinary ideas had no charm for him," an early biographer noted.[16] From his youth, Seward showed a strong natural aptitude for politics. He proved himself a shrewd, articulate, and highly principled lawyer, known as a man who would defend the penniless as readily as the rich. His fame spread.

The great William Gladstone, British prime minister, would write to Charles Sumner that "Mr. Seward's argument in the Freeman case is the greatest forensic effort in the English language."[17] Staunchly antislavery, Seward extended his compassion to the Native American. He deplored that "a people so gifted by nature, so vigorous and energetic, and withal so docile and gentle in their intercourse with the white man, can neither be preserved as a distinct social community, or incorporated into our society."[18]

During the 1840s, Seward first began to articulate a grand, comprehensive view of America's place in the world. He saw global politics in simple moral terms as a struggle between forces of right and wrong, a battle between freedom and despotism. America's role was clear. In Albany on April 6, 1848, Seward eulogized John Quincy Adams, whom he admired more than any other statesman, reiterating a sentiment that Adams himself had voiced: "The establishment of the republic of the United States of America is the most important secular event in the history of the human race."[19]

Seward had high expectations for America. In a letter sent to the Chautauqua convention in 1846, he predicted that "our population is destined to roll its restless waves to the icy barriers of the north, and to encounter Oriental civilization on the shores of the Pacific."[20] Or put in verse he like to quote:

> Abroad our Empire shall no limits know
> But like the sea in boundless circles flow.

Seward's view of empire did not lie within the conventional territorial sense. He believed the United States was unique, a political "alembic," and a harbinger of an ultimate global unity of races. America's role was to fuse "the exhausted civilizations of Asia" with the ripening ones of western Europe, renewing Asia by means of injecting American principles of religion, philosophy, economy, politics, and morality through the instruments of "the Bible, the Printing Press, the Ballot Box, and the Steam Engine."[21]

Seward was not averse to the use of force in international politics but only if other means should fail. Force he thought unnecessary because the rest of the world would inevitably and freely accept American values. "I would not seize with haste, and force the fruit, which ripening in time, will fall of itself into our hands."[22]

Like wanderer John Ledyard and merchant William Sturgis, William Henry Seward saw a natural linkage between the American Pacific and the Asian Pacific. The United States, Seward argued, was already the only real power on the Pacific. And the Pacific, "its shores, its islands, and the vast regions beyond, will become the chief theatre of events in the World's great Hereafter." Seward anticipated that trade on the Atlantic would be exceeded by trade on the Pacific "within a generation."[23] In principle, he was right, although off by a century in his calculations.

The Pacific rim would be the site for a new commingling of cultures as well as of commerce; Europe would sink in relative importance. Seward predicted in 1850 that in one hundred years the United States would be a nation of two hundred million,[24] with unequaled resources, and "with moral energies adequate to the achievement of great enterprises, and favored with a government adapted to their character and condition, [which] must command the empire of the seas, which alone is real empire."[25]

The United States, Seward argued, had the natural resources, the human skills, and the geographical position to wrest mastery of world commerce from British hands. New York City should rightfully replace London as the nerve center of a global commercial network. The rewards would be immense, and not only for Americans. In his sublime national egocentricity, Seward believed an American-dominated world would be beneficial to everyone.

CHAPTER SEVEN

The Clipper Ship, Maury the Pathfinder, and the Great Circle Route

The elegant and swift clipper ship is an apt symbol of Seward's era, when American sails whitened every sea, even more than its humdrum prairie counterpart, the Conestoga wagon, when Americans were pushing out their zones of settlement. Both originated in America, and both served as instruments of America's manifest destiny. The clipper ship stirred the artist—painter, printmaker, song writer, or historian—as has nothing else in the history of transportation. "They were more than things of wood and hemp—those old ships. They were at once the flower and symbol of all that was true and great and fine in a passing civilization" was a typical rhapsody.[1] Historians, swept away by the romance, have tended to invest the clipper with more economic importance than it probably warrants.

Americans were not the only fans of the clipper. When, late in 1850, the American ship *Oriental* sailed from Hong Kong to London in ninety-seven days, she caused a furor in British maritime circles. Admiring the "youth, ingenuity, and ardour" of Americans, some Englishmen glumly predicted "the extinction of the British Mercantile Marine."[2] With the repeal of the Navigation Acts in 1849, American ships could carry cargo from third nations into British ports, and Americans seemed likely to seize the lucrative tea trade from British hands. The *New York Daily Times* exulted:

Our clipper-fleet outstrip the wind, and leave their competitors of the Honorable East India Company, quite in the back-ground. American ships are apparently destined to engross the carrying trade. London boat-builders and ship-masters are gathering about a Yankee clipper, in the Thames, which has just brought a cargo of teas from Canton in ninety days. These are nautical marvels. Hitherto they have passed for extravagant fables; every clipper Captain has been a Sinbad, and his astounding log-book a chapter from the Arabian Nights. Now the evidence is before their eyes; faith has its anchor within the Thames, and they have only to look, wonder, and believe.[3]

The British may have built similar fast ships (and they were the only others to do so), but even they acknowledged that American designs were superior, the "cut and set of [American] sails" the best in the world.[4] Furthermore, American ships were more efficient, requiring smaller crews because of "their use of deck winches, patent sheaves, light Manila running gear, and large blocks, where we [British] . . . [are] content with common sheaves, stiff hemp gear, and the hard worked handy billy."[5] In the late 1850s, the British began to fight back for the tea trade with their own clippers like *Cutty Sark*. These were composite ships using oak and teak for keel and deck, iron frames, and copper sheathing for their bottoms. For the British they were cheaper to build than all-wood ships; they were rot resistant and had generous cargo capacity.[6]

Despite the machinery, labor costs per ton of cargo were high aboard the clipper ship. Relatively speaking, the clipper did not carry much. The ship was designed for speed not capacity; it was to carry passengers and high-value cargo as fast as possible. For that purpose, the clipper was supremely successful, and it was a long time before any steamship could set a better day's record than a clipper.

The clipper and those who sailed it seemed to embody much of what Americans liked to identify with the spirit of the nation: a ready acceptance of challenge and an exuberant sense of adventure, a relish for speed and a delight in power, an ability to combat and conquer the elements. The clipper ships were crafted with an intrinsic grace, an elegance and style expressed in a soaring verticality, their enormous sails seeming to touch the clouds. "America's Gothic cathedrals," Samuel Eliot Morison would later declaim; in the towering form of their spars and sails, they foreshadowed the skyscraper, the later American innovation on the urban architectural scene.

Matthew Fontaine Maury flatly proclaimed the clipper ship to be "the noblest work that has ever come from the hands of man."[7] The proud names proclaim it: *Rainbow, Great Republic, Chariot of Fame, Flying Cloud, Sovereign of the Seas*. Built of oak, pine, and rock maple; cut, mitered, and fitted with exquisite precision—the typical clipper had a black-painted hull sporting a crimson or gold stripe and an elaborately carved and gilded figurehead at the prow. Because shipowners wanted to attract passengers, the cabins would house tasteful and costly furniture, perhaps fittings of rosewood, mahogany, or satinwood, boasting elegance of workmanship as well as fineness of materials.

The clipper ship is part of a general tendency, beginning about 1815, to build merchant ships that were larger, with greater spread of sail, and of sharper design. *Clipper* is an imprecise term, first creeping into slang usage in the mid-1830s. The ship represents an improvement technology rather than a revolutionary one. One looks in vain for an inventor or for the first clipper. Nor is it invariably clear what was a clipper ship and what was not. But by the late 1840s, the clippers emerge as a recognizable type, identified as American. They are perhaps best described as long and narrow, with concave, needle-sharp, "inside-out" bows flared at the top, designed to slice, rather than to push, and cutting, instead of plough-ing, through the water.[8] The shape of their hulls and the quantity of the canvas they carried gave the clippers their great speed. In 1853, *Sovereign of the Seas* broke all records by sailing more than four hundred nautical miles in twenty-four hours.[9]

Donald McKay, the most famous builder of clipper ships, turned out *Staghound* in his East Boston yard. She was christened in Medford rum on December 7, 1850, and a huge crowd of fifteen thousand turned out to watch, despite "cold so bitter that tallow froze and boiling whale oil . . . [had to be] poured on the ways."[10] *Staghound* cost around $75,000, but her first voyage alone would make that sum. McKay's profits prompted a contemporary observer to say of him that "his business ca-pacity for mercantile transactions . . . [is] scarcely less conspicuous than his skill as a mechanic."[11]

McKay's masterwork was the *Great Republic*. Upon launch, in 1853, she was the world's largest sailing ship. She displaced 4,556 tons, was 334 feet long and 53 feet wide, with masts towering more than 200 feet high. Her masts at deck level were more than a yard thick, composed of sev-eral massive timbers bound together by iron hoops. Her sails, if spread flat, would have covered one and a half acres. The tendency among builders, egged on by shipowners, was to make ships of greater and greater size, until they reached the virtual limits of what wood could do.

During the War of 1812, Americans had become interested in speed; fast privateers could dodge British blockades. Speed demanded more and bigger sails, which required greater ship size, more crew, and greater cost. But less time at sea meant less money spent for wages and victuals. Speed also meant quicker recovery of an investment and quicker carriage of goods, some of them perishable. The tea trade put a premium on speed because tea tends to deteriorate at sea, and the first crop of the season from China would always command top price.

But without the California gold rush, also in 1849, the clipper ship would probably not have been commercially feasible.[12] On September 19, 1848, news of the discovery of gold in California reached New York via Mexico in what was touted as the record time of forty-four days from the Pacific to the Atlantic.[13] A mania seized the public; everyone wanted to go to California. A San Francisco newspaper reported on November 20, 1850, that "the number of vessels entering our harbor is really a matter of wonder. Within the forty-eight hours ending on Sunday night, nearly sixty sail entered the Golden Gate. The history of the world presents no comparison."[14] This sudden new demand was a powerful encouragement to build clippers, so well suited to the great unbroken spaces of the Pacific, particularly for the run around the Horn to California, a domestic commerce that by law Americans monopolized.[15] More than any other instrument, the clipper helped bind newly acquired California to the east coast core of American life.

General cargo could go via square-rigger; passengers would pay any price to get out to California as quickly as possible. The isthmian route was so congested and so disagreeable before the railroad spanned it that many chose to go via the Horn.

In California, gold was cheap, but all else was dear. High prices pushed freight rates up to five times what they had been before. Furthermore, a California-bound clipper could vastly increase profits if, instead of returning to the American east coast in ballast (for California had little except gold to send to New York), she sailed on from San Francisco across the Pacific in order to pick up a lucrative cargo of China tea for carriage around the Cape of Good Hope to England.[16]

The clipper would split the time required to sail from the North Atlantic to the China Sea by more than half. The pioneering *Empress of China* took fourteen months and nineteen days for the round trip from New York to Canton; the clipper *Rainbow* would do the same in six months and fourteen days.[17] Speeds were advertised, competition among builders and operators was keen, and the general public followed it all avidly. *Flying Cloud*'s record-smashing voyages were hailed as national triumphs, like America's twentieth-century first flights into space.[18] Never before had anyone traveled over such great distances so fast by either land or sea.

These intricate machine-like structures of wood, canvas, and hemp commanded utmost artistry not only from the designer and the carpenter but also from the mariners who worked them. The clipper was a complex, sensitive, and capricious instrument to be played upon by the captain with all the subtlety and skills he could muster. He required a highly competent and exceptionally hardworking and dedicated ship's company if he were to be successful.

The common saying was that it took three years to become a sailor, and any man wanting to master the art should certainly be "on the ratlines" by the time he was fourteen, training his hands to work on the rigging "making every finger a fishhook"—knotting, splicing, seizing, mastering all the art of the marlinspike—and also learning "wind sense," the art of exercising the tiller.[19] One seaman recalls that he and his fellows had to know by name and location, even by feel (for often it would be dark), each of "131 different halyards, clewlines, bunting or braces."[20]

Any mistake could carry catastrophic consequences for the individual or for the whole ship's company. Wear and tear, on ship and seaman alike, was great. "Only the hardiest could do a man's work on a clipper and like it."[21]

Ideally the captain was a humane master just as the crew were sober, conscientious, and skilled seamen. Because the U.S. Navy and Army remained small and the United States had no colonial empire and no East India Company, the merchant marine offered the best opportunity for an American boy wanting overseas adventure. The American elite, unlike the British, did not despise commerce. In cities like New York and Boston, the merchant took an honorable place in society. He had no aristocratic rival. Therefore, just as oceanic enterprise attracted American investment capital, the merchant marine, for a time, tapped some of the brightest and most ambitious of America's young men for its officers and its seamen.

But on both sides of the mast, the quality tended to be uneven and that of the crew to decline sharply during the clipper era. With the enormous increase of American shipping, demand for good seamen outran the supply. Press gangs prowled the waterfronts, and employers began to grumble that they could recruit "men fit only to keep the bread from molding."[22]

In their obsession with speed, captains drove their ships and their crews to the limits, crowding on the canvas to its utmost stretch. If there were no passengers, the captain lived in solitary majesty with "no companion but his own dignity."[23] The captain enjoyed absolute power on board, with terrible consequences to officers and crew if he abused his authority.[24] The men would then learn soon enough about "handspike hash" or "belaying pin soup," rawhide applied vigorously to the back and shoulders, sloshed down by a bucket of saltwater.

The appearance as well as the performance of his ship concerned the captain. If the moon shone brightly, he might have his men holystoning the decks even at night.[25] Many an exhausted sailor, in a weakened and malnourished condition, succumbed to disease or, working on the yards high above deck in stormy weather, fell to his death below, with howling winds and roaring waters to sing his requiem. Men who fell overboard, and there was scarcely ever a voyage when someone did not, were hardly ever saved.

On happier and more relaxed days, with blue skies, warm sun, and fair winds, the sailor could wash and mend his clothes, smoke his tobacco, swap yarns with his shipmates, and enjoy the sibilant swishing of the water, the slapping of the sails, the rhythmic creaking of the masts and spars, and the humming of the wind through the yards, punctuated by the warning cries of the lookout and the quick chiming of the bell.

Sometimes the men sang as they worked. When heaving a windlass or hauling a halyard, one man would sing out to establish a rhythm and others would follow. A song was, they said, "as good as ten men, [and] as necessary to sailors as the fife and drum to a soldier."[26] All hands esteemed a sailor's ability to sing well.

Leisure was not a significant part of the seaman's life. "American shipmasters," Dana observed, "get nearly three weeks' more labor out of their crews in the course of a year, than the masters of vessels from Catholic countries. As Yankees don't usually keep Christmas, and shipmasters at sea never know when Thanksgiving comes, Jack has no festival at all."[27] The old saying went that "sailors worked like horses at sea and spent their money like asses ashore."[28] Sailors aboard clippers were treated better than on other ships of the time, American or foreign.

Many American ships did not provide alcohol, unlike the British, for example, and as a result insurance underwriters wrote cheaper policies. Boiled coffee, sweetened with molasses, was the substitute. The cook was often Chinese or African American, but no hint of ethnicity seems to have enlivened the cuisine. Flour and water mixed with dried apples or raisins were boiled down in a canvas bag to make a staple item "duff" or "clagger." "Plum duff," its elegant variation, was reserved for Sundays. "Scouse," or "lobscouse," was another common dish, a hashlike combination of broken pieces of biscuit soaked in water, with added bits of beef and grease or perhaps bread, chopped potatoes, or onions. The mixture then was baked. Beans, potatoes, dried peas, salt beef or pork, hard bread, and coffee or tea rounded out the menu.

Fresh food of any kind was a luxury. Passengers often brought along their own supplies of wine or spirits and favorite delicacies. Bullocks, sheep, pigs, and poultry were kept in pens or in the longboat, to be butchered en route. The largest were eaten first; pigs were the best sailors, therefore surviving longer. But the objective always was to butcher the animal before it died.

Little was wasted. Sailors used the refuse grease from the galley to slush down the masts and to keep the ropes pliant so that the ship could be handled more easily. All aboard had to endure the rancid odor. Food aboard a mid-nineteenth-century clipper or ordinary merchantman was perhaps better than that served aboard the Manila galleon, although only marginally so. But at least the voyage was short enough that scurvy was not a problem. The day of refrigeration would soon change all this for the sailor, and for the transoceanic passenger it made a lavish menu a routine experience.

The successes of the clipper in carrying people and freight so fast and over such great distances were due not simply to the art of the shipwright and the skills of the shipmaster but in part also to the research of American naval officer Matthew Fontaine Maury, known to history as the Pathfinder of the Seas. Maury showed captains where they might best sail. Nowhere was this more important than on North Pacific routes to Asia.

On a four year (1826–30) trip around the Horn and across the Pacific aboard *Vincennes*, the sloop subsequently used by Wilkes as his flagship, Maury learned firsthand that the only charts available carried insufficient as well as incorrect information. He began to write pseudonymously about this and other deficiencies of the U.S. Navy. He developed both a propensity to write for publication and a style attractive to the public.

Condemned to shore duty by an accident to his leg, Maury was named superintendent of what would eventually be called the Naval Observatory and Hydrographical Office. There he began to collect voluminous data about winds and weather for use by sailing captains. The same year (1842) that Samuel F. B. Morse was experimenting with undersea telegraphy in New York harbor found Maury collecting information at his desk in Washington. He put down on a chart the tracks of many vessels making the same voyage, but in all seasons, at different times, and over the years. He then projected the winds and the currents met by these ships, thus making available on one piece of paper the body of accumulated experience.

First digging his information out of logbooks, Maury then began to solicit it directly from naval officers and merchant mariners. Constantly craving more information, he enticed captains to help him. Every navigator submitting an abstract log was eligible to receive a free copy of the charts and sailing directions to which he had contributed.[29] What mariner would not hunger for such information?

Maury's charts shortened the time at sea and lessened the danger. A captain could be sure that he was pursuing not only the fastest path known but also the safest. He was now far less likely to pile up his ship on some unknown rock or shoal. The Boston merchant community were among the first to recognize the value of Maury's work. China merchant Robert Bennet Forbes offered to raise $50,000 to buy Maury a surveying ship, and Forbes supplied him with many ships' logs.[30]

Self-confident, articulate, persuasive, and experienced with ships and the sea, Maury captured enormous and sustained popularity from the public. On the publication of his *Sailing Directions* (1854), *Hunt's Merchants' Magazine* proclaimed that "since the invention of the mariner's compass, and its great adjunct, the chronometer, no such boon has been given to Commerce, and through it to civilization, as this book confers."[31] *The Physical Geography of the Sea* (1855) would remain in print for twenty years and be translated into half a dozen European languages.[32] Maury's literary, "nervously eloquent" style and its heavy religiosity appealed to the contemporary audience.[33]

In the introduction to his major book, *The Physical Geography of the Sea*,

Matthew Fontaine Maury (Courtesy, National Archives)

Maury delightedly quotes a letter of appreciation he received from an American merchant captain: "I feel that, aside from any pecuniary profit to myself from your labors, you have done me good as a man. You have taught me to look above, around, and beneath me, and recognize God's hand in every element by which I am surrounded."[34] Maury drew plaudits from the critics—if they were not scientists. One review declared that "Lieutenant Maury will be numbered among the great scientific men of the age and the benefactors of mankind."[35] But the scientific community was, with reason, skeptical, if not hostile. Writing from a twentieth-century vantage, John Leighly says that "as a scientific treatise *The Physical Geography* fell below the level of the best contemporary knowledge."[36] Maury was good at assembling data, but his science was not rigorous. Whether Maury even was a scientist is arguable. He contributed only modestly to the development of theoretical knowledge; he was interested in theory only insofar as it contributed to practical knowledge. Sometimes touted as "the father of oceanography," he made only a negative contribution to that science.[37]

But Maury did make a substantial contribution to oceanic navigation. He seems to have been the first American to cast aside the Mercator view of the world and the first to perceive and propose the great circle route across the North Pacific. When looking at the Pacific, he suggested, the map should be discarded in favor of the globe.

Maury observed that travel from California to China is much farther via Hawaii than via the Aleutians, despite what a Mercator chart would show, and that the arc of the North Pacific is "*the great highway from America to the Indies,* and will hereafter be regarded the great *commercial* circle of the Pacific Ocean."[38]

The great circle route invested the California coast with a new strategic importance, especially the town of Monterey, Maury suggested. San Diego was also a possible oceanic port for trade with Asia, but it stood on the edge of a desert which limited its opportunities for growth landward. San Francisco was situated farther out of the way of the great circle than either of the other two. Monterey, Maury argued, was therefore the logical terminus of the American trans-Pacific China trade. And it was logical terminus also, he said, for a future transcontinental railroad.

Maury anticipated a voyage between Shanghai and Monterey as taking twenty-six days, including a one-day stop midway en route, for coaling in the Aleutians. He adds: "The intelligence brought by each arrival would be instantly caught up by telegraph, and as instantly delivered in New York and Boston."[39] An Aleutian stopover on the great circle route would require permission of the Russians; Maury hoped that could be negotiated before the Russians gained a true understanding of its commercial significance.[40]

The Russians were making spasmodic, largely unsuccessful attempts to keep Americans out of their territories because unscrupulous Yankee traders were continuing to sell liquor and firearms to the indigenous peoples, in defiance of Russian law. But at the same time, the Russians continued to want and depend on American suppliers for a wide range of goods.

Maury pointed out that of the estimated global population of eight hundred million people, six hundred million of them "are to be found in the islands and countries which are washed by the Pacific." It would therefore be difficult to exaggerate the "value and importance to the Republic of a safe and ready means of communication through California with those people." Pacific islanders, Chinese, and Russians are all potential customers for American products, he suggested. "Do you suppose that the laboring classes of China would live and die on the unchanged diet of rice if they could obtain meat and bread?" he asked.[41]

Maury wanted to know more about the winds and currents, the hydrography and meteorology of the huge and little-traveled North Pacific. He conjectured that the overall pattern was probably similar to that of the North Atlantic although more uniform since the expanse is wider. But only Yankee traders and whalers seemed to know anything about this part of the ocean, and no one had collated their information.

To a steamship captain, distances in miles were of key importance to plotting a course, but weather and stopover opportunities were also significant. The fogs and storms as well as the uncharted rocks of the Aleutians discouraged the mariner. And these islands, with their handful of people, provided little of intrinsic commercial interest, with small opportunity to pick up or drop off cargo or passengers. Unless fuel consumption were the only criterion for a voyage, the Aleutians' Dutch Harbor could not compete with Hawaii's Honolulu.

To the captain of a sailing ship, winds and currents were more important than distance in miles. The shortest distance could prove to be the longest voyage. Because of the prevailing winds, plying the great circle route across the Pacific was less good for the ship under sail than taking a more southerly course, particularly if the ship were running westward. All sailing ships were in the habit of stopping at Hawaii because in addition to their other attractions the islands lie within the trade wind region.

Above all else, transportation is a matter of routes. Routes are determined by politics and by technology, as well as by markets and sources of supply. Russian ownership of the Aleutians certainly inhibited any American use of the great circle route effort requiring a stop at Dutch Harbor. National sovereignty often dictates where a ship can obtain that which it requires. The sailing ship normally needed to stop only for food and the fuel for cooking it. The coal-powered ship, driven by its inexorable need for fuel, not to mention the crankiness of its machinery, which demanded frequent repair, would necessarily follow a different course from the wind-powered ship.

CHAPTER EIGHT

Americans in Far Pacific Waters: Expeditions

The large size of the United States put a premium on exploiting the telegraph, the steamboat, and the railroad, but no quick and easy route to the Pacific yet existed. Conestoga wagons lumbered into the Willamette and Sacramento valleys, driven by exhausted but eager pioneers across the "Great American Desert" and over the "Stoney Mountains," as the Rockies were first called, drawing the attention of those left back home to Pacific horizons.

Novelists like Herman Melville and James Fenimore Cooper put the primary American frontier on the sea, suggesting that America's destiny was more maritime than continental.[1] Whalers were simultaneously widely crisscrossing the waters of the Pacific. Americans acting independently of government were ready to make the North Pacific Ocean and at least its American rimlands theirs.

The frontier of commerce in East Asia was beginning to interact closely with the frontier of settlement in California as the latter began to move closer to the former. Sea transport created and sustained both. The United States, like Russia, had leaped to the Pacific while leaving a large continental space to be organized and settled later. The North American Pacific coast from Mexico to Alaska remained a series of "islands" until well along in the nineteenth century (and even later in the case of Alaska), the interior largely unexplored and unsettled. It was easier to travel from New York to Canton or Shanghai than to the Rocky Mountains or the Great Salt Lake. First Honolulu, and later San Francisco, arose as New England transplants, owing much of their commercial life to Yankee merchant mariners, and the stamp of Boston would persist in local mores long after the fading of its commercial influence.

Before the 1840s were over, Great Britain had yielded all claims to Oregon, Mexico had surrendered California, and an overstretched Russia, pushed far to the north, was already contemplating total withdrawal from the American continent. People began talking of an isthmian canal because America had fresh need of a secure path between the two oceans.

Just as the first American Pacific cities like San Francisco and Portland were taking form, American merchants were shifting their commercial networks northward along the Asian Pacific littoral; in response to the increasing commercial and military presence of the Atlantic world in the Asian North Pacific, new coastal cities were emerging. Within twenty years' time, Shanghai, Tientsin (Tianjin), Port Arthur (Lushun), Vladivostok, Kobe, and Yokohama would be founded as commercial ports or naval bases, interacting economically or strategically within the North Pacific world.

In the China trade, Canton's ancient routes stretched out toward Southeast Asia. The Portuguese and the other early European visitors, as well as the first American arrivals, like the British had simply slipped into the old patterns and moved across the Indian Ocean to reach them, not across the Pacific.

But Canton, in the new North Pacific international era opening in the 1840s, was rapidly giving place to Shanghai as the major port on the China coast. By 1871 Shanghai would handle 71 percent of China's external trade, Canton only 13 percent.[2] Unlike Canton, Shanghai looked eastward out into the Pacific.

Situated midway on the China coast between north and south, Shanghai lies at the head of the world's greatest commercial inland waterway system on the delta of the Yangzi, able to tap one of the world's most populous and greatest potential markets. Shanghai is China's natural maritime gateway, interposing itself between the foreign maritime world and the vast peasant economy of central China. That Shanghai had only a poor harbor, highly susceptible to silting, seemed almost irrelevant. Shanghai's role in modern history carries an environmental inevitability.

First visited by the British in 1832 and captured by them in 1842, Shanghai was opened to foreign commerce on November 17, 1843, as a result of China's defeat in the Opium War. Shanghai was the farthest north of five treaty ports then opened to foreign settlement and soon by far the most important. The first resident American merchant arrived in 1846.[3] Shanghai was already drawing down Canton's trade. Canton and Hong Kong were nearer to India. Shanghai, to the benefit of Americans, was closer to California, and to Japan as well. That proximity would become important after Japan's reopening in the late 1850s.

Foreigners found Shanghai a more spacious and agreeable place, with a better climate than Canton.[4] Shanghai's tidal mudflats were soon dredged and wharfed by jetties and bunds; gracious wooden-frame, two-story mansions wrapped upstairs and down by sweeping verandahs seemed a transplant of British life in India; trees and flowers softened the landscape. A forest of foreign masts and funnels, first sailing ships and soon steamers, joined the thriving junk traffic.[5] Shanghai became the radiating center for the diffusion of North Atlantic commercial, industrial, and religious culture in the Chinese world.

In the early 1850s American sailing ships carried almost half of China's foreign trade merchandise. Even after the decline of sail, American shipping remained important in Chinese waters. Americans, preeminent with river steamboats, saw an entrepreneurial opportunity in China's lack of steam navigation in its coastal and riverine traffic. The Chinese were receptive not only because of the commercial opportunities of the new technology but also because they believed that foreign ships were less likely to be attacked by pirates.

Russell & Co. of Boston, the first American firm in Shanghai, created the largest merchant steam fleet in East Asia. Its Shanghai Steam Navigation Company, founded in 1862 and sold to the Chinese in 1877, served coastal towns to the south and to the north as far as Tientsin, but the Yangzi formed the heart of the system. On land the Chinese objected to steam power; railroads disrupted natural harmonies and disturbed the ancestors, and China long resisted the building of a rail network. Steam power at sea provoked no such sentiments.

The American boats were wooden coal-burning side-wheelers, most of them New York or Brooklyn built, very much like those used so successfully on the Hudson and other east coast rivers. The larger craft (four hundred tons or more) could be safely sailed out to China, their own floating cargo; the smaller ones were knocked down and put aboard a seagoing vessel for shipment. The British despaired of competing with this Yankee enterprise.[6]

Just as the clipper ship was nineteenth-century America's chief contribution to the technology of transport under sail, the paddle-wheel steamboat was its nineteenth-century chief contribution to the technology of steam transport. Curiously, both were obsolescent modes even as they were introduced, but Yankee ingenuity made each highly effective for specifically appropriate uses.

The American steam riverboat fleet, the world's finest, pushed maritime commerce and travel deep into the heart of continental America. There in the 1850s the steamboat reigned; railroads were still primitive and their network thin, intended for the most part simply as connectors between bodies of water. Once a dense rail system was built, and this happened very fast, the steamboat faded as a major means of transportation. The age of glory for the river steamboat was no longer than that of the sailing clipper.

The success of the Americans in China with this form of marine technology was due not simply to marine architecture and engineering. Superior American business management, entrepreneurial energy, and imagination were important too. Furthermore, the Americans seemed to possess a certain "cultural malleability," an ability to get along well with the Chinese, at least by contrast with the British, although Americans were prone to exaggerate their aptitude for intercultural relations.[7]

American dominance in the local shipping world gave the illusion there of an American oceanic preeminence. Frank Blackwell Forbes, a major figure in the Shanghai Steam Navigation Company, predicted that "the Pacific Mail and our company will probably in a few years monopolize most of the carrying trade of Eastern waters."[8] The Pacific Mail Steamship Company embarked on the first regularly scheduled, large-scale trans-Pacific service in history on January 1, 1867, with the wooden paddle-wheel steamer *Colorado*. But the British were way ahead of the Americans with oceanic steam transport in the Pacific, as everywhere else. Steamers flying British colors passed through the Magellan Strait in 1840 to serve Valparaiso, and via the Indian Ocean they linked the China coast to Britain in 1844.[9]

Visiting American naval officer Robert Wilson Shufeldt wanted to open the Yangzi to American commerce as far as I-chang, gateway to Szechuan Province, some eight hundred miles upstream, seeing this as advantageous to Americans and Chinese both. Shufeldt, writing in 1867, claimed that "China and Japan—are both looking toward America—with most friendly gaze—not only for the trade & intercourse which they expect from the Pacific—but with a sort of feeling that the American Element, is an element antagonistic to that European power whose encroachments they dread."[10] Although its base in reality may have been slender, this was a thought in which Americans often sought comfort.

By 1862 the population of Shanghai reached 1.5 million, with one-third of its people, Chinese and foreign, living in the foreign settlements. The rising commercial city inspired an exuberance, a frontier boom mentality like that of the contemporary American West, undaunted by the fury of the T'ai-p'ing Rebellion (1850–64), probably the bloodiest civil war in world history.[11] Shanghai, the closest Chinese port to the sources of supply, came to export about half of the tea and three-quarters of the silk China sold to the United States.[12] Roughly equidistant in shipping time and distance from the American east coast and western Europe, Shanghai is where China juts farthest out into the sea toward America. It is China's point of tangency to the great northern crescent of the Pacific and where the Chinese, before the Communist triumph in 1949, would interact most closely with the North Atlantic world.

Along with the territorial establishment of the United States on the shores of the Pacific, at mid-century the biggest event in North Pacific history was the reopening of Japan and the first stirrings in modern times of any Japanese oceanic mentality—an interest that would ultimately project Japan far out into the Pacific. The reopening of Japan on the direct Pacific path to China would further encourage the geographical shift of international commerce into the North Pacific to which Shanghai was contributing so heavily.

Beginning in the seventeenth century the Tokugawa shogunate governing Japan had decided that national security demanded severely limiting Japan's intercourse with the Atlantic world. Within that nation, the aggressiveness of Iberian Christianity had appeared to threaten a newly fashioned and delicate balance of political power. The Portuguese and the Spaniards, their priests and their friars, were therefore banished.

Ultimately, only the Dutch, who were profit seekers and not proselytizers, were permitted—and under highly restricted conditions—to bring their trade to Japan from Europe. The Japanese continued to allow and even to engage in maritime trade with the East Asian world via Tsushima and the Ryukyu Islands, offshoots of the Japanese archipelago. But these constricted outlets were more important as conduits for information than as pipelines for the flow of goods.

Offshore fishing and coastal shipping remained important to the Japanese; huge quantities of rice were regularly moved by sea to centers of consumption like Edo (Tokyo), even then one of the world's most populous cities. But the Tokugawa government, fearing the ideological contamination of the aggressive Atlantic world, refused to allow the building of any ships of a size adequate for oceanic travel and forbade Japanese people to travel overseas.

Before the Tokugawa era, Japanese mariners had frequented the China coast and sailed to places as far as Luzon and Malacca, but they had never ventured out into the wide Pacific except when carried there by the vagaries of wind and current. Japan, like the rest of East Asia at mid-nineteenth century, remained a passive force in the newly unfolding world of the North Pacific of which Americans were prime initiators.

Virtually from the birth of the Republic, Americans were expressing interest in Japan even if they knew practically nothing about it. In 1791, the journal *American Museum* praised the American appetite for oceanic adventure, which was carrying American ships in new directions everywhere, specifically across the Pacific:

Perhaps no species of traffic has promised more lucrative advantages than the fur trade from the North-western coast of North America and the adjacent islands, across the Pacific Ocean to China. If the voyages be prudent and industrious, if they do not waste their time in the voluptuous enjoyments of the tropical islands which lie in their way; but steadily pursue their business, and are faithful to their employers, there is no doubt but large fortunes may be made in this traffic.[13]

En route to China lay Japan. The Japanese produced tea, porcelain, and silk—the same range of goods as the Chinese—and the Dutch found trade with them to be lucrative. With all the frustrations of the tightly controlled China traffic, would Japan not offer an excellent supplementary market? American furs should be a welcome commodity to the Japanese, and "the people there will soon be convinced that we have no other views than trade."[14]

Captain David Porter is the first on record (1815) to suggest a commercial and scientific expedition to Japan. He was quite aware of the political difficulties and the failures of other nations to persuade the Japanese to open up, but having served with Stephen Decatur at Tripoli in 1804, he suggested a similarly tough approach to Japan. The administration hastily put him in a position out of harm's way.[15]

Aaron Haight Palmer, a New York entrepreneur with an enormous appetite for statistical information, was what we would call today a public relations man. During the 1840s he tried unsuccessfully to organize an isthmian canal project and pushed for an American global trade. Asia and the Pacific held a special interest for him; he was convinced that Japan would be an excellent market for American cotton goods and whale oil.

But it would be some time before any Americans would be welcome in Japan for any reason. And when they did finally come, it would not be to sell furs, cotton goods, or whale oil. The initial interest of Japan to Americans was largely extrinsic: it lay athwart the major future route to China. President Millard Fillmore pointed out, in a letter to the emperor of Japan carried to Japan by Commodore Matthew Perry, that recent geostrategic changes had brought Japan and the United States much closer. The United States now reached from the Atlantic to the Pacific; California was of growing importance; new transportation technologies meant that American ships could theoretically get to Japan in less than three weeks. Serious American interest in negotiating with Japan developed only with the prospect of steam navigation across the Pacific, and for this new technology Japan developed an intrinsic interest as a source of coal, "that great mineral agent of civilization."[16]

Not all Americans then favored "civilizing" other nations or "liberating" the oppressed. Not everyone was enthusiastic about opening Japan. Some people grumbled that it would be better to "open New Mexico" to improved mail and roads than to open far-away Japan.[17] To Henry David Thoreau,

the whole enterprise of this nation, which is not an upward, but a westward one toward Oregon, California, Japan, etc., is totally devoid of interest to me, whether performed on foot, or by a Pacific railroad. . . . It is perfectly heathenish,—a filibustering toward heaven by the great western route. . . . What end do they propose to themselves beyond Japan? What aims more lofty have they than the prairie dogs?[18]

The Perry expedition (1853–54) was the last of several American attempts, each of which approached Japan from Asia, north from Malacca, not westward across the Pacific. Perry certainly had a Pacific perspective, and he saw Japan ultimately as Far West instead of Far East, but he could not choose his route because his steam warships demanded frequent stops for coal. The Pacific offered none.

Furthermore, the United States had no naval dockyards on the Pacific coast; Mare Island, purchased for that purpose in 1853, was not yet built. The navy used Atlantic dockyards. American warships in East Asian waters were obliged to put into British-controlled ports for any substantial repairs.[19] Perry's squadron took eight months to get to Japan via the Cape of Good Hope and the Indian Ocean.

Perry had drafted his own orders; Secretary of State Daniel Webster was too ill to do so. But doubtless Webster would have wished much the same. Massachusetts man that he was, Webster's interests were strongly maritime. Of all the United States, New England remained the region most tied to the sea and the international economy.

Webster had long thought of the Pacific as a natural zone for the extension of these interests. For Webster the Pacific was the last link to forge in a great global chain binding the world, "as far as civilization has spread," into a new oceanic steam transportation network.[20] He defined Hawaii as an American sphere of interest for commercial, strategic, and religious reasons. Hawaii was territory not to be annexed—for that Americans had neither will nor means—but not to be yielded to any foreign power.

Honolulu, on Oahu, and Lahaina, its Maui counterpart, formed the nurturing center of the North Pacific whaling industry and encouragement to the growth of American influence in the islands. Only after 1860 would the plantation supplant the whaleship as the foundation of Hawaiian commercial prosperity.[21] Missionaries were drawing fresh American attention to the islands as a possible proving ground for efforts farther to the west, on the Asian mainland. And now that the United States possessed major deep-water ports on the Pacific, Hawaii assumed new geopolitical interest. Britain, France, and Russia had all expressed interest in Hawaii at one time or another, and both Britain and France were expanding in the South Pacific—one to New Zealand and the other to Tahiti.

Whale fishers certainly reminded Americans of the existence of Japan. Herman Melville writes that "if that double-bolted land, Japan, is ever to become hospitable, it is the whaleship alone to whom credit will be due; for she is already on the threshold."[22] But although much talk was bruited about in Washington about the desirability of improving the situation of American whalers in the North Pacific by making Japanese ports havens for them, the whalers themselves did not lobby for such governmental assistance. They were more interested in better charts than in anything else. Their plight seems simply to have provided additional ammunition to those interested in opening Japan for other reasons.

Even before Perry lifted anchor, the Japanese had promised to treat American castaways decently and to victual any foreign ships requiring it.[23] The Japanese did not want a commercial treaty with the Americans (or anyone else), and the Americans knew it.[24] But an earlier reluctance on the part of the American public to support a policy of extracting commercial privileges by force faded in the 1850s.[25]

In his official published account of the expedition Perry wrote that its purposes were "to procure friendly admission to Japan for purposes of trade, and to establish, at proper points, permanent depots of coal for our steamers crossing the Pacific."[26] A myth grew that Japan was a veritable "Pennsylvania of the Pacific," its coal making it even more attractive as a stopover en route to China.[27] Hawaii was also a strategically located stopover, but the islands were more than four thousand miles from the China coast, and they had no coal to offer unless it were stocked there. No other stopovers were yet thought of.[28] Maury's shorter great circle route via the Russian-held Aleutians could not compete with the delights of Hawaii, where the Americans were at least commercially preeminent.

Perry was much interested in the transport of mails and had in fact been earlier given the responsibility of overseeing the construction of mail steamers under U.S. government behest. Fast mail service across the Pacific would, he thought, "complete the circle of bi-monthly communications around the entire globe" and make it possible for American merchants to get important information from China before the British could.[29]

Perry was steam conscious, unlike many of his American counterparts, and he had pushed for the adaptation of steam propulsion in the American navy. His trip to Japan along the British steam route across the Indian Ocean and through the Strait of Malacca, and his difficulties in obtaining coal, showed him how vulnerable Americans could be without their own fuel sources. Perry wanted American naval bases in the western Pacific. He wanted American coaling stations, and he wanted American colonies, or "offshoots" as he skittishly called them; he was vague about what their precise political relationship with the United States might be.[30]

Perry was a bluffer. The United States may have been commercially assertive and giving the British a run for their money in East Asia, but the U.S. military sinew was thin and the resources of the nation still largely undeveloped. The population of the United States stood at twenty-five million, less than that of Japan. And only a quarter of a million or so lived west of the Mississippi. The Perry expedition was a major strain on U.S. naval resources; the commodore was unable to collect the number of ships he would have liked.

The shallow waters of Edo's approaches sheltered the Japanese capital from Perry's guns, which, although shell firing, were short in range. The biggest weapon the Americans could use against the Japanese was the threat of Britain's Royal Navy. The Opium War (1839–42) revealed the long-range striking power of the British fleet and the Japanese were well aware of it.

But in Perry's grand view, the entire Pacific Ocean north of the equator lay simply waiting the grasp of America. No American before him had seen the Pacific so comprehensively or in such specific terms. The rivets of Perry's new steam-linked empire would be Hawaii (which he did not visit), the Bonins, the Ryukyus, and Taiwan. Commerce would lubricate the mechanism, and this commerce would benefit not only America but also Asia. His vision was like that of Seward.

Perry believed Naha on Okinawa, the largest of the Ryukyus, was essential to a future San Francisco–Shanghai steam packet line. He foresaw that Shanghai would become the commercial heart of the China trade, its teas and silks borne by steamship to California. "It is impossible to estimate . . . the advantages that may grow out of an intercourse so rapid and so certain," Perry declared.[31] He visited Naha five times, making it the headquarters for his activities along the coast of Japan, and he established a coal depot there, which he rented for ten dollars a month.[32]

Perry liked the Bonin Islands (Ogasawara), which lay nearly on the same latitude as the Canaries. Granted, their soil was poor, but their proximity to Japan—only two days' steaming time[33]—gave them "a peculiar importance and interest."[34] For a ship traveling to China from Oregon, Japan would furnish the most convenient stopping place. But for the California-China route, the Bonins would be better. Bayard Taylor, journalist with the expedition, wrote (1855) that the commodore was attracted to the Bonins as a coaling station on "perhaps the only spot in the Pacific, west of the Sandwich Islands, which promises to be of real advantage for such a purpose."[35] Perry bought a piece of land there for offices, wharves, and coal storage.

But the commodore perceived the whole sweep of the Pacific as open to American expansion with a divine inevitability about the whole process: "The history and fate of nations are doubtless directed by an overruling Providence, and probably we could not, if we would, change their course, or avert our ultimate destiny."[36] The United States must become a "highway for the world." In the steam age, the shortest route between East Asia and Europe would lie across North America, and so to Perry it seemed "that we might with propriety apply to ourselves the name by which China had loved to designate herself, and deem that we were, in truth, 'the Middle Kingdom,' "[37] "The people of America will, in some form or other extend their dominion and their power until they have brought within their mighty embrace multitudes of the Islands of the great Pacific, and place the Saxon race upon the eastern shores of Asia."[38] Finally dropping any reluctance to use the word, he argued, "Colonies are almost as necessary to a commercial nation, as are the ships which transport from one country to another the commodities, in the interchange of which commerce subsists."[39] Forty years later, arch-imperialist Alfred Thayer Mahan could say it no more bluntly.

Perry saw Great Britain and the United States as embarked on a collision course of commercial competition in the Pacific, with war the likely result. Britain's imperial center of gravity had shifted eastward from the Atlantic after the Napoleonic Wars, from North America and the Caribbean toward India and China. The Indian Ocean became virtually a British lake.[40] But the British did not extend their sphere eastward beyond the China coast, their Pacific trading diaspora developing as a Far Eastern extension of that. Because of newly acquired Oregon and California, the Pacific seemed to offer new opportunities of naval and maritime superiority for the United States.

Perry did not much like Russia either, partially because of its threatening commercial potential and geostrategic rivalry but more for ideological reasons. He was pessimistic about the U.S.-Russian relationship in the long term. "With harbors on the coasts of Eastern Asia and Western America, opening on a sea which must be the seat of an immense and lucrative commerce, [Russia] might aim to be a great maritime power, and to rule mistress of the Pacific."[41] If Russia should gain control over Japan, its resulting naval and commercial power would menace the United States. In any case, it seemed likely that Russia would extend its reach south to China, to meet Americans, with "Cossack struggling against Saxon" in a giant contest of absolutism versus freedom, with immense, incalculable consequences.

The Russians gave Perry ammunition for his argument by racing him to negotiate with the Japanese. A Russian squadron under the command of Admiral Evfimii Putiatin sailed to Japan, first to Nagasaki, later to Shimoda, to try to secure the opening of one or two ports to Russian ships and to delineate the national boundaries with Japan. Putiatin's visits and talks culminated in a treaty (February 7, 1855) in which Russia gained much the same benefits as had the United States, as well as an agreement that the island of Sakhalin should be jointly occupied.

Putiatin negotiated successfully without black ships, big guns, or bluster. But he had no choice; his major ship *Diana* was beached and destroyed at Shimoda by a typhoon. The hospitable Japanese helped him build a replacement, which he sailed home, carrying *Diana*'s guns on board.

Commodore Perry saw the United States as still living in its youth, and for Perry, history was a continuing process in which the United States was "destined at some *indefinite* time to attain a full and vigorous manhood, and then alas, like all earthly governments, to fall into decadence, to decline in power, and at last, to fall asunder, by the consequences of its own vices and misdoings; thus making room for some new empire now scarcely in embryo."[42]

This was a matter upon which he made no further speculation, but the thought was unusual at the time. Americans who did ruminate about such things apparently saw history as coming to an end with the rise of America to global supremacy. Interestingly, Perry seems not to have thought much about Japan and the consequences for that nation of his visits. In his preoccupation with Great Britain and Russia, Japan to him was no more than a passive force and possible pawn.

Like his naval predecessor David Porter, Perry wanted to push the U.S. political presence to the shores of East Asia. Like Porter, Perry was far ahead of the current of government policy and public opinion. Americans did not want a naval station at Naha any more than they had wanted one in Nukuhiva. The secretary of the navy found it "embarrassing . . . [it would be] rather mortifying to surrender the island, if once seized, and rather inconvenient and expensive to maintain a force there to retain it."[43]

Washington repudiated Perry's actions and ignored his proposals. His geostrategic perceptions would have found more sympathetic ears there forty years in the future; Perry would have been far more comfortable with Theodore Roosevelt than he was with Franklin Pierce. Pierce may have been an instinctive expansionist, but he operated by administrative paralysis. Roosevelt would have relished and responded vigorously to Perry's aggressiveness.

Despite the hoopla it caused in the United States—and Perry possessed great skills of self-advertisement—his treaty was not much. Richard van Alstyne calls it "a mere shipwreck convention."[44] Perry secured the promise of decent treatment for American castaways—rights equal to those that the Japanese might accord any other foreign power—and the opening of two ports, Shimoda and Hakodate, as coaling and supply depots. The Japanese asked Perry why, if his mission were a peaceful one, he brought four warships to deliver one letter? The Commodore replied that it was a greater compliment to the Japanese emperor.[45]

More agreeable to the Japanese were the presents the Americans brought, especially a magnetic telegraph and a small railroad track with locomotive and car, symbols of the revolutionary changes underway in the world. The Americans were impressed by Japanese knowledge and sophistication, "though with Japanese self-possession they concealed much. They laughed, and were untiring in their attention to cherry brandy," one observer remembered.[46]

American visitors immediately after Perry were frustrated by Japanese unwillingness to trade. "In diplomacy I'd put the Japanese against the world," businessman George Francis Train complained.[47] But at least the commodore opened the way for the diplomat. Perry was followed by Consul Townsend Harris, who secured a real treaty, effectively opening Japan to American commerce. Perry's visits set off a domestic crisis in Japan that led to a new government for the Japanese, the reopening of the nation to unrestricted relations with the North Atlantic world, and a new Japanese consciousness of the Pacific.

The Ringgold-Rodgers expedition (1853–55), another American naval North Pacific reconnaisance, pursued science while the Perry expedition was pursuing strategy. It had a far broader geographical scope than that of Perry, which was confined largely to Japan and the Ryukyu Islands. But in terms of drama, Perry triumphed. It was he who captured the imagination of the public and the pen of the historian.

In pursuance of an act of Congress passed on the motion of Senator Seward and prompted by groups of east coast businessmen, the North Pacific expedition sailed June 11, 1853, from Hampton Roads, Virginia, with Commodore Cadwalader Ringgold flying his flag aboard the trusty sloop *Vincennes* (Ringgold himself had served with Wilkes on that great expedition). Four other ships came, including only one steamer, *Hancock*, not a paddle-wheeler but a screw-propelled ship.

Ringgold was stricken with a fever while his little squadron was riding at anchor in Macao. The strenuous treatment of quinine, morphine, and opium he was given brought him physical recovery but mental shakiness. Commodore Perry then summarily relieved Ringgold of his duties and replaced him with his old friend John Rodgers. Since Ringgold had previously quarreled with Perry, the latter's motive was later questioned. Another wrinkle in the case was Perry's frustrated desire to embrace the surveying expedition within his own command. Ringgold later was vindicated, but Perry died before any inquiry could be made into his action.[48]

Rodgers was mindful of the importance of his assignment, writing of the Pacific as the ocean in which "we of all the world have the deepest interest."[49] His primary objectives were to chart the coasts of China and Japan, making them less hazardous to whaleships and other passersby, and to explore the upper reaches of the North Pacific and possible routes for future steamship traffic between California and China. Secretary of the Navy William Alexander Graham had told the Congress that

one vessel in every twenty that went there [the North Pacific] during the summer of 1851 has been left behind a total wreck, and the lives of their crews . . . put in jeopardy, mostly for the want of proper charts. No protection that our squadrons can at this moment give to our commerce . . . can compare with that which a good chart of that part of the ocean would afford to this nursery of American seamen.[50]

As Rodgers said, Americans could not expect the British to chart the Pacific as they had so much of the rest of the world's oceanic space. "Self interest would rather counsel their putting an impassable barrier, were it possible, between our country and China."[51]

Rodgers was working off Japan before Perry was able to negotiate any agreements with the Japanese, but Rodgers's assumption was that Perry would secure ex post facto Japanese agreement to his work. Lieutenant John Mercer Brooke, who served the expedition as astronomer and hydrographer, surveyed much of the eastern coast of Honshu. Working from an open boat, manned by fifteen men who camped out nightly on the shore, Brooke cavalierly ignored Japanese sovereignty. Rodgers wrote the secretary of the navy (February 15, 1855) to say,

We are not war-vessels, and can not display much force, but I have come to the conclusion that the [United States] government would not be unwilling I should risk a collision with the Japanese in endeavoring to carry out our right. The trade is desirable, but the survey is a necessity. . . . I shall bring temper, watchfulness, determination and courtesy into the discussion."[52]

Brooke ended up at Hakodate, one of the two Japanese ports opened as a result of the negotiations of Commodore Perry.

Commodore Perry wrote approvingly of "the spacious and beautiful bay of Hakodati, which for accessibility and safety is one of the finest in the world."[53] The Americans viewed Hakodate with particular interest, not only because it would serve as a port of entry into Japan. Hakodate was also the closest seaport to the North Pacific whaling grounds and could be expected to have considerable importance as a haven for American whalers, a place for refreshment of crews and repair of ships. Rodgers anticipated that more than forty whaleships might winter in Hakodate, and he worried because "whaling crews have the reputation of too often behaving riotously on shore." That problem could be solved if an American warship were stationed in the harbor or if American authorities were on shore.[54]

The harbor of Hakodate was splendid, almost landlocked, "not unlike

Gibraltar in general character and position, but far less imposing," was a British verdict.[55] Like Gibraltar, a high promontory was connected to the main shore by a low neck of land. The town was strategically situated to command the Tsugaru Strait and the entrance to the Sea of Okhotsk. All the commerce of the Amur valley, for which expectations were running high, would naturally flow out into the Pacific via this channel. American merchants could, they hoped, supply underpopulated Pacific Russia with all manner of foodstuffs and manufactures in exchange for Russian money that could be used to buy goods in China and Japan for the American market. Hakodate would serve splendidly as headquarters for such trade.

Another asset recommending Hakodate to Americans was the relative lack of Englishmen. The British maintained a consulate there for a time, as did the Americans, French, and Russians, but Hakodate lay beyond the network of the old East India Company and the China trade.[56] British ships and British merchants remained few, unlike at Nagasaki or so many other East Asian seaports. The Russians used the harbor as a winter refuge for a warship or two, and had the reputation for eagerness to buy anything drinkable.

All of the foreign visitors noted that copper coins called "cash" were very cheap in Hakodate. Exporting them was illegal, but the profits seemed worth the risk of being caught smuggling. A dollar would buy 4,200 cash there. The cash could be sold in Shanghai at 1,200 or 1,300 to the dollar.[57] Because of Japan's lengthy absence from international commerce, the gold-silver price ratio was similarly skewed, offering immense opportunities for quick returns.

Since the people of Hakodate seemed not particularly cordial to visitors, foreigners took the precaution of carrying revolvers.[58] But the town was more serene and politically relaxed than Yokohama in those tense years when the Japanese were first reluctantly confronting the Atlantic world. Americans in Yokohama then found it difficult to persuade anyone to sell them a life insurance policy.

As a follow-up to the earlier work of the Rodgers expedition, the secretary of the navy ordered John Mercer Brooke in April 1858 to survey a steam route to China. Brooke's westward path, by way of Hawaii and the Marianas, would track much of the twentieth-century route of Pan American Airways' seaplanes. Brooke did not visit Midway, but he found Guam, an important West Pacific haven for American whaleships, to be of great potential importance; it was the only harbor in the Marianas he judged suitable for a coaling station. Caught by a typhoon, Brooke's tiny sloop, *Fenimore Cooper*, was beached and wrecked on the coast of Japan. Happily the crew, the instruments, and the records were all saved.[59]

Brooke himself finally returned to the United States in February 1860 in a stormy passage as a passenger and adviser aboard *Kanrin Maru*, the first Japanese steamship to cross the Pacific. Seeing Japan as a potential friend 'to the United States and as a rich market for American cotton, John Brooke strongly supported establishing a steamship line across the Pacific from San Francisco to Japan and the mouth of the Amur River.[60]

Both Rodgers and Brooke were friends of Matthew Fontaine Maury, which meant that their findings found circulation through his work, specifically in later editions of his *Physical Geography of the Sea*. Maury was intensely interested in what they might have learned about the North Pacific since that ocean was so little known. He wanted information about weather patterns, harbors, possible coaling stations. He was particularly curious about the currents and could only speculate about the possibility of a North Pacific analogy to the gulf stream of the North Atlantic. Such a current, he wrote earlier, would "exercise great influence upon the course of navigation and upon the commerce of that ocean."[61] The eruption of the Civil War prevented the publication of a full report and a complete set of charts.[62] Perry's report, and the visit of the Japanese envoys who had traveled aboard *Kanrin Maru*, aroused great interest among Americans. Walt Whitman watching them parade down Broadway, thinking perhaps of the old adage "westward the course of Empire," observed in *A Broadway Pageant* (1860):

> The sign is reversing, the orb is enclosed,
> The ring is circled, the journey is done.

CHAPTER NINE

Americans in Far Pacific Waters: Entrepreneurs

Whaling, "nursery of American seamen, and prodigy of Yankee enterprise," became in the first half of the nineteenth century a major economic engine and America's first global industry.[1] It was peaking at about the time of the Perry and Rodgers expeditions. In 1852 William H. Seward reminded the U.S. Senate that "we are the second in rank among commercial nations. Our superiority over so many results from our greater skill in shipbuilding, and our greater dexterity in navigation, and our greater frugality at sea. These elements were developed in the [whale] fisheries."[2]

The importance of whale fishing far transcended shipping and the economy. Whaling stimulated exploration, gave Americans a widened perspective of the Pacific, and, like the clipper ship, nourished literature and the arts. American success in whale fishing cultivated American national self-esteem.

Even before independence, Americans made themselves conspicuous in this epic enterprise, causing Edmund Burke to declare in Parliament (1774) that "neither the perseverance of Holland, nor the activity of France, nor the dexterous and firm sagacity of English enterprise, ever carried this perilous mode of hardy industry to the extent to which it has been pushed by this recent people—a people who are still, as it were, in the gristle, and not yet hardened into the bone of manhood."[3]

The Revolutionary War suspended whaling for Americans, but they were quick to resume and intensify it. The brig *Bedford* out of Nantucket, loaded with 587 barrels of oil, tied up at the port of London in February 1783, the first ship to sport "the thirteen stripes of America in any British port."[4] No foreign nation could compete with the Yankees in this sphere, and yet the American effort became itself international, an exotic microcosm of the American nation, international in geographical scope and international in blood. The Native American supplied a skilled part of the enterprise; Melville bows to this in choosing *Pequod* as the name for Ahab's ship, and he tells us that by the 1840s fewer than half of those men serving before the mast aboard whaleships were American born though almost all the officers were.[5] Many of the men were from Africa, particularly the Cape Verde Islands.

As waters closer to home became fished out, the lure of Leviathan pulled American ships deeper and deeper into the spaces of the Pacific. There the whalers plunged their harpoons into waters ranging from the fringes of the Antarctic to the far north. The cold waters of the polar seas, rich in krill, nourished a large whale population.

From 1835 until the sharp decline of the industry after the Civil War, the whaling grounds of the North Pacific, more hospitable than the Antarctic, would yield some 60 percent of the total oil collected by the American whaling fleet.[6] By the mid-1840s American ships formed more than 75 percent of the world's whaling fleet. Russians were annoyed by the overwhelming American presence on their shores; the Japanese, still wrapped within their own self-imposed isolation, could only stand on shore and count the American ships as they passed through the Tsugaru Strait into the Sea of Okhotsk.[7]

Indifferent to national boundaries, American whalers viewed the great ocean as a single geographical area and one belonging as much as or more to them than to anyone else. Whether a place was already known and already bore a name, the Americans did not hesitate to apply their own. Siberian landmarks, regardless of what the Russians called them, were commonly known by such names as Bowhead Bay, Plover Bay, and Cape Thaddeus.[8]

The proprietary attitude of the Americans alarmed the Russians, and one official advised the future Tsar Alexander III to send a warship to the Russian Far East because otherwise "the non-Russian natives of that coast will altogether forget that they belong to Russia. Already so many Chukchi speak English."[9] American goods, brought in as a side business by the whale fishers, also found a growing market on Siberian shores. And as late as the 1920s American and Canadian schooners freely visited the shores of Kamchatka and Chukotka, hunting for furs and trading with the local peoples.

But the Americans were often pioneers in uncharted seas, coursing "where no Cook or Vancouver had ever sailed," as Melville reminds us. "Scores of anonymous Captains have . . . in the heathenish sharked waters, and by the beaches of unrecorded, javelin islands, battled with virgin wonders and terrors that Cook with all his marines and musket would not have willingly dared."[10]

Whalers with their sentinels standing at masthead, alert for uncharted rocks and reefs as well as for the monster of the seas himself, shattered the isolation of the central Pacific and opened the way for merchants and missionaries, naval explorers and scientists, finding, claiming, and naming (sometimes after themselves) many islands that would not seem particularly important until later. Whaling ships passing in mid-ocean to "speak" to each other or pausing to visit in a "gam" swapped the news and passed on the gossip, furnishing also an effective way of spreading geographical information rapidly.

International history of the Pacific during the first half of the nineteenth century belongs primarily to the whaler. The whalers' sphere of activity and their number of contacts then exceeded those of all other Americans in the Pacific put together.[11] By the early 1850s, the annual value of whales taken in the North Pacific, at $9 million, exceeded by nearly $2 million the sum of the highest annual imports from China.[12]

Melville and others convey something of the higher art and mystery of pursuing the whale. The work was dangerous, difficult, and dirty; the men working at it were customarily paid in "lays," or fractional shares of the profits, and often abused and exploited. An ordinary seaman might claim a lay of 1/200; if he protested, that portion might be "increased" to 1/300.[13] The voyage was hazardous for the investor, who was obliged to wait a long time for uncertain returns on his money, and for the mariner, who was obliged to seek his quarry through ice and fog, shoal and storm. Desertions were heavy and crews green; during a typical three-year cruise, loss of life for officers and men averaged 10 percent.[14]

The whaling chronicle may be one of courage, but the heroism was adulterated by cruelty to man and to whale and by the crassness of the overall enterprise. Whale fishing for the Atlantic peoples was, after all, simply a large-scale, commercial, extractive undertaking. They gave little thought to anything but the relentless pursuit and capture of the hapless animal.

The ways of the American whaler seem crude and inconsiderate in contrast to those of the indigenous people of the North Pacific rim. For them the whale was not an industrial good but a sensitive animate object, commanding respect as a source of especially delicious food as well as for much else. They found a use for every part of the whale: its bone, sinew, and flesh. The hunter attached elaborate rituals to the catch, and whaling took place within the religious life of the community. Song celebrated the whale, and the hunter honored it by wearing his best clothes during the chase.

The ritual was not confined to the arena. Back home, simultaneously with the chase, in at least one North Pacific tradition, "the wife of a . . . whaling captain represented the whale during the hunt; by lying quietly in the house beneath a bark mat, her stillness was imparted to the whale, making it easier to approach and harpoon." According to common belief, the whale was not simply caught; by mutual agreement with the hunter, it allowed itself to be taken.[15]

For the Americans and Europeans, the realities of whaling quickly rubbed off any romance. Whaleships—"blubber boilers," as Melville called them—were stout and seaworthy craft that might serve for thirty or forty years but were utterly without style and could be sailed only about as fast as "you can whip a toad through tar." In the history of the industry, the big innovation had happened a century before any whaler had entered the Pacific. This was putting the tryworks or firepot onboard ship, enabling the voyage and the hunt to continue while the corpse of the whale was processed. The whaler therefore became seaman, hunter, and butcher.

Cutting into the animal's flesh, the crew would unroll the blubber in large circular strips, throw it into the great brick and iron boiler on deck, and reduce the fat to oil. "It is not very pleasant work," remembered one captain's wife, enduring "the soot, smoke, smell, and grease which prevailed for about two days and nights. But then it has to be done, and we can bear it."[16]

Baleen, the horny substance taken from the creature's mouth, was as valuable as the oil. Strong but supple, manufacturers chose baleen to make canes, buggy whips, bustles, and the circular weights attached to the bottoms of hoop skirts. Spermaceti, a waxy substance found only in the head of the sperm whale or cachelot, made superb candles that burned with a brilliant light.

The new American network of coastal lighthouses and the introduction of machinery into manufacturing increased the demand for whale oil, for both illuminating and lubricating. But when the American petroleum industry got underway on the eve of the Civil War, cheap kerosene and petroleum jellies rapidly drove whale oil out of the market. Animal-derived lubricants went rancid; petroleum did not. Animal oils were always in limited supply and therefore expensive; petroleum became abundant and cheap.

Gaslight supplanted candles, and spring steel eventually replaced baleen in the corset industry. Furthermore, with the rise of manufacturing in New England, the rich found new and safer places to invest their capital. New Bedford, Massachusetts, became as well known for its cotton textile factories as for its whaling industry.

Like whaling, the extraction of guano was very much in the pattern of activity pursued by the Atlantic intruders into the Pacific: explore, exploit, exhaust (and exit). At a time when other natural fertilizers were in limited supply, farmers especially prized guano, the excrement of birds, bats, and seals. Of the three sources, bird deposits were of the highest value. Guano contributed by the so-called guano birds, including cormorants, boobies, pelicans, and gannets, offers the highest percentage of nitrogen and phosphoric acid and the most value for fertilizer.

Demand for guano arose from the need for high quantities of food for rapidly growing populations, especially in Europe. Furthermore, farming techniques of the time did not allow for adequate replenishment of land nutrients. Even parts of the United States, not so long ago broken to the plough, were by mid-nineteenth century showing signs of decreasing fertility. Guano proved many times more effective than ordinary manures, and legends sprang up recounting its seemingly incredible powers: "Boys fell asleep on bags of guano and awoke eight feet tall. Rains fell into guano-laden ships and the masts suddenly sprouted into leafy bowers."[17]

The Pacific is the chief source of this valuable stuff, and the best quality and highest concentration of bird guano in the Pacific region is to be found on islands off the coasts of Peru and Baja California. On the Chinchas, off Peru, the deposits lay as much as two hundred feet deep.[18] Two phenomena contributed to this wealth. First, the waters adjacent to these areas are home to huge populations of anchovies upon which birds thrive. Second, the climate of each of these areas and the topography of the islands is such that the birds can roost densely in vast numbers, thus concentrating their droppings, while the lack of rain prevents the washing away or diluting of these materials.[19]

The great guano rush began in the late 1840s when American consumers became disgruntled with the high and rising price of the Peruvian article handled either directly by the Peruvians or by the British acting as their agents. Captive Chinese laborers, sometimes working in ball and chain, were the usual guano diggers. For them, the reality was wheezing, coughing, and watering of the eyes. Loosening the piles stirred up clouds of thick yellowish-gray dust, pungently permeated by ammonia fumes. Downwind the clouds could be seen and smelled a hundred miles away.[20]

The agents charged a high price and fed the market only irregularly, thus frustrating American consumers. American entrepreneurs, finding it impossible to break into the Peruvian traffic, sought and obtained U.S. government support for the exploring and exploiting of remote and uninhabited "guano islands" farther out in the Pacific. These were, they claimed, "important benefits which Providence has placed in our path."[21]

The plea was that American farmers were suffering from the consequences of a foreign monopoly and the American merchant marine was losing the opportunity for continuing employment. New York and Boston guano speculators gained the sympathetic ear of Senator William H. Seward. As a result, the Guano Act was passed in 1856 to provide federal legal and military support to any American company or individual wanting to extract guano from any island not under the jurisdiction of another country and not occupied by citizens of any other country, as long as they marketed the guano solely to American customers. The act specified that the government did not undertake to retain possession of any guano island after removal of the guano.

The U.S. government had never claimed any islands by right of discovery and had repudiated or ignored attempts by individuals like Captain David Porter who tried to assert such claims. The Guano Act was characteristic of Seward, who did not share this governmental reluctance and was eager to exploit any means of projecting the American presence deeper into the Pacific.

Within a twenty-year period after 1856, eager would-be guano traders filed bonds for harvesting on fifty-seven Pacific islets and atolls, including Baker, Howland, Canton, Palmyra, and Johnston, which would later take on great strategic significance. The British, the Americans' chief maritime Pacific rivals, ignored any American claims, sometimes themselves subsequently occupying the same places. At the time this posed no problem, but the issue would resurface, unresolved, in the 1930s when the matter of landing rights for aircraft took on vital importance.

As for guano, it provoked dreams of fortunes in the minds of many a mariner. But again it is a story of greed vanquishing reason. Overharvesting and maltreating the birds threatened to destroy the whole enterprise. By 1860 nearly all the accumulated Peruvian supply of the precious stuff had been stripped and shipped out, mostly to Europe. Furthermore, Chilean nitrates, as well as phosphates newly discovered in the Carolinas and Georgia, plus synthetic fertilizers, began to compete successfully with the birds. Interest in guano waned, and the guano islets of the Pacific were forgotten, at least temporarily.[22] The importance of guano mining, whaling, and other oceanic extractive activities for the American reach to the Orient was that they broadened geographical knowledge of the Pacific and prepared the way for the development of trade routes.

CHAPTER TEN

The Russian Connection

The acquisition of Oregon (1846) and California (1848) and the signing of new treaties with China (1844) and Japan (1858) had drawn American attention to the North Pacific as never before. The Russian Far East posed special attractions: wild and undeveloped, presumably rich, and accessible via sea. Whalers had first aroused an American consciousness of Siberia.

The Russians, eager for commercial and technological assistance, were both attracted and alarmed by the Americans, but to some the Americans appeared to be comfortably remote from Siberia, too far away to be politically dangerous.[1] Some influential Russians even discussed a Siberia independent of St. Petersburg, perhaps even a republic with some kind of special relationship to the United States.[2]

Alexander Herzen, refugee from tsarist tyranny, had proclaimed the Pacific Ocean to be the Mediterranean of the future. But, in his words,

The dead hand of the Russian government that does everything by violence, everything with the stick, cannot give the vital impetus which would carry Siberia forward with American rapidity. We shall see what will happen when the mouths of the Amur are opened for navigation and America meets Siberia near China.[3]

A small but steady stream of American mariners, merchants, and adventurers had begun to visit Russian shores, eyeing the commercial possibilities of furs, fish, timber, and ice. Americans helped the Russians to prospect for coal on the island of Sakhalin. The Russians in turn seemed glad to buy almost anything the Americans had to sell. Most of the foreign merchants in eastern Siberia were Americans; the Boston firm of Boardman and Cushing was the first.[4]

Some Americans talked very optimistically about Russia's future on the Pacific: "At the mouth of the Amoor she can, and no doubt will, establish a large commercial city and a vast naval depot. When this is done, she has all China and Japan at her immediate command, and . . . she can there lay the foundations of one of the mightiest commercial cities in the world."[5]

Hunt's Merchants' Magazine commented that before the settlement of California, North Pacific Asia seemed too remote to offer any real commercial possibilities to Americans. But now America's new Pacific coast lay only thirty days' sail from Asia; Japan was no longer closed to American shipping; and Russia was manifesting new interest in the Siberian Far East under the vigorous leadership there of Governor General Nikolai Muraviev, who acted largely on his own initiative. In two treaties with China's Ch'ing (Qing) regime, in 1858 and 1860, Russia added to its empire the Primorie (Maritime Province), the Amur delta, and, upstream, the entire northern bank of that river, for a total of about 400,000 square miles, an area nearly twice the size of France.

To some Americans, settling and developing the Amur valley opened the possibility of a global trade shift promising "as great a revolution in the commercial world as . . . the discovery of the passage to India by the way of the Cape of Good Hope."[6]

Perry McDonough Collins, a charming and imaginative mid-nineteenth-century American entrepreneur, like John Ledyard saw geographical spaces in new ways. Collins envisioned the possibility of the United States circumventing British-dominated global trade routes by establishing new ones to the northwest, stretching across the North Pacific Ocean by the great circle route and penetrating deeply into north Central Asia by means of the Amur River, a natural road to the ocean and the "Mississippi of Asia." Despite the challenging climate of the region and the difficulties of navigating the river (frozen over more than 170 days a year), which Collins does not mention, he saw the Amur valley as a potential home for fifty million people, with steamboats chugging up and down the river just as they were doing on the Mississippi.

Collins persuaded President Pierce to appoint him as American commercial agent for the Amur River area, providing an official cover for what was really a private endeavor. Collins left for St. Petersburg in April 1856 and traveled extensively across Russia. He and a companion, Bernard Peyton, a Virginia businessman, were, as far as we know, the first Americans to cross the Urals after Ledyard. Collins wrote, "That the waters of Lake Baikal can be connected with the Amoor I think there is no doubt, and thus open the very heart of Siberia to our Pacific commerce," a new "passage to India," Collins declared.[7]

Russia, Collins argued, should do with Manchuria what the United States did with the Louisiana Purchase, "for the whole of Manchooria is as necessary to the undisturbed commerce of the Amoor as Louisiana was to our use of the Mississippi."[8] In short, Collins saw Russia as logically pursuing a pattern of expansion in Pacific Asia analogous to U.S. expansion in Pacific America. And he hoped that Pacific Siberia, "hitherto unapproachable, unknown, isolated," would soon "awake to the scream of the steam engine and the lightning flashes of the telegraph."[9]

For all his naiveté and the slenderness of his knowledge of Russia, Collins did sense that Siberia was somehow different from the rest of Russia and could potentially experience a different kind of development. Collins's genius was to perceive the potential unity of the North Pacific world and the possibility for Americans to weave it together using the new technologies of transport and communication.

In his view, Siberia was not only Russia's new Far East but also America's new Far West. Here lay a frontier for the steamboat, the railroad, and the telegraph in a pattern of linkages allowing the United States to dominate the major pattern of world commerce. North America, over which the United States was creating hegemony, would furnish the vital economic link between Asia and Europe.[10]

A homing pigeon supposedly carried the news of the French defeat at Waterloo to Nathan Rothschild in London, to his immense advantage on the stock market. But the pigeon was not totally reliable, and the semaphore was of limited use. The electric telegraph, like the steam engine, provided a new predictability to movement, in this case, to the flow of information. The speed of the telegraph carried enormous advantage to decision makers in peace and in war. Wires and cables also interjected new means of controlling access to information. He who owned the lines was master of a flow to which the outsider was not privy.

The American telegraph network was growing very fast, much faster than railroads. Construction was relatively cheap and easy; the demand was instant and large. Within eight years of the first American line, the system had seventeen thousand miles of wire.[11] Within thirty years, most of the globe was wired together; the telegraph was a factor in international affairs before the railroad or the steamship. As with other nineteenth-century inventions, the telegraph was first used in the North Atlantic world core, from whence it spread globally. And as with other new technologies, it made a powerful instrument for commercial—and political—domination.

Information from China could by means of steam and electricity reach London faster via North America than by the traditional Indian Ocean route. Since the United States is located midway between Europe and East Asia, by creating and exploiting a network of steamships, railways, and telegraphs, American hoped to make both Europe and Asia dependent on them for information from the other.

Perry McDonough Collins chose the telegraph as his instrument for developing a new American intercontinental commercial primacy. He seems to have got the idea when he was traveling across Siberia in 1857. He proposed spinning a sixteen-thousand-mile telegraph system connecting the United States with Russia by means of a submarine cable under the Bering Strait, which at its narrowest is only about fifty miles.

The line would run from the western end of the American transcontinental system, which was about to be built by Western Union (completed in 1861), north through the unbroken solitudes of British Columbia and Russian America, across the floor of the Bering Sea at the straits, and southwestward along the Asian Pacific coast to the mouth of the Amur, connecting there with the far eastern terminus of the Russian transcontinental wire then under construction. The Russian government was eager to build telegraphs so as to tighten control over its far eastern territories, so remote from St. Petersburg. Russia also wanted to be part of the new international information network. Being capital poor and needing technical advice, the Russians were open to Collins's proposal of cooperation.

In October 1861 the Atlantic-Pacific transcontinental line across America was completed. Submarine cables were much more expensive than overland wires, and the experts feared that a long undersea cable would never work. In the early 1850s, successful cables were laid across the English Channel and other short waterways.[12] But Cyrus Field's ambitious attempt to span the Atlantic had so far failed.

In 1863 Western Union was prepared to gamble that Field never would succeed, and therefore to go westward across the Pacific to Europe. Samuel F. B. Morse assured Collins that a far northern route would pose no special technical problems.[13] The Western Union Extension Company was thereupon organized with capital of $10 million. Its stock soared.

After first refusing, the tsarist government subsequently agreed to allow the Americans to construct a connection over Russian territory to the line they themselves planned to build between the mouth of the Amur and European Russia. The Russians had an obvious stake in speedy communication with their newly acquired Asian Pacific territories east of Lake Baikal. To the extent that costs were important, extensions of this Russian main line such as Collins proposed were desirable as a means of enhancing revenues. Siberia was too empty to generate much traffic.

Collins was eager to include a link to China in his system, and he tried to use this possibility to entice the Russians to agree to the project. He warned that otherwise China would be tied into a British-dominated system running across Eurasia, which might divert European traffic from Russia. The American entrepreneurs were unable to resolve all their differences with the Russian authorities but decided to go ahead with the project anyway. No problems arose on the North American side. The British, surprisingly, did not object to allowing a line to be strung along the British Columbia coast.

The Collins route had the advantage of necessitating only fifty or so miles of cable under the ocean, and the system offered the glittering possibility that the United States could dominate intercontinental communications, to immense commercial advantage. Before the British line could get there, the Russian network would join with those of western Europe, West and Southwest Asia, and even China. London would be obliged to communicate with Shanghai or Tokyo via New York and San Francisco. Thus, Americans would "hold the ball of the earth in our hand, and wind upon it a network of living and thinking wire, till the whole is held together and bound with the same wishes, projects, and interests."[14]

Not surprisingly, Secretary of State Seward became an ardent supporter of the Collins project. The advantages of the medium were obvious. "To be without it," Seward said, "is to be isolated. Other conditions being equal, the country that has the largest extension and the most thorough radiation of the telegraph wire enjoys the most active and profitable system of domestic commerce."[15] Seward judged the project feasible as well as useful.

The distance and the topography were no problem. The poles for the most part could be cut locally; other materials were easily transportable. The wire and insulation necessary for one mile weighed not more than four hundred pounds. Although the winters were severe on this northern route, wood is less perishable in cold climates, and less insulation is required for the wires. President Lincoln allowed Western Union to borrow Colonel Charles S. Bulkley, who had developed his knowledge of telegraphy while supervising the building of a line in the demanding environment of the American Southwest, pushing through Apache country. Bulkley proved an able engineer-in-chief.

Seward saw an opportunity in this new work with Russia. "Russia actually invites us to put forth our national energy . . . and apply [it] . . . in the great work of renewing and restoring the long-languishing civilization of the region where our race first impressed its dominion upon the globe."[16] In other words, the telegraph provided a perfect means to spread American ideas throughout the world.

By June 1865 a plan of operations was established, the work divided among three parties, and construction began. George Kennan, a young telegrapher and subsequently a successful journalist and lecturer, America's first Russian expert, got his initial experience of Russia in Siberia as a member of the construction team.[17] Joining the team and sailing to Siberia from San Francisco, Kennan later reflected that the venture was in some respects the most remarkable undertaking of the present century. Bold in its conception, and important in the ends at which it aimed, it attracted at one time the attention of the whole civilized world, and was regarded as the greatest telegraphic enterprise which had ever engaged American capital.[18]

Living mostly off the country, Kennan traveled north up the Kamchatkan peninsula by boat, horse, dog and reindeer sledges, and by foot, in order to reach the projected telegraph route between Okhotsk and the Bering Strait. He found Kamchatka to offer wild and picturesque scenery, punctuated by volcanoes and deep valleys, with flowers growing in almost tropical luxuriance and a rich bird and animal life. Coming there "with mind and mouth heroically made up for an unvarying diet of blubber, tallow-candles, and train-oil," Kennan was delighted early in his trip to report sitting down with his traveling companions, "to an excellent supper of cold roast duck, broiled reindeers' tongues, black bread and fresh butter, blueberries and cream, and wild rose petals crushed with white sugar into a rich delicious jam."[19]

The Russian government sent the steam corvette *Variag* to help the Americans make soundings and to lay a (British-made) cable under the Bering Strait. The Russians entertained the Americans aboard ship. Kennan writes that nearly all of the thirty some officers spoke English; "the ship itself was luxuriously fitted up; a fine military band welcomed us with 'Hail Columbia' when we came aboard, and played selections from Martha, Traviata, and Der Freischutz while we dined."[20]

Life in Siberia was not always so pleasant. Traveling twelve hundred miles by dogsled with companions with whom you had no language in common, "cutting poles [21 feet long and 5 inches in diameter] on snowshoes," Kennan remembered, "in a temperature ranging from 40 degrees to 60 degrees below zero, is in itself no slight trial of men's hardihood."[21] To the severe winter weather one must add the sufferings of hunger and the persisting threat of starvation.

The success of the North Atlantic cable in the summer of 1866 spelled immediate challenge for the North Pacific telegraph. Even more important, one month earlier, Western Union had absorbed Field's American Telegraph Company and could tap his Atlantic profits. The company had no need for a Pacific line to compete with its Atlantic one.[22] Western Union had become America's first large industrial monopoly, perhaps the most powerful corporation in the nation.[23]

After spending $3 million, the company could nonetheless afford to abandon the Collins route. Thousands of poles were left to rot; glass insulators and spools of wire were left behind to provide drinking glasses and fishing tackle for imaginative indigenous peoples.[24] Spruce and pine sprang up to fill again the wide swath cut by the telegraphers through the wilderness. The expedition disbanded and departed. George

Kennan chose to return home, not the easy way across the North Pacific but on Ledyard's route, by dogsled and post horse, five thousand miles across Siberia to Europe.

The telegraphic expedition explored some six thousand miles in Asia and America and collected enormous amounts of data on the soil, timber, and minerals of this largely unknown region. Robert Kennicott, a young man whose health was unequal to his enthusiasm, was selected to head a small group collecting information on flora and fauna. Kennicott was the first to map the course of the Yukon, and that river would cost him his life. He suffered a fatal heart attack when trying to rescue a member of his team from drowning. The expedition provoked new American interest in the North Pacific fringe, causing Henry M. Bannister, a member of the team, to assert that "its greatest result was the annexation of Alaska."[25]

William Henry Seward argued consistently that transportation and communications were the key to commerce and commerce the key to world power. In his own time, he had seen not only the first electric telegraph but also the first steamboat and the first railroad. He thought the United States must build an intercontinental railroad, an isthmian canal, and an intercontinental telegraph system in order to gain global commercial leadership.

When a group of New York investors was forming the Isthmus Canal Company in 1869, Seward attempted to encourage them. The telegraph, he said, enables the exchange of ideas, but goods in bulk require cheap and frequent water transport. A North American transcontinental railway would be "profitable and useful" only as "type and shadow" of a Darien ship canal in Panama.

The world needed two interoceanic canals, Seward asserted. Suez would not suffice. Suez would deflect American Atlantic commerce eastward through the Mediterranean and Indian Ocean:

It would be a reproach to American enterprise and statesmanship to suppose that we are thus to become tributaries to ancient and effete Egypt, when by piercing the Isthmus of Darien we can bring the trade of even the Mediterranean and of the European Atlantic coasts through a channel of our own, so palpably indicated by nature that all the world has accepted it as feasible and necessary. We have undertaken to develop the resources of our own continent, and to regulate and restore the Asiatic nations to free self-government, prosperity, and happiness. The Darien ship canal is the only enterprise connected with the great work of civilization which remains to be undertaken.[26]

But the time for an American isthmian canal had not yet come. William Henry Seward's immortality would come from the purchase of Alaska (1867).

Russia had wanted to sell its American territories for some time. The declining fur trade and the financial difficulties of the Russian American Company were important reasons for the decision, along with grander geostrategic considerations. Governor General Muraviev, expansionist in Asia, was a retractionist in America. In the wake of Chinese decline, new opportunities loomed in the Amur valley and along Russia's Japan Sea coast, where the city of Vladivostok would be founded in 1860.

Muraviev was sobered by the defeat his nation suffered in the Crimean War. A French and British squadron had bombarded Petropavlovsk, the Russian naval base in Kamchatka. Russian America had escaped attack and possible conquest during the war only by means of a private neutrality pact between the Russian American Company and Hudson's Bay Company. Furthermore, Muraviev was mindful of Russia's global contest with Great Britain and of the need to construct strategic counterbalances. In March 1853 he wrote to the tsar of his belief that Russia should withdraw peacefully from the eastern shores of the Pacific, transferring the activities of the Russian American Company from Sitka to Sakhalin, in order to retain the friendship of the United States. "Due to the present amazing development of railroads, the United States will soon spread over all North America. We must face the fact that we will have to cede our North American possessions to them."[27]

Americans were pushing for the annexation of Russian America perhaps as early as the van Buren administration. Senator R. J. Walker claimed suggesting it to President Polk in 1845. Subsequently the Russian government made unsuccessful overtures to President Pierce.[28] Muraviev sought to concentrate Russia's energies on its Asiatic coast, a theme simultaneously pursued by Russian minister Edouard de Stoeckl in Washington. Writing to his foreign minister, de Stoeckl argued that "there [in Asia] we are upon our own soil and we have the products of a vast and rich province to exploit. We shall take our part in the extraordinary activity which is developing on the Pacific; our establishments will rival in prosperity those of other nations and ... are destined to gain, in this great Ocean, the chief consideration which belongs to Russia."[29]

The Grand Duke Constantine, younger brother of the tsar, favored the sale of Russian America to the United States because, in his judgment, "Russia must do all it can to strengthen itself in its center, in those compact, native Russian regions which in nationality and faith constitute its real and main power." He feared that if Russia did not yield its North American territories to the United States, Americans would "in the natural order of things" ultimately take them by force.[30]

On the evening of March 29, 1867, de Stoeckl called on Seward while the secretary was at his home playing whist. The news had just arrived by cable from St. Petersburg—one of the first uses of the new Atlantic cable system—that the tsar was willing to sell if the Americans would buy. Seward was eager, but the treaty required approval of the president and other members of the cabinet, two-thirds of the Senate, and a majority of the House. Public opinion had to be on his side. No popular demand existed to acquire Russian America, but no substantial opposition either. Only one newspaper fought the treaty, and that was the *New York Herald* whose editor, Horace Greeley, detested Seward. Seward's challenge was to educate the nation about the merits of what he so passionately desired.

The secretary began, as the *Herald* puts it, "working the telegraphs and the Associated Press in the manufacture of public opinion night and day."[31] The press had a lot of fun with the issue at Seward's expense: "I think we would do well in buying these possessions, for I never saw a place that was so much in need of buying as this; and as a place to emigrate from it has advantages possessed by none."[32] Seward, too, amused himself by reading from old newspapers some of the reactions to the acquisition of Florida and Louisiana, described as "noxious, snake-infested swamps."

The *New York Times*, pro-annexation, reported that

the main importance of this acquisition grows out of its bearing upon our future trade with Japan, China and other countries of East Asia. . . . Many now living will see the day when the Pacific Coast will be as thickly studded with ports and cities as the Atlantic is now, and when the Pacific Ocean will be covered with commercial fleets, exchanging between the Asiatic and American Continents the productions of each. And it seems inevitable that all the commerce should be American.[33]

A Philadelphia newspaper argued that annexation would "have the useful effect abroad of serving to show the world that the great republic, so far from having culminated and begun to decline, as some supposed from the Civil War, was really on the threshold of its greatest era."[34]

The potential wealth of the territory and the good price ($7.2 million) proved the most persuasive of all the arguments to buy Russian America. But Russian friendship was also deemed important. The Russians had sent their fleets to visit northern U.S. ports during the Civil War, and this was widely interpreted as a friendly gesture at a time when both Britain and France seemed to favor the Confederacy. This was more a matter of appearance that reality. American amicability with Russia was possible because relations overall remained so thin. Few Russian visitors traveled to the United States; few Americans visited the Russian centers of St. Petersburg and Moscow. Scientific or cultural exchanges were only spasmodic, and commerce remained a small fraction of each nation's trade with other nations.

Seward lobbied long, hard, and skillfully for his treaty. For balky members of the Congress, "he even held sumptuous banquets ... at which it was reported that both solid and liquid refreshment was liberally served."[35] General Nathaniel P. Banks of Massachusetts, chairman of the House Foreign Relations Committee, spoke fervently in favor of the treaty. He reminded the House that many people were slow to see the benefit of earlier territorial acquisitions to the United States—Louisiana, for instance, or Texas. Banks, briefly a professional actor, prided himself on his oratory. To support his case, he now invoked the shade of the late John Quincy Adams who, serving in the Congress in the last years of his life, would "lift his aged and palsied arm, as one treaty after another came under discussion, all of which had enlarged the boundaries of his country and given it new sources of wealth and power, to exclaim ... 'It was this hand that wrote this treaty.' "[36]

The strategic position of Alaska seemed attractive. Banks said it would bring the United States close to the Asiatic coast, to "such a point that the citizens of this country can pass in an open boat, not being at any one time more than two days at sea." Alaska was the key to the Pacific, the Aleutians a "draw-bridge between America and Asia ... stepping stones across the Pacific."[37]

Seward's most important convert was Senator Charles Sumner, the highly respected chairman of the Foreign Affairs Committee, who later said he thought the United States was already committed to go through with the matter and that he "hesitated to take the responsibility of defeating it."[38] The majestic Sumner rose in the Senate and in a style likened by Henry Wadsworth Longfellow to "a cannoneer ... ramming down cartridges," delivered a powerful and persuasive three-hour oration explaining why the Senate should ratify the treaty.[39]

Sumner was the first person to use the Aleut name, Alaska, or "Great Land," for Russian America. Artfully fusing high idealism with crass materialism, he offered many reasons to support his argument. First he described the advantages of the new territories to the American Pacific Coast: the abundant furs and fisheries, the ice that Californians customarily enjoyed from the island of Kodiak, and the many new harbors, all closer to Japan and China than those in California. San Francisco itself, the senator pointed out, is closer to Japan by way of the Aleutians than by Hawaii. By abetting American trade with Japan and China, the treaty would help "to unite the east of Asia with the west of America."[40]

"The archives of the State Department," Sumner reported, "show an uninterrupted cordiality" between the United States and Russia, and the cession of territory now "seems a natural transaction entirely in harmony with the past. It remains to hope that it may be a new link to an amity which, without effort, has overcome differences of institutions and intervening space on the globe." The treaty offered the opportunity to extend democracy in North America and to deny Great Britain the territory. By ratifying it, Sumner said, "We dismiss one more monarch from this continent."[41]

Sumner did offer a caveat. He did not want this treaty to be "a precedent for a system of indiscriminate and costly annexation." Sumner argued "there is no territorial aggrandizement which is worth the price of blood. Only under peculiar circumstance can it become the subject of pecuniary contract. Our triumph should be by growth and organic expansion in obedience to 'preestablished harmony,' recognizing always the will of those who are to become our fellow citizens."[42]

Yet neither he nor anyone else ever discussed the wishes of the indigenous peoples or the antiquity of their cultures. Nor did he speculate on the thinness of the Russian presence in Alaska. Most of the Russians chose to return home after the annexation, leaving the United States with an indifferent or hostile local population. Alaska became a place for the adventurous to escape the burden of authority. To the immigrant it could not exercise the Edenic appeal of Kentucky or California, and even today it attracts more sojourners than settlers.

In Seward's grand plan, Russian America was to be only a preliminary step in the rounding out of the United States in North America. The *Saint Paul Press* of April 10, 1867, described the acquisition of Alaska as "providing a new anchorage for that policy of northward expansion by which Mr. Seward hopes, before long, to absorb the immediate British possessions."[43] London was keenly aware of this, as was British Columbia. A Victoria newspaper commented that an American Alaska "places the whole of Her Majesty's possessions on the Pacific in the position of a piece of meat between two slices of bread, where they may be devoured at a single bite."[44]

A railway connection was the key to the allegiance of British Columbia, and Seward hoped that American entrepreneurs would provide it, linking that far western outpost to the United States instead of to the eastern Canadian provinces. "Commercial and political forces . . . render a permanent political separation of British Columbia from Alaska and Washington Territory impossible.[45] British Columbia," he scrawled, on the margins of text, "—we do not want it now, but we shall—we shall have it."[46]

In Seward's mind the process had a grand historical inevitability. In a much earlier speech (St. Paul, September 18, 1860) Seward had said:

Standing here and looking far off into the northwest, I see the Russian as he busily occupies himself in establishing seaports and towns and fortifications, on the verge of this continent, as the outposts of St. Petersburg, and I can say, "Go on, and build up your outposts all along the coast up even to the Arctic ocean— they will yet become the outposts of my own country—monuments of the civilization of the United States in the northwest." So I look off on Prince Rupert's land and Canada, and see there an ingenious, enterprising and ambitious people, occupied with bridging rivers and constructing canals, railroads and telegraphs, to organize and preserve great British provinces north of the great lakes, the St. Lawrence, and around the shores of Hudson bay, and I am able to say, "It is very well, you are building excellent states to be hereafter admitted into the American Union."[47]

Seward was at the peak of his power when secretary of state (1861–69) but his ideas by then ran against the grain of American popular thinking. Furthermore, in a long political career, Seward had made many enemies, and during his last years in office, he was inevitably identified with a president who was singularly unpopular. The public, at first distracted by the Civil War and then emotionally exhausted by it, wanted peace and quiet. It had changed its views since the 1840s and 1850s; Seward had not. Moreover, the frontier was wide open and the American economy hard pressed by the demands for reconstruction. America had no capital to invest in overseas enterprises. And after the war, the maritime industries slipped into a profound and persisting decline. Trade with foreign nations continued to grow mightily, but it was carried by foreign, not American, ships.

Late in August 1868, Boston held a great banquet to celebrate the visit to the United States of Anson Burlingame and his diplomatic mission. Burlingame had served as American envoy to China. Now he was traveling on behalf of China. The orators of the day were both numerous and prolix; among the guests present were Charles Sumner, Caleb Cushing, and John Rodgers.

Oliver Wendell Holmes, in a poem he composed for the occasion, looked to the time, he said, when "Erie blends its waters blue, with waves of Tung-Ting Hu, [and] deep Missouri lends its flow, to swell the rushing Huang-Ho!" Ralph Waldo Emerson spoke of China and Japan now suddenly stepping into the "fellowship of nations . . . an irresistable [sic] result of the science which has given us the power of steam and the electric telegraph."[48]

Congressman Nathaniel Banks rose to tell the crowd of reading that very morning a letter in a newspaper lamenting that "the commercial flag of the United States had been swept from the seas of the world." But Banks argued that the Burlingame mission traveling to Boston was evidence of the recovery of American commercial prestige and power. On the Pacific, "bolstered by the friendship of Russia, China, and Japan," he asserted "we shall reinstate the commercial flag of the United States and raise our power, prestige and prosperity in that line of human enterprise to an elevation which the mind of man has never yet been able to conceive."[49]

Changes in the Pacific world had been revolutionary in the space of one generation. By 1860, its oceanic shores had been explored and charted. For the first time in history, most of its people had been brought into contact with each other and with the rest of the world. The United States was the only nation then pursuing trade across the North Pacific. Trade figures remained modest, expectations enormous. Belief was more important than fact, realities more psychological than commercial. Americans had led in spinning together the first delicate webs of a North Pacific community.

Americans saw the Pacific functioning as a new binder for a culture free of Europe's dominance, recognizing that they could not compete in the Atlantic world. But the Atlantic world was the past, and it was small in contrast to the Pacific. The Pacific, they liked to say, was the future site of a civilization higher than that of the Atlantic.[50] This seaborne culture would be ineluctably American because, as Commodore John Rodgers put it, Americans were "the only powerful race" in the North Pacific.[51]

PART FOUR

GIRDLING THE EARTH, 1869–1914

But why drives on the ship so fast
Without a wave or wind?
. . .
The air is cut away before
And closes from behind.
Samuel Taylor Coleridge, The Rime of the Ancient Mariner

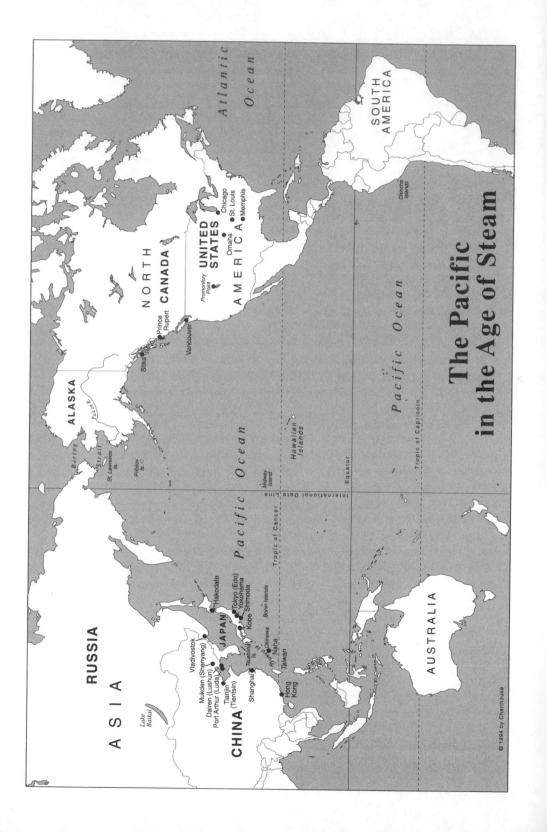

The Pacific
in the Age of Steam

© 1994 by Charthouse

CHAPTER ELEVEN

Suez, British Ascendancy, and American Maritime Decline

The year 1869 was one of marvels in the history of global transportation. The Suez Canal was opened to traffic on November 17; eight months earlier Americans drove a golden spike to celebrate completion of the last link of a North American transcontinental railroad system. Both events were phenomena of steam power. Growth in the use of steam on land and at sea had been gradual, but these two specific events made a sudden and stunning effect. Both exercised an influence on trans-Pacific transport, one negative, the other positive. The canal reaffirmed the importance of the Indian Ocean route to East Asia, which for Europe was the Far East. The railroad drew the North Atlantic closer to the North Pacific, strengthening the sense for Americans that Asia was the Far West.

The piercing of the Suez isthmus under the leadership of French diplomat and businessman Ferdinand de Lesseps accomplished what the Egyptian pharaohs and the Greek Ptolemies had tried and failed. The opening of the canal provided the occasion for a grand international party to celebrate an engineering and entrepreneurial triumph. The French empress Eugénie was only one of the royalties who came to add sparkle to the occasion. Verdi composed *Aida* especially to entertain the guests (although the work did not actually have its premiere until a new Cairo Opera House opened in December 1871).

Suez inspired rhetoric from Europeans similar to that which flowed from Americans when they contemplated "the commerce of the Orient." Alphonse Lamartine wrote that "it is essential that the Mediterranean, this great lake which is neither French nor European but international, should once more become the theatre and the vehicle of an incalculable volume of commerce and ideas." The canal, bringing Asia closer to Europe, will "help to weld the whole universe into one great unit, politically, industrially, and religiously."[1] And of course that "one great unit" would be dominated by North Atlantic Europe.

Because a railway already ran alongside the canal, the new waterway made little difference to the speed of transiting passengers or mail. But for freight the canal was extremely important because it eliminated breaking bulk, the time and expense of unloading and reloading.

Suez would prove more important to Great Britain, the world's largest shipper, than to any other major nation. Throughout the nineteenth century three-quarters of its traffic would be British, and the canal would form the most strategic segment of the most direct route to India. The canal cut the distance from Liverpool to Bombay over the Cape route from 10,680 miles to 6,223, a saving of 42 percent.[2]

Steam propulsion made Suez possible. Sailing ships found it extremely difficult to pass through the long trough of the Red Sea with its many calms and tricky currents. Sailing ships would have required a towing system to move through the canal itself. Thus, in addition to the shifting of global transport routes, Suez sped the demise of sail because it encouraged the use of the steamship.

Suez represents a European counterattack on trans-Pacific trade and on grander notions of Pacific (and North American) global centrality. Canal traffic was largely intercontinental, not local, and its influence was enhanced by the intercontinental telegraph and cable system, which, passing through Egypt, wired the China coast to western Europe two years later in 1871. For China, the cable concentrated foreign trade at cities where it touched. It deepened the growing gulf between the Pacific China of the treaty ports and the vast village China of the interior, still almost unaffected by the Atlantic world.

Suez shortened the distance from London to Hong Kong by about thirty-five hundred miles, bound East Asia more tightly to Europe, and reinforced the notion that East Asia was the Far East. The canal reaffirmed a role for both the Mediterranean in global trade patterns and North Atlantic centrality within these networks. For the British, the Cape route remained a secure alternative oceanic pathway to Asia with coaling stations and colonies along the way, all protected by British global dominance in naval power.

By 1869 a new international economic order had replaced the unintegrated national economies of 1800. The rate of technological innovation was exploding exponentially. Exploitation of newly discovered and seemingly unlimited supplies of natural resources accelerated. Capital formation swelled enormously. In all of this, Great Britain led the world, and as long as Britain maintained its primacy in metallurgical industries, British wealth and world leadership were ensured.

Britain's large industry demanded heavy foreign trade. Cotton and woolen cloth, ships, coal, and iron and steel products formed the base of nineteenth-century British exports. Britain imported even more than it exported but the invisibles—shipping, insurance, investment income— balanced the account. The far-flung geography of the British empire provided ample sites for coaling stations, sustaining British commercial and military power.

British domination of the international monetary system, the mechanisms of world trade, and commercial information flows would pull British world supremacy into the twentieth century, long after the United States had become the world's greatest manufacturing nation. Until 1914 the British owned about 80 percent of the world's submarine cables, and London lay at the heart of the global cable network.[3] Britain's cable preeminence contributed mightily to London's position as the center of world trade and finance. Americans chafed under this British dominance and until the twentieth century saw the British as a rival and even a potential foe.

In the Pacific world, Great Britain controlled geographical access, at both Cape Horn (so long as the Falklands remained in British hands) and the Strait of Malacca, commanded by British Singapore. Malacca offered a shorter route from Suez to the China coast than the former favorite passage, the Sunda Strait. Since Sunda was tucked into the Dutch East Indies, the change was strategically beneficial to Britain.

An obsolescent technology characterized the American maritime presence on the Pacific. Americans clung to sail while the rest of the world was turning to steam. In shipbuilding, the shifts from wood to iron as well as from sail to steam benefited the British and bolstered Britain's commercial power over that of the United States. And so the great clipper ships, quintessence of American sail technology, proved to be, as Samuel Eliot Morison observes, "monuments carved from snow. For a few brief years they flashed their splendor around the world, then disappeared with the finality of the wild pigeon."[4]

Americans may have invented the steamship and an American steamer may have been the first to cross the Atlantic, but the British soon firmly grasped the lead in oceanic steam technology. Steam navigation had begun in the 1820s; ten years later, British ships were steaming as far as India. By the 1850s the iron-hulled screw-propelled steamer, assisted by sails, dominated British trade in the Mediterranean. In maritime commerce, Great Britain moved far ahead of the United States during the American Civil War, but signs of American decline were apparent even earlier. Inland navigation was soaking up American maritime energies.

American sailing ships set the world standard, yet Americans seemed complacent, content to brag of their "smartness and ingenuity" and unwilling to consider change. "Americans seem to regard it as nationally detrimental, as well as a dereliction of independence, to copy any nation, and more especially the English, in anything," the *New York Times* complained, later judging the American failure to push ahead with steam navigation to be "disastrous to both the welfare and the reputation of the United States."[5]

Many, the *Times* suggested, were looking to a new Pacific trade after the Civil War to revive the slump in American shipping. Using fueling stops, screw-propelled steamers could even navigate the long voyage across the Pacific, but the United States had not one ship of this type large enough to compete with the British. And whereas the British were experimenting with very large ships, "we have done, and are doing, literally nothing."[6]

In the new machine age, the U.S. Navy offered no help to the merchant marine. The navy had concentrated its efforts on exploring rather than experimenting; its interests were more geographical than technological, more theoretical than practical. The navy served more as an instrument of science and diplomacy than of war.

Comfortable in its continental isolation, remote from the great powers and European rivalries, the U.S. military establishment, both before the Civil War and after, saw no need to push for innovations. For the merchant marine, the U.S. Navy offered no technological prods or spinoffs, in either ship construction or ship propulsion.

During the latter years of the Civil War, the navy had briefly been the most powerful in the world, but its primary roles were coastal defense and blockade. It was not a blue-water fleet. Its ships, like the *Monitor*, the first steam-powered ironclad warship in history to fight another steam-powered ironclad, reflected that limited function.

William Rowland, builder of the *Monitor*, testified to the Congress in 1869 that the U.S. Navy did not then have a warship that "would not be a laughing-stock if sent abroad as a first-class naval vessel." Admiral David Dixon Porter (son of Captain David Porter of Nukuhiva fame) remarked of the *Monitor* class, "They cannot go to sea. We send them to sea now and again, because we have nothing else to send, but they all require two or three vessels to go with them, in case they should break down or get out of coal."[7]

The only seaworthy American warships were wooden and obsolete. After the war, most Americans saw little use at all for a navy, and congressional appropriations reflected that sentiment. America had no colonies to defend, and domestic markets were far more significant to the economy than were foreign ones.

The metallurgy and the mechanics of shipbuilding in America in the new age of iron and steam remained small scale and comparatively backward for a long time. Americans could not build ships competitively. High tariffs on imported shipbuilding materials deterred American constructors, and American labor costs were simply too high, reflecting contrasting standards of living, American and European. A Clydeside shipyard worker was content with bread, cheese, and beer; his American counterpart wanted meat every day. For the British it was a simple matter not only of cheap labor but of cheap coal, cheap iron, and cheap capital compared to the less-developed United States.

The Civil War and the opening of the West interrupted and rearranged old American economic patterns in many ways. At the outbreak of war, owners of all U.S. ships, overwhelmed by soaring insurance rates, rushed to put their vessels under foreign flag. War disrupted traffic in America's leading export, raw cotton, and accelerated the decline of American merchant shipping. Federal merchant ships were scattered widely in foreign waters and were hard to protect from Confederate raiders like the *Alabama* or *Shenandoah*. The latter vividly demonstrated the vulnerability of American ships in the North Pacific by decimating the Yankee whaling fleet, just as Captain David Porter had destroyed the British whaleships in the War of 1812. After 1865 that enterprise never again would recapture its prosperity. In 1855 three-quarters of America's exports and imports were shipped in American vessels; in 1869, two-thirds of that total were carried by ships flying foreign flags.

In the same period American foreign trade doubled. But by 1865, not one U.S. steamship was regularly trading with Asia (or Africa or Europe, for that matter).[8] America's shipping had declined precipitously in both relative and absolute terms. America on land was far more successful than America at sea.

Investment capital flowed out to the newly opened great spaces of the West, which lured the boldest farmers. Back home, the best men began to go into factories and engineering shops or to work on the railroads instead of putting out to sea. The men followed the money. And within the American romantic imagination, the prairie schooner would displace its seagoing counterpart. The steam locomotive, as Walt Whitman would have it, became "the pulse of the nation."

Thus, the maritime life of the United States began to fade into history, memories to be encased within museums, libraries, and learned societies.

CHAPTER TWELVE

The Great Transcontinental
Pacific Railroads

The period 1869–1914 proved a triumphant one for the American railroad, and American interest in the new medium of transport had sprung up a generation before that. As Leo Marx has pointed out, "the iron horse," in both form and function, embodied the new machine technology: fire and smoke, noise and smell, rationality, impersonality, speed, precise timing.[1]

In American factories, steam power was not so important as it was in British. The spinning mills of Lowell, Massachusetts, ran on waterpower, and as late as 1869 steam was generating "barely half of primary power capacity in United States industry."[2] But steam-powered agricultural machinery helped open the prairie, and steam-powered boats greatly increased riverine transport, making it possible to use great rivers like the Ohio and the Mississippi in both directions, against the current as well as with it.

The river steamboat, such a splendid technological and commercial success, established a level of amenities for the American traveler that other modes of transportation could only attempt. Pullman cars, for example, when they began to appear, and the first transoceanic aircraft tried to approach this standard. Aboard the steamboat one could find bathtubs, barber shops, poker tables, libraries, and all manner of services, most notably food, not to mention "the fullest possible facilities for sluicing and gentling the patrons with wines and strong waters."[3] In short, here existed a luxurious mobile world in miniature of comfort and elegance.

In the United States roads had been unable to link together waterways effectively. Railroads could. The railroad thus greatly changed internal patterns of movement, giving a new east-west thrust to American life.

Other machines were producers of goods; railroads and riverboats were "producers of territory," enlarging the sphere of American life.[4]

For years, Americans had dreamed of a railroad to span North America. Charles Sumner pronounced that it "will mark an epoch of human progress second only to that of our Declaration of Independence."[5] Other orators liked to compare a continent-spanning railway to the Seven Wonders of the Ancient World—unfavorably to the latter. As early as 1832, when the world's first railroad, the Stockton and Darlington, had been running in England only seven years, an American newspaper made the stunning proposal of connecting the Atlantic to the Pacific by rail.[6] A businessman named Asa Whitney, aptly dubbed the Father of Pacific Railroads, was the first serious advocate of such a project, beginning his promotional campaign in 1845 during the memorable administration of James Knox Polk.[7]

Born near Groton, Connecticut, home town of John Ledyard, Whitney went to New York and entered the dry goods business, becoming an importer and buyer, duties that carried him abroad. In England in 1830, he rode on one of the first railways, the Liverpool and Manchester, and saw, he later said, how the new mode of transport abbreviated the time separating British manufacturers from Chinese consumers by speeding goods from factory to dockside. Shortening the distance between the United States and China became a major concern to Whitney.

The panic of 1837 brought hard times and ultimate disaster to his business. Whitney fled New York for China in 1842, a bankrupt widower, determined to start his life anew and to do something that would benefit humanity. While he was in Asia, he picked up a lot of statistical information about the Chinese economy and made enough money in the export trade to generate an adequate income for the rest of his life. More important, he developed the idea for social betterment that would make him famous and project America toward the Orient.

Returning to the United States just after Caleb Cushing got his treaty from the Chinese in 1844, Whitney presented his first proposal to Congress in January 1845, outlining a stupendous idea. The essence of his proposal was to build a railroad across North America that would cut the travel time to China from a sea voyage of 100 to 150 days to thirty days on land and at sea. Although Whitney was not the first to suggest bridging the Great American Desert, he was the first to make a detailed proposal of how to organize the enterprise.

Hunt's Merchants' Magazine pointed out that such a railroad would make it possible to go from New York to California in three or four days (optimistically), and the journal offered its readers some historical perspective: the same trip by whale ship or merchantman required six months; the clipper had reduced it to four; steamships to and from the

Panama isthmus cut the journey to one month; the isthmian railroad had shaved it to three weeks. Now we were down to a matter of days, the magazine said.

Whitney tended to refine the details of his proposal as he went along, but the gist of what he wanted was a land grant to finance the building of the railroad. He asked that the Congress reserve a strip of land sixty miles wide stretching from the western shore of Lake Michigan through the southern Rockies to two points on the Pacific coast; the mouth of the Columbia River and San Francisco Bay. The United States did not yet even own the latter but very shortly would.

In Whitney's scheme, commissioners appointed by the federal government would sell the land grant in ten-mile segments; the sale of one segment would pay the construction costs of the next. Whitney himself would undertake to build the first ten-mile segment. Whitney would own and manage the railroad until it became profitable, at which time he would turn it over to the government. In this fashion, no large sums of capital were immediately required, and the railroad could be built without risk to the government. Whitney would profit only by selling any of the land grant not required for construction or initial operating costs. Meanwhile, he asked only for a four-thousand-dollar annual salary for supervising the construction. To many people, Whitney's project appeared to be both unfeasible and suspect. Why should the government give so much to any one single person?

In 1845, the United States had less than three thousand miles of railroads, although the trackage was expanding at an explosive rate. For bulk cargo, water remained far superior to land transport, especially with the canal just reaching its peak traffic, but the railway would challenge this. In the United States the river systems had determined the pattern of transportation, with roads and canals feeding the rivers. Major rivers like the Connecticut, Hudson, Delaware, and Mississippi flowed north-south. The great value of the Erie Canal was that it provided a major east-west link across the barrier of the Alleghenies. But all canals in the North, including the Erie, were frozen and useless during the winter, hence a powerful attraction of the railroad.

People noticed that Asa Whitney bore a strong resemblance to Napoleon Bonaparte, a likeness sufficient to embarrass him whenever he visited Paris. But Whitney's behavior was not Napoleonic. His ideas may have been flamboyant, but his manner was not. A correspondent of the *New York Tribune* described him as a "dark complexioned, stout, and good looking man, very little the worse for the wear—his language is plain, pointed, unadorned, and business-like—and he sticks to his text, the 2,400 mile Railroad."[8]

The simplicity and directness of Whitney's manner was attractive. Whereas he bored newspaper editors almost to death because of his awesome persistence, it paid off: "He gets the notice and they get rid of the annoyance."[9] Whitney was impatient with engineering problems and tended to brush off questions on such details. He preferred to dwell on the grandeur of the results of the Pacific Railway. The press came to find him good copy, and he managed to keep his subject before the public.

Traveling widely throughout the country, Whitney personally reconnoitered the railway route, traveling by log canoe 750 miles down the Missouri River and visiting places hitherto unknown, adding colorful firsthand information useful to his argument. He wrote articles and pamphlets and penned letters to influential people. He successfully lobbied state legislatures to back the prodigious enterprise, all the while refining the details of his proposal. His simple language and earnest manner proved highly persuasive, at least outside Washington.

To the Congress, Whitney's plan seemed too altruistic to be credible. Early builders of railroads were often more interested in land speculation than they were in running a transportation company. Big money was to be had by selling off lands granted to support construction. Washington's response to Whitney was therefore skeptical, and the Congress increasingly found his persistence a nuisance. He admitted that "the work proposed is so large, and the results promised so immense, that it is not surprising [that] those who would not take the trouble to investigate, have pronounced it impracticable and visionary."[10] He argued in rebuttal that "if I have been troublesome to, and interrupted members of Congress, it was not for myself, but for my country."[11]

The essence of the proposal, as expressed by a Whitney convert, was that the Pacific Railway would revolutionize world commerce by itself carrying the great bulk of it, making the United States the commercial heart of the world, "without the outlay of one dollar by the nation, or any burden or tax upon the people."[12]

Whitney, the "prince of projectors,"[13] as the press labeled him, for all his persistent eloquence, could not combat sectionalism; no one could agree on the best route for the Pacific Railway. Although the terrain to be covered was daunting, technical difficulties did not bar any of the projected routes. The chief problem was political: competition between North and South over where the eastern terminus should be. Thomas Hart Benton wanted St. Louis; Stephen A. Douglas, Chicago; southerners like Matthew Fontaine Maury would have been happiest with Memphis. But by 1850, everyone seemed at least to agree that San Francisco was the logical western terminus.

The discussion of routes moved people to think more about local benefits rather than simply the railway as a grand international highway. The acquisition of Oregon and California gave new importance to communication among states, overshadowing matters of foreign trade. But Whitney was still thinking in intercontinental rather than transcontinental terms. To him it was always the "Pacific" railway, although he was prepared to modify his rhetoric to please his audience. What really excited him was the geostrategic implications of the project. As he described it to the Congress:

You will see that it will change the whole world, and you will see, that each and all of you have the power, without cost or price, to do more than all mankind before you have done ... [because the railway will be] the greatest, the most magnificent work of all ages and of all time. A work which will bring the vast world together as one nation, one family; a work which shall allow us to traverse the vast globe in 30 days; a work which must civilize and Christianize all mankind; a work which must place us in the center of the vast world; Europe on the one side, and Asia and Africa on the other, compelling all Europe to pass through us to Asia and Africa.... I ask that our destiny as a nation may be accomplished.[14]

Iron rails could forge a new reality of American dominance over the commerce of the Orient. Twenty years later a contemporary observer would argue the same point—that a railroad to the Pacific would mean "the transfer of the world's commerce to America, and the substitution of New York for Paris and London as the world's exchange. In the train of these immeasurable events must come the wealth and the culture which have hitherto been limited to Europe."[15]

Now "all is east from us," Whitney was saying. Build the railway, and America will be in the center of the world, with Oregon the most important part of the globe. Without the railway, Whitney feared that the Pacific coast would either become independent or be taken by some European power. He implored the Congress to act quickly while public lands necessary to fund the railway were still available for distribution.[16]

Congress did not act. When the British expressed some interest in using Whitney's plan to build a railway across Canada, Whitney traveled to England to talk on behalf of the project to people there. Unfortunately, his visit coincided with the 1851 Crystal Palace exposition. The Colt revolver, McCormick reaper, and other marvels of American technology usurped any attention a railway across the Canadian wilderness might otherwise have attracted, and the British press had some fun with Whitney." If ... our friends should really get from the Mississippi to Oregon, it will be a thousand pities that they should stop there. A tubular bridge across Behring's strait would literally put a girdle round the earth—and then the predilection of American citizens might be gratified by the establishment of a perpetual circulation."[17]

President Polk's success in rounding out the frontiers of the United States demanded the railway, and in 1853 Congress finally appropriated money for a survey of the proposed routes. After having spent at least seven years on his campaign, Whitney retired into comfortable obscurity at a country estate outside Washington. Although he would never build his Pacific railroad, more than any other individual he persuaded the American people of its merits. What had originally appeared foolish increasingly came to seem reasonable, in part because of Whitney's enthusiastic persistence. And Whitney's plan had basic features that ultimately would be realized, with the grant of public lands to railroad builders and the fusion of private effort and public support in the construction of railroads.

Yet other than surveys, nothing substantive was done about the Pacific railway until July 1862 when, in the midst of the Civil War, Congress passed an act granting aid for the construction of a railroad and telegraph from the Missouri River to the Pacific Ocean. The South was now out of the decision. The North could decree the eastern terminus, and Omaha, the choice, was oriented toward Chicago rather than St. Louis or Memphis. The route was split between two companies: the Union Pacific, charged with building the line from Nebraska to the western edge of Nevada, and the Central Pacific, which had already been chartered by the California legislature to build east from the Pacific. The government made grants of land and money in the form of bonds.

The Central Pacific brought in to California its Pennsylvania-made iron rails, carried by sea around the Horn. The Union Pacific could draw on the eastern rail network to transport its building materials. But this network stretched westward only as far as the frontiers of settlement. The Union Pacific had the added problem of fending off attack from affronted Native Americans seeing their lands infringed upon. Work parties routinely carried arms; marauding Indians, defending their lands, occasionally wrecked trains and killed their crews.

In the longer range, the builders of the Union Pacific had to worry about traffic and the balance sheet; perhaps it is not surprising that for many years the railroad was a financial failure. Until the area was settled, there would be no local passengers or freight, on which real profits depended. The builders worked on the promise of profit, not the actuality of it. Construction was fast and sloppy, requiring continuous improvement and replacement, and demanding heavy further outlays of capital. Cobwebby wooden trestles, untreated cottonwood ties that were prone to rapid decay and too soft to hold spikes very effectively, and wrought-iron rails instead of the new and much more expensive steel ones characterized much of the early construction.

British visitors commented tartly on the contrast with the beautifully cut stone viaducts and well-ballasted roadbed characteristic of British railways. One touring British sportsman outside Cheyenne actually saw tracks being laid on the grass, with a bit of dirt shoveled beneath them here and there where uneven ground demanded it. The first good rain-storm would cause a washout, he scornfully noted.[18]

Yet the use of cheap materials for initial construction was probably wise. As routes became rationalized, grades were lowered and curves straightened. Trains could become longer. Stone or earthen embankments replaced wooden trestles. Rolling stock became steadily heavier, making entirely unanticipated demands on the roadbed.

The Union Pacific recruited Irish immigrants for much of its construction crew. The Orient came across the Pacific to help build the Central Pacific in the form of Chinese contract labor, hired originally because no one else was available at such low pay for such dangerous and difficult jobs. Blasting out tunnels, putting down ballast, and laying track in the midst of the blizzards of the High Sierras, "that terrible pile of snow-crowned peaks, of deep-sunk ravines, of jagged ridges and perilous chasms," the Chinese won grudging respect from their co-workers.[19] They showed themselves to be quick learners as well as hard workers; they did not fight, they did not drink, and they did not strike. Their employers were well satisfied. Supervising engineer Grenville Dodge said the "only trouble is, we cannot talk to them."[20]

Chinese coming to the United States were sojourners, here without family, intending to make money and then return home. They were generally treated badly, as they were in South America or Southeast Asia. Only occasionally a protesting voice might be raised. Aaron Hayes writing in the *Atlantic Monthly* suggested that the American missionary ought to "convert his own countrymen before he presumes to teach the Chinese."[21] Few Americans would have agreed with him, and the Chinese government did little to help its nationals abroad; China remained a passive presence in nineteenth-century international affairs. Few Americans appreciated that the Chinese diaspora to the American side of the North Pacific rim contributed to bringing America closer to its goal of reaching the Orient.

Civil War delayed the beginning of construction, and the Union Pacific laid no rails until August 1864. Progress thereafter was extremely slow, less than three hundred miles a year. Finally, in 1868, the process was accelerated to four miles a day. The great event when Union Pacific met Central Pacific occurred on May 10, 1869, at Promontory Point, near the northern shore of Great Salt Lake, close by Ogden, Utah.

An occasional quick burst of sunshine helped Colonel Charles Savage, the official photographer, by breaking the cloud cover. In his speech just before the driving of the ceremonial spikes, Grenville Dodge, who had been a member of the first survey party crossing the Missouri in 1853, shouted, "This is the way to India."[22]

Three spikes were driven to signal the meeting of the two lines. California sent a golden one; Nevada's was silver, from the Comstock Lode;

Arizona's gift was fashioned of gold, silver, and iron. Historian Patricia Nelson Limerick points out that the event is scarcely a frontier metaphor to cherish or one to call upon as a precedent. Leland Stanford, on behalf of the Central Pacific, took up the first sledgehammer and missed the spike, hitting the rail instead. Thomas Durant, representing the Union Pacific, next swung—and missed.[23] Derisive laughter broke out on the fringes of the crowd. But the strokes of the hammers, not the guffaws, were picked up by the telegraph, nervous system to the railway, flashing the great news to the rest of the nation almost instantly.

The telegraph could not convey the raucous atmosphere. Sidney Dillon, a director and later president of the Union Pacific, remembered that "there was not much formality in the demonstration that followed."[24] Colonel Charles Savage's photograph captures some of the exuberant untidiness, but the champagne bottles triumphantly raised at the center were discreetly whitened out in later versions. As the two locomotives touched each other, cowcatcher to cowcatcher, champagne was ceremoniously poured on the last rail. No foreign dignitaries attended, nor amazingly, did any high-ranking U.S. government officials. The contrast to the opening of the Suez Canal was striking.

The high spirits of the occasion were not what Leland Stanford wanted commemorated. He commissioned a painting to show the occasion as he wished it had been, all limned with appropriate decorum and dignity, with the faces of a number of people who had not even been there, including one who had been dead for years.[25] The transcontinental railway is a chronicle of cruelty and corruption, waste and incompetence, but the mythology utterly transformed it. The accomplishment, it seems, was ultimately all that mattered.[26]

The nation rejoiced. The *New York Times* reported that San Francisco held the largest parade in its history. In Sacramento, the Central Pacific ranged thirty locomotives in front of the city, ready to blow their whistles when the great news came.[27] Vice President Colfax was visiting Chicago where a vast impromptu parade formed, at least seven miles long, they said. Philadelphia assembled a large number of steam fire engines at Independence Hall with whistles screaming and bells ringing. People there were reminded of the excitement roused at the news of Lee's surrender in 1865.

New Yorkers flew the flag everywhere, church bells pealed, cannon roared in salute, and the chamber of commerce dispatched a congratulatory telegram to their San Francisco counterparts. At Trinity Church, on Wall Street, the Reverend Dr. Francis Vinton preached to an "immense" congregation. He spoke of the events being "one of the victories of peace—a victory grander than those of war," of a "triumph of commerce . . . indicating free trade as a future law of the nation. . . . When the ocean route was discovered around the cape of Good Hope, it was very properly regarded as a blessing to mankind—hence the designation by which it is known; but the completion of this mighty work, which connects the two oceans, is a still greater blessing. . . . It will preserve the Union of these States." In the rector's conclusion he arrived at what undoubtedly was his most important point: "So this Pacific Railway is a means, under Divine Providence, for propogating [*sic*] the Church and the Gospel from this, the youngest Christian nation, to the oldest land in the Orient, now sunk in Paganism and idolatry."[28]

Harper's was cautious in assessing the advantages of the railroad. In its favor was its immense strategic importance. In the case of war with an oceanic power, the United States could now safely and swiftly send troops to the Pacific coast, without risk of delay or interference from the enemy. "In this single point of view every dollar which the Government has expended in aiding the construction of this road has been wisely laid out."[29] And on the commercial side, passengers would be likely to pay happily to cross the country in less than a week. But the savings in time provided by the railroad would not offset the high costs of shipment for bulk goods. Furthermore, the local traffic was likely to be slender for some time.[30] American railroads west of the Mississippi, unlike those to the east, were instruments for exploration and economic development. Generally they preceded people rather than following them.

Before Asa Whitney was swept away by typhoid fever in 1872, he had the satisfaction of seeing the first North American transcontinental railroad system completed and three other lines—the Northern Pacific, the Southern Pacific, and the Santa Fe—well underway. The debated routes of the late 1840s would all become realities.

Whitney's hopes for a land-sea traffic across the Pacific were shared by many. The U.S. Senate took note that raw cotton, flour, and tobacco had present or potential trans-Pacific markets and that the quality of these and other "animal and vegetable" substances was now damaged by the long voyage around either of the Capes. Either of these round-trip routes required crossing the equator twice. An American transcontinental railroad could not only greatly increase international oceanic trade flows but also change the possible mix of goods. "The products of the American soil will be exchanged for the rich commodities of Asia; and when the millions of mouths shall have tasted American bread, the high destinies of this commerce will have been fixed."[31]

Here then would be the means to redress the ever-lasting adverse balance of trade with China. Furthermore, the new "national highway" would stimulate the growth of a shipbuilding and shipping industry on America's Pacific coast, where the United States presented

a new front to the old continent. . . . The merchant and the traveller, and the curious, from all quarters of the civilized world, would crowd the cars and the steamships employed upon . . . [the new route]. Passing through the heart of America these visitors could not help but be deeply impressed by the over-whelming merits of American civilization. The principles of true liberty and of Christianity, as twin sisters, would present their engaging forms to the admiring stranger—first attracting his attention by their simplicity, and then engaging his affections by their virtues and intelligence.[32]

Just like Americans, early explorers in Canada had envisioned linking the Atlantic to the Pacific by a series of inland waterways. The great St. Lawrence gave them much encouragement, and optimistically looking to Asia, they chose the name Lachine for an early settlement on that river. By the middle of the nineteenth century, British railway enthusiasts began to tout the advantages of a transcontinental route. A trans-Canada railway appeared particularly advantageous because it offered the pos-sibility of faster travel from England to China than either of the isthmian routes, Suez or Panama, or than via the American transcontinental route to San Francisco. The *New York Tribune* fretted that a transcontinental railroad could transform British America (the future Canada) from a co-lonial dependency into a major international power.[33] Americans even worried that their northern neighbor might be first.

But British America lagged behind the United States in developing a rail network. When the United States boasted more than nine thousand miles of track in 1850, British America had only sixty-six.[34] British Amer-ica lacked both the capital for building railroads and the population to sustain them. Few people lived west of Lake Superior, and they were concentrated in coastal British Columbia. British America was a gener-ation behind the United States in developing its West. Nevertheless, some Englishmen were attracted to the idea of helping their colony be-cause they shared the same vision of Oriental commerce possessed by many Americans and the same geostrategic obsession that the nations controlling routes to the Orient would wield the commercial scepter of the world. Much of the literature discussing a Canadian transcontinental railway speaks of its destination as China, rather than British Columbia, as if the Pacific Ocean did not exist and the railway tracks could extend all the way to Shanghai.

As early as 1833, Sir Richard Broun first drew public attention to the possibility of an Anglo-Asian steam route via British America, which included a railroad from Halifax to the Pacific shore opposite Vancouver Island. From these ideas sprang British interest in the plans of Asa Whit-ney, prompting the comment that "our acute, formidable, enterprising neighbours, the Yankees, have actually made such a survey of the line as to render its success no longer problematical."[35] But the British gov-ernment did little except to sponsor a modest exploration of the territory west of Lake Superior. The subject stayed alive. Sir Edwin Watkin, pres-

ident of the Grand Trunk Railway, wrote in the *Illustrated London News*
in February 1861 that "our augmenting interests in the East demand, for
reasons both of Empire and of trade, access to Asia less dangerous than
by Cape Horn, less circuitous even than by Panama, less dependent than
by Suez and the Red Sea."[36]

Commercial prudence might have led Canada to tie into the already
existing transcontinental network south of the border, but politics dictated otherwise. The establishment of the dominion in 1867 increased
Canadian desire to cement British Columbia to the rest of the country
and to thwart U.S. desires to annex the whole of Canada's Pacific coast.
Canadians recognized the predatory instincts of the United States, which
were certainly not peculiar to William H. Seward. Did the United States
not seek the whole of Canada in settlement of the *Alabama* claims? Canadians not only wanted to preserve their independence coast to coast,
they also wanted to best the United States in competition for the China
trade.

In 1871, after some negotiation, British Columbia agreed to join the
Dominion, but one of the stipulations was that a trans-Canada railway
be constructed. The project was daunting. A trans-Canada railway would
be the longest in the world yet built, and it would need to combat a
harsh climate while crossing virtually unknown country and some of the
world's most demanding terrain. The Opposition ungraciously questioned whether British Columbia was worth the cost of the railway.

The dominion of Canada formed the world's second largest political
territory; only the Russian empire was bigger. Yet Canada had only three
and a half million people and even its eastern heartland remained undeveloped. The government wanted both British Columbia and a trans-
Canada railway. Sir John A. Macdonald put it simply: "Until this great
work is completed, our Dominion is little more than a geographical expression."[37]

In the words of a Parliamentary spokesman:

When we become possessors of British Columbia, we shall have a most magnificent inland sea of harbours such as between Vancouver and the mainland. It
appears as if set apart by a special Providence as a depot for the shipping of the
East, and as an entrance to the great highway for all nations across the British
American continent. Doubtless, in course of time the trade of China, Japan and
the Asiatic Archipelago will centre there. This is the prize that was as anxiously
sought after in ancient times as it is in modern times. Persia, Assyria, Carthage
and Rome prospered and held in fact, commercial supremacy while they controlled the trade of the East. Venice, Genoa, Lisbon, Amsterdam and London
each in turn held a proud commercial position, while it catered up the luxuries
of the East for the Western world. This is the inheritance of the Pacific Coast. . . .
This is the prize which we as a people must look forward to, and certainly it is
one which is well worth the endeavour to obtain.[38]

Canadians were well aware of the strategic advantages they enjoyed over the United States relating to distance from East Asia. The farther north, the better, it would seem. Yet Prince Rupert, British Columbia, which became a Pacific railhead in April 1914, remains even at the end of the twentieth century too isolated to prosper. Vancouver sprang up in 1886, its genesis due to the railway. Founded late, it is the youngest important North Pacific city and has not yet fully realized the advantages of its geography.

Sir Wilfrid Laurier declared that whereas the nineteenth century might be that of the United States, the twentieth century would surely belong to Canada, and Pacific trade would help make it so.[39] Laurier believed that trans-Pacific commerce would lessen Canada's dependence on the United States. But in 1911, Laurier was voted out of office; most Canadians did not share their leader's Pacific interests.

The Canadian Pacific Railway was begun in 1875 and completed ten years later. It started hauling passengers across the continent in the summer of 1886, and this service would last little more than a hundred years. The railroad immediately linked itself to an efficient trans-Pacific shipping service, part of its original plan. The first passengers traveled from Vancouver to Hong Kong in 1887, and two years later the imperial government granted a mail subsidy. The sleek white-hulled "Empress" class ships became known for quality travel.

The China trade for some Canadians remained as powerful a myth as it was for some Americans, and for both the realities disappointed. Despite imperial comradeship, British trade with East Asia made no spin-offs for Canadians, and the railway built to increase ties with China ironically made them worse, at least from a human relations point of view, as did the American railway too. The Chinese laborers who were such as important part of the construction crew were treated abominably. Yet paradoxically, as in the United States, the Chinese had shown themselves to be superb workers, quiet, diligent, and dexterous, undaunted by the terrifying challenges of their assignments. Both Canada and the United States passed legislation restricting Chinese immigration but only after the railways were built.

Canada has remained preoccupied with its neighbor to the south and has directed its overseas perspective overwhelmingly toward the Atlantic. Only with the late twentieth-century Asian immigration to Vancouver and the magnetism exercised by the newly industrializing economies of Asia does this attitude seem likely to change.

The Russians had the same problem as the Canadians of linking a remote Pacific oceanic periphery to a core of national power and culture more oriented to Europe than to Asia. The idea of a Siberian railway had been floating around for a long time, at least since the 1850s when

Governor General Muraviev was so dramatically expanding the Russian empire on the Pacific. Visiting Americans like Perry McDonough Collins had early on proclaimed the merits of railroads to receptive Russian ears. Russia began to build the longest Pacific railroad of them all in 1891.

Canadian success encouraged the Russians, but they also perceived the Canadian Pacific Railway as a threatening attempt by the British to extend their influence in the North Pacific. Because of the Suez Canal, the British already controlled the fastest sea route to East Asia from Europe.

For the Russians the extremes of climate were more severe even than those of Canada. The long, cruel winter was followed by a short, hot summer, with a myriad of mosquitoes rising from the many marshes, and the ground everywhere soft and squishy above the permafrost. But the challenge of topography was not generally as daunting as that faced by the Canadians or Americans. No mountains like the Rockies stood between Moscow and the Pacific, although the sheer cliffs and dense forests of the Iablonovyis were not easy to penetrate. The greatest heights are those around Lake Baikal, mere hills compared with the towering peaks of North America. The shores of Baikal had no natural terraces, and the builders had to blast out a path on the walls of the lake.[40] Yet for the Russians the greatest obstacle overall was bridging the formidably broad rivers, ultimately with massive metal bridges.

Like the Americans and the Union Pacific, the Russians threw up wooden bridges, slapped down the track, and built the railroad later. They economized on quality of rails and roadbed, which meant that trains could be neither heavy nor fast. The best trains in 1900 averaged 15 miles per hour.[41] American railroad men like James Jerome Hill considered the Trans-Siberian to be too poorly built and too poorly managed to be competitive to the American transcontinental systems, although the Russians hoped it would be so.

In Siberia, labor was in short supply, and the government fell back on the army and the prison to get their workers, but Chinese were recruited to build the far eastern sections of the Trans-Siberian. Unlike the other transcontinental railroads, the Russian one was purely a government project. Like the others, foreign capital was important. The Russians borrowed from the French. The Americans and Canadians had borrowed from the British.

The Russians saw the Trans-Siberian, billed as an "agent of civilization and progress," as a means of building a solid base for Russian power in Pacific Asia. They hoped that it would provide commercial as well as military advantage. Tea, for example, Russia's national drink, came from China, initially carried in brick form by caravan through Central Asia. The Suez Canal had made it easier to send the tea via the oceanic route into Black Sea ports. The Siberian railway now seemed the means for Russian hands to transport this and many other goods.

The Russians touted their railway as having international importance in part because it was a way of attracting the interest of foreign investors to the Russian economy. Yet in both domestic and international life, the Trans-Siberian would have a smaller impact than many people anticipated. Russia remained too isolated from the mainstreams of world commerce to have its great railway be successfully integrated into any global transportation pattern. Western Siberia, closest to the heart of Russian political and economic power, felt the greatest influence of the railway. Pacific Siberia was too far to permit economical rail shipment of any but the most valuable goods. And Pacific Siberia could hardly be compared to California for intrinsic attractiveness. The region today remains thinly populated and its natural resources largely undeveloped. What Gertrude Stein reportedly said of Oakland—"There's no there there"—would be more applicable to Okhotsk or Magadan.

Traffic density on the Trans-Siberian remained low, and travel was very slow.[42] But the speed increased with the gradual improvement of the roadbed, enabling the pace of the globetrotter to be "quickened to a gallop."[43] For the summer intercontinental traveler, the Siberian route offered a pleasant alternative to the sweltering Red Sea. The railroad sped the mails. Just prior to outbreak of the Russo-Japanese War in 1904, a letter could reach Shanghai from London by rail in sixteen days; by ship through Suez, it took six weeks. Jules Verne's fantasy of eighty days around the world could now be more than halved.

But the Trans-Siberian was not efficiently operated—American criticisms were justified—and crises like war with Japan in 1904–5 disrupted any patterns of customer loyalty that might otherwise have developed among foreign users. The Canadian Pacific, an integrated sea-land system that even the Americans could not match, offered far more reliable service from East Asia to Europe, despite the two oceans and North American continent to cross.

CHAPTER THIRTEEN

William Gilpin and the Cosmopolitan Railway

Milliam Gilpin was the first American to write of girdling the earth with a steam transportation network; he was, as Bernard DeVoto says, America's first geopolitician, but his were geopolitics for peace, not war. Railways were only part of his philosophy.[1] And he had a grand dream that they would make possible the building of a harmonious world community.

Gilpin, a man of high ideals but vague ideas, was no businessman or engineer. He had little knowledge of or interest in railroad construction or management. Gilpin's active life centered around politics; he served as U.S. senator and governor of Colorado. But his restless energies and versatile abilities also carried him into law, the army, and journalism. He would probably like best to have been identified as a political philosopher. Gilpin's ideas owe much to German geographer Alexander von Humboldt, but he put on them his own peculiar exuberance, patriotism, and rhetorical flourish.

Gilpin settled in Kansas City before the Civil War; later he would move west to Denver. Both cities would figure prominently in his geostrategic view. Gilpin studied the opening of the West as well as participating in it, and he gave considerable thought to analyzing the American people while constructing his theory of world civilization. He was especially interested in the problems of transportation, and he spent nearly fifty years thinking about it, beginning with the linking of the Atlantic to the Pacific. Humboldt had suggested digging a canal to connect the headwaters of the Missouri to the Columbia.

This idea was picked up by U.S. senator James Semple who incorporated it in a report he made April 20, 1846, to the Senate Committee on the Post Office and Post Roads, offering the usual rhapsodies about the ancient and continuing importance of Oriental commerce that Europe

William Gilpin (Library of Congress)

had made every effort to capture and now lay within the grasp of American hands.² Semple predicted that Humboldt's canal would be completed before the Panamanian isthmus was cut and that "a daily line of boats and cars may be run through from New York to the Columbia, with profit."³ Semple argued that an internal route, such as a canal, offered big advantages because it could capture local as well as through traffic, in contrast, say, to long oceanic passages. He also cited the "immense" overland Russian trade with China as evidence that the handicap of vast distance—in the Russian case, twice that of St. Louis to Astoria—could be overcome.

Semple invited Gilpin to contribute to his report, which the latter did at length. Within Gilpin's remarks lay the germ of many of his later ideas. He predicted that "across the middle territory of our Union . . . in less than twenty years, will be seen the European and Asiatic railway!"⁴ The "Cosmopolitan Railway," as he called it, formed the keystone of the intellectual structure Gilpin created, eventually publishing a book by that name in 1890. The Cosmopolitan Railway was to ring much of the globe, largely following the axis of the temperate zone of the Northern Hemisphere, the "zone of greatest accomplishment," the "zodiac of empires." In order to span the Pacific, the railroad would sweep to the north and carry its traffic across the Bering Strait by means of a ferry. From Lake Superior to the Alaska coast, the route would be an easy one, virtually at water level, and it could follow a great circle course, economical in distance.

For Gilpin the oceans were of no particular significance; appropriately for a midwesterner, he thought instead in terms of great continental land masses. His America was inward looking, focused on the great valley of the Mississippi. But he proposed that the international transportation systems of the three northern temperate continents be interwoven, thereby forming a "prodigious condensation of economy in the interchanges of the products and people of the world."⁵ Railways and steamships could bring Asia to Europe and solve "the geographical problem which has agitated the world before and since Columbus."

The global heartland of power, energy, and progress lies, Gilpin suggested, between the thirtieth and fiftieth degrees north latitude, within the "Isothermal Zodiac" described by von Humboldt. Within this Isothermal Zodiac runs the "Axis of Intensity," an undulating band roughly following the fortieth parallel. Here exists an ideal blend of the best climates, soils, and topography—the essential raw ingredients of high culture. Here—in western Europe, North America, and East Asia—are situated the world's focal cities and the world's "great permanent reservoirs of human population and activity."⁶ From here around the globe, north and south, culture both radiates and attracts.

Significantly, Gilpin noted, more of North America lies within this core of dynamism than does any other continent.⁷ North America also enjoys the benefit, as Gilpin saw it, of concave topography; the continent forms a great bowl centering on the Mississippi basin, providing a natural and orderly environment for communication and transportation and the means to achieve unity. Neither Europe nor Asia has the topography to encourage a natural unity; both are convex. Geography has therefore failed to integrate them. But the Cosmopolitan Railway could do so, Gilpin believed.

America is, he argued, the natural geographical intermediary and therefore arbiter between Europe and Asia. America is potentially both barrier and connector of the other two—barrier against war, connector for peace. America's destiny, Gilpin believed, was to lead the world into an era of permanent peace. In the fusing of the trilateral world core, Gilpin predicted that the United States, "fresh, pliant, and ductile," would "ascend over and absorb" the British empire. Great Britain was too small, "an area of land restricted to *pygmy dimensions*; insufficient bread; no production of groceries; no raw material of cotton; no ores, except tin and iron; exhausted fuel; a population paralyzed by want; unable to labor; no room; no elasticity; no democratic vigor possible." British power, he judged, was "artificial."[8]

Gilpin decried what he saw as the British tendency to denigrate the Chinese, whom he respected for the antiquity and polish of their culture and whom he recognized as the source for much of what was enjoyable and useful in American life: fruits, flowers, vegetables, silk, the magnetic needle, and the laxative calomel. Gilpin looked forward to the day when, for the exchange of ideas, savants like Benjamin Franklin would travel to Peking instead of to Paris.[9] But Gilpin was not sure of what might be the Chinese political role in the future world.

He had a clearer idea about Russia, which he saw as America's partner in building the great railway. The two nations had much in common. Each had recently overthrown social tyrannies: serfdom and slavery. Each was large in population and vast in extent of territory. Each was rapidly developing an industrial economy.

Build this railway between them, and America and Russia may join hands against all the rest of the world, on any issue, military, commercial, and industrial. [The railway] . . . will become the chief highway of the nations, the front and finishing line of progress, circling round the warm and hospitable Pacific, whose shores are pregnant with limitless undeveloped resources, leaving the cold Atlantic to those who choose to navigate it.[10]

America's "sublime and prodigious destiny," Gilpin proclaimed, was to "unite the world in one social family," and the Cosmopolitan Railway was the instrument by which this could be accomplished.[11] Like Asa Whitney, as we have seen, Gilpin was long on rhapsodic description and short on specifics. But his ideas would provoke American interest in the railroad as an instrument for reaching across the Pacific.

CHAPTER FOURTEEN

Steamships on Schedule: The Pacific Mail

D espite the generally miserable story of American shipping after the Civil War, Americans did pioneer in establishing scheduled steamship service across the Pacific. Service began because the Congress in February 1865 authorized an annual grant of $500,000 to subsidize carrying the mails to Japan and China. Federal mail subsidies had begun in 1845, in part because of apprehensions about using the British postal network. British underwriting of their system made it attractively cheap, but Americans disliked the strategic implications of depending on the British.

Payments by the U.S. government opened new opportunities for shipping, but to most voters, subsidies seemed public monies devoted to private purposes and private profit and to go against the grain of free market capitalism.[1] The result was a constant uncertainty for shipping companies, which could never be certain that the financial help upon which they depended would be renewed.

The Pacific Mail Steamship Company, founded in 1848, had successfully operated a route linking California to Panama. Because its service was coastal and domestic, the Pacific Mail was not handicapped by foreign competition like those American companies operating across the Atlantic. And thanks to the gold rush, the company did very well, carrying passengers out and gold home. Its major problem was keeping its crews from deserting ship for the goldfields.

The Pacific Mail was eager to take on a trans-Pacific service because of the looming threat of the American transcontinental railroad, which would make its Panama route far less desirable. The company saw the need for new business to replace the old; it also perceived the opportunities that the first railroad across North America would present. The

Congress was willing to help the company in order to stimulate American shipbuilding (only ships built in American yards could be used in a subsidized service), to provide a reserve fleet for navy use in the event of war, and to buttress "the supremacy of American commerce on the Pacific."[2] Congressman John Lynch, chairman of a committee to investigate the condition of the U.S. merchant marine, set his eyes particularly on the Pacific, "a great highway which we have only to occupy with vehicles of transportation."[3]

Despite the harsher realities of the China trade, the myth of the fabulous wealth of Oriental commerce and of what it might do for the United States persisted stubbornly. But China came to be perceived less as a source of luxury goods for the American elite market and more as a place for Americans to sell mass consumption goods.

The question, though, as R. B. Forbes, the veteran Boston China merchant put it, was that perhaps the Chinese would indeed like to eat American bread and meat, wear American wool and cotton, and smoke Virginia tobacco. But how were they to pay for it? The Chinese, or the Japanese too, for that matter, Forbes argued, would not want any more American goods than they could pay for in tea, silk, straw matting, and so forth. How much of these could the American market absorb? The youngest American alive, Forbes maintained, would "not live to see the Celestials smoking Virginia tobacco . . . nor cutting their paddy by the new reaping machine."[4]

The statistics bear out Forbes. Over the period 1795–1860, the China trade ranged in value between the modest 2 or 3 percent of total American foreign trade, both imports and exports, and never over 1 percent of ship tonnage.[5] American foreign trade continued to concentrate in North Atlantic flows, especially to England.

Yet just as rails were laid across the continent in the hope and expectation of towns to follow, steamers began their rounds across the Pacific in anticipation of traffic to come, as would air service sixty years later. Americans were the trans-Pacific steamship pioneers; the Canadians joined next, and finally the British and the Japanese. Considering their global preeminence, their dominance of the international trade of China, and their position in Canada, the British were almost conspicuous by their inconspicuousness in trans-Pacific traffic.

With no competition, foreign or American, the Pacific Mail Company offered the first scheduled service across the ocean, from San Francisco to Hong Kong via Japan, starting in 1867 with four wooden-hulled, "walking beam," paddle-wheeled steamers. This was thirty years after steamship service had begun across the North Atlanta.

These ships—*China, Japan, Great Republic,* and *America*—were the largest oceangoing side-wheelers ever built and among the largest wooden ships. They were obsolete when they were put into service, obsolete even when they first emerged from the shipyard. Their machinery recalled designs of the 1830s.[6] Cunard built its last paddle or side-wheeler in 1862, and by the mid-1860s the British and French had totally abandoned the paddle for the screw and the iron hull.

Paddles hammered the surface of the water, flat upon the waves, while adding little to the forward thrust of the ship. The screw was much more mechanically efficient even when the paddle wheel was totally immersed and operating optimally, which it rarely was. A side-wheeler carrying a full spread of canvas tended to roll her wheels alternately out of the water, increasing fuel expenditure. Advanced designs for screw-propelled ships incorporated compound engines, which greatly increased efficiency of fuel consumption. At nine knots, a side-wheeler would consume fifty tons of coal a day; an iron screw steamer could do thirteen knots and burn only twenty-five.[7]

Admiral David Dixon Porter favored the new type. Wooden hulls, he said, were injured by heat, and he was not convinced that a side-wheel steamer could be run to China as cheaply as a propeller-driven craft. Robert Bennet Forbes, who took a skeptical view of the prospects of the China trade, was also highly critical of the choice of paddle-wheel ships. He strongly recommended ships with full canvas and "powerful auxiliary propellers." At ten to twelve knots under steam or twelve to thirteen under sail, these would be fast enough "to ship all we shall want to ship from China for the next two hundred years."[8] Moreover, they would be cheaper to operate since sail could be used as much as half of the time and the machinery would last longer. Sail would always be available in the event of accident to the machinery. Forbes did not note that the paddle wheelers also carried sail. The performance of steamships, he observed, "ought to be received with great caution, as all know who have had anything to do with steam."[9]

Shipbuilders continued to hedge their bets. Not until 1889 did trans-Atlantic ships appear that carried no canvas. The transition between modes of power stretched out to fifty years.[10]

Whether Forbes had iron or wooden hulls in mind, he does not say. But had the Pacific Mail wanted to begin its trans-Pacific run with iron steamers, presumably one of the yards that turned out the many iron-clads built during the Civil War could have been converted to those needs. Why then did the Pacific Mail choose the ships it did? Its conservatism was not unique. Americans generally stuck to paddle wheelers, which had enjoyed such splendid success on America's rivers, long after screw propulsion was introduced. Paddle wheelers could be built with wooden hulls, whereas the vibration from the motion of a screw tended to shake a wooden ship apart. A propeller required the tensile strength of an iron hull.

But the Pacific Mail had additional cause to go for the paddle wheel: the lack of maritime infrastructure—no drydocks, no fully equipped repair yards, no marine engineering shops—anywhere on the North American Pacific coast until the Mare Island shipyard was established in San Francisco. The company was operating out of an undeveloped region, far from the nation's technological centers. The problem was compounded because Pacific Mail operations were conducted at distances even farther removed from that North Atlantic heart.

Pacific Mail steamships had to go all the way down to Panama to find a suitable place for beaching at low tide in order to effect repairs to the hull or paddle wheels.[11] Iron hulls, since they fouled so quickly, would have exacerbated this problem. As Joseph Conrad puts it, "After a spell of a few weeks at sea, an iron ship begins to lag as if she had grown tired too soon."[12]

In the early years of steam navigation, because the North American Pacific coast lacked proper drydocks, many ships had to be abandoned; elsewhere, they might have been repaired and restored to service. All steam engines of the time were at best cranky. Since the Pacific Mail Company knew that repairs would be a problem, it chose a type of ship with the least complicated engines, representing a satisfactory standardized and familiar design. Furthermore, the side-wheelers were relatively cheap to build, offering generous size for the money and comfort for the passenger. Charles Coffin, an early passenger, believed that the Pacific Mail, anticipating carrying a large number of Chinese passengers who would generate the company's chief source of revenue, chose a model of ship that would provide large space in steerage.[13] The company would in fact not only carry a lot of Chinese alive but also some dead, since Chinese always chose to be buried in the homeland if possible. Coffins and corpses were ubiquitous items of trans-Pacific freight.

The ships' machinery was supplied by the inappropriately named Novelty Iron Works of New York, which happened to be a big shareholder in the Pacific Mail Company. Perhaps, as John Kemble suggests, this was the "deciding factor" in the choice of wheel over screw.[14] Nonetheless, despite all the criticisms, these ships proved efficient and profitable, and they were impressive-looking craft, with gleaming black hulls, white sails, and huge churning paddle wheels, 120 feet in circumference, majestically beating the waves into a foam.

The side-wheelers required large spaces for stowing cargo and bunkering coal. The great distances of the Pacific strained fuel capacity. As it was, sometimes the ships ran perilously close to exhausting their supplies. In earlier days, passengers bound from Panama to California had the experience of having their ship make an emergency stop to cut and load wood. Crossing the Pacific, the side-wheelers carried fifteen hundred tons of coal when fully loaded and burned forty-five tons a day under optimum conditions. For a long time the company stocked coal at Midway for emergency use but apparently never had to tap it.

The side-wheelers had to fight the sometimes boisterous seas of the open Pacific, as well as the typhoons of the East Asian coast, but wooden ships suffered most from their special vulnerability to fire. Insurance costs were twice those for iron ships.[15] *America* and *Japan* both went up in flames, the latter with great loss of life. Marine disaster was common for all ships in that era. Uncharted coasts, errors in pilotage, and faulty equipment all took their toll. A British traveler aboard the *Great Republic* observed during an elaborate fire drill that there were not enough life-boats "to hold the half of us, and the nearest land is in the Sandwich Islands, so all this parade was bosh."[16]

The side-wheelers took precautions against another special kind of risk. They carried aboard a half-dozen cannon and a good supply of small arms, including cutlasses and pikes intended to use against any onslaught of pirates along the China coast or the dreadful possibility—which the ship's officers hardly dared mention—of a riot by the Chinese passengers, bursting out of their constricted spaces below.

Shortly after leaving office, William Henry Seward and his secretary, Olive Risley Seward, embarked on a world tour that included a voyage across the Pacific aboard one of these ships, the forty-three-hundred-ton *China*.[17] For Seward, the trip was a tremendous undertaking. His arms were paralyzed and his general condition parlous because he had never recovered fully from that terrible night in April 1865 when he was stabbed and the president shot.

China was carrying a cargo of agricultural machinery, carriages, fur-niture, flour, fruits, butter, patent medicines, and Mexican silver. The United States would have more and more industrial goods to sell to East Asia, but demand for these remained low because East Asian income levels did not permit buying such expensive goods in any quantity. This traffic across the Pacific then was not so dissimilar to that of the Manila galleon before.

Characteristically, the Pacific Mail would ship out flour, the mail, and treasure (gold and silver bars, Mexican silver dollars), bringing back tea, silk, rice, and a wide variety of exotic Chinese goods for the San Fran-cisco market. Eastbound cargoes were somewhat larger than westbound ones and generated a lot more income.

Olive Seward found the amenities of the *China* to be "surpassed only by the palatial boats on the Hudson River and Long Island Sound [on which they were patterned] . . . we enjoy an uninterrupted promenade seven hundred feet in circuit on the upper deck," from the poop to prow.[18] Parquet decking and black walnut furniture set an elegant tone. Staterooms were a generous eight by ten feet and enjoyed large portholes opening on the deck and doorways on both sides—one to the saloon, the other to the deck. The whole ship was scoured, tarred, painted, and polished as "clean as a Shaker meeting-house."[19]

One traveler describes the bath aboard *Great Republic*, located "in the paddle-box with a window a yard square. It is filled with fresh Pacific water, and I roll therein like the sea-lions . . . while I watch the birds. Now and then a whale blows. None of them can enjoy the air and water more than I do in the early morning."[20]

On Seward's voyage, only sixty cabin class passengers were aboard, with room for twice that number. And even this was higher than the average rate of 20 percent occupancy. The passengers whiled away their time by playing games. Deck sports were popular, whereas "the ladies had their music and their books." The ships offered well-stocked libraries. Evenings were enlivened by theatricals, concerts, and banquets. "An expert Japanese juggler entertains us in the cabin," Olive Seward recalled.[21]

Passengers found the fresh air, sunshine, and enforced relaxation delightfully restful once that dread malady, seasickness, was under control. A British traveler cautioned that no remedy existed for this except bed rest until the ailment "runs its horrid course."[22] Another passenger groaned that "one minute I was afraid I'd die—the next minute I was afraid I wouldn't."[23]

The food was abundant, including fresh meat from the animals carried live on board, but its quality, unlike that of the staterooms, was not the equivalent of a good hotel ashore. For Americans heading out to far-off and "semi barbarous" Asia, doubtless it was reassuring to travel in such modern luxury.[24] And the Chinese waiters and cabin stewards, with their black skullcaps, blue tunics, baggy white trousers, cloth shoes, and pigtails down the back, provided an exotic taste of the Asia to come.

The officers were always Americans; the crew was recruited in Hong Kong. The latter were cheap to hire and cheap to feed; the officers found them good seamen in fair weather and in foul. But the practice of hiring foreigners instead of Americans attracted some criticism at home. A high company official defensively told a congressional committee investigating the maritime industry that "a Chinaman can keep as good a deck watch and do as full an amount of work on deck as a man of any other nationality, and he does it better, because he does not require any one standing over him to see that the work is performed properly."[25] The passengers found the Chinese crew altogether satisfactory: quiet, courteous, and efficient.

With minimal amenities but decent Chinese food, hundreds of steerage passengers might be crowded below decks in a separate world. On Seward's outward journey, five hundred Chinese sojourners in America were returning home. These passengers did at least enjoy access to deck space and open air. Their passage is by no means to be compared with the horrors of the coolie runners, the Pacific equivalent of the Atlantic slavers. The Chinese passenger paid as little as forty dollars for his passage, but this was an important source of revenue to the company. First-class fare, San Francisco to Hong Kong, was three hundred dollars. Sometimes prosperous Chinese passengers, traveling cabin class instead of below decks, would nonetheless choose to eat below, opting for Chinese food instead of American cuisine.

General Horace Capron, traveling out to advise the Japanese government in the development of Hokkaido, was favorably impressed by the Pacific Mail Steamship Company, and he was a notoriously fussy man:

It is truly wonderful to what a degree of perfection they have brought the navigation of their ships. The vessel just passed [to which his ship *America* gave letters] was an extra ship running out of regular time; yet a telegraphic dispatch, via Europe and the continent of America to San Francisco, notified the agent of the line that she would leave the port of Yokohama, Japan, and our Captain gave us notice yesterday of the fact that we would probably meet her during the following day.[26]

Meeting another ship was always an important feature of the voyage and especially exciting because the steamer might not see any other vessel in the course of the entire voyage.

Early on, the Pacific Mail eliminated its trans-Pacific stop in Hawaii. The Honolulu harbor entrance was too shallow to permit entry by steamships large enough to make the run across the Pacific. More important was the advantage of using the great circle route for a shorter distance. On experimenting with the route first described by Maury, captains found that adverse winds and bad weather increased coal consumption. They therefore compromised between the demands of distance and those of weather by choosing a more southerly course, nonetheless well north of Hawaii, between the thirtieth and thirty-fifth parallels. This route added some 250 miles to the distance but provided a better trip. At the 9.5-knot speed dictated by company policy, the trip from San Francisco to Yokohama took about twenty-four days. The paddle wheelers could have made it faster, but coal was too expensive. Captains were forbidden to try to establish speed records.

Horace Capron was moved by the beauty of the paddle wheel: "How calmly and quietly and evenly this almost inspired piece of mechanism moves along."[27] Rough seas might tell a different story. One day out of Yokohama, the fury of a typhoon reminded him and everyone else aboard of their vulnerability. "The ship rolls and plunges fearfully, the captain and crew cannot conceal their anxiety."[28]

The company hoped to capture some of the Europe-bound passenger traffic from East Asia, but forty-four or forty-five days from Hong Kong to Liverpool could not be matched on the trans-American route. The sailings available on both French and British ships were more frequent, and the fares, at least from China, were cheaper. Japanese silk and green tea could reach London faster via the American route than by Suez, Japan being that much closer to the United States. But for bulk freight the canal was as much as 80 percent cheaper because no transshipment was necessary.[29] Sometimes other factors might enter—national prejudices perhaps. One British chauvinist advised "travellers to resist all temptations to travel by steamers not flying the British flag. Their ways are not our ways," he observed darkly.[30]

The Pacific Mail briefly engaged in local shipping along the Asian coast, sailing from Yokohama to Shanghai via Kobe and Nagasaki, plus offering service to Hakodate. These runs were bought out by Mitsubishi in 1875. The Pacific Mail also flirted with the idea of using its largest ships for the Japan-California line and putting on smaller ones for service beyond to Hong Kong. Eventually the company came to realize that the China traffic was the most important and merited the biggest ships. In 1875, it began service to New Zealand and Australia prompted by a mail subsidy provided by those governments. After ten years it ended; the traffic was insufficient to bear the costs.

By the early 1880s the wooden side-wheelers were all replaced by iron-hulled, screw-propelled steamers. Five of these joined the Pacific Mail in the early 1870s, most conspicuously the *City of Tokio* and *City of Peking*. Built in the Chester, Pennsylvania, yards of John Roche, at more than five thousand tons, they were, when built, the largest ships flying the Stars and Stripes.[31] The *City of Tokio* was lost when she piled up on a reef outside Yokohama harbor in 1885.

The Pacific Mail survived the withdrawal of its subsidy in 1876 caused by exposure of scandalous use of large sums of money by a former president of the company, Alden B. Stockwell, lobbying for favorable legislation. Subsidies were politically controversial anyway since the ownership of steamship companies tended to be concentrated in the Northeast and voters in many parts of the country felt little appetite for spending government money on specifically favored individuals and corporations, especially those out of state.

The shipping interests had argued that the potential of the China and West Pacific trade warranted government assistance. The postmaster general and the secretary of the navy proved far more receptive to these arguments than did the Congress. A promised huge increase in exports as a result of the mail subsidy did not happen. It was merely modest. Exports to China over 1856–66 were $35.7 million; over 1867–77, $41.8 million. Imports, on the other hand, did grow substantially, from $108.4

City of Tokio (Courtesy, Peabody & Essex Museum, Salem, Mass./Essex Institute Collections)

million to $183.7 million, reflecting renewed American demand for Asian silk.[32] Mail subsidies proved a futile means of generating commerce; the American merchant was still struggling to find something to sell to the Asian consumer.

In 1891, the Postal Aid Law provided federal assistance to the Pacific Mail by subsidizing a sailing across the central Pacific from San Francisco to Hong Kong every four weeks. Other routes were established across the South Pacific to Australia, and to Tahiti and the Marquesas. Under the tough and efficient management of former naval officer Rennie Pierre Schwerin, the Pacific Mail experienced more than twenty years of profits beginning in 1893. The company consistently enjoyed the reputation of providing excellent service despite the fact that its corporate image suffered from tales of unscrupulous management and financial manipulation.

John Kemble has pointed out that the maritime history of the Pacific is unique for the heavy role within it played by railroads. Perhaps this is understandable in view of the huge importance of the railroad in American economic life overall during the last quarter of the nineteenth century. The Pacific particularly lent itself to this phenomenon. The transcontinental railroad companies began to get interested in extending their networks on the seas, and the Pacific Mail was receptive to their courtship.

Such an arrangement carried mutual benefit. The western railroads had little local traffic and were looking to far horizons. And since the population of the American Pacific coast was still very small, it could not sustain much trans-Pacific trade. For a steamship company, a rail link into the American economic heartland was highly desirable to widen the market. In this fashion, American ships could better compete with foreigners using the two Capes or perhaps even Suez.

The Pacific Mail already enjoyed a controlling relationship both over the Panama Railroad and the steamers running from Panama to New York. Even after the Union Pacific-Central Pacific was operating, the Panama route could offer competitive rates, and it remained profitable for ordinary freight.[33] In 1873 Rufus Hatch, manager of the Pacific Mail, announced a decision to bypass the North American route in favor of the Central American route. By doing so, the Pacific Mail could control the flow of all priority through traffic between East Asian ports and the eastern seaboard of the United States.[34] Service would be slower than by the Central Pacific–Union Pacific but it could be made cheaper since the one company could offer one through rate.

The Union Pacific and Central Pacific tried unsuccessfully to buy the Pacific Mail, which they saw being run with increasing incompetence and financial recklessness. Some said it was no longer a San Francisco but "a Wall Street Company," more of a speculative venture than a shipping enterprise. Of course, the same comment could be made of most American railroads at that time.

In 1874 the Union Pacific–Central Pacific railroads started their own shipping company, the Occidental and Oriental. Its leaders were corporate heavyweights: Leland Stanford, Collis P. Huntington, Mark Hopkins, and Charles Crocker, known as the Big Four. The Occidental and Oriental, with four fast and dependable British-built single-screw steamers chartered from a British line, began to sail regularly from California to China. These steamers made better time than their competitors, doing the San Francisco–Yokohama run in fifteen to sixteen days.

A rate war led to an agreement to split the market with the Pacific Mail. Each line agreed to provide a monthly trans-Pacific service, with alternate sailings biweekly. A year later, the railroads, under the wily and furtive hand of Jay Gould, captured the Pacific Mail, and the two steamship companies, operating essentially as one, harmoniously divided and effectively controlled the trans-Pacific market until the entry of the Japanese at the close of the century. By 1901 Edward H. Harriman had added the Pacific Mail to his vast railroad empire; eventually (1915) it would become part of W. R. Grace and Company, of guano and, later, chemical fame.

CHAPTER FIFTEEN

Railroad Titans and the Beringian Route to Asia

The Union Pacific and Central Pacific did not long enjoy a monopoly of rail service across the American West. Other metal fingers soon began to stretch from the Mississippi to the shores of the Pacific. The Santa Fe got trackage to San Diego in 1885; the Northern Pacific completed its line from Duluth to Tacoma in 1883; James Jerome Hill's Great Northern reached Seattle in 1893. By 1903 a three-way competitive transcontinental rail system, north, south, and center, each with feeder lines, spanned the United States. Two more such lines would be put together in the early twentieth century. Punching through the trans-Mississippi frontier, the railroads opened up vast potential supplies of resources: ores and timber, food and energy. The result, in a contemporary judgment, was "one of the greatest industrial feats in the world's history."[1] Railway mileage was growing faster in percentage terms than the overall economy.[2]

The man who exercised control over the Great Northern system stands as a titan in the history of American transportation, James Jerome Hill. Becoming the nation's foremost railroad man, Jim Hill won the title of Empire Builder. His was a compelling personality and an extraordinary entrepreneurial talent.

Hill's massive head sat squarely on a burly body, neck somehow swallowed up in the union. A shaggy beard, moustache, and bushy brows covered most of his face but could not conceal a strong nose or bald pate. Even as a young man, Hill was bald. In his later years a fringe of steel-gray hair flowed down the back of his head from crown to collar. Thick-set and slow-moving, Hill's physique belied the volatility of his personality. His phlegmatism could rapidly dissolve into brief spasms of anger or boisterous humor. But withal he remained self-controlled. He was a man without intimates. His father died when he was fourteen, and

Jim went to work. Early hardship nurtured thrift, impatience, and ambition. Hill's learning was self-acquired, but he had a passion for reading
and relished taking in vast quantities of information. A good memory
later enabled him to recite mileage tables and freight rates by the yard,
but a fondness for detail did not obscure a probing intelligence and a
wide vision.

As a youth Hill dreamed of the Orient, of going to India to earn his
fortune running paddle-wheel boats on the Ganges. When he started out
from his Canadian home, he got no farther than the frontier town of St.
Paul, Minnesota, where he began working on the Mississippi as a steamboat man. After organizing his own successful transportation company
involving river boats and stagecoaches, Hill eventually was able to take
over a bankrupt railway. His career as a railroader would span the
American railway age from its beginnings to its peak and incipient decline.

Hill created the Great Northern system, the first American transcontinental railroad to be built without government land grants or subsidies.
To build it was a terrible gamble. The route Hill chose ran about a hundred miles north of the Northern Pacific, then teetering on the edge of
bankruptcy, and about an equal distance south of the heavily subsidized
Canadian Pacific. This was a narrow corridor of opportunity. Henry Villard, president of the Northern Pacific, scoffed, "Hill has got his road up
into the Rockies, but he'll never get it down again!"[3] But Hill reached
Puget Sound in 1893. In the financial panic of the same year Villard's
railroad went into receivership along with the Union Pacific, joined soon
after by the Santa Fe.

The terrain for the Great Northern was as challenging and as empty
of customers as any of the other transcontinental lines. But unlike the
others, Hill built well. The Great Northern had lower grades than its
rivals. "Mr. Hill," it was said, "can ignore the Rocky Mountains. His
engineers have removed them from the map."[4] Lower grades meant
lower fares, and Hill knew that curves were as costly as slopes to speed
and economy. The lower the grade and the straighter the track, the
longer the train could be and the faster it could travel. After the Great
Northern was opened in 1893, Hill's engineers went back and made solid
embankments to replace wooden trestles. A heavy, well-ballasted roadbed permitted the use of heavy equipment. Hill was careful to select
only the best rolling stock, constantly buying and constantly improving
the standard. Thus, the Great Northern was able consistently to carry
much heavier loads than any of its competitors.[5]

Three years after he finished the Great Northern, Hill, with the help
of J. Pierpont Morgan, was able to acquire a controlling interest in the
Northern Pacific. This effectively double-tracked his line. To the
Northern Pacific he later added the Burlington system, which gave him

direct access to the corn of the Midwest and the cotton of the South. Hill was not simply interested in his tracks but also in what lay beyond them, in the passengers and the cargo that would fill his trains. He sought to bring "men without land to lands without men."[6] Hill had well-developed ideas about agriculture and land use, and he shared Thomas Jefferson's view that the farm was more important than the factory for America.

Reading Washington Irving's classic *Astoria* inspired Hill to look westward, to think of highways to the Pacific and beyond to East Asia, as John Jacob Astor had done.[7] The Great Northern's crack passenger train was the *Oriental Limited*. Thick carpets, deep wicker chairs, and elaborate design work and fixtures conveyed an aura of luxury. Among the amenities the train boasted were a barber shop, library, and bath. "It is club-life carried through the journey," reported a grateful passenger, Vice President Adlai Stevenson, of a transcontinental trip, a statement Great Northern was happy to repeat in its advertisements.[8]

The Great Northern competed with the Canadian Pacific for the carriage of raw silk, the major American import from East Asia. The United States was now trading more with Japan than with China. Silk production was Japan's leading industry, and the United States bought 90 percent of what Japan exported, much of it used to make fine hosiery.[9] Handling silk required special equipment and special speed; it was high value and subject to rapid deterioration. Until the Great Depression, American customer demand for this luxury grew. Between 1925 and 1929 the Great Northern "averaged forty-three silk trains a year, including one that hauled a cargo valued at $5 million."[10] Sometimes special trains were used, setting speed records in their trips from western docks to eastern factories.

Over the years Hill's view swelled to global geographical scope. "By the cheapest transportation ever known, I will reverse the immemorial course of trade eastward over the seas, and turn it from Suez to Seattle," he boasted.[11] Hill's geostrategic interest centered on the Pacific. "You must realize," Hill once wrote, "that in this Oriental business we are not competing against the other railroads alone.... We are competing with the all-water route from New York to the Orient around the Cape and via the Suez Canal, and with European commerce by sea."[12]

Hill's philosophy in essence was that of William Henry Seward: transportation is the key to commerce, and commercial wealth is the essential ingredient of national power. Hill claimed that it was "not an exaggeration to say that the railway, next to the Christian religion and the public schools, has been the largest single contributing factor to the welfare and happiness of our people."[13]

Hill began his working life with ships, so when he went into railroading it is not surprising that he used ships to extend the range of his

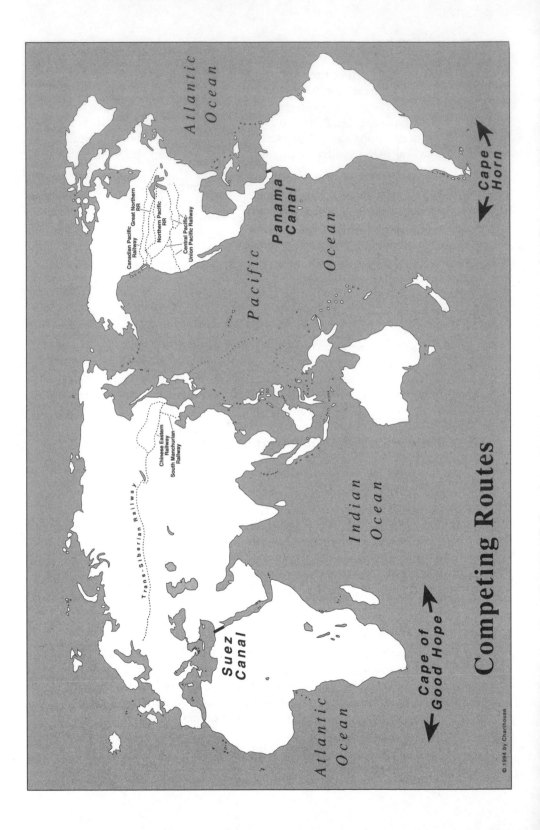

Atlantic Ocean

Panama Canal

Cape Horn

Pacific Ocean

Canadian Pacific Railway
Great Northern RR
Northern Pacific RR
Central Pacific-Union Pacific Railway

Chinese Eastern Railway
South Manchurian Railway

Trans-Siberian Railway

Indian Ocean

Suez Canal

Cape of Good Hope

Atlantic Ocean

Competing Routes

© 1994 by Charthouse

activity, on the Great Lakes and along the North American Pacific coast. Mindful of the geographical advantage of Puget Sound, "gateway of the United States to the Pacific Orient," Hill then wanted to run his own ships as the Canadian Pacific was doing, along the continuing great circle shoreline of the North Pacific, dispatching timber, steel, wheat, and cotton in great quantities to East Asian markets. Puget Sound ports had two great advantages over San Francisco: they were two days closer to East Asia and had locally available, hence cheaper, coal than what could be got in California.

Hill undertook to enter oceanic trade in a characteristically ambitious way. He planned four, and built two, gigantic ships, each with a dead-weight cargo capacity of twenty-seven thousand tons, the world's largest carriers at that time: *Dakota* and *Minnesota*. Each could carry a load equivalent to one hundred trains, each pulling twenty-five cars.[14] These ships were designed to become part of a "land bridge" across the North Pacific, and Hill expected lowered per ton costs because of their size.

They were constructed in a new shipyard in Groton, Connecticut, appropriately, in view of the anticipated destination of the ships, the birthplace of John Ledyard, and the site of the future Electric Boat Company–General Dynamics Corporation, builder of submarines. The *New London Day* proclaimed the launching of *Minnesota* on April 16, 1903, as "the most magnificent marine spectacle of the century."[15] The great ship could carry two hundred passengers in high comfort; some of the suites boasted telephones. Passengers were secondary in importance to cargo, but they were to be treated well, perhaps better than aboard any other ship at that time. Some well-known people would travel aboard these ships, including the Japanese peace delegation to the Portsmouth Conference ending the Russo-Japanese War in 1905.

The architecture of these giant merchant ships was innovative; the boilers were equipped with the world's first shipborne automatic stokers. But perhaps quirky is a better way to describe them. Hill himself took a hand in the design, his second mistake. His first was to choose an inexperienced yard as the builder. Cost overruns were huge, and Hill, disenchanted, later said, "I would rather undertake to build a thousand miles of railway than to build two ships."[16]

Hill wanted to keep his boxcars full going west as well as east. The empty car robbed him of revenue.[17] Diverting oceanic traffic from the Suez route to the Pacific seemed one good way to do so. The outbreak of war between Russia and Japan in 1904 helped because the Japanese wanted imports fast, everything from flour to steam locomotives, and the rail-sea route between the North Atlantic and East Asia via the North Pacific was faster than via Suez. The Japanese also wanted to import goods free of possible intervention by Russian warships. Here was another impetus to trade across the North Pacific. The Japanese islands,

The Great Northern Railway's Oriental Limited train at Smith Cove, Seattle, and the Great Northern Steamship Company's vessels, the *Minnesota* and *Dakota*. (Courtesy, Burlington Northern Railroad Company)

which then included the Kurils, thrust themselves protectively between the Russian fleet with its bases and the wide Pacific. American Pacific ports exceeded New York by a factor of eight in the value of exports to Japan.[18]

Hill was pleased to see that Puget Sound shipping was growing rapidly and seemed to be overtaking the California ports. Unlike that of the Atlantic merchant fleet, most of it sailed under the American flag. The railroads could offer exporters the benefit of through rates, one comprehensive charge for land and sea transport together. This provided a way to subsidize exporters by charging them less than domestic shippers had to pay for transporting freight by rail, and because the fee was comprehensive, the difference could be hidden.

The Interstate Commerce Commission issued new regulations in 1906 requiring that rates be published. The railroads protested, saying that doing so would jeopardize their relationships with domestic shippers, and without differential rates they could no longer compete with subsidized foreign steamships.[19] The New York *Journal of Commerce*, sympathetic to the plight of American transport companies, judged that growing U.S. governmental regulations were a greater threat to an "open door" for American trade across the Pacific than were any actions by the Japanese.[20] But the Japanese did not help matters by raising the tariff on wheat flour after the war was over.

Hill's two giant ships went into service out of Seattle in 1905. Deep hulled, with enormous carrying capacity, their blunt bows kept these monsters slow. Their construction was only the beginning of an unhappy story that would end for *Dakota* when she struck a reef off the coast of Japan on March 3, 1907, while traveling at full speed. Everyone aboard was saved, but *Dakota* became the world's largest and most expensive shipwreck.

Her surviving sister, *Minnesota*, was so slow at twelve to fourteen knots that she could make only four trans-Pacific round trips yearly and burned coal at a prodigious rate. Furthermore, the ship was so large that it was difficult to assemble an adequate cargo. When fully laden, she was unable to pass through the new Panama Canal, which limited usage. *Minnesota* made eighty Pacific crossings before being sold.

These ships shared with all other American ships working the Pacific an inability to compete with the Japanese because of their shipbuilding subsidies, lower wage scales and operating costs, and more casual safety regulations. The whole affair might appear to have been a complete fiasco, but Hill's ships did serve to siphon traffic into the railroad. The two ships were ahead of their time; they were bulk carriers before that era began in the 1950s.

Hill told a Minnesota audience,

When we built the Great Northern Railway to the Pacific coast, we knew that it was necessary to look to Asia for a part of our traffic. I sent a trained statistician to Japan and China and kept him there a year. He brought an abstract, a manifest of every ship that entered or left their open ports for a year, and I was quite delighted at the prospect for trade with Asia . . . but when I came to consider the question of carrying the Asiatic produce under the American flag upon the sea, I found that we could not do it profitably. I found that the little yellow man could do it a great deal cheaper than we could.[21]

Hill thereupon sent an agent to Japan who in February 1896 negotiated a contract with the Nippon Yusen Kaisha (NYK), resulting in Japan's first trans-Pacific liner service and, Hill hoped, the opening of a market in Asia for American wheat and other bulk commodities for which even a small per capita consumption would mean big business. Hill's knowledge of business conditions in Asia prompted his good friend Grover Cleveland to say that "for ten years he . . . spent more money than the Government in sending competent men to Japan and China to study the need of those countries."[22] The U.S. government did little to help American business overseas.

Hill made a strong case for the importance of foreign trade to the United States, pointing out that "the whole world, commercially speaking, is not as large as the states of the Union were before the Civil War. It is not so far from anywhere in the world to any other place in the world, considering the time or expense, as it was from Boston to San Francisco before the war."[23] Hill worried about the adverse balance of American trade, commenting that the United States bought some $35 million in imports from Japan but sold only about $5 million in exports, necessitating an American payment of $30 million in gold to balance the account.

The demand for American flour rose when the Japanese army began feeding bread to its own troops as well as to Russian prisoners, and Hill hoped that the export of wheat could redress the trade balance if the Japanese population in general (and other Asians) could be persuaded to eat bread instead of rice. The challenge was to grow it and ship it at a cheap enough price. "Our white bread," Hill asserted, "is like the lotus: no nation that once eats it will change to poorer diet."[24] Hill did his best to persuade Asians to bake bread, even distributing recipes translated into Chinese.[25]

Timber was another potential American export of great value, Hill believed. Not coincidentally, his Great Northern ran through the heart of the most magnificent forest on the continent and the greatest conifer forest on earth: virginal and ancient, stretching for some two thousand miles, from just north of San Francisco to the Alaska Panhandle. But timber enjoyed no domestic market because of the expense of transport.

It could not be shipped by rail to the east coast, where most of the potential buyers were, unless something could be found to put in its place for the trip back west.

Hill believed bulk products like timber, wheat, cotton, and steel were the most suitable American exports across the Pacific because American labor was too expensive to make goods cheap enough for Chinese or Japanese to buy. Although three-fourths of U.S. exports were agricultural products and raw materials, Americans were disproportionately interested in manufacturing, Hill believed. But he allowed that perhaps a market existed along the China coast for a narrow range of basic manufactures, among them American cotton cloth and American machinery, "until their manufacturing industry should be well developed. . . . Both China and Japan have inventive as well as imitative ability . . . [and] they will eventually become competitors such as we have never had to meet," Hill warned.[26]

Sales possibilities were staggering because of the numbers of people involved. Unconsciously echoing the earlier excitement of Lancashire textile manufacturers, Hill mused: "If the Chinese should spend only one cent per day per capita, it would amount to $4,000,000 a day or nearly $4,500,000,000 a year."[27]

Hill had high expectations of the Japanese, admiring the "scientific attention to details" that they were devoting to industry. Japan "is preparing and hoping to dominate the Oriental markets and to invade those of the rest of the world. . . . Presuming that Japan will come to be a great commercial nation, American trade on the Pacific Ocean should soon rival that of the Atlantic."[28] China too would industrialize, Hill predicted, and Americans could anticipate "building your railroads west of the Missouri with steel rails rolled in Shansi."[29] For Hill, history was not ending with U.S. supremacy.

In his book *Highways of Progress,* written toward the end of his career, Hill remarked that once the transcontinental railway reached Puget Sound, the United States was in a position to "realize a dream that has held the minds of men since the time of Alexander the Great."[30] But the nation had failed to capture commercial maritime leadership and "the history of our trade with the Orient is a tale of lost opportunity." In a growing worldwide trading network, Hill predicted that America's customers would soon become America's competitors.

Hill was frustrated by the paradox that the United States offered the world's cheapest transportation at home but could not extend it abroad. By 1900, the United States had more than half the world's railway mileage, yet "just as soon as we take our commodities to the salt water the other nations make us drop our bundles and they carry them at our expense and make us pay them for doing our work."[31] The United States needed more ships and low freight rates.

Both Hill and his great rival, E. H. Harriman of the Union Pacific, when complying with the ruling of the Interstate Commerce Commission requiring publishing of rates, declared they would give up their attempts to push trade with Asia.[32] Disgusted with what were to his mind an unreasonable ICC and an indifferent Congress, Hill wrote that "America is not a commercial nation . . . and until she has to make greater efforts to support her population than has been necessary in the past, I do not see how she will become important among the leading exporting nations of the world."[33]

By the late nineteenth century, three railroad systems came to dominate North America: the Canadian Pacific, Hill's system, and that of Edward H. Harriman. Unlike Hill, Harriman was a Wall Street financier who came to railroading only in the maturity of his career. The vehicle for his rivalry with Hill was the Union Pacific, bankrupt when Harriman took it over in 1897, restored to solvency, and carried into enormous growth by his shrewd and aggressive management. Hill built his line to the Pacific; Harriman bought his.

The railroads in late nineteenth-century America, major consumers of iron, steel, and coal, major carriers of people and freight, played a huge role in the American economy, as had the maritime industries fifty years before and as would the automobile industry fifty years later. Behind each of the major railroads stood a small group of powerful financiers. The Vanderbilts; James Stillman of the National City Bank of New York; Jacob Schiff, the head of the richest private banking house in the United States, Kuhn Loeb & Co.; and Henry Clay Frick sat in E. H. Harriman's corner. Hill drew the support of the great Pierpont Morgan and London's Baring Brothers. The Canadians enjoyed their own sources of money, both Canadian and British.

The Canadian Pacific, of course, monopolized Vancouver. In tonnage carried per mile, the Canadian Pacific compared favorably with either of Hill's transcontinental lines individually but not put together. Harriman controlled the major arteries of transport to San Francisco and Portland. Harriman's transportation empire was the largest in American history. But Hill held Puget Sound.

Import-export statistics showed San Francisco yielding to Seattle, seeming to vindicate Hill's judgment that geography and the great circle route favored ultimate Seattle leadership in U.S. trade with East Asia.[34] Hill appeared to hold the shortest transcontinental U.S. traffic routes to Asia firmly in his grasp, and yet a possibility existed for Harriman to circumvent this hammerlock by going north and building a railroad from Northwest America to Northeast Asia. That idea had been around for some time, and, as we have seen, William Gilpin was one early promoter of it. The Klondike gold rush (1897) gave the idea fresh interest.

In 1892, two years after Gilpin's *Cosmopolitan Railway* appeared, a young civil engineer named Joseph B. Strauss, as part of his studies at the University of Cincinnati, prepared a design for a Beringian bridge to link the future railways of North Asia and North America. Strauss's work was inspired by John Roebling, whose masterpiece was the Brooklyn Bridge. Like Roebling, the aesthetics of bridge building captivated Strauss, and although he would never span the Bering Strait, he would span the Golden Gate, designing perhaps the most beautiful bridge of all time.[35]

Rumors of a great intercontinental railway construction project had been floating around for some time, even before Gilpin's book. In 1886, John Arthur Lynch of Washington, D.C., petitioned the U.S. Senate to commission a survey of a line for a railway from the northern border of the United States through British Columbia to Alaska. At some suitable harbor on the Alaskan coast, Lynch proposed establishing a steamship line connecting on the shore of Northeast Asia with a railroad as yet unbuilt by the Russians. Lynch argued that the line would open to Americans direct intercourse with the huge population of Asia, to immense commercial advantage. He asserted that the natural obstacles to such a rail line would be no greater than those recently overcome in the building of the Pacific Railway.

To his petition Lynch attached a couple of letters in an attempt to buttress his case. The most prominent writer was the scientist Joseph Henry, who remarked on the magnificence of Lynch's plan and agreed that "whatever tends to facilitate intercommunication of nations has an important bearing on advance of civilization" but cautioned that the project would require a very large amount of capital and international cooperation.[36]

The petition died, but in response to a Senate bill passed in April 1886 intended to encourage the settling and development of Alaska, Major J. W. Powell, chief of the U.S. Geological Survey, did make a report about a railroad. Drawing heavily from information compiled by the Collins telegraph team, Major Powell suggested three different routes for a railroad between Montana and the Bering Strait, with a branch line en route out to Wrangell. He ended his report by saying, "The Director does not feel called upon to express any opinion as to the wisdom of constructing the railroad under consideration."[37] Nothing further happened.

In the fall of 1890, the *New York Times* reported that a group of New York capitalists, including Henry Villard of the Northern Pacific Railroad, was planning to build a railroad from Puget Sound to Alaska and that the line to Juneau would get underway in the spring of 1891. Reportedly St. Petersburg capitalists were also interested because the Alaska line would connect with Siberia by means of ferryboats across the Bering Sea, where the railroad cars would be put on a Russian railroad to be built "across the desert wastes of Siberia." Besides seal fish-eries and lumber, abundant coal in Alaska should provide an inducement to investors.[38]

Nothing happened.

As the building of the Trans-Siberian neared conclusion, the *New York Times* reported from St. Petersburg on April 4, 1899, that the "Russians are confident that, as far as concerns traffic between the West and the Far East, the locomotive will eventually conquer the steamship, and some of the most serious and enterprising men in the United States are preparing to clasp hands with them across the water."

Late in 1901, the press again picked up stories of an intercontinental railroad. This time, French capital was supposedly interested. The visit to St. Paul of Robert Barbier, manager of the Russo-China Bank of Pe-king, strongly hinted at James Jerome Hill's participation. Why else would Barbier visit Minnesota? A St. Paul newspaper reported that the Frenchman anticipated that within two years of the completion of a Ber-ingian railroad, the population of Alaska would soar to 1 million since many immigrants would be attracted there from western Europe.[39] An-other report had it that a new company was being formed in Seattle, the Trans-Alaskan Railway Company, which would build and operate a sys-tem of railroads in Alaska connecting with Siberia by ferryboats.[40]

About the same time, Harry DeWindt, a dapper English globetrotter sporting an enormous waxed moustache and a generous sense of self-worth, motivated either by a love of science or a love for publicity, or perhaps both, decided to explore a route for transcontinental travel from New York to Paris, accompanied only by his manservant. DeWindt got as far as the Siberian side of the Bering Sea, where he planned to get dogsleds, guides, and equipment in order to continue his journey. Since DeWindt refers to the Chukchi as "a race of people filthier, if possible, in their habits and habitations than the Alaskan Eskimos," the basis for good intercultural communication between him and his hosts would seem to have been slender.[41]

Indeed DeWindt's travel plans were cut short. The local chief refused to help him, instead confiscating his provisions and drinking up his li-quor. DeWindt had brought along a tiny Union Jack, which he thereupon nailed to a whalebone and propped up on the shore. Miraculously, al-though the season was over, a whaling ship saw the flag, stopped, and rescued DeWindt and his manservant.

Undaunted, DeWindt ventured forth again on his intercontinental ad-venture, this time starting from Paris in December 1901. More than six-teen thousand miles later, he arrived in New York, having collected enough material along the way for a book and a lecture series. DeWindt wrote that his main object had been to determine the feasibility of rail travel from Paris to New York, and he claimed to be the first to have covered the route by the means then available. The preferable way, he said, was Irkutsk-Okhotsk, then north to the Anadyr and East Cape (Cape Dezhnev), and from there across the narrow waters to Alaska. DeWindt thought that many a martyr to seasickness would cheerfully endure a very long train ride in preference to the unspeakable miseries of a stormy passage across the Atlantic.[42]

An intercontinental railroad would be quite possible, DeWindt concludes, but he acknowledged that the cost would be enormous. The many miles of tundra in the Great Arctic desert would demand that pilings be driven to keep the track from submerging in the summer swampiness above the permafrost. And the Bering "subway" would be hugely expensive. Who would pay? And would it pay?

The "prominent Russian officials" with whom DeWindt consulted ridiculed the project. Theodore Roosevelt, intrigued by DeWindt's adventures, invited him to the White House for lunch and a chat. The president thought the idea of an intercontinental railroad was a great joke, asking that DeWindt be sure to reserve him a first-class compartment on the first train to leave New York for Paris. And yet for an age in which seemingly grandiose projects like interoceanic canals and transcontinental railways were becoming realities, the idea was not preposterous. A Beringian bridge or tunnel would be only about twice the length of a Panama canal and slightly longer than the world's now longest undersea rail tunnel (thirty-four miles) connecting Honshu and Hokkaido. The straits are about twice the width of the English Channel, but the Diomede Islands break this distance into roughly two halves.

The same year of DeWindt's trek, 1902, a Frenchman, Baron Loicq de Lobel, describing himself as a scientist and having spent some eighteen months traveling in Alaska and the Arctic collecting information about the natural resources of the region, visited St. Petersburg in order to sound out the possibilities of building a railway that would connect the Bering Strait with the Trans-Siberian mainline, following the route surveyed by George Kennan and the Collins telegraph expedition. The biggest challenge, it seemed, would be the strait—whether to throw a great bridge across or to tunnel beneath.[43]

The Baron de Lobel suggested a tunnel.[44] This elicited a response from a reader of *Engineering News* who instead favored building a thirty-foot-wide causeway from the mouth of the Yukon west over St. Lawrence Island to the Siberian mainland. The distance is longer than at the strait but the water shallower, he believed. Therefore the volume of rock required would be no greater, and the entrance to Siberia would lie farther to the south. The Asian railroad connection could thus be made shorter. The letter writer speculated that such a dike, by preventing the flow of currents, might modify the climate of the region.

The editor commented that he understood the depth of water to be much greater than the writer of the letter did and that anyway "it is yet to be demonstrated that any one really desires to travel from New York to Paris by way of Behring Straits and Arctic Siberia."[45] But even Edward H. Harriman, it seems, was flirting with the idea of an all-land route connecting Europe with the United States by way of Siberia.

If anyone could have carried out this mammoth project, it was Harriman, the "Napoleon of railroading." Not one to talk much about his plans and thought to be cold-blooded, brusque, and friendless, Ned Harriman sprang into national and international prominence only a dozen or so years before his death in 1909 at the age of sixty-two.

Harriman was as dynamic as Theodore Roosevelt, in the opinion of one man who knew them both, but in appearance and manner, Harriman was Roosevelt's antithesis. The president's daughter, Alice Roosevelt Longworth, who met Harriman in East Asia, saw only the outside: a "small, brown, taciturn man who never seemed to play," yet she was impressed that he shunned the pomp of wealth in his pursuit of power.[46] His voice was soft, his manner subdued; he seldom smiled; he never talked at length about anything. He had "no quality of being picturesque."[47] At 125 pounds, his was not an imposing figure, especially by the ample standards of the day. Nonetheless in the business community "E. H.," as he was known, seems to have commanded respect because of the quality of his mind.

A minister's son, Harriman went to work at the age of fourteen like his great rival, Hill. He started in Wall Street as a quotation boy and quickly manifested his amazing talent for making money. By his mid-thirties he had gained financial independence. Harriman's first encounter with railroading was in 1880 when he was elected to the board of directors of a tiny railroad in upstate New York. To Harriman, money was incidental to power, and in his maturity he found the power he wanted in railroads. Although in later years he was unwell, and he died relatively young, he fought for good health. Accomplished at sports, he kept an exercise bar in his private railroad car, which he used religiously.

Harriman was an improver, an organizer, and a rebuilder. He turned the Illinois Central into one of America's best-managed railroads. The elegance of the financial skills Harriman exercised there prompted Robert A. Lovett to marvel that "somehow or other . . . [the Illinois Central] never had bonds for sale except in times when bonds were in great demand; it never borrowed money except when money was cheap and plentiful."[48] Lovett said that Harriman *planned*; he never *speculated*.[49]

Harriman's success was based on a superb brain that worked fast, extensive knowledge rooted in a command of infinite detail, a splendid assurance, and a steely persistence. In his last years, Harriman controlled one-third of total U.S. railway mileage, and he would be judged the single most powerful man in the United States.[50]

In 1897 Harriman acquired the Union Pacific, described then by financier Otto Kahn as a "rather pathetic object," "two streaks of rust" across the desolate wastes of the great plains.[51] Here rested an enormous opportunity for Harriman's talents. His administrative style was direct and original. For example, in Wyoming the Union Pacific suffered from attacks of outlaws, who would hold up the trains and fleece the passengers. Harriman's tactic was to buy the hardiest and speediest horses he could find, hire the most accomplished hunters and guides to mount them, and move them around by fast train to confound any attackers. Soon the trouble stopped, and the railroad acquired a reputation for safety.[52]

The Union Pacific was large enough to give Harriman national scope and to enable him to aspire to something even more: a global steam network. With the financial resources of Kuhn, Loeb to draw upon, Harriman successfully reorganized the Union Pacific and bought into other railway companies such as the Southern Pacific, which had shipping interests and could serve as projections of commercial power across the Pacific. Robert A. Lovett suggests that Harriman's vision extended beyond railroads or ships; he was thinking about the overall development of the United States west of the Mississippi, of empty plains to be populated and arid lands to be irrigated.

Harriman was thinking also of the world beyond the United States, of the value of foreign commerce to the national economy. His means of access to that world was the Pacific. But Hill's northern transportation system enjoyed a geographical advantage over Harriman's. Hill's empire lay closer to Asia.

This may be part of the explanation for Harriman's Alaska expedition of 1899, billed as a vacation (for a man who did not normally take vacations). Harriman wanted to bag a brown bear, they said; the bigger, the better. Perhaps he also wanted some favorable publicity as a patron of science since he was aware of the philanthropic kudos some of the other men of his wealth were receiving for their museums and their libraries. In terms of the prominence and number of its scholarly participants, the expedition is to be ranked even above that of Wilkes. And, of course, it was all paid for by Harriman.

This was an enterprise on a grand and lavish scale. Harriman chartered a luxurious steamship for his party, which consisted of himself and his family (including his young son, Averell, future ambassador to the Soviet Union, who thus made his first entrance to Russia via Siberia instead of Europe), a couple of friends, and some two dozen distinguished scientists. John Muir and John Burroughs were among the company, along with two photographers and three artists. This was, in effect, a floating university offering a regularly scheduled series of lectures aboard.[53] A magnificent multivolume illustrated narrative of the experience was subsequently published, as well as many scientific papers resulting from observations made during the expedition.

From Seattle where the party congregated, the ship moved up the Alaska coast, stopped at Dutch Harbor, visited the Pribilov Islands, and touched the shores of Siberia because "Mrs. Harriman expressed the desire to see Russia." Alaska made a strong imprint on Harriman. In a press interview after his return he said, "To you older people let me say this: if it is at all possible for you to do so, be sure and see Alaska before you die. To the younger generation let me say: see the rest of the world first before going to Alaska, for after you have seen its majestic mountains, glaciers and other scenic wonders, no other scenery will ever satisfy you."[54]

E. H. remained silent about a Beringian railroad, and whatever interest he may have had in it did not lead to surveys or other substantive action. Instead he apparently began to think about a railroad-steamship combination, knitting together lines already in existence, which was, after all, much more characteristic of the Harriman operating style. E. H. was a buyer rather than a builder.

Harriman traveled to Japan in 1906 to negotiate control of the South Manchurian Railway, which Japan had just acquired as part of the fruits of victory over Russia in 1905. The SMR connected the Chinese Eastern Railway, which was a shortcut for the Trans-Siberian, to the great naval base, Port Arthur, and commercial port of Dairen (Dalien) at the tip of the Liaodong Peninsula. The road, like the Chinese Eastern and the Trans-Siberian with which it connected, was in poor shape. It needed a new roadbed and new locomotives, cars, and other equipment; all its bridges had been destroyed.[55] This required a large infusion of capital and the administrative reorganizing at which E. H. was so expert.

Harriman scarcely needed the opportunity for such an investment, nor did he need the possible profits. He simply liked the idea of one transportation system linking four of the world's greatest concentrations of population: China, Russia, Japan, and the United States. His was a North Pacific view, and what he contemplated was without doubt the most ambitious international business project in American history.

Perhaps, as Michael Hunt suggests, the opportunity to work in the international sphere, beyond the increasingly vexatious web of federal government regulation, appealed to Harriman. Perhaps the United States had become too confining for a man of Harriman's entrepreneurial ambition and energies.[56] But patriotism was also a motive for Harriman to push overseas. He said he wanted "to save the commercial interests of the United States from being entirely wiped from the Pacific Ocean in the future."[57] And he wrote to Secretary of State Philander Knox that he remained involved in Manchurian ventures because of "patriotic motives. . . . This may seem queer from a business standpoint, but sentiment enters into [it] more than sometimes we think."[58]

The end of the war in Northeast Asia seemed to open up new opportunities for Americans. Harriman's mind was again ranging beyond transportation. Manchuria, undeveloped, underpopulated, potentially rich, attracted him. Bigger in area than France and Germany put together, with broad plains, high mountains, and dry continental climate, Manchuria was more than a little reminiscent of the old American West, with all the opportunities that region seemed to offer.[59] Manchuria's Russian-built towns, springing up along the railroad, had broad streets laid out in a geometrical pattern like those of midwestern America. It had only 15 million people at the turn of the century, and U.S. senator Albert J. Beveridge, an early visitor there, thought it capable of sustaining 50 million.[60] Perhaps railroads would provide the means to open up the untapped resources of a large and potentially very rich land, just as they were doing in America.

Furthermore, Manchuria was a potential market for American machinery and American foodstuffs, for cotton cloth, kerosene, flour, and timber. In manufactured goods, Americans thought they ought to be able to outsell even the Germans because Europe was so remote. Transportation costs from the American Pacific coast offered American exporters a real advantage. On his tour Senator Beveridge noted approvingly the legend "Baldwin Locomotive Works," on "an American engine, running on American rails, spiked down to a Russian railway grade in Chinese Manchuria!"[61]

Harriman's international interest ranged beyond Manchuria. American minister in Tokyo Lloyd Griscom remembers him saying in an uncharacteristically forthcoming fashion:

Griscom, there's no doubt about it. If I can secure control of the South Manchuria Railroad from Japan, I'll buy the Chinese Eastern from Russia, acquire trackage over the Trans-Siberian to the Baltic, and establish a line of steamers to the United States. Then I can connect with the American transcontinental lines, and join up with the Pacific Mail and the Japanese transpacific steamers. It'll be the most marvelous transportation system in the world. We'll girdle the earth.[62]

Harriman expected the Japanese to be glad to do business with him because the war with Russia had left Japan financially exhausted. Some Japanese agreed, thinking a Harriman investment in Manchuria might provide a useful strategic buffer between the Russians and the Japanese, discouraging any Russian desire for revenge.[63] Street riots in Tokyo, protesting the Portsmouth settlement, discouraged American visitors then, but Harriman was greeted with warm politeness, if for no other reason than his association with Kuhn, Loeb, which had lent Japan substantial sums during the war when the Japanese had desperate need for money to buy weapons and war materiel.

The time was not propitious for signing the contract Harriman wanted, but he left Japan thinking he had made a deal. In San Francisco a message he received from the Japanese consul informed him otherwise. The reason offered by the Japanese for their change of mind was that they could not sell Harriman a railroad in Manchuria without Chinese approval because Manchuria belonged to the Chinese, and China had not yet agreed to the transfer of the railroad from Russia to Japan. But China did not then make the important decisions for Manchuria. Foreign military power did—the Russians in the north and the Japanese in the south. After 1905 the Russian sphere contracted in favor of the Japanese with no room for investment or trade involving other nations.

As early as September 1905 the Japanese had plans underway for the development of south Manchuria in which the rail system was to be the key element. The Japanese found that they could raise capital in London, which, to the chagrin of the British, they chose to spend on American rails, cars, and locomotives, judging them to be the world's best. The South Manchurian Railway in Japanese hands proved to be immediately profitable and ultimately extremely lucrative. The railroad served as a means to colonize and colonialize a large territory, creating an informal empire for Japan. Yet Americans continued to hope. Manchuria would remain a psychological frontier for the United States, a frontier of expectation; it never became a tangible one.

In his negotiations Harriman may well have been done in by his New York competitors' promising to lend money to the Japanese with no strings attached.[64] Whether true or not, another American financial crisis, the panic of 1907, removed that possibility. The general shortage of capital and confidence wrought by the panic handicapped Harriman more than it did the Japanese in the pursuit of other opportunities in Manchuria.

Willard Straight, consul general in Mukden (Shenyang), was trying to encourage Harriman to consider building a railroad to the west and parallel with the South Manchurian line.[65] And Harriman was trying to persuade the Russians to sell him the Chinese Eastern Railway, negotiating in Europe by means of a French agent of the Russian Finance Ministry.[66] George Kennan, the erstwhile telegrapher and Harriman's admiring biographer, suggests that if Harriman's plan had been successful, a double-tracked Trans-Siberian, equipped efficiently, might successfully have supplied the Eastern Front in World War I, kept Russia in the war, and changed history.[67]

But Harriman had overlooked both Russian pride and Japanese nationalism—Japan's desire to operate independently on the Asian mainland—and the Japanese ability to tap the London money market for their capital needs. Harriman's shrewdness in business did not extend to foreign affairs.

Harriman continued to think about alternatives in Northeast Asia and sent his agents to reconnoiter. One attractive possibility was to build a rail line from Peking across the Gobi through Mongolia to Irkutsk and the Trans-Siberian mainline. This, the route of the Trans-Mongolian railway, would ultimately be built, but not by Harriman and not until after the establishment of the Chinese Peoples Republic in 1949.

One year after his Japan visit, Harriman was dead.

Another mammoth rail project bruited about at this time was a Cape-to-Cape line, running from Cape Horn to the Cape of Good Hope, an around-the-world trunk road of twenty-five thousand miles. The enthusiasm for this project welled up out of the completing of the Trans-Siberian and the excellent progress being made toward digging the Panama Canal, a project abandoned by the French as impossible and now being carried to success by American hands. Andrew Carnegie reportedly was interested in promoting a rail route from New York to Buenos Aires, hoping in this fashion to wrest the trade of South America from European hands. Alexander Cassatt, president of the Pennsylvania Railroad, served as chairman of a committee to investigate this possibility.[68]

For the British, the strategic implications of these railroads appeared largely negative, affording instead new opportunities to the United States, Russia, and other continental powers like newly rising Germany, with its dream of a Berlin-to-Baghdad railway, to challenge British domination of intercontinental transportation routes. British geographer Sir Halford Mackinder even predicted a new age of strategic dominance by railways, in an influential lecture, "The Geographical Pivot of History," delivered in London in January 1904. His was a counterattack against the American notion of a coming centrality for the Pacific.

In his talk, Mackinder suggested that it was time to subject geography to "philosophic synthesis," time to enlarge Bishop Berkeley's fragmentary formula. Mackinder proclaimed the end of the age of exploration, an end to the Columbian era in which the North Atlantic maritime nations had come to dominate the world primarily by means of sea power and the machine.

The world core, he said, remained a power system rooted in a small space, but the interactions of its parts now provoked global reverberations. The world had both expanded and contracted. Much of the mystery of global space had by now been penetrated. The global surface was largely known and politically defined; the world had therefore become a larger theater for international events. At the same time, in a dynamic and continuing process, steam and electricity were revolutionizing the speed of transportation and communications, thereby making the world a smaller space.

The railroad, a British invention, Mackinder saw as ironically shifting the center of gravity in world affairs away from Britain and maritime Europe to the center of Eurasia. This space, Mackinder suggested, was the world's heartland. Oddly he placed the heartland even farther to the east than the core of Russian power—not around Muscovy or within Ukraine but far out in the almost empty steppes of Central Asia. Mackinder's dictum was the opposite of Berkeley's: *eastward* the course of empire, he declared. Russia, without sea power or the machine, had swept to the Pacific in a thrust almost as significant, he believed, as those of da Gama and Magellan.

Steam power, enhanced by the Suez Canal, originally appeared to give advantage of mobility to the sea, but Mackinder put great stress on the impact of intercontinental railroads and the superiority of internal lines of communication. The long-distance railway, he argued, would eliminate the need for costly transshipments of raw materials and processed goods, which instead would flow "directly from the exporting factory into the importing warehouse."[69]

Mackinder offered a concept of a Euro-Asia—one continuous land mass, three times the size of North America. North America was peripheral to what he called the "world island." The United States enjoyed no particular importance on Mackinder's strategic map, yet he saw the nation as more of a Pacific than an Atlantic power, "the real divide between east and west is to be found in the Atlantic ocean." And, he predicted, "the century will not be old" before the Eurasian world island is laced by railways.[70] A vast interconnected world would thus develop, for the most part inaccessible to oceanic commerce and impervious to seaborne power.

Mackinder saw his heartland as a space around which might coalesce an "empire of the world." One can understand the excitement that Mackinder's theories would arouse among German geographers and the inspiration to what would be called geopolitics. Mackinder's message made far more of an impact on Germans than it did on Englishmen, for it offered Germany the opportunity to gain an enlarged and dominant position in world affairs.

Rising from the audience at the close of Mackinder's lecture, the prominent political figure Leopold Amery presciently questioned the future roles of both the railway and the steamship by suggesting that sooner or later aircraft would supplement them as a means of locomotion, and indeed the Eurasian railways Mackinder anticipated never got built.

Furthermore, Amery queried, will location be so important in the future? "The successful powers," he asserted, "will be those who have the greatest industrial basis. It will not matter whether they are in the centre of a continent or on an island." Science, industry, the power of invention will be the key determinants of national power, he argued.[71] Americans paid small attention to Mackinder or to Amery choosing instead to continue to dwell lovingly on the advantages that dominating the Pacific might bring.

CHAPTER SIXTEEN

Grasping the Western Pacific

Despite the profound maritime and naval weakness of the United States, in the early 1880s President Chester A. Arthur gave at least lip-service to the importance of a healthy merchant marine, a prosperous foreign trade, and the means to protect it. Arthur's exceptionally able secretary of the navy, William E. Chandler, was responsible for the navy's first modern steel warships.[1] And naval officers serving in the Pacific continued to talk as expansively as David Porter or Matthew Perry had. Rear Admiral Henry Haywood Bell, commander of the Asiatic Squadron immediately after the Civil War, had wanted to show the world who were "masters of the Pacific."[2] His subordinate, Robert Wilson Shufeldt, who would become best known as the opener of Korea in 1882, enthusiastically shared this ebullience.

Shufeldt's rhetoric could have been drafted by William Henry Seward; Bishop Berkeley and Timothy Dwight would have nodded approvingly. The Pacific, Shufeldt declared, is "the ocean bride of America." With China, Japan, and Korea the bridesmaids and California "the nuptial couch . . . [the] Ocean *is* & *must* be essentially American. Through it & by us—China & Japan must acquire a new civilization & adopt a new creed—for it is in this sense that 'Westward still, the Star of Empire takes its way.' "[3]

In the war with Spain (1898), the need to destroy the Spanish navy swept U.S. arms into the Philippines. Once the Spanish fleet was destroyed at Manila Bay, the uncertainty began. Washington had not anticipated the next step: acquiring a naval base, all of the island of Luzon, or the entire Philippine archipelago?

Ultimately the United States annexed the Philippines, "lest some other power do so or the islands themselves sink into anarchy," the imperialists argued. And indeed the Germans were hanging around expectantly. But no one seems to have thought out the future in terms of American (or Philippine) national interests. The result was to thrust American power—or American vulnerability—deeply into the western Pacific. China seemed nearer, but this was more perception than reality. The Philippines were touted as a springboard to the East Asian coast, but they would not actually serve as such until long-distance air travel began.

Guam fell to the Americans almost as an afterthought,[4] and a few months later the United States formally claimed Wake Island, largely because of its presumed value as a cable relay station. The United States had an easy opportunity to take all of the Marianas but failed to do so. No one seemed to realize that Saipan was almost as valuable as its neighbor Guam. A few months after the Treaty of Paris (December 1898) ended the war, Spain sold the rest of the Marianas to Germany. A few years later Japan would get them as booty from World War I, with grim consequences for Americans during World War II.

Americans had earlier established a presence in South Pacific Samoa. In 1872, Commander Richard W. Meade, USN, in the aggressive David Porter tradition, had independently tried to secure a naval base there at Pago Pago. Washington failed to support him. But in 1889 a conference in Berlin established a tripartite protectorate among Germany, Great Britain, and the United States. Thus, Americans thereafter held another potential stopping-off place on the route to China.

Hawaii, already a commercial dependency of the United States, had assumed renewed importance as American interest in the Pacific began to reflect a big increase in the size of the navy. In 1887 the navy obtained a lease to Pearl Harbor as a potential base. Captain Alfred Thayer Mahan, whose influential book *The Influence of Sea Power on History* was published in 1890, believed that the Pacific Ocean and eastern Asia were increasingly the world's "predominant objects of interest"[5] and that the Pacific would be the meeting ground between two great civilizations, the "East" and the "West."[6] Annexation of Hawaii was in the air long before it happened in 1900. Republicans favored it; Democrats did not. It required the vote of two-thirds of the Senate. The McKinley administration lacked that support until the Spanish-American War, which underlined the strategic importance of the islands.

Mahan had argued that the United States must not allow any potentially hostile maritime power to hold a valuable coaling station in Hawaii, within twenty-five hundred miles of the American Pacific coast. Hawaii he perceived as a nerve center in America's new push out into the Pacific. Hawaii lay on the direct route between a future isthmian canal and China; all shipping passing through Panama en route to East Asia would naturally stop at Honolulu for food and coal. Hawaiian resident Lauren Thurston pointed out that within the whole Pacific Ocean, from the equator to Alaska, and from Japan to California, "there is but one spot where a ton of coal, a pound of bread, or a gallon of water can be obtained by a passing vessel, and that spot is Hawaii."[7]

Many Americans perceived Great Britain as the primary threat, aiming at taking Hawaii in order to build its own strategic lifeline across the Pacific from Australia to British Columbia, thus barring the American reach to East Asia. Communications formed an important part of any such strategic network. In 1902, the British completed their own "all-red," as they liked to call it, trans-Pacific cable line, connecting Canada with Australia. This line necessitated the longest unbroken reach in the world, stretching from Vancouver to Fanning Island. The British had hoped to find a place en route for a relay station. In 1894 they tried to establish claim to the rocky treeless islet of Necker, about four hundred miles northwest of Kauai in the Hawaiian archipelago. Necker is less than three-fourths of a mile long and without any other conceivable value. The Hawaiians, still independent, learning of the British plan, sent out their own ship to Necker, raised their flag, and forestalled the inter-lopers.

A British line was not needed for commercial purposes. Australia already enjoyed cheap and efficient cable service via Asia to Britain. But the British wanted privacy in communication across the Pacific. As Charles Bright put it: "There may yet come a moment when the Mother Country and her children will have things to say to each other which strangers should not overhear."[8]

The British tried also to compete with the Americans in transportation across the Pacific. In 1898 the British firm of Bowrings started steamship service between China and Japan and San Diego, connecting with the Atchison, Topeka, and Santa Fe Railroad. They hoped to generate traffic in wheat, cotton, and manufactured goods in exchange for Asian silks and teas. After only four years they gave up; the demand was simply insufficient.

Britain was not prepared to compete in a strategic sense with the United States in the Pacific, or anywhere else for that matter, particularly after signing an alliance with Japan in 1902. That agreement signified the need of the Royal Navy to draw down its forces in the Far East in order to reinforce those in home waters facing a rising German menace. The alliance also marks the coming of age of Japan as a power in the North Pacific, and Japan's victory over Russia three years later cemented the international reputation of the Japanese.

Captain Mahan assured American businessmen that Hawaii could serve as a "half-way house" to the huge markets of East Asia. There, American surplus goods could be sold and American fears of the perils of plenty assuaged. China, it seemed, could save American industry, relieving what Philadelphia shipbuilder Charles Cramp called the threat of "national apoplexy."[9]

Historian Brooks Adams, grandson of John Quincy, also looked to the Pacific, asserting that since "George Washington's empty continent" had been filled, the proper new American sphere is an expansion of the old North Atlantic core civilization into a Pacific-centered one, extending across both the Atlantic and Pacific Oceans, brushing one wing over the British Isles and the other over East Asia, "much as the Romans encompassed the Mediterranean."[10] Adams believed that the Pacific offered simultaneously a frontier to stir the imagination and an ingress to the oldest world of all, Asia, awaiting rejuvenation by the superior American hand.

China, he ventured, would pose the greatest problem of the future and offer Americans the greatest opportunity because of its huge undeveloped natural wealth and its unlimited cheap labor. America's "geographical position, our wealth, and our energy pre-eminently fit us to enter upon the development of eastern Asia, and to reduce it to a part of our economic system."[11] America's new Pacific orientation would make the United States "a greater seat of wealth and power than ever was England, Rome, or Constantinople."[12] American diplomat John Barrett exulted, "We are a world power in the Orient"; Admiral George Dewey's "great victory" at Manila Bay instantly made this so.[13]

During the Boxer Rebellion (1900) in China, U.S. Marines joined the march on Peking to relieve the besieged foreign legations there. And this further drew the eye of the American public across the Pacific. Secretary of State John Hay tried to forestall the carving up of China by persuading the powers to adhere to an open door policy there. Subsequently President Taft tried to encourage American investment in China, but despite America's new Western Pacific territorial empire, flows of commerce or investment across the Pacific failed to accelerate to anything like the volume or value of that moving across the Atlantic. And the hard fact was that until World War II, the United States had only very limited military power to project into the farther reaches of the Great Ocean.

On the other side of the Pacific, Japanese business leaders and government recognized very early the importance of the maritime industries to Japan's modernization. In this domain, Japan rose as the United States fell. For oceanic navigation, the new Meiji state in 1868 began with nothing—no ships, no technology, no money, and no trained people. Japan experienced a long, slow start with little achievement until the turn of the century. Until then, Japan had no steel or engineering industries, and the first modern shipyards in Japan were obliged to fashion their own steel plates or buy them abroad.[14]

War with China in 1894–95 sharpened the Japanese sense of urgency concerning both shipping and shipbuilding, and in 1896 the government legislated subsidies to encourage both industries, with significant results. The North Pacific became Japan's maritime focus, but the initial commercial thrust outside that region was to the south and on to India instead of to the east and the United States. The Mitsubishi group dominated both shipbuilding and shipping, and its yards at Nagasaki built all the major ships to come out of Japan at least until 1914. Its shipping line, the Nippon Yusen Kaisha (Japan Mail), founded under that name by Iwasaki Yataro in 1873, would ultimately become the world's largest shipping enterprise.

In the international sphere, the NYK and other Japanese shipping companies would benefit from low operating costs, as well as government subsidies, and enjoy competitive advantage drawn from business alliances within Japan. In 1893 NYK began service to Bombay; by late 1896 its ships were sailing regularly to Australia, through Suez to Europe, and across the Pacific. But tonnage carried on the trans-Pacific route was less than half that taken by the line to Europe.

Since two-thirds of Japan's exports by value to the United States were raw silk and speed was important in the shipment of this precious commodity, Puget Sound, closer to Japan, was more attractive than California as a means of entry for the Japanese. Seattle could offer transport to the U.S. Atlantic coast one day less than San Francisco.

NYK and James Jerome Hill's Great Northern signed a contract in July 1896 enabling the Japanese to quote through-freight rates to U.S. destinations, but the 1908 U.S. Interstate Commerce Commission ruling about proportional rates for the land and sea segments caused a problem to the relationship. The sea portion of the charge was increased in favor of the rail, which caused NYK's income to decrease. NYK had other problems too: rising competition from both the British and other Japanese companies.[15] Toughest competition of all was the Canadian Pacific because Vancouver was even closer to Yokohama than Seattle, and the Canadians put together a highly efficient rail and sea system for the rapid shipment of silk.

American trade across the Pacific suffered because two major exports, machinery and raw cotton, were both produced in east coast states. For these items, time was not a major consideration, and shipping them all the way by sea made breaking bulk unnecessary. Therefore, Atlantic ports held a cost advantage over Pacific ports, even if they were much farther from Japan.

CHAPTER SEVENTEEN

Theodore Roosevelt, the Pacific, and the Panama Canal

The Great War of 1914–18, coming so soon after the Russo-Japanese War of 1904–5, has caused the earlier conflict to be "forgotten." Yet it was immensely significant for its participants and for the United States and other powers also. The peace settlement brought new international prominence for a U.S. president, Theodore Roosevelt, and new international prestige for the United States.

Roosevelt by education and natural ability was one of the most competent men ever to have presided over the White House. He possessed a high intelligence, a well-furnished mind, exuberant energies, and an enormous taste for information, coupled with an exceedingly clear image of international politics and the position of the United States within its framework. Roosevelt perceived the modern interdependence of business and finance, but his concerns were more strategic than economic.

Dubbed "Theodore Rex" by Henry James, Roosevelt was fascinated by power, by the study of it and by the use of it. Roosevelt's tragedy, as his biographer Howard Beale points out, is that his extraordinary abilities were not matched by as extraordinary values, at least by the judgments of today.[1] His instinctive aggressiveness and his ardent imperialism would now seem to remove him from the ranks of the greatest U.S. presidents.

The cosmopolitan Roosevelt was the first chief executive to travel outside the United States while in office, and he considered travel to be an important part of his education. His reputation abroad was high; he was the first U.S. statesman to be taken seriously by his European peers and to be regarded as one of the club. And he was able to make skillful use of a network of friends to circumvent conventional diplomatic channels.

With a keen historical sense, Roosevelt saw the United States to be the heir of a declining Great Britain as keeper of the balance of power, but now that role was global, not simply European. The United States was to play the central role in an emerging world community, in Roosevelt's opinion. The United States held a special geographical position, operating from a massive territorial base halfway between Europe and Asia, at the continental intersection of the oceanic world. Roosevelt wholeheartedly incorporated Asia and the Pacific in his worldview, seeing that region as part of the mainstream, and he recognized that U.S. relations with Russia were more important in Asia than they were in Europe.

In a speech delivered in San Francisco on May 13, 1903, after charting for his audience the geographical shifts of world civilization, beginning with Mesopotamia, Roosevelt proclaimed the era of the Pacific. "Now, men and women of California," he said, "in our own day, the greatest of all the oceans, of all the seas, and the last to be used on a large scale by civilized man bids fair to become in its turn the first in point of importance."[2]

The growth of population and wealth on the North American Pacific slope; the anticipated completing of the Panama Canal; the possession of Alaska, where Roosevelt seemed as interested in preserving wildlife as he was in shooting it elsewhere;[3] the annexation of Hawaii and the Philippine Islands; all drew the presidential eye toward the Far West. Roosevelt felt no animus toward the Russian people, but he loathed the tsarist system of government.

The evils of tsarist despotism had for some years been vividly described by the erstwhile telegrapher George Kennan, now a popular journalist and lecturer. Kennan delighted in presenting himself to entranced lecture audiences dressed in the clothing and chains of a Siberian exile. American public opinion, which had been so warm and friendly toward Russia during the Civil War and immediately after, shifted to the negative toward the close of the century. In large part this was because of Kennan, now accepted as the nation's leading authority on the subject. But tsarist pogroms and the flight of Russian Jewry to a new life in the United States certainly had something to do with American distaste for tsarism.

Roosevelt interpreted Russia's power as a function of its strategic position on the Eurasian land mass. Geography could be the only explanation for the apparent contradiction between Russia's influence in international affairs and its internal poverty and backwardness. A thin and glossy veneer of imperial magnificence covered profound inner structural rot, as Roosevelt saw it. But Russia's internal weakness did not inhibit its outward expansion. To Roosevelt it seemed that Russian encroachment in Korea and Manchuria was likely to squeeze out any American commercial or even missionary enterprise. But the United States lacked the military muscle to do anything about this. Japan seemed the ideal surrogate to keep the Bear at bay. The Japanese, Roosevelt exulted, were playing "our game" in Asia.[4]

Roosevelt was the first U.S. statesman to take Japan seriously. He was deeply interested not only in the outward marks of Japan's successful modernization, which he likened to that of Germany, but also in the civilization that lay behind the success. He thought that the warrior ethos about which he read avidly in Nitobe Inazo's *Bushido*, a book he tried to push on his friends, was something Americans might well emulate. He not only read and talked about Japan; he also took up judo, attractive to his thirst for exercise as well as to his new intellectual interest. "In a dozen years," Roosevelt wrote admiringly in 1905, Japan "will be the leading industrial nation of the Pacific . . . as formidable from the industrial as from the military standpoint. She is a great civilized nation; though her civilization is in some important respects not like ours. There are some things she can teach us, and some things she can learn from us."[5]

In his annual message to the Congress in 1906, Roosevelt pointed out that "our nation fronts on the Pacific, just as it fronts on the Atlantic. We hope to play a constantly growing part in the great ocean of the Orient." But he warned that Americans would not enjoy the commerce with Asia for which they hoped unless they extended to Japanese immigrants "the same measure of justice and good treatment which we expect to receive in return."[6]

Many Californians would not agree with him, and the treatment of Japanese immigrants was one of the most grievous issues with which Roosevelt wrestled. San Francisco segregated its schools, local laws impeded Asians from buying land, and the Japanese government could not understand why Washington could not stop such discriminatory practices.

Japan, "the England of the Orient," in Secretary of State John Hay's phrase, was destined, Roosevelt thought, to be an outpost of Western civilization in Asia. But as the war with Russia progressed, a sense of unease began to grip him. "In a dozen years," he mused, "the English, Americans and Germans, who now dread one another as rivals in the trade of the Pacific, will have each to dread the Japanese more than they do any other nation."[7]

Should Russia be totally destroyed on the Pacific, Japan would fill the military vacuum. The president had no desire to see a "Slav Peril" replaced by a "Yellow Peril." He was torn between his admiration of the Japanese and his fear of them. He worried about the rapidly growing naval power of Japan in the Pacific and its possible threat to American interests. He sought counterweights—continental pressures that would deflect Japan from maritime expansion yet allow Americans the opportunity to compete on equal terms in Northeast Asia. Roosevelt's ideal for

Northeast Asia would have been not a balance of power but a balance of impotence.

At Portsmouth, New Hampshire, foreign belligerents met on U.S. soil for the first time in history to seek peace under the guidance of a U.S. president. Theodore Roosevelt initiated the conference and kept it from failing. For this accomplishment, he would later receive the Nobel Peace Prize, the first head of state and the first American to be so honored.[8]

Although U.S. interests in Manchuria and elsewhere along the Asian North Pacific littoral remained largely inchoate, the stuff of dreams, writing in June 1905 in one of his many letters Roosevelt maintained, "I believe . . . our future history will be more determined by our position on the Pacific facing China, than by our position on the Atlantic facing Europe."[9] The president's words are reminiscent of those of William Henry Seward spoken some fifty years before. They were vindicated in Japan's triumph over Europe's most populous nation, long considered one of the world's foremost powers. Russia's defeat set off global reverberations and invested the North Pacific region with new strategic importance.

The president's insatiable curiosity and phenomenal energies led to intensive interaction with friends, some of them formidable intellects, including Brooks Adams, William James, and Sir George Otto Trevelyan. In voluminous correspondence and protracted conversations, over the dinner table and during spirited hikes in Washington's Rock Creek Park with an exhausted group of companions struggling to keep the pace, Roosevelt was constantly shaping and refining his judgments. He was, after all, still only in his forties. His "ideology of civilization" furnished him a means to interpret the past and understand the present and reinforced his pride in what he defined as the singularly superior U.S. mix of political stability, industrial success, and military power, forged in America's encounter with its continental frontier, propelling the United States into the Pacific.[10]

Roosevelt could personally identify with the opening of the American West and the "winning of the frontier," a phrase he chose as the title of an early book. The Pacific interested him intrinsically as much as its Asian shores. Roosevelt's concerns were not commercial so much as strategic, reflecting his strong interest in national power. In his words, "it is better for a nation to produce one Grant or one Farragut than a thousand shrewd manufacturers or successful speculators."[11]

Roosevelt was a navalist. For him the navy was a symbol of national greatness, and from his youth, imbibing stories from his two Confederate naval officer uncles, the Bulloch brothers, he had been concerned with strategic matters. His first book had been a naval history of the War of 1812, published in 1882 at the nadir of the U.S. Navy. When President

McKinley offered him his first federal post, that of assistant secretary of the navy, he wrote to his sister, "I am intensely interested in our navy ... and know a good deal about it."[12] He was correct, and, armed with that knowledge, Roosevelt took this relatively insignificant job and, suffusing it with his enormous energy managed to make himself famous. British journalist W. T. Stead drily commented on Roosevelt's enthusiasm for a strong navy: "He does not say in the Kaiser's phrase that America's future lies upon the sea, because he would scorn to confine America's future to any element, even to that which covers three-fourths of the world's surface."[13]

Roosevelt was captivated by Mahan's *Influence of Sea Power upon History* and did his best to make its author famous. But he was thinking about sea power long before Mahan began writing about it. Mahan, being a professional naval officer, could speak with an authority on these matters that Roosevelt lacked. Roosevelt used Mahan to decorate his ideas, and obviously the enthusiasm of the president was equally useful to Mahan.[14]

Roosevelt as president would boast that he "more than doubled the navy."[15] And in a dramatic flexing of this new muscle, he sent the U.S. battleship fleet on an around-the-world cruise in 1907–9 in what has been called "the most significant peace-time naval demonstration in modern history."[16] Naval visits, paradoxically, have usually been interpreted as gestures of friendship. The president said that the cruise of the Great White Fleet and the digging of the Panama Canal impressed the world more than any other events of his administration. Although he later admitted that his "prime purpose was to impress the American people," the cruise also had large international impact, especially resounding on Japanese-U.S. relations.[17] The fleet visited Japan upon invitation, receiving a thundering chorus of *banzai*, the waving of flags, smiles, and songs from thousands of greeters lining the streets to greet the visitors. But the visit served also as a reminder to the Japanese government that the United States was a greater naval power than Japan.

The suddenness of Japan's emergence as a power had stunned and sobered Europe and seemed to threaten the comfortable old order in the Pacific. The *Melbourne Age* was prompted by the arrival of the U.S. fleet in Australia to write of Japan as threatening any "Anglo-Saxon predominacy" in the Pacific.[18] Australia was even more worried about and hostile to Japanese immigration than the United States then was.

The U.S. battleship squadron was accompanied by a train of nearly two dozen colliers, all flying foreign flags. In the age of coal, the United States did not have the merchant shipping necessary to support a blue-water navy. In the event of war, neutrality laws would have required these support ships to vanish. The whole exercise therefore was artificial, at the time an unreal projection of U.S. maritime power. In the age of petroleum, beginning shortly before World War I, the fleet would be less vulnerable.

The global cruise of the fleet showed why the United States needed an isthmian canal. It also stimulated an investigation of possible coal deposits in British Columbia and Alaska and led to pressuring for the improvement of ship repair facilities at Bremerton, Mare Island, and Pearl Harbor. When the fleet returned to Hampton Roads, Roosevelt said, "Nobody after this will forget that the American coast is on the Pacific as well as on the Atlantic."[19]

We know that Theodore Roosevelt believed building the Panama Canal to be one of the major decisions of his tenure of office. Da Gama and Magellan had opened the first two great global oceanic routes around Africa and around South America: the Cape and the Horn. The Suez Canal had largely displaced the Cape of Good Hope. Panama would do the same to the Horn, and Roosevelt told the Congress in his first address to them that "no single great material work which remains to be undertaken on this continent is of such consequence to the American people."[20] Panama radically cut transport distances between the American Atlantic coast and the Pacific. From New York to San Diego via Cape Horn is 12,600 miles; via the Panama Canal, 4,800.[21]

North Atlantic initiative had developed or constructed each of the four great waterways. The Cape and the Horn were natural passages, and during the preindustrial age they served to thrust North Atlantic interests and activities into areas lying deep in the Southern Hemisphere. The Capes could preserve some of their importance into the industrial era because of the wide-ranging demands that industry was making for natural resources. Sailing ships long continued to use the far southern sea routes for haulage of relatively nonperishable bulk cargoes like coal, grain, guano, or wool.[22] But Suez and Panama, artificial waterways, created new, shorter primary global sea routes that were closer to the North Atlantic world core. The canals brought a new strategic consideration into international affairs: they were more vulnerable to control or to closure than were their Cape counterparts.

Both Suez and Panama were originally land routes; Alexandria was linked to the Red Sea by rail in 1854, one year before rails spanned Panama. These railroads began the siphoning of priority traffic, mail and passengers, from the Capes. Because of lack of American concern for maritime trade, strategic needs, not commercial ones, finally dictated the digging of the Panama Canal. Suez certainly was far more international than Panama and built for commercial rather than strategic purposes. For millennia the isthmus had been a crossroads for the confrontation and interaction of the cultures of three continents.

Not only was the Suez Canal's ownership international, but also, and more important, its traffic, although in reality the British dominated both, having taken over Egypt de facto in 1882. The United States dominated

Panama. One-third of the ships going through that canal were American, and a lot of the traffic was intercoastal, the chief beneficiary being the American Pacific coast. Suez was privately owned; Panama was not. Suez wanted to make a profit and the tolls reflected it; Panama was cheaper to transit.

Suez and Panama are canals very different in physical character. Suez, twice the length of Panama, is no more than a ditch dug through the flat desert sands; Panama with its locks, can be described as an elaborate piece of machinery, its waterway cut through a mountainous tropical jungle.[23] The two canals did not compete; each enjoyed its own geographical domain. The North Pacific was untouched by Suez. The farthest northern point on the China coast at which Suez could compete with trans-Pacific traffic lay somewhere between Hong Kong and Shanghai. This meant that all of North China, Korea, and eastern Siberia, as well as Japan, rested within the orbit of potential American oceanic commercial influence.

With the formal opening of Panama in 1914, the great age of Suez—and of Great Britain in world affairs—was over, although most people at the time did not recognize it. A symbolic coincidence lies in the passage of the first oceangoing ship through the Panama Canal. *Christobal* made her voyage on August 3, 1914, the same day that catastrophic war erupted in Europe.

The North Atlantic world core created the two interoceanic canals and used them as instruments for the global expansion of its influence. But with the worldwide retraction of British naval power beginning in the new century and its disappearance from the Caribbean, Panama lay beyond any European strategic grasp. Its location put it outside the major routes of European international commerce. Mahan predicted that the two canals would mark globally "a line of division, south of which the efforts of commerce and of politics will be intrinsically much less important than those which occur to the north."[24] But this had always been the case, even when the Capes were essential to interoceanic travel.

Despite American rhetoric, the world in 1914 was still Atlantic centered, and world trade was still dominated by Europe. And the Atlantic was the real focus of American interest. The Atlantic was where most Americans had come from; the Atlantic was home of the civilization Americans admired and studied; and the Atlantic was the center of world economic activity and political power.

Panama simply provided a new route to a developing area, the Pacific. A second new route, the belated discovery by Norwegian explorer Roald Amundsen of a Canadian Northwest Passage, provoked little interest in Canada or the United States until much later, when the discovery of Arctic oil in 1968 gave new need for transportation across the top of the world.[25]

A third route to the Pacific along the Arctic shores of Eurasia, the Northeast Passage, was a subject of much interest to the British and the Dutch in the middle of the sixteenth century when the two Capes were claimed by the Iberian powers. But the northern Europeans seriously underestimated the length of the Siberian Arctic coastline, supposing that it might be possible to sail to China from the mouth of the Ob River.

The Northeast Passage was successfully navigated for the first time not by a Russian but by a Swedish explorer, Adolf Erik Nordenskjold, who rounded Cape Dezhnev in July 1879. Lack of investment capital, competition from the Suez Canal, and, ultimately, the Trans-Siberian Railway discouraged the exploitation of Nordenskjold's feat. No one would follow him until after the Bolshevik Revolution of 1917 and the Soviets closed their nearby seas to any foreigners. The Arctic still awaits its time. As the age of steam was expiring, Panama, the "Southwest Passage," dominated entry into the eastern Pacific, as the Suez-Malacca "Southeast Passage" commanded the approaches to the western Pacific. Neither of the two far northern routes, east or west, proved then of any real use or interest.

Although rich in resources and replete with confidence, the United States was a debtor nation in 1914 and its investments overseas, although they stood at a respectable 7 percent of gross national product, were modest compared, say, to those of the British. The amount Americans had invested in Asia was a tiny part of total American overseas holdings: only $120 million out of $2.65 billion.[26] Asia failed to attract much American financial interest because of its remoteness, geographically and culturally, because of the ignorance of Americans about Asian cultures, and because of the low per capita income of most Asians. For Americans, Europe, highly developed and seemingly stable, was a far more attractive place in which to invest and a far more lucrative market. Trans-Pacific commerce shows this; in 1914 it made up only about 14 percent of American foreign trade.[27]

American technology by 1914 was probably the most significant element of the American commercial presence abroad, across the Pacific and elsewhere. Americans seemed to be pioneers in all the most modern industries, at least those that most enriched the life of the consumer: the telephone, camera, photograph, the electric trolley car, the typewriter, and the automobile. Americans did not invent the automobile, but they democratized it, making it available to the average person.

These new industries were highly profitable, paid their workers well, and formed a nucleus for further growth of American export trade. W. T. Stead said that American successes had come in areas where the British had failed to compete. Another British journalist declared that "England has slept while commercial rivals went ahead . . . [but] the future still lies before England if England will but have it."[28] The British could learn from the Americans and be "energized" by them.

Throughout the nineteenth century the British exported coal, textiles, and machinery such as railway equipment. Iron and steel shipbuilding, as Correlli Barnett puts it, was the "quintessential expression" of British supremacy in the technology of the first industrial revolution.[29] Britain enjoyed certain competitive advantages as a builder of ships. It was its own best customer and floated the world's largest merchant fleet. British coal, iron, steel, and engineering industries were world pioneers. But in the last quarter of that century of greatness, steam began "hissing its own funeral dirge," and a second, science-based industrial revolution came to flower, built on chemicals and electricity and dominated by the United States and Germany.[30]

The United States felt itself to be the world's richest and most powerful nation because of the success of its technology as well as the attractiveness of its ideas, and American rhetoric overflowed with confidence. Oddly, the miserable position of the nation's merchant marine did not seem to enter any calculus of national power except to those most intimately involved with the maritime industries. These people told the Congress that American steamships were handling only 8 percent of U.S. foreign trade and that 20 percent of the world's tonnage would be required to handle that trade. Foreign shipping exacted a "tribute" of more than $100 million every year to render this "humiliating" service to the United States. A Cleveland manufacturer testified that he had been "around the world three times, and I cannot recall ever meeting the American flag on the high seas."[31] Yet most Americans seemed not to care.

Shipping magnate Robert Dollar, a Scottish-born immigrant like Andrew Carnegie, came to the United States at the age of twelve in 1856, settling in San Francisco in 1888. Dollar waged a vigorous struggle on behalf of the U.S. merchant marine and organized trade missions to China and Japan as an attempt to encourage trans-Pacific commerce. The results were discouraging. Reluctantly Dollar accepted that Americans would have to keep on building ships in British yards, and flying them under the British flag, as he himself was obliged to do. But "if we ever get into war,—the day of reckoning will come, and our politicians will get a rude awakening."[32] The realities were that overseas business remained peripheral to American domestic investment and the heart of the American economy. Shipping reflected the fact. Lack of an oceangoing merchant fleet was entirely consonant with American notions of national self-sufficiency, and on the practical side, investors saw a dollar bringing greater return if it were not put into shipping or shipbuilding. Only a few people thought of a merchant marine as useful, even necessary, to the cultivating of new markets overseas for American goods.

Even Captain Mahan, who had extolled the importance of the maritime industries, once having published his first great work in 1890, says little more about America's need for merchant shipping.[33] Mahan saw the country grow rich, build a battle fleet, and acquire colonies, all without a merchant fleet. The case of Great Britain proved Mahan's theory of sea power; the United States disproved it. He chose to overlook the American case.

In 1914 Europe was home to one-third of the world's people and controlled three-fourths of the world's shipping tonnage. Markets and prices had become global. Bulk items like ores, grains, and fibers were the dominant cargoes; the steamship had increased global economic interdependence. Sailing ships still carried items like cotton or wheat for which neither speed nor punctuality was particularly important. The North Atlantic world, where the life of the United States was still largely focused, despite all the rhetoric about the Pacific, overwhelmingly dominated global politics, trade, wealth, and international culture. Put simply, the North Atlantic was the world city; the rest was farm.[34]

PART FIVE

CONQUERING THE SKIES, 1914–1941

For I dipt into the future, far as human eye could see,
Saw the Vision of the world, and all the wonder that would be;
Saw the heavens fill with commerce, argosies of magic sails,
Pilots of the purple twilight, dropping down with costly bales;
Heard the heavens fill with shouting, and there rain'd a ghastly dew
From the nations' airy navies grappling in the central blue.

Alfred Tennyson, *Locksley Hall* (1842)

CHAPTER EIGHTEEN

World War I and Pacific Transport

Although ultimately called a world war, the great 1914–18 conflict was essentially confined to Europe, the Pacific was incidental. For Americans the war proved a marvelous stimulus to the rise of economic and military power. An "imperial country," as Thomas Wolfe puts it, "for the first time gathered the huge thrust of her might." Europe's catastrophe became America's opportunity. The deflection of British foreign commerce to wartime needs and the virtual disappearance of German foreign trade opened new global market opportunities to erstwhile outsiders like Americans and Japanese.

In 1914 trade across the Pacific may have still been very much smaller than trade across the Atlantic, but Americans carried a much larger share of the former than they did of the latter. No one nation dominated trans-Pacific traffic as the British ruled the Atlantic. Overall, in the Pacific, Britain held but a slight lead over Japan and the United States.[1] In the early years of the war, the Japanese share of trans-Pacific shipping increased enormously and the British share declined. Japan, far away from the real fighting, could only benefit from it.

New demands kept Japanese factories busy turning out ammunition, armaments, and a wide variety of manufactures for new customers unable to buy elsewhere. Within the North Pacific world, for Japanese and for Americans too, the supplying of Russia by way of Vladivostok emerged as a major enterprise. The demands of the global wartime economy prodded and pulled Japanese manufacturing technology to new levels of knowledge and competence. Building on this higher plateau of achievement, Japanese shipyards twenty years later would be turning out some of the world's fastest merchant ships and largest warships.

All of the nations of the North Pacific ultimately joined the Allied powers. The Japanese, who entered early, polished off the Germans in short order in China, and this was the only fighting in the North Pacific during the war. At war's end, as Russia plunged into revolution, the Americans joined the Japanese in sending troops into the Russian Far East, the Primorie (Maritime Province). The Americans went there in a misguided attempt to keep the huge supply of weapons and ammunition piled on the docks at Vladivostok from falling into the hands of the Germans now that Russia had surrendered. Checking the Japanese furnished part of the motivation, but this temporary attempt at expanding the reach of American power served only to nourish Soviet suspicions of capitalist aggression, reinforcing the old tsarist fears of a special American expansionist interest in Siberia.[2]

After the outbreak of the war during the fall of 1914, near panic broke out in commercial circles along the American Atlantic coast. Demand for shipping outran supply. Germany's forced withdrawal from oceanic commerce meant an immediate shortage of shipping, and as German ships vanished, German submarines began to do their best to make British ships do the same. Insurance rates soared.

Suddenly no ships were available to carry American commodities like cotton and wheat, lumber, flour, and kerosene for overseas sale. These high-bulk, low-value cargoes could be carried profitably only when rates were cheap. Trying to help out, the government allowed American owners to shift any ship registrations back to the American flag and suspended the law that all officers serving aboard must be U.S. citizens. For American shippers the resulting transfer of tonnage eased the immediate crisis.

The heavy demands of war in the North Atlantic drew ships from elsewhere. James J. Hill's great bulk carrier *Minnesota* left the Pacific permanently; the Pacific Mail Company temporarily took all its thirteen ships out of Pacific service, selling two of them to a Japanese company, Toyo Kisen Kaisha; and Robert Dollar sheltered much of his fleet under Canadian registry. These actions did not reflect much solicitude on the part of American shippers for the building of export trade across the Pacific. The companies were, it seemed, solely interested in their profits, wherever they might be found.

American shipping interests blamed the La Follette Seaman's Act of 1915 for increasing their costs and driving them to the shelter of foreign flags. This law, reflecting a new official concern for the lot of the exploited seaman, decreed in its concern for safety that not less than three-quarters of all men shipping out under the American flag must be able to understand English.[3] For ships operating in the Pacific, this meant no more cheap Chinese crews.

American trans-Pacific trade depended more than ever before upon using British and Japanese carriers. Both those nations were understandably inclined to favor the interests and needs of their own nationals over those of Americans. The British, eyes on Europe, were preoccupied with winning the war; the Japanese were preoccupied with increasing their share of the world market. Governmental subsidies and controls aided Japanese shipping companies. American traders found that on westward voyages, Japanese shippers charged higher rates than on eastward ones, where they were kept quite low, an effective means of discouraging American exports and increasing Japanese sales in the United States.[4] This mercantilistic device acted as a pseudo-tariff. But the need to supply Russia swelled the freight moving westward from the United States to Asia and offset, at least temporarily, the impact of this Japanese practice.

A group of Chinese investors took the initiative in trying to establish a shipping company to carry trade from China directly across the Pacific, through the Panama Canal to the American industrial east coast. U.S. minister in Peking Paul Reinsch encouraged these efforts, hoping that they would increase opportunities for American merchants and manufacturers by combating the growing Japanese commercial and political presence in China. Here many Chinese felt a community of interest with the Americans. A group of rich Chinese-American businessmen in San Francisco also tried briefly in 1915 to establish a shipping line across the Pacific.[5]

The demands of war caused American exports to skyrocket. The United States became the chief armorer and manufacturer for the Allies, and a variety of weapons, munitions, and finished goods began to stream across both the Atlantic and Pacific. Shipping rates soared, and the profits were reminiscent of the best years of the old China trade. A single voyage could earn the cost of a ship. But because American tonnage was so small, most of the shipping charges fattened foreign, not American, pockets.

In his third annual message to the Congress, President Woodrow Wilson pointed out the problem:

It is necessary for many weighty reasons of national efficiency and development that we should have a great merchant marine. The great merchant fleet we once used to make us rich, that great body of sturdy sailors who used to carry our flag into every sea, and who were the pride and often the bulwark of the nation, we have almost driven out of existence by inexcusable neglect and indifference. ... It is high time we ... resumed our commercial independence on the seas. For it is a question of independence. If other nations go to war or seek to hamper each other's commerce, our merchants, it seems, are at their mercy, to do with as they please. We must use their ships, and use them as they determine. We have not ships enough of our own. We cannot handle our own commerce on the seas. Our independence is provincial, and is only on land and within our own borders.[6]

The president could persuasively present American shipping to the American people as a specific means of winning the war as well as a general means of promoting national power and wealth. A healthy U.S. merchant marine would also give the economy greater flexibility and independence. Thus, Wilson could subtly encourage sentiments of isolationism along with those of interventionism.

The Shipping Act of 1916 put the U.S. government heavily into the maritime business. The act passed with the enthusiastic support of everyone who had suffered from high shipping rates. Midwestern wheat farmers became sudden converts to the need for government intervention in the shipping market; only the shipping interests were opposed, but they were appeased by the knowledge that the new governmental shipping corporation that the act established could operate for only five years after war's end.

Congress provided the money; the president acted, in a situation demanding that he do so immediately. Congress ultimately appropriated enough money to build a fleet twice the value of the world's pre-1914 oceanic merchant fleet, more than seventeen million tons of ships.[7] The government paid the costs, but the ships were built and operated by private companies.

The navy produced a long shopping list, including colliers, oilers (reflecting the new and growing use of oil as fuel), hospital ships, and other auxiliaries. When the United States actually entered the war in 1917, the government faced the problem of transporting an army of two to three million men with all its equipment across the North Atlantic, without the ships to do it. Consequently, over half of the American Expeditionary Force had to be carried to France aboard foreign ships.[8]

Purchase, charter, and requisition proved more effective than construction. Building was done in a costly and inefficient manner, and it simply took too long. Even the first of the "Hog Islanders," the steel cargo carriers turned out rapidly in multiple copies at Philadelphia's mammoth Hog Island yard, did not slide down the ways until nearly a month after the signing of the armistice in November 1918. Once the American shipbuilding effort did get going though, American yards produced more ship tonnage in shorter time than ever before in world history.

Never before in history had the Congress spent so much for so little. The quality of some of the ships suffered from the speed with which they had been built; the wooden, concrete, and composite-hulled vessels proved to be virtually worthless, and maritime engineering technology was then shifting so rapidly from coal to oil and diesel power that many of the ships were obsolete as soon as they hit the water. Yet the Wilson administration was looking beyond wartime needs in the anticipation that the new American merchant fleet could be even more important in peace than in war. At the end of the war, the Shipping Board owned nearly 2.5 million tons of new ships; that figure would swell ultimately to 9.3 million tons. The Jones Act (Merchant Marine Act of 1920) sought to transfer this enormous fleet to private hands and also to define trade routes essential to the national welfare. The U.S. merchant marine, many hoped, might sustain the prosperity of wartime, enjoying the benefits of cheaply acquired ships, postal subsidies, and cabotage—a monopoly on service between domestic ports.

Edward N. Hurley, head of Wilson's U.S. Shipping Board, even saw the fleet as a means of selling abroad American ideas as well as American goods.[9] But most of the world came to greet Wilsonian idealism tepidly, and Wilson himself found his government increasingly enmeshed in an intensity of rivalry with the Europeans, especially the British, as Great Britain struggled to recapture global shipping dominance.

As part of the postwar settlement Americans hoped for a universal maritime agreement on freight rates, working conditions, and wages, a sort of global La Follette Act. Other nations evinced no such desire. American shipping circles maintained the perennial argument that the national interest, defense, and trade promotion demanded a strong merchant marine. A strong merchant marine required either the direct means of government participation by building and operating ships or the indirect means of subsidizing the private sector to do so. No one seemed to question the validity of the premise. The dispute concerned the method to achieve it.[10]

The war left the United States with immensely enhanced power, and it had enriched rather than impoverished the nation. The former German emperor, from his Dutch exile in Doorn, observed the favorable strategic position of the United States, standing advantageously on the periphery, not hemmed in, holding "the balance in world politics, the decisive weight in any scale of peace or war."[11] In the Pacific, for Americans the war brought great change by severely weakening the European presence while simultaneously strengthening the rising international power of Japan.

Despite the perennial American hopes for a thriving commerce with China, Japan had become America's leading Asian trade partner well before the turn of the century. At about the same time, shadows began to fall in the political relationship between the United States and Japan. In 1897 Admiral R. R. Belknap, lecturing to the Naval War College, had judged war with Spain, Great Britain, or Japan as equally probable.[12] After the Japanese defeated the Russians in 1905, Japan became the most likely enemy and the target for U.S. war games.[13]

Amicability slipped into alienation and ultimately animosity, and the two nations found themselves increasingly competing for a place within a politically disintegrating China. Each nurtured its own myths about China. Neither Americans nor Japanese, in their self-centered ways, realized that the Chinese Revolution held no place for them; China wanted independence, not guidance. The United States and Japan temporized during the years between 1905 and 1921, concluding a series of bilateral agreements that reached climax in the arms limitation and other agreements of the Washington Conference of 1921–22, which ended Japan's alliance with Great Britain.

Japan had showed an eagerness to expand its international power by the Twenty-One Demands it tried to impose on China in 1915 when the powers were distracted by war in Europe, and by intervention in Siberia in 1918. But in the 1920s the trend shifted. Japan seemed to be headed in the direction of a functioning liberal democracy and an amiable working relationship with the English-speaking democracies. The United States was willing to withdraw its naval power eastward to Hawaii. The Washington settlement appeared to promise peace in the Pacific, leading the *New York Times* to predict, "Luckily, there is no prospect of political incidents ever affecting Japan's trade with the United States."[14]

During the world war the Germans virtually disappeared from East Asia and would never return in a territorial sense. The Japanese benefited from the departure by picking up the German colonies in Micronesia—the Marshalls, Carolines, and Marianas—which would prove to be immense strategic assets. For the European Allies, the costs of victory had been too great for them to return to the Pacific with the full energies of former times. But Britain sustained its large commercial interest in China, centering in Shanghai, and British shipping sustained an honorable place in the Pacific, better able, it seems, to compete with the rising Japanese than could the Americans. International shipping tonnage in trans-Pacific trade increased more than five times, reflecting both the success of Japanese industrialization and the impact of the opening of the Panama Canal.

Trans-Pacific trade still suffered under the handicap of comparative distance, and its volume tended to fluctuate widely. Much of Japan's international trade was still with neighboring Asia and Europe. It did not cross the Pacific. Passenger traffic between the United States and Asia remained very small compared with the flow across the North Atlantic. Asians were not permitted to immigrate to the United States. Canada did not want them either. The lack of close cultural and commercial ties across the Pacific and the cost of passage, as well as the time it required, inhibited tourists. Most Americans still looked toward Europe as the place for vacations or study trips. In 1937, for every hundred trans-Atlantic passengers, fewer than ten crossed the Pacific.[15]

But the disparity in levels of economic development between Japan and the United States was beginning to shrink, thereby broadening trading opportunities, for, as Ellsworth Huntington pointed out long ago, "The greatest trade of all is between countries that are most alike."[16] Trade ties between the two nations continued to deepen; by 1928 the

United States was taking more than two-fifths of Japan's exports (largely in raw silk) and furnishing Japan with a third of its imports.

The Japanese silk farmer was even more dependent on American customers than the American cotton grower had been on English customers. American textile manufacturing was concentrated along the Atlantic coast. With the Great Depression and the collapse of the market for the highest-quality raw silk, Japanese shippers began to use the all-water route via Panama to supply American manufacturers, thereby depriving American transcontinental railroads of a lucrative business. But new artificial fibers began to supplant silk and eventually destroyed the market for Japan's biggest earner of foreign exchange.

Americans continued to send lumber, grain, flour, and petroleum to Asia; by the mid-1930s, scrap metal and wood pulp largely supplanted the grain and the flour. And by volume, petroleum had become the most important American commodity to flow across the Pacific, reflecting the increasing heft of Japanese industry. Japanese shipping dominated this carrying trade.

The Great Depression plunged all shipping and trade worldwide into crisis. Too many ships were chasing too few cargoes. Foreign merchant fleets recovered before the American. Strikes and continuing labor turmoil, as well as rising costs of operations, handicapped American ability to compete. Again, a declining amount of American foreign trade came to be carried in American bottoms. The American share of trans-Pacific trade dwindled to a minor 15 percent of the total. But the emergence of a new medium of transportation in which the United States would triumph drew attention away from this poor performance on the seas. Americans would have a new opportunity to capture the wealth of the Orient.

CHAPTER NINETEEN

The Early Air Age

Dcember 17, 1903, is that consequential day at Kitty Hawk, North Carolina, when the first motor-driven, heavier-than-air machine successfully flew. Its trip covered 120 feet, lasted twelve seconds, and attracted remarkably little comment. Transportation had entered a new dimension, but few people then recognized it.[1]

A mere seven years after the Wright Brothers' epochal flight, in 1911, a great grandson of Commodore Matthew Calbraith Perry (and a grandson of Commodore John Rodgers), Calbraith Perry Rodgers, became the first person to fly across the United States, finding his way for the most part by following railroad tracks from Jersey City out to Pasadena. The Armour Company sponsored his flight in return for the opportunity to name his plane for a soft drink they were then touting. *Vin Fiz*, an obsolete Wright airplane, took forty-nine days for its journey, the time stretched out by repeated mishaps and crashes, with no serious consequences to the pilot but many repairs to the plane.[2]

After his epic trip, Cal Rodgers, receiving the accolades of a hero and dubbed King of the Air, was photographed at the edge of the Pacific, a jaunty smile on his face. Clenched between his teeth was a cigar; beneath his leather flying jacket and boots, he wore a white shirt, necktie, and business suit. The unflappable Cal was as formal in dress, if not in manner, as his great grandfather Perry. A few months later, flying a new plane, the hero crashed and died instantly in the surf at Long Beach when trying to avoid—or perhaps to chase—seagulls.[3]

Out of such modest and uncertain beginnings American airline companies were offering scheduled flights for passengers as early as 1914. Four years later, a letter could be sent by air, revolutionizing written communication. World War I gave an enormous push forward to aviation. At first the belligerents used planes primarily for scouting. Aerial fighting began when one side tried to prevent the other from collecting information in this fashion. Ultimately, gunfire duels led to bombing sorties. The number of airplanes soared. Great Britain began the war with 110 planes and ended it with 22,000.[4]

The demands of war made the entire aviation industry, including the building of airplanes and airports and the training of pilots and mechanics, grow fast. An industry rising overnight began frantically to build airplanes without any idea of how they might be used. Both the strategy and the tactics of air power were as yet unformed. America's first great achievement in the new industry proved not to be airframes but the Liberty engine, and the fine combat record established by American fliers was won for the most part using foreign aircraft.

After the war, though, the aircraft industry collapsed. The military market was uncertain, and a civilian market did not exist. The government offered the industry no plan and no help. Planes were abundant, and plenty of pilots were eager for any employment. The battles of the air aces had captured the imagination of an admiring American public and led to a postwar boom in short charter hops and stunt flying—barnstorming, they called it. One young barnstormer named Charles Lindbergh turned to flying the mails for a while and was lucky to survive to do bigger things. Mail pilots aspired not to be the best but the oldest. Lindbergh liked to tell the story of instructions he received from his boss: "Never land between stops, unless you run out of gas or the engine quits—in either of these events you are permitted to land but you must immediately report to me, at any time of the day or night, three things—first, how is the airplane, second, how is the mail, third, how is the pilot?"[5]

Americans worried that they were falling behind Europe in this exciting new field, and for a time their apprehensions were well founded. The war had made a greater impact on European aviation than American, but the American domestic market would prove so rich and provide such a competitive opportunity for American aircraft manufacturers and airline operators that by the mid-1920s the American aeronautical industry would begin to outstrip the rest of the world.

In 1916, the U.S. Post Office first commissioned a private carrier to fly the mails.[6] The Post Office and the airplane seemed to be natural partners, but scheduled service did not begin until a couple of years later and not very happily at that. In 1918, President Wilson attended an inaugural take-off of regular airmail service from Washington to Philadelphia and New York City, an occasion marred by repeated failures to get the aircraft started because of insufficient gas in the tanks. Once airborne, the pilot headed off in the wrong direction and crash-landed after going only twenty-five miles.[7]

The Kelly Act of 1925 relinquished the airmail service to private hands, but before then many army pilots were killed flying the mails. Airplanes were fragile machines, the weather was always a potential menace, and pilots had to fly without benefit of any navigational aids, often plotting their courses by using road maps. Night flying was too risky to be undertaken on any regular basis. The Kelly Act gave momentum to aeronautics. Because private carriers were obliged to compete for contracts, they wanted the best planes they could get; they sought economy and demanded efficiency. Airline companies and airplane manufacturers were all engaged in a healthy competition.

Charles Lindbergh's 1927 great solo flight across the Atlantic, the world's first and at the time longest nonstop flight anywhere, furnished a benchmark in aviation history and made Lindbergh an instant hero. He did it on his own initiative, alone, and without any help along the route. Young, handsome, pleasingly shy, mechanically adroit, undoubtedly courageous, a "pioneer," and perceived as quintessentially American, the "Lone Eagle" satisfied all the requisites for heroism.

At a time when America craved heroes, Lindbergh proved more satisfactory material than Calvin Coolidge or Herbert Hoover. At a time when the old spatial frontiers had gone, Lindbergh was showing the world a new one, and his feat seemed an assurance that a young and vital United States would lead the world into it. "More than any other single factor, his flight sold the American people on commercial aviation."[8]

During the 1920s and 1930s airmail became an important part of the national economy, and the government could use it as a reason to subsidize a struggling young industry of immense but as yet undefined potential importance. The aircraft manufacturing industry boomed along with everything else in the United States during the late 1920s, but expectations outran realities. The total output of airplanes in 1929 would not be again equaled until 1940, when the market began to recover from the depression.[9]

In 1930, the Post Office, under the energetic leadership of Walter Folger Brown, began to let its contracts by the "space-mile" rather than the "pound-mile," rewarding the carrier for cubic capacity (whether used or not).[10] The implication is obvious: the larger the airplane, the larger the stipend. Brown wanted to rationalize the industry by concentrating it in a few companies. He was partial to the European example of "chosen instruments," officially designated carriers. Some would-be competitors complained that they were left out of "the club," and later Brown's system would be severely criticized and become the subject of government inquiry. Brown had created, in effect, a government charter system, encouraging the airline companies to buy large aircraft and develop their passenger business under its protective framework.

But what kind of aerial transport machine would prove most suitable for the varying needs of people and cargo, in war and in peace was not at all clear in the late 1920s and early 1930s. Might there perhaps emerge a system of three different complementary types: landplane, seaplane, or the dirigible? Or would one form prevail? If it were the dirigible, as some believed, the Americans were far behind. The Germans were world leaders. In aviation, it seems, the Germans hoped to find at last their place in the sun.

CHAPTER TWENTY

The Zeppelin: First Over the Pacific

The German Zeppelin gripped the popular imagination briefly and appeared the most likely future means to span the enormous spaces of the oceans. This airship was the first long-range instrument of air power, and air power held formidable political implications, offering the opportunity to governments to control huge, uninhabitable areas on the cheap. Nowhere else was this more important than the North Pacific, with its vast and still-unknown Arctic fringes. Trans-Arctic air routes, flying over the pole, could potentially revolutionize patterns of intercontinental transportation and open up for Canada and the Soviet Union alarming possibilities of foreign incursions and territorial changes. The Russians feared that the imperialist powers might try to create a closed aerial artery—a Suez or Panama Canal for airships.

Modest fuel requirements made it possible for dirigibles to travel nonstop distances then unthinkable by airplanes. Count Ferdinand von Zeppelin, whose aerial experience went back to sailing a balloon with General Grant's army in Virginia, conceived the rigid airship at the beginning of the century, but neither the engines nor the strong light alloys were then available to make such an aircraft commercially feasible.

During World War I the airship came into some prominence, the Germans using it with great success for scouting over the North Sea and the Baltic, capitalizing on the ability of the airship to stay aloft far longer than any airplane. Zeppelins were also used as the first strategic bombers, weapons of terror. They bombed London; theoretically they could have done the same to New York. But the enormous size of the airship and the use of hydrogen to elevate it heightened its vulnerability to attack and curtailed its usefulness, especially as the number of airplanes increased. Hydrogen was so prone to explosion as to turn any mishap into potential disaster, a severe handicap even in peacetime.

After the war, Americans began to experiment with German airships acquired as fruit of victory. The U.S. Navy was particularly attracted to the dirigible because of its ability to carry out long-range reconnaissance, and it entered the field with the American-built *Shenandoah*. Wrecked in a storm, the airship broke into pieces, but Commander Charles E. Rosendahl was able to maneuver its stern portion, kept aloft by its helium-filled bag, safely to the ground, and most of the crew survived.

A primary reason for Rosendahl's survival in the demise of *Shenandoah* was that it used helium instead of hydrogen as the elevating agent. Hydrogen is the lightest gas of all; helium is the second. Helium is not only more expensive but also has lower lifting ability than hydrogen. Airships using helium must carry a smaller payload. Hydrogen burns or explodes if exposed to the oxygen in the air; helium is far safer, being inert, and the only fireproof lifting gas for airships.

The United States and the Soviet Union had the only known deposits of helium. The Russians were not building airships and not producing any helium. Because the United States eventually forbade its export, the Americans held a virtual monopoly on the future of interoceanic airship travel.

Yet Germany consistently led the world in airship technology, despite a postwar hiatus in its development. And the Germans would be the only ones ever to offer scheduled passenger airship service. After the war and before 1926, under the terms of the Versailles settlement, Germany was forbidden to construct large dirigibles.[1] After the ban was lifted, *Graf Zeppelin*, the first of the intercontinental airships, took off on its first flight as a commercial demonstration airship on September 18, 1928, and would enjoy a long and brilliant career.

Airplanes could not begin to compete with the standard of comfort or even safety that the dirigible offered, particularly those ships built at the maturity of the form. *Hindenburg* would be more than twice as big as the pioneering *Graf*. From experience with that early model, designers and businessmen learned that an airship had to go faster and carry many more passengers than the *Graf* in order to compete successfully with ocean liners.

The amenities were important too. Compartmented spaces for the passengers were almost as generous as those of a ship, and the service was comparable. Stewards would shine passengers' shoes left in the passageway outside the cabin. The airship traveled so quietly that the passengers could hardly realize they were moving; a combination of low-altitude flights and cruising speeds of eighty miles per hour made it possible to enjoy a rich scenic panorama below from cabin windows or a promenade deck. Space for passengers to move around and to exercise was essential because of the long time aloft. The bigger zeppelins were planned to include a lounge, smoking room, dining saloon, and showers. The *Hindenburg*, three city blocks long, even boasted a grand piano aboard, especially made out of aluminum so that it weighed less than four hundred pounds. On its maiden flight across the North Atlantic in May 1936, "one evening the moon was so bright that all the lights were turned out as a pianist played the 'Moonlight Sonata.' "[2]

Zeppelins took pride in the food they offered: fresh fruit and pastry, caviar and fine meats packed in dry ice, and, of course, appropriate wines and spirits. With its fuel tanks topped off, a ship of *Hindenburg* size could stay aloft for a week at a time. So smooth were the flights that no cases of airsickness were ever reported aboard either the *Hindenburg* or the *Graf Zeppelin*.[3]

The most spectacular instance of what the dirigible could make possible was the around-the-world flight of *Graf Zeppelin* in late summer 1929. Such a flight had been achieved only once before, and by airplane, not airship, when in 1924 a group of U.S. Army fliers took more than five months and stopped at more than eighty places.[4]

The *Graf Zeppelin* made only three stops in its twenty-one-day cruise: Friedrichshafen, Tokyo, and Los Angeles (twelve flying days). The *Graf*'s time was about three years and six days better than that achieved by the Magellan expedition. The circumnavigation was a German triumph, likened to the recent record-smashing trip when the liner *Bremen* captured the North Atlantic blue ribbon. The charming and well-known Hugo Eckener, commander of the *Graf*, acknowledged master of the art of the zeppelin and wearer of the mantle of the great count himself, said he wanted to prove that the airship was not simply a "fine weather ship" and that it could fly over the oceans and the great continental spaces.[5]

Eckener had to raise money for his trip. Stamp collectors would provide much of it, but almost half ($100,000) was put up by William Randolph Hearst.[6] The *Graf*'s trip actually began and ended at its home port of Friedrichshafen. But for Americans, because of Hearst, it began with a trans-Atlantic flight from the U.S. Naval Air Station at Lakehurst, New Jersey, and ended with a trans-American flight from Los Angeles back to Lakehurst. The chauvinistic newspaper tycoon decreed that in return for his money, the circumnavigation must begin and end by circling the Statue of Liberty.[7]

The passengers came down by special train from New York, serenaded by a band and cheered by thousands of wellwishers. Hundreds of sailors and schoolboys worked together tugging the ropes that brought the *Graf Zeppelin* out of the hangar and ready to rise, nose first. The crew of thirty-three was German, with Dr. Eckener at the helm. An alligator and a Boston terrier came along as freight in a cargo limited to twenty-eight-hundred pounds in the first Atlantic segment of the trip. No freight was carried on the leg from Germany to Japan, with the exception of a wreath commemorating prisoners of war. Inscribed "To German Heroes Buried in Siberia," it was dropped en route, just east of Yakutsk.

The fewer than two dozen passengers were an international group, including Arctic explorer Sir Hubert Wilkins; Colonel Merian C. Cooper, a descendant of novelist James Fenimore Cooper; a Russian geographer; the Spanish court physician to King Alfonso; and Japanese and American naval office observers, including Commander Rosendahl of *Shenandoah* fame. For those who paid the fare, it was a tidy nine thousand dollars.[8]

The most dangerous leg of the global journey was across what Eckener called the "dreadful wastes" of Siberia, along the great circle route, passing over hundreds of miles of beautiful but desolate tundra. In the event of an emergency landing, no people or equipment were below to provide help, and Eckener supposed that even an unfriendly greeting was possible from indigenous people. The route lay far to the north of the Trans-Siberian Railway, the only consistent belt of settlement across Asiatic Russia. Over this largely unknown territory, Eckener had to navigate his airship by dead reckoning, as if he were at sea. The Stanovoi Mountains proved to be much higher than the maps showed, and the dirigible nearly scraped their crest.[9] Information about the weather was scanty because radio stations were few, and no one knew very much about the air currents over the great Eurasian land mass.

The result was a triumph. The *New York Times* was not surprised at the enthusiastic reception given the dirigible by the Japanese, because, the *Times* said, they were so sensitive to "the significance of modern mechanical and engineering triumphs."[10] What would have been a twelve-day journey at best, by train and ship, from Berlin to Tokyo was compressed into four by the great airship. When the *Graf* put down on Japanese soil and the mail sacks came off, never before in history, it could be said, had letters traveled so fast from Europe to Japan.

The first nonstop flight across the Pacific was accomplished in sixty-nine hours, shore to shore. The editors of the *Times* again, remembering John Keats's reaction to Chapman's Homer and the first European view of the American Pacific, speculated on what the poet would have thought of the sweep across the Pacific skies by "a ship of the air greater in size than all the twelve Homeric ships that Ajax brought from Salamis."[11] A Japanese passenger during the Pacific crossing spoke optimistically of the narrowing of the ocean between Japan and America: "We are only three days apart now and I hope it brings the two countries together as well in a friendly and peaceful relation and understanding between each other."[12] Alas, perhaps more symbolic than the speed of the voyage and the shortening of distance was the thick fog and dense cloud through which the airship passed during most of its trans-Pacific journey.

The *Graf* could have forgone its stop in Japan, and Eckener flirted with that idea. The airship had enough fuel to carry it straight on to the

United States. But the commander decided not to disappoint the Japanese. Weather patterns had directed him northward in Russia, and he had therefore failed to appear over Moscow. After treating Berliners to a view of his ship flying the length of the Unter den Linden at a low altitude, neglecting the Muscovites was bad enough for his international public relations. He did not want to commit any other gaffes of that sort.

Because of difficulties incurred from the changing weight of hydrogen, Eckener had a near disaster taking off at Los Angeles. The *Graf* missed some high-tension wires by only about three feet, and its stern scraped the ground, but with no serious injury other than the temporarily shaken nerves of its commander. *"Gott sei dank"* (God be thanked!") Eckener is said to have uttered as the great ship settled down at Lakehurst.

A primary concern to all potential users of this new mode of transportation was the safety of the aircraft and those aboard. Dr. Eckener attempted to allay any fears for future travelers by compiling a record of how *Graf Zeppelin* had thus far performed. In the event of engine failure, the ship could make port safely with only 20 percent of its power available, Eckener claimed. And as for weather, the German said that it was merely the difficulty in getting an airship out of its hangar and ready for flight when weather conditions were not good that caused delay in flying. These delays, he pointed out, were to be found with ocean steamers also.

Once aloft, an airship could determine its precise route according to local meteorological conditions. Thus, Eckener and his colleagues introduced a new method of navigation into long-distance travel; they threw out the unchanging mariner's chart and replaced it with freshly drawn weather maps compiled along the way. "The airship," Eckener maintained, "is capable of coping with every situation of wind, weather and fog."[13]

Eckener wanted faster ships and bigger ones, shorter but with greater girth, to increase their commercial feasibility. His success inspired the founding of two American companies ready to leap into this exciting and highly promising new mode of oceanic transport. One company was established to study the commercial feasibility of airship passenger and freight service between Europe and the United States across the North Atlantic. The intention was to develop a cooperative enterprise with a German group.

The second company, Pacific Zeppelin Transport, backed by the Harriman interests among others, planned to establish airship service between California and Hawaii, with the prospect of extending it beyond, to Japan and the Philippines. Two eight-engine airships, each carrying eighty to one hundred passengers, would fly across the Pacific to the islands in a thirty-six-hour service. Because these ships were to use helium, the risk of fire was greatly diminished. This meant that the engines as well as the spaces for the passengers could be contained within the hull, reducing the air resistance set up by protruding structures like isolated gondolas hanging below the great gas envelope.

Technical problems were not the difficulty. Airship service over the Pacific to Hawaii did not get off the ground because a preliminary study showed that a government mail subsidy would be requisite to its financial success.[14] This was not forthcoming.

Thinking about the heavily traveled North Atlantic corridor, Jerome Hunsaker, aeronautical expert and vice president of the new International Zeppelin Transport Company, said he was prepared to gamble that the public would patronize this new form of travel—if the rates were less than twice those of deluxe steamer fares. The pool of potential passengers was large, and the four airships contemplated for trans-Atlantic service could carry only a small fraction of the passengers then traveling first class by ship. And this did not take into consideration new business that would be generated by the new mode of travel. Hunsaker quoted shipping magnate R. Stanley Dollar as saying that "if airships will carry our business representatives abroad in half the time, they will go oftener, get more business and inevitably create more passengers and freight for the regular steamship lines."[15]

Hunsaker saw airships not as competing with steamships but as offering a supplemental service to passengers demanding high-speed travel. Since it is far more expensive to run a ship at high speed than at cruising speed, he reasoned, the need to cater to travelers in a hurry makes an uneconomical demand on the steamship company. Airships also need not compete with airplanes, the latter having their own special market, which was small loads carried short distances.

Many years later Charles Lindbergh was asked his opinion of airships, and he said he found them attractive because of their relatively great range and the comfort they could provide their passengers. Their defects lay in their unwieldiness in ground handling—the hundreds of hands required to haul the great ship out and put it away afterward—and, Lindbergh believed, their vulnerability to adverse winds and weather. Contrary to Eckener, he thought these problems would affect scheduling and therefore costs.

"We studied dirigibles carefully," Lindbergh wrote, "in laying Pan American Airways' plans for over-ocean routes. We lost interest in them rather rapidly as airplane speeds and ranges increased and as navigational facilities improved."[16] But this was an opinion Lindbergh reached only after some time had elapsed. Immediately following the *Graf Zeppelin* flight, Lindbergh told the press that he thought the dirigible was superior to the airplane for transoceanic flying and that he looked forward to the establishment in the United States of a lighter-than-air passenger service as well as airplane service. He saw no conflict between the two modes. "Increased use of one would benefit the other. . . . There always will be both means of travel, I think," he asserted.[17]

The 1937 fire and explosion of the *Hindenburg* at Lakehurst shattered all the glamor attached to airship travel and effectively killed American interest in airships, although, to that moment, not a single one of the thousands of passengers traveling on a commercial zeppelin had ever suffered injury.[18] By this time airplane technology had moved so fast that the airship was no longer of much interest to the major entrepreneurs in American aviation. And the Germans, without helium, virtually gave up the field.[19]

The end of the dirigible represents more than a failure of a mode of transport. Something aesthetic was lost by the departure from the sky of these great slow-moving silvery-gray shapes, elevating the spirits of those watching from below even if they knew they would themselves never ride in them. The disappearance of the dirigible meant an end to a commitment to comfort over speed, and, for passengers, some sense of the environment through which they were passing.

The goal of the airplane manufacturer became simply to build a machine that would convey passengers to their destination as quickly as possible; genuine comfort was given up as unattainable within the constricted dimensions of even the largest aircraft. This remains true even today.[20] Travelers had become "living parcels," John Ruskin observed about railway travel, and his phrase became even more apposite for travel by plane.[21]

For the railway traveler and the airplane traveler, speed dictated a new way of looking at scenery, perhaps not seeing it at all, and it forced the passenger for the first time to seek diversion in reading and other pursuits. The traveler was increasingly untouched by the environment through which he or she passed. Ruskin laid down the dictum that "all travelling becomes dull in exact proportion to its rapidity," a sentiment that any long-distance air traveler today would fervently echo.[22]

CHAPTER TWENTY-ONE

Juan Trippe and Pan American

Juan Terry Trippe is next in our story of Pacific aspirations and the building of transportation networks. His fame derives from building America's first great international airline, Pan American. Trippe clung to the desirability of comfort, even luxury, for the traveler long after most of his colleagues had given it up. To that end he had flirted with the idea of the commercial zeppelin, and he consistently pressed airplane manufacturers to provide space for the amenities. Trippe had a sense of the drama of air travel, of its character as being something out of the ordinary.

Trippe was an airman first, a businessman second. His own life is one of riches to riches; his company's story is an American tragedy of rise and demise. What Trippe sought and then earned was not a great fortune (money did not interest him that much) but great power: the position of dominating a new transportation technology. From the first oceanic flights at least until after World War II, Trippe was clearly the world's dominant figure in international commercial aviation. More than anyone else, he brought the United States to leadership in that field, and the Pacific would be particularly important to that success.

Trippe's company, which he built and ran singlehandedly, was the only private organization among the international airlines and the youngest, largest, and most innovative of them all. Unlike the others, Pan American flew only international routes, and it was the first airline to fly the Pacific.[1]

Not long before that happened, the *New York Times* commented that until 1929 and the Great Crash, "we heard a great deal about the Pacific Ocean supplanting the Atlantic Ocean as the arena of world history. Westward and eastward from Europe, moving simultaneously in both

Juan T. Trippe (Courtesy, Pamela Trippe)

directions, the course of empire was taking its way." The forecast of
Pacific supremacy might ultimately be realized, the *Times* suggested, but
not yet. This is not because of any failure in "this new historic basin,"
but because the world's vital interests were still being shaped by events
in Europe and Americans were reaching a fresh realization of that fact.[2]
Trippe would heartily agree. He held no special brief for the Pacific. He
was simply an entrepreneur who pursued opportunities where he found
them.

Trippe was of Maryland ancestry and the son of a prosperous New
York banker. He was four years old when the Wright brothers were

making their first experiments at Kitty Hawk. A few years later when he was ten, his father took him to see the famous brothers fly around the Statue of Liberty. While a Yale undergraduate, when the United States was preparing to enter the world war in 1917, Trippe joined the Naval Reserve Flying Corps and became a founder of what was called the Yale Aero Club. There he learned to fly a wood-and-canvas biplane flying boat.

After going to Wall Street to sell bonds as so many of his classmates did, Trippe found his true vocation in the new airline business. Losing money with his first company, Long Island Airways, which took passengers on sightseeing trips and supplied charters, Trippe came to realize the opportunities that government subsidies for mail carriage could provide to an air transport company. With the help of some rich friends, including William Rockefeller and Cornelius Vanderbilt "Sonny" Whitney, Trippe formed a company in October 1927 that successfully obtained mail contracts and eventually became the Pan American Airways Corporation.

Trippe's most conspicuous early success was obtaining landing rights in Cuba. His company was founded only nine years after the British and French had begun to run commercial aircraft over the English Channel, and it was the same year as Charles Lindbergh's celebrated solo trip across the Atlantic, which so captured the public fancy and alerted the world to the possibilities of the new medium.

The year 1927 also marked the first successful flight from California to Hawaii. Although overshadowed in the public eye by Lindbergh's feat, the chief of staff of the U.S. Army was quoted as saying that "it was the most significant accomplishment since the completion of the Panama Canal."[3] Because of the air age, the map of the world took on new meaning. In the Pacific almost every island suddenly assumed new importance, as a "filling station" perhaps, or as a base for a radio transmitter.

Trippe would later reminisce about air transportation in the 1920s. The aircraft, he said, were frail and temperamental, and nothing existed on the ground to help the pilot—no radio beacons, no airports. "It was not a business," he remarked; "it was scarcely a hope of one. Postal revenue from the few pounds of mail carried hardly paid for the gasoline and you couldn't find a passenger revenue dollar with a telescope."[4] Even as late as 1928, Betty Stettinius Trippe, Juan's wife, recalls in her diary that Adolph Ochs, editor of the *New York Times*, was "barely polite when Juan spoke of the future of aviation."[5]

Trippe's was a complex personality. Inarticulate, except about business, and secretive, Trippe appeared almost painfully shy. Because of what seemed a disarmingly ingenuous naiveté, people sometimes made the mistake of underrating him. Trippe was affable but did not cultivate

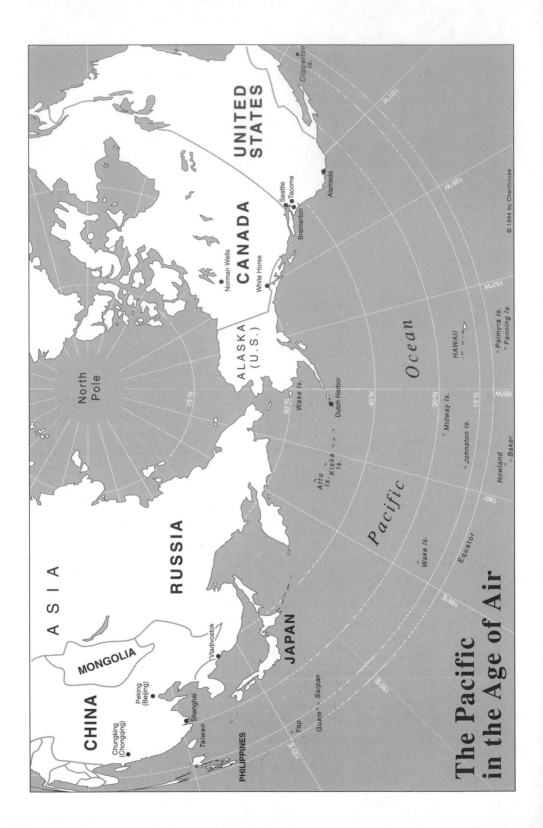

UNITED STATES

CANADA

ALASKA (U.S.)

CHINA

MONGOLIA

RUSSIA

ASIA

JAPAN

PHILIPPINES

Taiwan

Chungking (Chongqing)

Peking (Beijing)

Shanghai

Vladivostok

Yap

Guam ○ Saipan

North Pole

Seattle
Tacoma
Bremerton

Alameda

Norman Wells

White Horse

Wake Is.

Dutch Harbor

Attu Is. ⚬ Kiska Is.

HAWAII

Midway Is.

Johnston Is.

Howland ⚬ Baker

Palmyra Is. ⚬ Fanning Is.

Wake Is.

Pacific

Ocean

Equator

North Pole

75°N

60°N

45°N

30°N

15°N

180°

165°W

150°W

135°W

120°W

165°E

150°E

135°E

Clipperton Is.

© 1994 by Charthouse

The Pacific
in the Age of Air

close personal friendships. He could be described as a loner. Polite and puritanical, he seemed almost old-fashioned. Perhaps this is because Trippe became a great entrepreneurial success when he was still very young, and his manner and sense of dignity rapidly became that of a much older man.

A mixture of realist and dreamer, Trippe possessed a strong analytical mind and yet was equally intuitive, stirred by a vigorous imagination. He built a company, as his friend, poet Archibald MacLeish saw it, "capable as few corporations ever have been of dreaming. And what it dreamed of was a sea which would unite mankind rather than divide it as the waters for so long had done—a sea of air."[6]

But Trippe's practical sense remained strong. He was remarkable for identifying what he wanted and for his tenacity in achieving it. Adept at the art of politics, he could be immensely persuasive, and his dogged persistence tended to wear down his opponents. Yet he could be evasive when he did not want to commit himself.

To those who worked for him, Trippe seemed to be able to look into the future, an image he was careful to cultivate, and indeed he was fond of asking: "What, two years or five years or ten years from now, will I have wished I had done now?" Trippe's ruminations and speculations were not always right, but it was enough to be right part of the time, as one of his associates observed.[7] Trippe clearly perceived one big thing before most other people did: the airplane would soon become an extremely important global instrument.

One of Trippe's greatest assets was his ability to attract brilliant people to work for him, men like operations manager André Priester who developed Pan American's extraordinary training system. Priester required employees to type at the bottom of all internal memoranda the following phrase: "The air like the sea is not inherently dangerous but is terribly unforgiving of incapacity or neglect." It was he who said, "What we want is old women pilots."[8] Engineer Hugo Leuteritz was responsible for the radio direction finders essential to long-distance oceanic flying, and he established a pattern of weather reporting that would become the world standard. Public relations expert William Van Dusen should be added to the list for his breathtaking abilities at manipulating the press. And Trippe was fortunate enough to be able to recruit the renowned Charles A. Lindbergh in 1929 as a consultant to the company. The association of the Lindbergh name with Pan American was worth millions.

Trippe liked to compartmentalize both operations and information. He did not want his scribbled memoranda shared, and as one subordinate recalled, "He carried the company around in his vest pocket."[9] He did not keep extensive files.

To those in whom Trippe had confidence he would allow a wide latitude of freedom to work independently within a particular sphere, and he was satisfied simply to receive the results. He did not ask how they were achieved. Yet one of Trippe's greatest failings was a tendency to exploit his workers; he had to be forced to create a pension plan, perhaps because he himself had no need of one.[10] Much of the criticism Trippe received from the outside world was unwarranted and unfair. His ruthless pursuit of success inspired admiration from much of the general public but provoked enmity from those whom he bested on the way.[11]

Juan Terry Trippe created what was the world's greatest airline, synonymous with the best equipment and service, and virtually the overseas commercial totem of the United States. At its peak, Pan American—Pan Am, as it came to be called—could rightfully boast of setting the "World's Standard for Air Transportation."[12]

One of Trippe's great accomplishments as a businessman was his success in identifying his company with the nation. Pan American, its planes prominently sporting the flag, remained an American institution no matter how far from home that might be. Its station managers, rendering services to American travelers and businessmen sometimes analogous to those provided by the Foreign Service, were treated with the respect accorded government officials.

Paradoxically, Pan American rose and prospered while the nation was suffering the greatest economic depression in its history and when the state of the merchant marine would imply that the United States as a power in international transportation was sinking into permanent decline. The company was obliged to scramble for capital, not simply in order to buy its aircraft and hire its people but also to create the entire infrastructure for a new mode of transport. Perhaps the most amazing part of the accomplishment is its comprehensiveness, both functional and geographical. Trippe was prepared to take on any operational challenge and to put the whole world within his grasp.

The Europeans were keen competitors for a place in the air. The Versailles settlement permitted Germany to develop civil air transport only, and the Germans pursued this with a vengeance, putting all their formidable collective energies into the new field. They were active in South America and in China, organizing lines ultimately aimed to become segments of a German global network. Their zeppelin, as we have seen, was first across the Pacific.

The Dutch was the first international air carrier to reach the Pacific, beginning to fly from Amsterdam to Batavia (Jakarta) in 1930, over what was then the longest scheduled route in the world. The French followed, in 1931 first providing service from Paris to Saigon. The British reached Singapore in 1933 and Australia one year later.[13] The Japanese were active also, but as minor players, flying only in Asia, establishing a north-south network along the western Pacific rim and into Southeast Asia, following the old patterns of the Chinese and British. But none of these national efforts, even the British, was oceanic; all were rimland routes, hugging the shores, leaping from island to island or from continent to island, broken by frequent stops.

By the early 1930s, five great intercontinental air systems existed: British, French, Dutch, German, and Pan American. All served abroad as symbols of national power and a new technological frontier. The first four were governed by politics; Trippe had only to think of profit. Britain's Imperial Airways, for example, was obliged to recruit British pilots only and to use British aircraft only; the French and Dutch had to lay out their routes according to the demands of their colonial empires. The western European airlines were from the start international because they were operating from such small home territories, and those companies were either governmentally owned, or "chosen instruments," selected to fly certain routes in return for a guaranteed "fair" return. In exchange for this franchise, the airline agreed to make available to the government its planes and pilots in any national emergency. For the western European nations commercial air became a "stepchild" to the military.[14]

The American air transport companies—Pan American and the four great domestic lines (United, Eastern, American, and Transcontinental Western)—unlike their foreign counterparts, received direct governmental subsidy only for carrying the mails. Also unlike the others, the American operators sought their aircraft from private manufacturers and shared development costs with them. The overall lively competitive spirit of the American aeronautical industry stimulated initiative, encouraged innovation, and propelled the Americans into world leadership of the field.

Willy-nilly, Trippe was thrust into the realm of international diplomacy by the need to get landing rights with foreign nations. Over the seas or over unclaimed lands, the skies were free to all comers. But the Paris Convention of 1919 affirmed that each nation held sovereign rights to its air space and could permit or deny entry to it as it chose. Unlike shipping companies, which enjoy the freedom of the seas, airlines had to negotiate their routes because so much of their flying was overland.[15]

Before the U.S. government began to undertake to do this for American airline companies, Trippe did it himself, sometimes hiring former U.S. diplomats to help him. Before the United States entered World War II, Pan American Airways had secured the right to fly into thirty-eight countries, more than any other nation or company enjoyed.[16] Always it was Trippe alone who orchestrated the program. His accomplishments are all the more remarkable because he had little to offer in return for what he wanted. Trippe could not provide reciprocal landing rights; only the government could do that.

Fortunately for Trippe, many of the countries to which Pan American flew did not care about reciprocal rights because they would have been unable to exercise them. But at various times the United States denied British, Dutch, German, and Japanese requests to fly into the United States or its territories. The Dutch wanted to fly from the East Indies into the Philippines, and both the Dutch and British asked for landing rights in Hawaii. The Americans were particularly sensitive about Hawaii and disliked the possibility that foreign aircraft, particularly Japanese, might fly over military and naval bases there. In fact Canada was the only foreign nation regularly to fly into the United States before World War II.

Federal legislation providing subsidies for the carrying of airmail was an inducement to expand air services, both at home and abroad. For his first route, Trippe chose the shortest overseas international one possible, Key West to Havana, under one hundred miles. Flights began in October 1927, five months after Lindbergh's epic trip to Paris in May and four months after the first aerial spanning of the widest stretch of the Pacific, from California to Hawaii. Despite the name of his company, which might indicate a Western Hemisphere focus, Trippe did not want to build an airline with overseas operations only to South America. From the start Trippe wanted to build a global airline.

The limits of aircraft range were the most vexatious problem for airlines, and this was especially relevant to oceanic flights. In the first years of commercial air travel, crossing the oceans was virtually unthinkable, but distances in the Caribbean were mercifully short. There the longest over-water hop is from Kingston, Jamaica, to Barranquilla, Colombia, some six hundred miles.

These spaces provided an ideal laboratory for more ambitious oceanic flights. Here Trippe could experiment with radio for navigational guidance, with the collecting and disseminating of meteorological information, and with using multiengine aircraft. Trippe liked that redundancy—an airplane that could stay in the air if an engine should fail. Because aviation was just emerging from the stage of regular engine failures, this could mean the difference between survival and death.

Trippe and Pan American would rise to initial fame and success on the wings of the seaplane, or "flying boat." This aircraft gave Trippe the vision of an aerial marine service, offering luxury and safety analogous to that of the celebrated passenger ships then crossing the North Atlantic. Pan American's earliest flying boat, the Sikorsky S-40, set the tone with its life preserver hanging prominently on the "bulkhead" of the lounge.

Trippe craftily drew instant tradition for Pan American from the U.S. Navy. His officers wore gold stripes on their dark blue uniforms, the seniors sporting "scrambled eggs" on the visors of their white caps. The chief pilot aboard was identified as the captain; he exercised the authority and demanded the respect that his surface counterpart commanded.

Flight attendants were called "stewards." *Galley, bow* and *stern, port* and *starboard* were common parlance aboard. Aircraft speeds were calculated in knots, time in bells, and distances in nautical miles. And Trippe followed maritime custom in christening his "ships." On Columbus Day 1931, Mrs. Herbert Hoover smashed a bottle of Caribbean water against the bow of the *American Clipper*, guaranteeing good press coverage for the event and giving it virtually the stamp of official approval. Other first ladies would participate in subsequent Pan American christenings.

Trippe put huge technical demands on the flight crews of Pan American. The company developed some three hundred manuals, textbooks, and correspondence courses for its employees, with a sequential series of certified levels of competence, ranging from apprentice pilot to master of ocean flying boats. The company would pay half the cost of any correspondence course successfully completed.[17] In an emergency, one man aboard was expected to be able to assume the functions of another, the stewards being the only nonfungible crew members.

Even when the company was moving away from the seaplane, Trippe said, "It makes no difference whether it be a landplane or a flying boat, the traditions of the sea play a large part in the safe and reliable operation of the modern airplane."[18] All this was carefully calculated to give to the public a sense of solidity and confidence in what was still a dangerous form of travel, and one rich with imagery of daring dogfights, aerial acrobatics, crash, flame, and violent death.

"Too often, I'm afraid," Pan American public relations man William Van Dusen recalls with rare frankness, "we wrote not to reveal, but to conceal. The airplane was such a frightening thing we had to go to lengths to put the most attractive face on things, so as not to frighten off the politicians whose votes we needed, or the public. . . . Sometimes we had to invent: our cause depended more upon sympathetic understanding than it did on truth in the absolute."[19]

The choice of the name *clipper* for Pan American's new flying boats supposedly occurred during a conference one evening at Trippe's East Hampton, Long Island, home, discussing the new flying boats about to be delivered. Trippe's eye fell on a Currier and Ives print of a clipper ship hanging above the mantle, and he said, "I've got it!"[20]

The Trippe family's Baltimore origins gave special relevance to the choice. One of the first clipper ships, *Ann McKim*, was Baltimore built, and the Glenn Martin Company, builder of flying boats, was located just outside Baltimore. Trippe made the choice not simply because of these associations or the romantic image of the great ships. He was attracted to their competitive success; they had outsailed and outcarried their British competitors. He sought the same success and in a speech delivered in 1937 spoke of the importance of foreign trade to the prestige and power of the major nations, arguing that transport was their "chief weapon."[21]

The flying clipper first took commercial wing in the Caribbean. Ultimately, like its surface predecessor, it would be most strongly identified with the Pacific, the first ocean it would regularly cross. When Pan American announced its intention to fly the Pacific, the *New York Times* suggested, "Like the merchant clippers of old days, they will carry the American flag to the Far East at a speed and with an expert handling which can hardly fail to arouse again the admiration of the world."[22]

Flying clippers, like their sailing counterparts, filled a new need in transportation with brilliant success and enjoyed a flashy but short career, swept away all too soon by the accelerating onrush of new technologies. But Trippe was canny enough to apply *clipper* to his landplanes too, thus holding on for Pan American all the power of imagery that the old name evoked.

Trippe knew that the sailing clipper era had been brief and that at other times American shipping had proved noncompetitive because of the high internal price level of the United States—its high wages and its high tariffs. He was convinced that international air traffic would inevitably reflect the same pattern; foreign costs would inevitably be lower than American, and any American airline would need to cultivate special abilities and make an extra effort in order to survive.

CHAPTER TWENTY-TWO

"North to the Orient"

A s Juan Trippe looked at the big globe he liked to keep in his office, he realized that the great circle routes of the Northern Hemisphere had taken on a new relevance in the air age. Between America and Asia, the great circle not only provides the shortest aerial path but also offers the opportunity for frequent stopovers en route. In the summer of 1931, Charles Lindbergh, accompanied by his wife, Anne Morrow Lindbergh, made a flight over that route "north to the Orient," as she called it in her book recounting the adventure. Whereas more than seven hundred people had by then crossed the Atlantic, the Pacific was still an aerial frontier, open to pioneering.[1]

The Lindberghs' survey was the first flight from the "western part of the world to the East by way of the North."[2] The Lindberghs were aware of the rich historical imagery their trip evoked and the ancient attraction of their destination. Anne spoke of the power of the imagery "the Orient" conveyed, its "color, glamour, curiosity, magic, or mystery. . . . Our route was new; the air untraveled; the condition unknown; the stories mythical; the maps pale, pink and indefinite."[3]

But the journey, not the destination, despite its glittering imagery, was what concerned the two travelers. Their plan was to make their way in short hops, seeking no records; flying distances were well within the range of their plane. Like all other aircraft in that era, theirs was very much a part of its ground environment, usually visible to the flier and always of great importance. Fliers were not detached as they would become when airplanes came to fly habitually above the clouds. As Lindbergh wrote, you could look at a globe and lay out a highly rational course, following the great circle route, but the globe was abstract. It did not convey the terrors of howling winds and ice-choked seas, of glaciers,

Juan T. Trippe and His Globe (Courtesy, Pan Am Historical Foundation)

fogs, bitter cold, and isolation. The Lindberghs were all too aware of these.

The only precedents for the flight were two: an around-the-world U.S. Army flight from Seattle in 1924, which was the first trip by airplane from the United States to Japan with the longest single hop from Sitka to Seward (605 miles), and a Soviet flight from Moscow to Seattle and on to Washington in 1929, with Lindbergh there as an enthusiastic greeter of the Soviets.

Such was the rapid advance of airplane technology that the speed of Lindbergh's plane was twice that of his U.S. Army predecessors. His flight proved that a northern route to Asia was technically possible, despite the formidable risks of bad weather and poor radio reception. Dense fog settled over the Kurils six days out of every seven, making it easy for the flier to lose his way going down that island chain where airfields did not exist and protected anchorages possible for seaplanes were scarce.

The Lindberghs used a Lockheed Vega, the *Sirius*, an all-wood, low-wing, one-engine monoplane modified with lengthened wings expressly at Lindbergh's specifications. He wanted an exploratory vehicle that would be fast and fuel efficient and have a low landing speed adaptable to primitive airports. The airplane was completed and first flown in October 1929. Subsequently Lindbergh had the plane equipped with pontoons instead of wheels. The plane's speed was 118 miles per hour and its range twenty-one hundred miles. The pontoons carried extra gas as well as providing infinitely more landing places than wheels would have allowed. Lindbergh even claimed that "a pontoon landing on ploughed or soft ground is safer sometimes than a landing with wheels."[4] But he took no chances.

The route the Lindberghs chose—New York to Ottawa, Moose Factory, Churchill, Point Barrow, Nome, Kamchatka, the Kurils, keeping the numerous lakes of Canada well in eye and hugging the shores of the Arctic and North Pacific—was carefully planned so that the aircraft would be at all times within gliding distance of water—river, lake, or protected seacoast—in the event of the need for an emergency landing. In their trans-Pacific segment the Lindberghs flew close to today's heavily traveled nonstop intercontinental pathway.[5]

The two cockpits front and rear were each equipped with controls so that Mrs. Lindbergh could spell her husband. She took primary responsibility for operating the radio that transmitted as well as received, making constant communication possible with ships crossing the North Pacific below. The Lindberghs found that air-ground radio worked, despite the magnetism of high latitudes. Seldom-used high frequencies, they learned, could overcome magnetic disturbances. The plane also carried a rubber raft with food and water adequate for two months. The

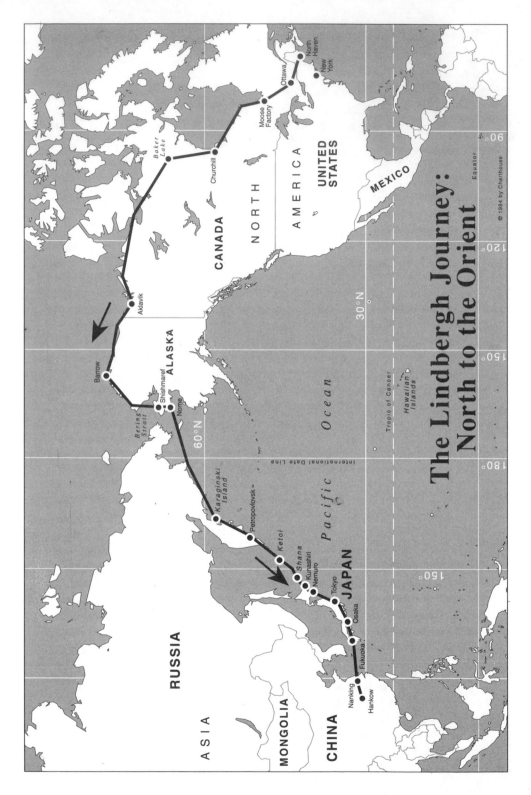

The Lindbergh Journey: North to the Orient

216

Lindbergh's *Sirius* (Yale University Library Archives)

flight menu provided cold baked beans on crackers, supplemented with army rations. Charles and Anne each carried only eighteen pounds of personal luggage.[6]

Lindbergh said that four years earlier, when he made his celebrated solo flight to Paris, he had originally planned to keep on going around the world, returning to the United States by way of Siberia, Bering Strait, and Alaska, but Ambassador Houghton in Paris had dissuaded him from making the attempt. So the *Spirit of St. Louis* was boxed up in a "coffin," as Lindbergh put it and shipped home by sea.[7] The hero himself sailed home aboard a warship to New York and a tumultuous greeting.

Like the Harriman northern voyage, the Lindberghs' trip was billed as a vacation, but its real purpose was to survey the Alaska edge of the Arctic and beyond in order to ascertain the possibility of connecting the eastern coast of the United States with the commercial parts of Siberia and other parts of Asia.[8] In Anne's subsequent book, she says that "it was Arctic air-routes, and the conditions to be encountered following them, which we hoped to study on our voyage to the Orient," routes of "indisputable" future importance.[9] Behind the enterprise loomed the stocky figure of Juan Trippe.

Once out of North America, diplomacy became important for the two American travelers. The State Department made arrangements with the Chinese and Japanese governments for landing privileges. With the Russians, Lindbergh had to negotiate himself because the United States and the Soviet Union still did not maintain formal diplomatic relations.

Whatever the arrangements, whatever the explanation, Lindbergh emphatically did not want the phrase "good-will flight" used, for this or any other of his flights. He hated the expression. To him it carried "a connotation of namby-pambiness that was distasteful. . . . I am under the impression it began as a newspaper concoction."[10] Lindbergh said that he "conceived, organized, and financed this flight personally," but since he was on Juan Trippe's payroll as a consultant, he gave Pan American all the relevant information he gleaned.[11]

Perhaps we can say that Lindbergh's position vis-à-vis Pan American was roughly analogous to the company's position vis-à-vis the U.S. government. The plane belonged to Lindbergh, and he paid all his expenses. "I considered," he said, "that such a policy was desirable because of my independent position as a consultant to airlines, etc. I wanted the freedom that personal ownership and operation gave me."[12] But Pan American helped the Lindberghs by negotiating arrangements with foreign authorities for radio services en route, and the company also planned, built, and installed the radio equipment the *Sirius* carried, including a watertight set put on the rubber raft for use in the event of an emergency ditching.

The flight began at Flushing Bay, New York, on July 29, 1931, and ended on Lotus Lake, Nanjing, China, September 19. Rapid mechanical progress was steadily reducing the risks of flying, and the dangers the Lindberghs faced crossing the Pacific were far less than those Charles had mastered crossing the Atlantic four years before. And this time he had a companion. The worst experience on the Pacific was one night en route from Kamchatka to Hokkaido, with the *Sirius* lying at anchor and the exhausted fliers trying to get some sleep. Rough seas and a high wind caused a mooring rope to be cut through by friction on the rocks. Only prompt help from friendly crewmen aboard a nearby Japanese ship saved the plane.

After arriving at the little fishing port of Nemuro on the northeastern tip of Hokkaido, Lindbergh met the press and expressed confidence that regular air service would soon be established between Japan and the United States. "The air route, I think, will be nearly the same as the one we took along the northern coasts. Although it was not my aim to discover a new route, at times I thought a more southerly course might have been better. We met very thick fogs, but I think ample weather reports would enable the route to be used where fog is less prevalent."[13] Sometimes the fog forced him to fly as low as fifty-seven feet above the surface of the sea.[14] Writing much later in his *Autobiography*, Lindbergh was far more candid than he then was to the press or even to Pan American. The flight, he said, "convinced me that Arctic routes to Asia would be the last ones developed. Flying boats could not operate from ice-covered water."[15]

Manila wanted the Lindberghs to come there too, hoping that a visit from them might raise lagging enthusiasm for commercial air traffic. But the Lindberghs stopped in Nanjing where the *Sirius* landed on flooded lands outside that ancient famine-struck city. Hundreds of curious and hungry people who had perhaps never seen a plane before crowded around the aircraft and nearly swamped it. Lindbergh saved his plane that time, but shortly afterward it was damaged in the Yangzi and had to be shipped back to the Lockheed factory in California for repairs.

Lindbergh's immediate judgments on the trip were sufficiently positive that Pan American decided to go ahead with further study of this northern route to Asia. In October of the same year (1931), two Americans, Hugh Herndon and Clyde E. Pangborn, not associated with Pan American, flew nonstop from Japan to the United States via the same great circle route: forty-five hundred miles in forty-one hours, fifty minutes. But establishing commercial air service was something else. It would require a lot more knowledge of how to operate aircraft in such a challenging environment, as well as necessitating the tricky business of negotiating landing rights from unfriendly, or at best indifferent, foreign governments. No plane could yet fly the distance from the centers of population in North America to those in Asia without refueling.

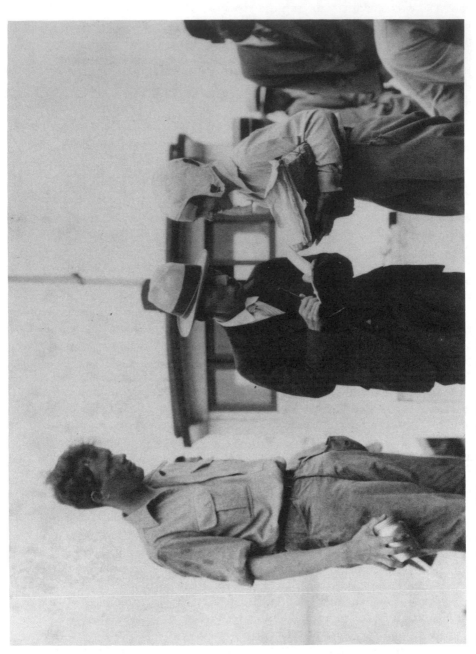

The Lindberghs in Japan (Yale University Library Archives)

The northern passage following the great circle via Alaska, the Aleutians, Kamchatka, and the Kurils appeared as not only the best but also the only route between North America and East Asia since the great distances of the central Pacific barred that more hospitable path to airplanes. Alaska therefore took on sudden new strategic significance, important in the event of any difficulties for the United States involving the Soviet Union or Japan. Alaska is not only close to Asia but almost as close to Hawaii as California is. Because Alaska was so large, so undeveloped, and so underpopulated and because it was also unfortified, it was highly vulnerable to foreign attack or even seizure.

Pan American saw Alaska in simple commercial terms, yet the company appreciated that it was important for American national defense to have a strong airline there. Organized flying had begun in Alaska in 1929, and the two largest companies were teetering on the verge of bankruptcy when Pan American bought them in 1932 to form a new subsidiary called, significantly, Pacific Alaska Airways. The U.S. military was alarmed at the prospect of the ending of an Alaskan air transport system because of its implications for national defense. Alaska, along with Hawaii, were keys to the protection of the U.S. Pacific coast; together they provided the opportunity for U.S. military planes to protect vital sea-lanes of communication. And for people living in Alaska, the disappearance of air cargo, mail, and passenger service would mean a reversion to the dogsled.

What Pan American got for its new Alaskan subsidiary were two dismal balance sheets, a collection of small and obsolescent aircraft, and a series of disconnected mail routes in a sparsely settled, enormous, and challenging natural environment with no satisfactory airports. Travelers seemed to demand nothing more; the market potential was poor.[16]

Why then did Pan American decide to enter the scene? Because of the long-range possibilities. Like the Caribbean, Alaska could serve as a laboratory, in this case for the study of Arctic flying, with the opportunity to reorganize and modernize what was in Alaska already and to extend these lines to the southeastern part of the territory and on to the United States below. An Alaskan network could also feed future trans-Pacific operations, and study of the Arctic would also be important for developing a suitable route to Europe. Pan American made great efforts to learn about flying conditions in Greenland, Iceland, and the far north in general because these areas provided the shortest possible intercontinental routes.

During the first year in Alaska, Pan American studied how to reorganize what was there and what equipment might best serve to improve service. The mail system depended on linkages furnished in the winter by dogsled and in the summer by river boats. Juan Trippe later was quoted as saying that "I thought that a territory where people paid $400 for the privilege of walking behind a dog sled for twenty days was a good prospect for an airline."[17] Much of the passenger traffic was on a charter basis, and Alaskans used planes in ways still uncommon elsewhere, for moving doctors to the sick and vice versa, for example. Planes had to operate under adverse or primitive conditions, using river bars or tiny clearings in the forest, adapting their landing gear to the change of season. Pan American lost money heavily in Alaska while it struggled to cope with a challenging entrepreneurial situation.

Apart from the physical difficulties of flying, the airline had to combat attitudes. Alaskans were indifferent, even hostile, to schedules and to paying cash on the line at a fixed rate. Traditionally no hours or even days were fixed for service; rather it was provided on demand and on credit. Fares might vary according to passenger load and flying conditions. The idea of reservations was unknown, and the company found it sometimes had to send messengers out to remind passengers that it was time to leave. The shift to scheduled operations had to be gradual; at first just the date was fixed, only later the hour.

Pan American had to construct a radio system to communicate from ground to ground and between air and ground. Weather reporting was of top priority. Eleven radio stations were set up, in addition to the one already operating at Fairbanks during 1934 and 1935. At some of the sites, everything, including building materials, had to be brought in. At Juneau, Pan American had to buy land and build an airport before any service could begin. Planes had been landing on tidal mud flats, and after years of operating with ski and pontoon landing gear, the company decided that wheels were necessary. But wheels demanded prepared hard surfaces—gravel, earth, perhaps snow. In all cases, labor and expense were involved. Fuel had to be stockpiled. Here the company had to yield to local custom and allow its supplies to be tapped by itinerant fliers, often without adequate compensation. Even the fuel drums often disappeared since they could be so easily converted into stoves.

Severe cold put great demands on machinery, and Pan American had to devise means of preheating engines, preventing carburetors from icing, and coping with the differential contraction of dissimilar metals. All this experience provided a great deal of information of immense value to the U.S. military, which Trippe was careful to note. In 1934 he pointed out to the Federal Aviation Commission that Pan American's operations within Alaska were of great importance to national defense. Aircraft operating from bases there, he said, could "command the sea lanes between the Orient and the United States."[18]

The problem was that the company's expenses in Alaska continued to run about twice the size of its revenues from operations there. Only the promise of the future sustained it—the opportunity to tie Alaska to the

United States and possibly to Asia and thus establish a potentially lucrative long-distance route.

Pan American focused its operations within Alaska at Fairbanks, establishing a trunk route system with runs to Nome and Bethel, and ultimately to Juneau with an eye to extending that line to the United States proper. Because of the weather, high mountains, and lack of intermediate fields, the company sought and obtained rights from the Canadians to stop at Whitehorse, Yukon Territory.

In 1932 Trippe engaged the Arctic explorer and scholar Dr. Vilhjalmur Stefansson, a Canadian of Icelandic descent, as a special consultant to the company. A year later, in November 1933, the United States recognized the Soviet Union, and Stefansson joined a group of Pan American officials who attempted to wring an agreement out of the Soviets. The Americans proposed to survey routes between Alaska and Vladivostok, and Alaska and Peking, with the view toward establishing an airway along either or both of these routes. The Russians were certainly interested in obtaining advice and assistance from Pan American, but politics mired negotiations, and landing rights were not forthcoming. Pan American's private view was that the Soviets were primarily interested in obtaining technical information from the Americans, giving very little in return.[19]

Stefansson was a great optimist for the Arctic, arguing that the challenges of its climate were exaggerated and that the realities of the air age gave the region new commercial as well as strategic value. He liked to compare what he considered to be the "myth" of the Arctic with the earlier myth of the American West, the "Great American Desert." Stefansson believed that ultimately civilization would be moving far north toward the Arctic, with new Chicagos, Winnipegs, and Edmontons springing up in Siberia and elsewhere in the boreal sub-Arctic.

Stefansson was the first to point out that the Arctic Ocean, more accurately a "gulf running north from the Atlantic . . . [is] a mediterranean sea separating North America from Asia somewhat as the old Mediterranean separates Europe from Africa." Air travel would transform it, he thought, from an impassable space to a well-traveled route, especially in summertime.[20] Stefansson anticipated that "dirigibles will fly at all seasons on straight routes, like ocean steamers, one of them completing the whole voyage. The airplanes will fly on routes less straight, for they will have to travel by relays as our railway locomotives and transcontinental air mails do now."[21]

A decade before Anne Lindbergh, Stefansson pointed out that you can go east by flying north, and that Arctic routes could supply the shortest path for travel from Europe or America to Asia. His was a new way of looking at the map.[22] Polar routes offer a number of advantages in addition to being short. Summer travel could be largely in daylight with

safety advantages, and, for airships, it offered stability of hydrogen supply (little expansion or contraction, resulting in little loss of buoyancy or
need to jettison ballast). On the Arctic route, ice floes would be available
for emergency landings, and there would be no need to think in terms
of floating airstrips anchored at intervals, as some thought the North
Atlantic might then require.

In the 1920s, Stefansson pondered three aerial routes from North
America to East Asia. The first, a mid-ocean route from San Francisco
by way of Hawaii to Tokyo and on to China, would be possible only by
dirigible because of the length of the jumps, especially that from California to Hawaii. The second possibility would be from Seattle or Vancouver to Tokyo or Vladivostok, via southeast Alaska, the Aleutians, and
Kurils. Seaplanes would be used. This route would be difficult because
of the excessive fogs along much of it, dangerously high mountains that
the planes would need to cross, and frequent temperatures of around
the freezing point producing sleet and icing. Stefansson favored a third
choice, from someplace in Siberia, such as Anadyr, to a corresponding
North American terminal on Great Slave Lake. Each of these points
would serve as a marshaling ground for cargo, mail, and passengers
gathering from points south. Anadyr, for example, would tap the rail
traffic of the Trans-Siberian and perhaps draw from Japan as well.

Compared with the other two choices, route three was shortest; it
avoided the Rocky Mountains with its traffic moving northward well to
their east and no mountains to cross higher than six thousand feet. Furthermore, the route was much less foggy (no foggier overall, Stefansson
suggests, than New York City). Perhaps the greatest advantage of this
third alternative was the number of emergency landing places it offered,
for lakes abound in the spongy tundra of the Arctic fringes. From On-
tario to the Bering Strait, the portion of this route Stefansson knew best,
"you would never be twenty miles, and seldom five miles, from a good
emergency landing field—lakes on which you would use pontoons in
summer and skiis in winter."[23]

As for the Asian portion of the route down to China, "no part of this
sector," Stefansson thought, "should prove more difficult than the present New York–Cleveland run," and it should be safer than the trip from
New York to Los Angeles. "It will take a number of years of this safety
to convince the general public, but eventually the facts will sink in and
through-passenger traffic will become great in proportion to the motive,
which is the saving of time." Outsiders might learn from people who
live in the North. Those there who could afford to travel at all did so by
air, Stefansson said.[24]

Stefansson recognized that "there would be a great many tourists who
. . . [did] not understand the advantages and pleasures of Arctic winter
travel," but that this too might change with experience. Here Stefansson

noted a similarity with the Canadian Pacific Railroad. When the rails were first stretched across the Rockies, many people in eastern Canada believed that the railroad would be unusable, at least for passengers, in the worst months of winter. Passengers, they said, would never endure the hardships of travel in storms and severe temperatures. The reality, Stefansson says, was that "the railway could more easily keep its Pullmans comfortably warm in winter than comfortably cool in summer. The snowflakes of the blizzards could be shut out completely while the dust of the sandstorms of summer would penetrate everywhere."[25]

Stefansson observed that weather forecasting and information would be extremely important to travel in the Far North, particularly at the change of seasons. Ice or open water would determine which landing gear a plane should carry—skiis or pontoons. Fuel could be brought in during the summer and stockpiled at strategic intervals along the way, permitting airplanes to fly with maximum payload.

Pan American made a special flight in September 1934 from Juneau to the Soviet Far East in an attempt to demonstrate the feasibility of a far northern intercontinental route. The flight had to be ended at Wellen instead of its intended terminus at Anadyr because of bad weather. Meanwhile, Trippe began to chafe at the delay. He had expensive new long-range aircraft coming on line and had to use them.

The North Atlantic run was still potentially the most lucrative, but although Lindbergh had made a series of successful survey flights for Pan American preparatory to developing that route, politics was making it impossible. The British had no aircraft able to fly the Atlantic, and they did not want to allow the Americans to do so. They would not agree to essential landing rights in Newfoundland, and that foreclosed the possibility of a northern route. Meanwhile the Portuguese, perhaps inspired by their British ally, were dragging their feet over yielding landing rights in the Azores. Without these there could be no southern route to Europe for Pan American.

In any event, the national interest, as Trippe saw it, dictated that trans-Pacific service be undertaken as soon as possible. Otherwise the Europeans would bind East Asia via the Middle East to their growing international air systems, thereby increasing their hold on the international economy of East Asia, to the detriment of the United States. European long-range air routes now were threatening to shape patterns of air traffic as the Suez Canal had earlier done so successfully with patterns of maritime traffic. Early in 1935, Trippe decided to go for a central Pacific route, giving up, at least temporarily, the idea of the North Pacific great circle. In the meanwhile, he had been paying careful attention to securing an anchor on the China coast, a terminus for whatever his Pacific oceanic choice might yet be. He had begun talking with the Portuguese about landing rights in Macao as early as 1930, and when he secured them in January 1936, he used this as leverage to extract the same from the British at Hong Kong.[26]

CHAPTER TWENTY-THREE

China Clipper

Trippe wanted to grasp the Orient. His Pacific destination was Shanghai, still the pulsating center of China's foreign commerce and still the gateway to the Yangzi heart of central China. But direct access to Shanghai was made impossible by the old most-favored-nation clause, first negotiated by Caleb Cushing in 1844, whereby China was obliged to give other powers any privileges exacted by any one of them.

What this meant was that although the Chinese might have been willing to give the Americans landing rights in Shanghai, they certainly did not want to yield any to the Japanese. Yet giving to one inevitably meant giving to the other. A way around this would be for the Americans to get landing rights at British Hong Kong or Portuguese Macao and arrange service from there, via a Chinese carrier, to Shanghai.

China had long been attractive to American aviation interests. Clement M. Keys, a Canadian-born American like James Jerome Hill, of whom he was said to be a great admirer, was an investment banker. He became head of Curtiss-Wright, pioneer in the American aircraft industry and particularly known for its military work. Keys wanted to establish a global aeronautical business, to make airplanes and to fly them too, and he was joined in this venture by another investment banker, Clarence Dillon. Keys was drawn to China because of the enormous size and needs of the market there. He wanted to combine trading and transport—buying and selling goods, carrying them over large areas that were dangerous or otherwise unsuited to ground transport. Early in 1929, Keys sent out an exploratory mission to investigate the possibility of obtaining rights to establish scheduled mail service between major Chinese cities, where oil and gasoline would be available for airplanes. He was prepared to put up a good sum of money.

Rather rapidly Keys's proposal ran into difficulties. The Nationalist government at Nanjing had achieved only an imperfect national political union, and within that government, vicious bureaucratic infighting handicapped any attempts by foreigners to secure lasting agreements. The problems in fact were similar to those faced by Americans who had wanted to build railroads in China at the turn of the century.[1]

The crash of the New York stock market in October 1929 ended any serious interest or ability on the part of Keys to invest in Chinese aviation. His company, now known as the China National Aviation Corporation (CNAC), became "an unwanted stepchild," tolerated by its American co-owners only because it might provide a means for them to sell to the Chinese military aircraft of which Curtiss-Wright was a major manufacturer.[2]

At the time, one other Chinese airline existed. This was Eurasia Aviation, a company in which the Germans had a minority interest. Using exceptionally fine Junkers aircraft, the Germans hoped to make Eurasia an arm of their international system. Plans to carry airmail from Berlin to Shanghai foundered on Russian reluctance to permit flights over Soviet territory. Eurasia had then to content itself with domestic Chinese routes. Happily the Eurasia network complemented the routes of the CNAC, avoiding the need for the two companies to compete directly.

In 1933 the wily Trippe managed to buy the American-held shares of CNAC at a good price. CNAC held a potentially valuable franchise for an air route between Shanghai and Canton and would therefore provide the final link for a trans-Pacific service. Trippe sent to China as his agent a former St. Louis banker named Harold Bixby who had been one of Lindbergh's backers for that first trip to Paris. Bixby, described by Lindbergh as quick thinking, wise, and humorous, took on the assignment of making sure that CNAC carried out its responsibilities on the Shanghai-Canton run.[3] He also supervised survey flights between the China coast and Manila for a Philippine link-up with Pan American's future trans-Pacific service. In August 1933, flying in a specially equipped Sikorsky S-38 two-engine amphibian, Bixby made history's first round-trip by air from Manila to Hong Kong.

By buying into CNAC, Pan American got routes and also the services of an experienced group of American pilots well acquainted with the tricky flying conditions around Hong Kong.[4] But the equipment CNAC was flying when Pan American took it over was primitive and the company insolvent. The situation was not unlike that in Alaska. CNAC planes were cramped and noisy, cotton for one's ears the only soundproofing. Bixby remembered that "the vibration gave the passengers lots of exercise" and that ventilation in the cabin was so generous "you had to tie your hat on."[5] Pan American sent out two Sikorsky S-38s to fly the mail, and Bixby undertook a series of trips throughout China to familiarize himself with some of that huge country, traveling by air, boat, train, bus, sedan chair, and even, he said, by wheelbarrow.[6]

Like South America, China was without a highly developed system of ground transportation and thus offered splendid opportunities for the development of travel by plane. Pan American's Latin American experience was therefore applicable to China. Trippe told the Federal Aviation Commission in 1934 he thought that "next in importance to Latin America, from the standpoint of American trade, diplomacy and national defense, is the great trade route to the Far East," which was then coincidental with Pan American's chief interests.[7]

The benefits to Pan American of operating in China were not simply the link to Shanghai, center for a potential twentieth-century North Pacific aerial China trade. China coast weather data were immediately valuable to Pan American meteorologists charting forecasts for the air traffic from Guam to Manila and on to Hong Kong. In large parts of the Pacific, the weather patterns were still unknown. Great storms could be born and could die without anyone the wiser. CNAC developed a meteorological service only gradually. The first planes flew with no weather information, as well as no radios and no maps. Pilots used the compass and relied on their knowledge of major landmarks below. Passengers probably closed their eyes during much of the flight; airsickness was common. But at least the passengers knew that they were saving a lot of time. The journey on the ground might be days, even months, if a sedan chair were the alternative.

When, in March 1935, the first Douglas DC-2, a glistening metal fourteen-passenger airplane that could travel 190 miles per hour, was offloaded at the Shanghai docks, aviation in China made a great leap forward. The DC-2 was soon followed (although not until a bit later in China) by the similar DC-3, the most successful of the first modern airplanes and one of the most successful in history. The DC-3 could make a profit without carrying mail or cargo but by its twenty-one passengers alone; it was known as "the first airplane capable of supporting itself economically as well as aerodynamically."[8]

After the small and unreliable Stinsons and Loenings, a new era of flight instruments and variable pitch propellers had arrived in China with the Douglas aircraft. CNAC flew under its own markings but profited by using the Pan American purchase and supply system, by drawing on Pan American experience and management skills, and by harvesting some of the prestige of being associated with the famous American company.

Yet CNAC remained more a political than a commercial organization.[9] Ignoring the large American interest in the company, the Chinese sought to use it as an arm of their government, even to ferry ammunition. This jeopardized the commercial status of the airline and made it increasingly susceptible to Japanese assault. The Americans were unable to persuade the Chinese to leave them alone. And while American arrogance offended Chinese sensibilities, Chinese corruption and graft grated on American perceptions of correct business practice. The marriage was often uneasy.

When war with Japan erupted in 1937, the Japanese began to move into China in earnest. The airline was reorganized, with new people and new routes. CNAC had to serve the needs of a China now cut off from the coast and isolated from almost all major centers of population. Fleeing Nanjing, the Nationalist government fought on, its headquarters deep in the interior, beyond the reach of the Japanese. Communications by air were essential both to keeping "Free China" together and to moving important people and priority cargo between the Nationalist redoubt and the outside world. The Chongqing (Chungking)–to–Hong Kong route was the most important, flown at night and ideally in bad weather so as to minimize the possibility of being shot down by the Japanese.

U.S. relations with Japan worsened with a new and growing U.S. governmental involvement in China in the late 1930s. The United States began to lend money to the Chinese Nationalist government, and Japan came increasingly to perceive the United States as preventing Japanese victory in China.

The Central Pacific was longer than the northern course to Asia, but its weather was better and posed no special challenges for Pan American's flying boats. Above all, it was attractive because of its potential for an all-American route to China. No international negotiations were necessary because the loot of the Spanish-American War, gathered almost casually in its wake and then hardly appreciated, gave the United States the necessary piers for an aerial bridge to China. At that time only Luzon had been thought of in terms of access to East Asia. The dawn of the air age invested many Pacific islands with new significance. Hawaii took on a new value to long-distance transportation, perhaps unequaled in its extreme isolation by any other place on the globe.[10]

Trippe's decision to fly the Pacific was bold. Many doubted that such commercial flights were possible. Two members of Pan American's board resigned, protesting Trippe's announcement that he was going for it.[11] But Trippe knew that he was about to receive large aircraft. If he could not use them in the Atlantic, he would use them in the Pacific. As we have seen, international jealousies were excluding Pan American from acquiring the landing rights essential to flying to Europe. Not until the British had their own aircraft capable of flying across the Atlantic were they willing to give Pan American rights to land at Nova Scotia, Newfoundland, Ireland, and England itself.[12] And so, oddly, the densest, the most heavily used oceanic corridor of all, the North Atlantic, which had been the first great leap to be successfully undertaken commercially by the steamship, was the last to be undertaken commercially by the airplane.

The distance from San Francisco to Honolulu (some 2,080 nautical miles) was the world's longest space with any interesting potential for commercial air traffic. Two navy seaplanes attempted the flight from California in 1925. Their original plan, far too ambitious, was to go from the United States to Australia, by way of Hawaii, Midway, Wake, Guam, Japan, and the Philippines. One of the two aircraft was able to reach Hawaii only by putting down on the surface for the last four hundred miles of the trip, rigging some canvas torn from the fabric of the airplane wings for a sail. Meanwhile, the other airplane had given up and returned to California.

Two U.S. Army fliers, Lieutenants Lester J. Maitland and Albert F. Hegenberger, were the first to fly successfully from the mainland to Hawaii. They did so in June 1927, completing the twenty-four hundred miles in twenty-five hours, forty-eight minutes. The two army officers used radio guidance; they were the first to benefit from a radio direction finder, but they also used the stars.[13] Flying a big brown three-engine Fokker landplane, they sometimes went as high as ten thousand feet above the clouds in order to get celestial fixes. Dressed in cotton clothing, the two shivered much of the way.

Maitland and Hegenberger wrote of their exploit in the *New York Times* that they saw Hawaii as a "frontier defense post" for the United States and that "from a military viewpoint it was highly desirable to link our island territory with the mainland, so that in the event of an emergency an important officer or exceedingly confidential message and plans could be sent across the distance in twenty-four hours."[14]

To Hawaii was only the first step. The overall air travel distance from the United States to China was greater than that between Miami and Buenos Aires, or the Dutch line between Amsterdam and Batavia. It was twelve times the distance across the Caribbean.[15] Yet bridging it was essential to an important American commercial presence in East Asia and to any around-the-world air service.

For Pan American, Igor Sikorsky built his first four-engine amphibian, the S-40 American Clipper, at its time (1931) the largest commercial plane to be designed and built in the United States. Sikorsky was one of the great figures in early American aviation, a man possessed with a rich sense of the importance of what he was doing. Writing the year before his death in 1972, Sikorsky remarked, "I personally believe that the discovery of human flight may be considered, with reason, the most dramatic development ever attempted by man from the discovery of fire to the start of space travel."[16]

Sikorsky had designed the world's first multiengined aircraft, a bomber used by the Russian army in World War I. Coming to the United States as a refugee from the Bolshevik Revolution, he founded the Aero Engineering Company in 1923 and began to build airplanes.[17] His S-38 was known as "the world's safest airplane" although unkind critics described it "as a collection of airplane parts flying in formation."[18] Sikorsky's airplanes were always distinctive in appearance. He would be particularly identified with seaplanes and, in his later years, with the helicopter. Sikorsky liked to design big aircraft, and he wanted them to be comfortable for passengers. Trippe appreciated that.

The S-40 had a cruising speed of 115–120 miles per hour, carrying a normal load of thirty-two passengers for a trip of up to about seven hundred miles, which was all the range required by the Caribbean. Sikorsky himself, with Charles Lindbergh, took the plane on its maiden flight from Miami to Panama. The S-40s were designed as amphibians, but by 1933 their land equipment was taken off, and they were used solely as flying boats. Lindbergh later said he was not at all happy about the design of the plane with its high wing resting on what appeared to be a clutter of struts and braces, as odd in appearance as its S-38 predecessor. Lindbergh frequently referred to the S-40 as a "flying forest."[19] But "Sikorsky convinced me that it was the wisest 'next step.' In spite of the improved performance [over the S-38], I felt the design was of the past rather than of the future."[20] Trippe would go the next step with Sikorsky but thereafter take a separate path.

A Pacific survey flight by the Sikorsky S-42, a much-improved and cleanly designed S-40 and the best-performing flying boat yet built, demonstrated that California could be linked by commercial air to Hawaii. But the normal range of that aircraft was fifteen hundred miles and to cover such a great distance required its conversion into a virtual flying gas tank. No room would be left for passengers or even for very much mail. Pan American used S-42s for all the survey flights in the Pacific from 1935 to 1937, ultimately relegating them to serve only the final short lap of the Pacific route trip, from Manila to Hong Kong.

Trippe abandoned Sikorsky and turned to the Baltimore manufacturer Glenn Martin for a new airplane, ordering three seaplanes from him even while the Sikorsky S-42 was still undergoing test flights. Sikorsky's vision and intuition, his skills as a designer, were tremendous and his aircraft performed superbly. But they were expensive to build and expensive to maintain.[21] Trippe was consistently ruthless in his pursuit. His eye was fixed on the far horizon of aeronautical technology, and his people now worked closely with Martin to push that technology to its very limits. Such was the pace of change that the newest aircraft model might become obsolete in as short a time as three years. Crashes often took care of obsolescence.

Yet airplane technology was improving at such a staggering rate in speed, rate of climb, and load capacity as to raise unreal expectations from the public. In 1936, the *New York Times* speculated that within ten years or so air passengers could anticipate "liners" flying across the Atlantic to Europe in ten hours' time, with large recreation spaces, bars and a real dining room, staterooms and showers, even a dance floor.[22]

Out of the three flying boats he built for Pan American, Martin got a lot of good publicity, valuable experience, and heavy financial losses.[23] All American aircraft manufacturers were constantly teetering on the edge of bankruptcy. Theirs was a highly specialized art; unlike the automobile makers, they could not enjoy any economies of scale, and unlike other manufacturers, they did business with only a very few customers.

Trippe was adept at persuading airplane manufacturers that they could build better planes than they knew they could and at prices he could afford. Charles Lindbergh believed that this pressing of the state of the art had powerful results. "One may ask," he wrote, "why we could not have waited a few years for more advanced equipment. Competition forced us to take the lead. Also, we wanted to take the leading position, and if we had not taken it, the 'advanced equipment' available in later years would have been very much slower in coming. This pressing of the state-of-the-art, exemplified throughout Pan American's existence, has resulted in America's outstanding leadership in present-day aviation."[24]

The first all-metal, high-wing Martin rolled out on November 30, 1934, 91 feet long with a 130-foot wing span, described by a Baltimore paper as "a streamlined mass of shining silver and black, the largest flying boat ever built on the American continent."[25] It would be named *China Clipper* and Humphrey Bogart would immortalize it in a film by that name. *China Clipper* would be joined by *Hawaii Clipper* and *Philippine Clipper*. These great ships carried forty-eight passengers and a crew of six up to thirty-two hundred miles without refueling. Sadly, all three ultimately were lost.

The Martins, mainstays of the Pacific run, were supplanted at the end of the decade by the Boeing 314, the last and greatest of the commercial flying boats. But Trippe was asking for something better than the Martins even as they were entering his service. Pan American would eventually buy nine of the Boeings; they had almost twice the horsepower of the Martins. More of these would serve in the Atlantic than in the Pacific. They could carry seventy-four passengers nearly four thousand miles at a speed in excess of 180 miles per hour. The world's largest civil air transport until the Boeing 747 more than thirty years later, the flight deck alone of the flying boat was larger than the passenger compartment of the DC-3, that stalwart of flying over land.[26]

These first aerial clippers were literally flying boats, carrying their "air-

fields" along with them. Flying boats demanded water routes; their test-
ing required an ice-free climate. The flying boat, when adopted by and
built in some numbers for the U.S. Navy, thus gave early encouragement
to aircraft manufacture in southern California, the first major manufacturing industry for the American North Pacific.

Los Angeles provided not only warm, sunny weather year round but
also a good supply of labor, both skilled and unskilled. Consolidated
Aircraft moved there to begin building the famous navy patrol craft, PBY
Catalina. The northeastern United States remained the center for the
making of propellers and engines, Pratt and Whitney the most well
known, but by the late 1930s California had become the nation's center
of airframe manufacturing with Douglas, North American, Ryan, Vultee,
and Lockheed, as well as Consolidated, located there.[27]

Flying boats reassured nervous passengers. The stout bulbous hulls
conveyed a sense of solidity, and it was easy to imagine that in an emergency, a flying boat could at least theoretically move on the surface of
the water and perhaps get itself either to land or to the vicinity of a
passenger ship for rescue. And these craft provided much more space
and comfort than any landplane of the time.[28]

But the weight of the aircraft demanded long takeoffs, and hulls were
vulnerable to corrosion and barnacles. Moreover, the flying boat design
was an uneasy compromise between the demands of two media, water
and air. The heavy hulls required to withstand the shock of hitting the
water put a burden on the engines. The stepped hull necessary to break
the adhesive quality of the water surface at takeoff and the rounded
shape required for movement in water worked against aerodynamic efficiency.

Inland cities posed a dilemma. Where could the aircraft come down?
And winter ice was to be found in any temperate area. This did not
occur in the central Pacific, but elsewhere even a port as far south as
New York City could not accommodate flying boats at certain times in
the winter. In cold weather Pan American had to use Baltimore. Even in
fair weather and mild climates, flying boats were highly vulnerable to
debris floating across their paths of takeoff and landing. But in the early
years of commercial aviation when airports were few, the flying boat
offered a lot of flexibility.

Lindbergh wrote to Trippe in 1936, "I am glad that you are developing
a land plane in addition to the new flying boats. I believe it is probable
that the landplane will replace the flying boat on all important routes in
the future. I think the only exception will be in places where landing
fields can not be obtained or where the traffic is so low that the construction of a field is not warranted."[29] But the flying boat was an awesome
craft and attracted much admiration. Until the late 1930s it was the only

airplane that could cross the ocean; landplanes were not large enough to fly such distances commercially.

Like the sailing clippers, the flying boats were dependent on dead reckoning and celestial navigation. But unlike the early sailors, the aviators had directional radio to help them. Pan American studied the logs of nineteenth-century navigators to learn about the characteristics of the Pacific: its temperatures and weather patterns, the height of waves in storms, the winds and cloud formations. The new clippers were as dependent on these phenomena of nature as the old clippers had been. The flying boats were even more dependent on the vagaries of wind and weather than were the ships steaming along below them.[30]

Nowhere were airmail subsidies more important than in the Pacific, where costs remained high and volume of cargo and passengers low. As late as March 1935, Pan American did not have the essential Pacific mail contract in hand. The Post Office Department was favorably disposed, but Congress had not yet appropriated funds. When the bids were let, Pan American submitted the only one, and it was accepted on October 24, 1935. Payment for mail to China was to be two dollars per mile for a load up to eight hundred pounds. Anything in excess of that would be one dollar per pound per thousand miles. Flying as far as Manila would suffice to satisfy the contract; Trippe covered himself in the event he could not obtain landing rights in China. The first trans-Pacific flight took off on November 22, 1935; passenger service would begin eleven months later.[31]

Pan American's proposed new service put the United States closer to China than any of the European powers were: five days from San Francisco as opposed to ten days from London, prompting *Fortune* magazine to comment admiringly that "the key to world power is not expansion but compression. The success of the modern state depends on how small it can make itself and the rest of the world. This is the function performed for the U.S. by Pan American Airways."[32]

Only the French, because of their strategically placed island possessions, had any possibility of competing with the Americans across the Pacific, but their potential route, southerly via the Marquesas and across to the tiny island of Clipperton and on to the Mexican coast, was not nearly as commercially attractive as the American route, and the French did nothing to develop it.[33] The Americans felt that they were in a race not for flying across the Pacific, in which they triumphed, but for the aerial grasp of East Asia. European airlines like Lufthansa had reached the very doors of China, increasing the handicap effect that distance imposed between American industrial centers and the highly competitive markets of the Orient. Americans feared that with Eurasian intercontinental air routes, the Europeans would be able to dispatch mail, passengers, and priority freight to East Asia for one-third of the time required for American steamers to cross the Pacific.

The British seemed the most likely to be able to spin a global network in aerial transportation as they had done so successfully in communications. Americans had been able to complete their own trans-Pacific cable in 1904, via Hawaii, Midway, and Guam, the only line across the central Pacific. At Guam the line split into two extensions; one running via the Bonins to Japan and the other to Manila. The line was long and unproductive because it could not generate local traffic. Clarence Mackay, its builder, explained that he had to make an agreement with the two British-dominated companies in China, Eastern Telegraph and Great Northern Telegraph, to obtain landing rights for his system to join theirs.

The fact was that Mackay's "American" company, the Commercial Pacific Cable Company, was largely owned by British interests. Perhaps this is why American senders found rates across the Pacific so high and service so poor. Most customers found it more to their interests to use routes via London. High cable costs across the Pacific inhibited the flow of news and undoubtedly lessened American press coverage of East Asian affairs. From China one could cable Europe at five or six cents per word; to New York City the cost would run thirty-five to thirty-nine cents.[34]

Much of the world was already part of the British realm, but in crossing the Pacific by air, geography ran against them. The British faced an enormous strategic disadvantage because they had no well placed spot where planes could be refueled. Unless the British could obtain landing rights in Hawaii, existing aircraft ranges precluded a global British aerial transportation network analogous to their cable and telegraphic network. Canada could not, with existing aircraft, be linked by air with Australia without using Hawaii. Furthermore, the British did not have a suitable long-distance aircraft; the Americans had the only planes that could then span the Pacific. Without buying American-built aircraft, the British and everyone else could continue to fly only on the fringes of the great oceanic spaces.

The dawning air age in the Pacific rekindled ancient national territorial rivalries. Many Pacific islands had only shadowy ownership; some of the claims were intertwined with the guano trade. And, characteristically, Juan Trippe's name would crop up in association with a guano company that began to raise questions of access to these islands. Canton in the Phoenix group was one such case, particularly interesting to the U.S. Navy because of its excellent lagoon, ideal for seaplane use. But the U.S. claim to Canton was weak and required tactful negotiation with the British. Because war was looming in Europe, the British did not want to pick a fight with the Americans. North of Hawaii, there is no land until the

Aleutians; east, none until California. South and west of Hawaii, islands abound. Although the central Pacific route offered the tremendous advantage of providing stepping-stones already under the U.S. flag, the route, especially at Guam, was extremely vulnerable to interdiction by the Japanese.

An alternative southwestern route to Asia from Honolulu offered greater security from the Japanese but opened vexatious questions of territorial rights. President Franklin Roosevelt took a strong personal interest in the matter and put it quite bluntly to both the State and Navy Departments: "We want several Islands in as many parts of the mid-Pacific as possible which will be useful for aviation purposes, including safe anchorages in still water."[35]

The Americans had two issues to dispute with the British. The first was the matter of island sovereignties; the second was a matter of obtaining landing rights for Pan American in New Zealand without yielding reciprocal privileges in Hawaii. Here Pan American was able to play on New Zealand's desire for an international airmail connection. The British did not yet supply it and New Zealanders feared that Imperial Airways might be planning to bypass them. For Americans, these southern air routes did not lead to North Pacific Asia, to China or Japan, but they were significant because they strengthened American ties to New Zealand and Australia and provided a safer link to the Philippines.

Yet the U.S. government formed no realistic, consistent, or coordinated strategic policy regarding Pacific islands and articulated no clear national objective for the Pacific. Administrative responsibilities were scattered among various departments—Interior, Treasury, War, and Navy—and no one knew or even seemed to care what the United States actually did own in the Pacific.[36] Until the gathering clouds of the mid-1930s, a general official apathy prevailed.

Pan American was not the only company interested in flying the Pacific. In the fall of 1934, the South Seas Commercial Company, its president the aircraft manufacturer Donald W. Douglas and its vice president Harold Gatty, navigator for Wiley Post in the circumnavigation of 1931 and navigation tutor to Anne Morrow Lindbergh, told the federal government that they wanted to fly to the Philippines via Honolulu and by means of either a central or south Pacific route from there. They therefore sought long-term leases on a number of islands, including Johnston, Howland, Baker, and American Samoa, as well as Midway, Wake, and Guam. South Seas was interested in using landplanes perhaps in addition to seaplanes. The Douglas DC-2, not surprisingly, is what they had in mind.

The navy was prepared to allow the South Seas group the opportunity to construct the bases that company wanted, South Seas having agreed that Pan American or any future American company would be free to use them. The navy's chief concern was that no foreign aviation company be let in. Potentially South Seas challenged Pan American, but it was a new company and without any record of performance. Pan American had the advantage of experience, equipment, and people and had already developed in the Caribbean a close relationship with the navy. Instead of fighting the competition, Trippe embraced it. Donald Douglas joined the Pan American board of directors, and Harold Gatty became an officer of the company, with the responsibility first of negotiating landing rights in Auckland, New Zealand, and ultimately of representing Pan American in New Zealand and Australia, which he did from 1935 to 1941. Nothing else was to be heard from the South Seas Commercial Company.

In similar fashion Trippe removed another challenge to Pan American's monopoly raised by the Inter-Island Airways of Hawaii, which, in association with the Matson Lines, proposed entering the trans-Pacific air transport business. Matson settled for carrying by sea Pan American's heavy baggage from California to Hawaii, that segment of the Pacific Division where weather conditions, number of passengers, amount of cargo, and requisite amount of fuel were always in delicate balance.

The U.S. Navy and Pan American Airways were silent partners. The company could do things the navy wanted to do but for political reasons could not. Admiral William D. Leahy, when acting secretary of the navy, told Edward Noble, chairman of the Civil Aeronautics Authority, on April 20, 1939, that

Pan American Airways' activities from the beginning have been of great value to the Navy. Its pioneering work in equipment, methods, development of routes, establishment of aids to seaplane operations, and opening up of foreign territory to air activity, has done far more than can be measured in concrete terms to assist Naval aviation in its own development and progress. For this reason and because of Pan American's continuing close cooperation with the Navy, and its eagerness always to make available to the Navy its facilities, information and assistance, its problems merit all practicable support from the Navy Department in the interests of national defense.[37]

The navy's help to Pan American had been important from the start when the company began to lay out its route across the Pacific.[38]

Each of the island way stations selected for the route to China presented its own peculiar set of problems, yet each had to satisfy certain basic requirements. The flying boats needed moorings, buoys, floats for embarking passengers, fueling systems, repair shops, and a radio station. Offices, living quarters, and a hotel for passengers were essential. In that regard, Honolulu and Manila, both major cities, posed no problem, nor did Guam, the most isolated U.S. possession, a dot in a sea of Japanese-held islands. Although Guam was so remote that only one commercial freighter regularly called there to pick up the mail at three-month intervals, Guam at least provided space and people, and the government made available to Pan American an abandoned U.S. Marine Corps base there.

Midway and Wake required complete colonization, all of which had to be planned in New York and executed on the spot before a single dollar could be earned by the company. A chartered ship, *North Haven*, carried out to the islands some three hundred freight-car loads of equipment and supplies of everything from toothpicks to diesel engines.[39] The most important item was radio equipment, especially Leuteritz's long-distance (range up to fifteen hundred miles) direction finders. Each base was equipped with a motor launch with a thousand-mile range, prepared, if necessary, to make a five-hundred-mile rescue trip. Managers of the stations had to be proficient in seamanship. On board *North Haven* pilot Bill Grooch held classes in navigation.[40]

Offloading proved an enormous task for the construction crews. The ship had to anchor as best it could in deep water offshore and transfer all cargo in the heavy Pacific swells, at great risk of loss. Eggbeaters, poker chips, flower and vegetable seeds, aquaria for brightly colored fish, and clocks showing time simultaneously in several different places were among the specialty items. Not only was it a challenge to select the more than one million different objects required to stock five different airbases, but also the packing had to be done sequentially so that goods could be taken off for each destination in sequence. Midway and Wake each needed an eggbeater, but neither needed two.

The achievement was extraordinary; it was done fast and it was done well. Three naval officers came along aboard *North Haven* to photograph and to observe an operation that bore unquestionable military implications. Soon after the construction crews had finished their work, the navy was holding war games in Midway involving a fleet of forty seaplanes that staged a mock attack on Hawaii.[41] The U.S. Navy had eyed Midway appraisingly as early as 1920 as a possible base for military flights across the Pacific.[42]

Clearly, the five or more years of experience of Pan American's flying across the Pacific would be of immense later value to the nation in conducting war against Japan across the Pacific. Pan American had opened up some of the ocean's geographical mysteries. Wake and Midway would take on new meanings. It is not surprising that the Japanese looked at what was happening there in the 1930s with some unhappiness and showed it by refusing to share information about weather patterns in their sphere of operations. But the arms limitation treaties then in effect placed no restrictions on commercial aviation, and the Japanese could make no objections to what Pan American was doing.

Simultaneously with the laying out of the bases, the company was conducting a series of practice flights using the Sikorsky S-42. These flights were far away from the Pacific. The S-42 simulated the Hawaii run with an all-night, nonstop twenty-five-hundred-mile flight over water between Miami and the Virgin Islands and back. Its success was interpreted as readiness for the Pacific. Subsequently, the S-42 was ferried via the Gulf of Mexico and San Diego to Alameda on San Francisco Bay, and its work began. By the spring of 1935, Pan American pilots had surveyed all sectors of the projected Pacific route except the portion between Guam and Manila. These were new pathways hitherto unbroken by commercial aircraft. And all the surveys were flown without untoward incident.

The first possible stop across the central Pacific from Hawaii was Midway, so named in 1867 by the U.S. Navy Department because of its geographical position en route to Japan across the central Pacific from California. Midway is also roughly halfway round the world from the Prime Meridian at Greenwich. Midway is formed by a pear-shaped cluster of islets sheltered from the force of ocean rollers by an eighteen-mile circumferential reef.

Midway had no water and needed a distillation plant that required imported oil to feed it. A cable station had been built there in 1903 as part of the American trans-Pacific cable, and the landscape reflected the softening influence of the human presence. People had planted and carefully nurtured stands of ironwood trees and beach magnolias, Norfolk pines and banyans. Tropical flowers added color, and vegetable gardens offered promise of nourishment. Songbirds were imported. Yet most of the inhabitants of the island were a kind of albatross called the gooney, a bird species found nowhere else, which migrated to and from the Aleutians two thousand miles north. The goonies provided some amusement to visitors. The bird was tame enough to submit to being handled. One man remembers "teaching [them] to fly by holding them over our heads and racing down the beach."[43] Midway was subject to strong Arctic winds and bad weather blowing down from the Aleutians, and winters were disagreeably cold. For Pan American people it was "a difficult and uncomfortable station" that no one later was sorry to give up.[44]

Before Pan American arrived, little was known about Wake, an uninhabited horseshoe-shaped volcanic speck of three islands totaling about three square miles, with a lagoon in the center. Trippe began his investigations in 1932; later he would recall visiting the New York Public Library and poring over maps to try to find the essential stopover between Midway and Guam. The maps did not help him, he said, but clipper ship logs he found there did. Thus, Trippe asserted, he identified

Wake as possible for his purposes.[45] The *New York Times* had already (October 6, 1931) speculated that "it may be practicable for the United States to develop Wake Island and Guam as stopping places for an ocean airway between California and the Philippines. With better acquaintance the Pacific may turn out to be less hazardous than the Atlantic." So the idea was at least floating in the air before Trippe's library excursion.

Wake, the top of a volcano all but submerged in the Pacific, is surrounded by deep water. No easy anchorage is available. Wake's sudden enormous value was its unique position; the big challenge it posed was for the aerial navigator to find it. Charles Wilkes's *Vincennes* had touched there in late December 1841, and the expedition immortalized two of its own members by the names they gave to two of the minuscule islands forming the whole: Peale and Wilkes.

Trippe sent C. H. "Dutch" Schildhauer down to Washington to dig around for information and later out to visit the site. Schildhauer, a retired navy captain, probably knew more about flying boats than anyone else. His assignment was to study the microgeography of the central Pacific stopovers in terms of their usefulness for aircraft. Did the islands have enough smooth water for flying boats to land and take off safely? Was there space for a dock and a refueling barge? Atolls ringed by reefs and with sheltered lagoons were ideal. Midway was an atoll. But Wake was a mountaintop. Where could the flying boats safely land?

Schildhauer found that anyone living on Wake without recourse to outside resources would have a diet limited to fish and bird eggs, although the Polynesian rat and the hermit crab shared Wake with the birds. Of the islets, Wilkes was covered with jagged rocks and scrawny brush. Peale seemed much more hospitable with its rich loamy soil. The only wells yielded brackish water, so any residents would need to collect rainwater. The Spaniards, who had spotted the island and named it San Francisco, had passed it by, presumably because it was arid and because the highest elevation was fourteen feet, making the island and everything on it vulnerable to storm. "We always had some fear of a typhoon washing over parts of Wake Island," a Pan American official would later write.[46]

The lagoon at Wake offered only a six-thousand-foot length for takeoff, a bit short for the flying boat with full load and no wind. And even this range was made possible only by the laborious and dangerous blasting of coral heads one by one. Left close to the surface, they could rip out the belly of a flying boat. The coral lay at deceiving depths, some deep and others uncomfortably shallow. But the lagoon was essential because "the ocean around . . . is very deep, it is a question whether a plane could take-off in lee of the island as movements of the ocean would still be heavy."[47]

The new inhabitants planted trees around their prefabricated buildings, with vegetable and flower gardens like those on Midway, to try to soften the starkness of the surroundings. Some of those stationed on Wake or Midway found the isolation to be almost unbearable, on top of the low pay. Yet Wake was a fisherman's paradise, and one of the creators of this new world wrote, perhaps with tongue in cheek, that Wake would become an attractive resort. "The tired business man who wants real rest and relaxation can count on a complete absence of any form of temptation at Wake."[48]

Guam, the last of the small island stopovers, seemed continental by contrast with Midway or Wake. From a commercial and technical point of view, Pan American might better have flown from Guam on to Tokyo (1,575 miles) than to Manila. The distance to China was shorter, and China still loomed powerfully in the American imagination. In fact Japan, with its rising industrial economy, would have made a better Asian terminal than China and would have generated more business for Pan American than China could. But commerce was obliged to bow to politics. Americans had no choice; Japan then permitted no foreign airlines to fly into its territory.

Development of commercial aviation in Japan lagged behind comparably developed European nations. Perhaps this was because of Japan's geography; it was relatively mountainous and relatively small, with a highly developed rail network. Outside the home country, Japanese commercial air flew west to Korea and Manchuria and south along the China coast to Southeast Asia, following the pattern of Japan's ancient orientation to the mainland. The Japanese chose to put their aerial energies into military aviation, with good effect, as the Americans would soon ruefully learn.

Trippe considered doing business with the Japanese. In April 1935, President Roosevelt approved his request to invite them to use the newly established Pan American base at Guam. The possibility would then exist of Guam's serving as a link between Pan American and Dai Nippon, the Japanese national airline.[49] But Trippe subsequently thought better of it, telling the State Department that Japan was technically far behind in transoceanic aviation. Were Guam opened to them, it might simply prod them to greater efforts.[50] Trippe did not want competition from the Japanese any more than he wanted it from anyone else.

The Japanese move into China in 1937 shattered the possibility of making any new commercial agreements with them. Rising political tensions over naval rivalries, continuing American anxieties over the cruel character and effectiveness of Japanese military expansion in China, and extreme Japanese sensitivity to possible overflights of the Marianas or Bonins (foreigners were excluded from these island groups) made a harmonious aerial cooperation with the Japanese highly unlikely. Pan American navigators could sometimes trick the Japanese radio station at Rota near Guam into giving them a fix, but the Japanese were not inclined to be cooperative.[51] It was, after all, not to the interest of Japan's military government to help establish an American airline across the Pacific.

November 22, 1935, is the day the first flying boat took off on a scheduled flight across the Pacific, the first scheduled transoceanic airplane flight in history. It carried the mails from San Francisco to Manila, where Pan American had established its base at Cavite, not far from where the Manila galleons, the first ships to cross the Pacific on a regular basis, had been built. President Franklin Roosevelt noted that the flight was coincident with the one hundredth anniversary of the arrival of the first clipper ship in San Francisco.

Mindful of the historic significance of the event, Postmaster General James A. Farley came out to California to honor the inaugural flight, despite some ambivalence about Trippe and his methods. Farley calculated that travel time between America and Asia was now being reduced from seventeen days by fastest steamship to six days by flying boat. Pan American's image with the general public took on new luster.

The *China Clipper* had flown from the Baltimore factory to Miami, where Pan American made a few adjustments and became acquainted. Then it flew across the Gulf of Mexico and the isthmus of Tehuantepec, an unavoidable overland stretch before heading up the Pacific coast through Acapulco, San Diego, and to San Francisco, all the while hugging the coastline as closely as possible.

In the departure ceremonies at Alameda on November 22, 1935, a radio announcer declared that the Pacific would no longer be a barrier between the East and West:

And it is America, whose dynamic energy and courage to pioneer, whose aeronautical genius, whose far-sighted government has alone of all nations on the face of the earth made this tremendous achievement possible. Within a few feet of our platform the "China Clipper," studded with powerful engines, her great glittering whale-like hull resting gently in the water, stands ready . . . on the wings of these sturdy Clipper Ships are pinned the hopes of America's commerce for a rightful standing in the teeming markets of the Orient.[52]

Pan American's public relations department could have put it no better.

President Trippe dispatched the flight at 3:27 P.M. Pacific Time, on November 22, 1935, in proper nautical fashion: "Captain Musick . . . you have your sailing orders. Cast off and depart for Manila in accordance therewith."[53] The airplane was in good hands. For the epic flight, Captain Ed Musick was at the controls. Musick was regarded as Pan American's best pilot, and his first officer on this trip, R.O.D. Sullivan, was said to have "flown the Pacific so often he could recognize some of the waves as old friends."[54]

Heavy with fuel, the clipper was unable to fly as planned above the skeleton of the unfinished Bay Bridge; Musick had to go under those looping wires, followed by a convoy of escorting planes. Before arriving in Honolulu, Musick made his men shave (in cold water) and get back into well-pressed uniforms and spotless white caps. "Getting cleaned up," remembered one of them, "not only made us feel better—when the crew stepped off the Clipper all spic and span you'd have thought we'd just taken a swing around the harbor. It made the ocean crossing look routine."[55]

The trip would make a hero out of Ed Musick, putting his face on the cover of *Time* magazine and subjecting him to so much fan mail that Pan American had to employ a secretary to handle it. One woman requested the handkerchief Musick had carried on the first crossing.[56] The chief pilot was venerated by all his colleagues; they thought him the best. Musick was even more taciturn than Lindbergh and loathe to say anything to the press or to speak at any public occasion. To his co-workers, "he spoke little but when he did, everything was punctuated with profanity."[57]

Pan American began its regular trans-Pacific passenger service on October 21, 1936, making it now possible to travel around the world by scheduled commercial carriers in twenty-one days. Clipper travel across the Pacific attracted the rich, the famous, and the important—those whose time was especially valuable or thought it was. Fares were at a rate, adjusted for inflation, twice that of the Concorde today. A ticket from San Francisco to Manila and back cost $1,438.[58]

Trippe liked to equate the airplane with the ocean liner or the Pullman car in its amenities. The sense of luxury was a good antidote to fear. The popular imagery of modernity, of speed, the "streamliner," first applied to the train, and later to the airplane, conveyed a sense of a future that perhaps many would be able to share. The luxurious nature of travel could be enjoyed vicariously by a nation ground down by profound economic depression. Like the life depicted by Hollywood's romantic comedies, long-distance travel was, for the average person, something to be imagined and not experienced.

One early clipper traveler was playwright Clare Boothe, later the wife of publisher Henry R. Luce, who wrote of her experience for the readers of *Life Magazine*.[59] She spoke of the "common danger" and "high sense of adventure" shared by her fellow voyagers as they departed. Soon after takeoff, she remembered, the scenery lost interest. "The cold, inhuman, wide, horizonless, blue-and-white beauty of this detached sector of the universe soon begins to pall." The lifeless void of sea and cloud was unrelieved by the sight of any other planes. Even ships below were rare.

Passengers talked, played cards, worked crossword puzzles, or read. "Only the Army men don't read. Sometimes they play crap games. Mostly they sit, smoking great brown cigars, or stand in the passage like monoliths. They suffer visibly for exercise. Their jaws move tirelessly: they are always the last to abandon the chewing gum passed out on the take-offs, which 'helps your ears.' " Too many meals were served for the taste of Clare Boothe: coffee and sweet rolls at dawn takeoff; sandwiches in mid-morning; "hotdogs or soup" at eleven.

A buffet luncheon, a mammoth delicatessen of cold meat and variegated canned objects is served at any time between 12 and 3, depending on the hour of landing, or the feeling the two shrewd, amiable, efficient stewards . . . have about the state of boredom into which their passengers have fallen. When all else fails, passengers dig their way out of boredom with their teeth. By the third day out the cold buffet, spread on a white sheet on the long, narrow seat of a compartment, becomes known as "The Body of the Deceased."

After the only overnight flight of the journey, the clipper landed in Honolulu at 7:00 A.M., and the passengers had a full day and night to savor the pleasures of Hawaii before a dawn departure for Midway. The early departures inflicted by flying as much as possible by daylight tended to take the edge off the luxury of the trip.

Midway and Wake were much alike for those living there: hard work and heavy sun. For the traveler, a large dinner and sleep in a hot hotel, "whirring with electric fans that barely move the still, sand-baked air." But on Wake at least, one could swim in shimmering iridescent waters or enjoy a game of tennis.

By the third full day of flying, en route to Guam, the passengers got restless, Clare Boothe reported. "They walk up and down the narrow corridor, bored with cards, talk, reading, at long last even with eating. They are beginning to be faintly irritated by only being able to smoke in the main or saloon compartment which is also the hottest." The optimal altitude for the clipper was about eight thousand feet, but when it flew lower and the weather was good, the crew would open all the windows to relieve the heat.[60]

Fatigue for the crew was far greater than fatigue for the passenger. Pilots sat but the navigator would reach the end of the flight feeling as if he had walked across the Pacific; he rarely had time to sit down during the sixty hours of flying time. Pilot Horace Brock found the Martins "clumsy and unstable." The engines set up a high vibration, and the circulation of air in the cabin was poor. Brock remembered feeling as tired off duty as on, sweating in continuously high cabin temperatures, perhaps over eighty degrees, with not enough oxygen.[61] But the perils

Life aboard a Martin clipper ca. 1935. The galley, with stewards preparing refreshments. (Pan American)

Dining aboard the Martin clipper, complete with linen tablecloth, silverware—and waiter. (Pan American)

One of the private suites (of two) aboard the Martin M-130. (Pan American)

Double-decker berths of the Martin clipper. Night flights generally were made in the San Francisco–Honolulu leg; the flights were timed so that passengers could sleep at Midway, Wake, and Guam. (Pan American)

Decor of the Martin clippers was severely "moderne" in a characteristic thirties manner. This is a regular passenger compartment. In passageway behind are the curtains of berths. (Pan American)

The Martin *Clipper* (Courtesy, Pan Am Historical Foundation)

of making a mistake were so great as to be unthinkable and kept the crew alert.

Despite an increase in the mail subsidy to $3.35 per mile in April 1939, revenues remained inadequate to cover Pan American's costs.[62] Maintaining all the way stations was extremely expensive and not offset by passenger revenues. Even if every seat were full, the Martins held only thirty-two passengers, too few to make any money. And on the California-Hawaii lap sometimes only eight passengers could be taken because flying conditions required extra fuel. Only profits from the Latin American service kept the Pacific Division alive.

The year 1938 was a bad one for Pan American. Not only was the company losing a lot of money in the new Pacific service but Musick would die in the crash of his Sikorsky *Samoa Clipper* operating on a survey flight out of Pago Pago. A second disaster was the loss of one of the three then-irreplaceable Martins, *Hawaii Clipper*, which went down somewhere between Guam and Manila. Trippe talked darkly of Japanese sabotage, but this charge was never substantiated. No trace of the aircraft was ever found. Undoubtedly, it eased the pain of the loss to think that it was caused by sabotage rather than negligence.[63]

The weekly trans-Pacific schedule had to be curtailed because it required three long-range airplanes. The Sikorskys could not fly the requisite distance with a sufficient payload, and the Boeings were not yet ready. Trippe, having established a South Pacific route to New Zealand with an extension to Australia soon likely, was losing interest in the Pacific. The establishment of these far-flung route systems, planned and discussed, sometimes even before landing rights had been acquired or a mail subsidy nailed down, and long before suitable aircraft in adequate number were available to fly them, is characteristic of the audacity and fragility of the whole enterprise. It is characteristic also of the impatience and optimism of Trippe—never satisfied with handling only one problem at a time, always out in front and scarcely glancing behind to ensure that his troops were with him.

Everywhere Pan American was struggling to maintain its service with a limited number of aircraft. The delivery of the Boeing clippers was continually delayed while the manufacturer tried to work the kinks out of them. An inadequate Sikorsky had to be used to supplement the Martins, now that one of the three of those was gone. Even after the arrival of nine Boeings, the company remained chronically short of aircraft. Yet Trippe plunged ahead on all fronts. Adding to the stretch on resources were the war in China and the demands made by the European conflict after 1939, which caused Pan American constantly to rewrite its schedules and remap its routes.

During the 1920s, the world's airlines had begun to expand their markets from passengers and mail to a variety of "lightweight low-bulk com-

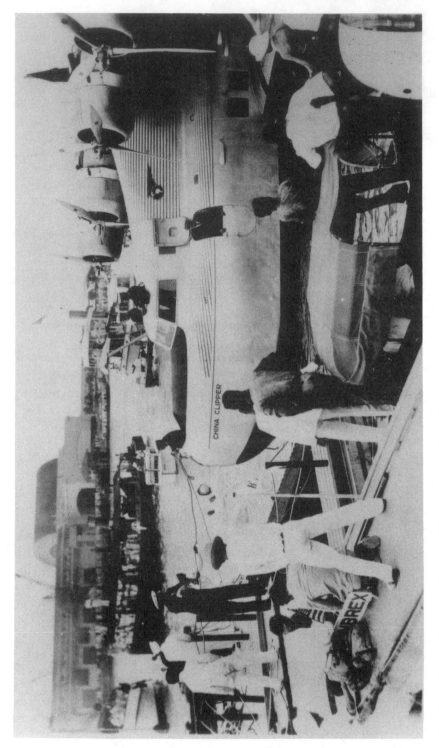

The *China Clipper* (Courtesy, Pan Am Historical Foundation)

modities with a high time-related value."[64] Film and flowers, tropical fruits, baby chicks, wedding gowns, newsreels, false teeth, machine parts, letters of credit, and bills of lading were the sorts of things that could be best sent by air. As the shadows of war deepened across the Pacific, military cargo increased in importance, and Pan American's prospects improved. American aviation, blessed by a huge and potentially prosperous domestic market, flourished despite the depression; the industry stimulated competition among airplane manufacturers and began to set the world standard, leaving Europe behind.

By establishing its routes across the Pacific, Pan American bound Asia and the Antipodes to the United States in a new way. J. T. Trippe had accomplished what E. H. Harriman had only hoped to do, creating a world transportation network with the Pacific as its center. War would both shatter and reshape this global pattern in unanticipated ways.

PART SIX

WAR, THE NORTH PACIFIC, AND "THE NEW AMERICAN FRONTIER," 1941–1945

The new frontier extends from Minneapolis, via our Pacific coast states and Alaska and through Siberia and China, all the way to Central Asia.

—Henry A. Wallace

CHAPTER TWENTY-FOUR

War Challenges Pacific Transport

War with Japan invested the Pacific with new prominence for Americans. Strategically the United States had hitherto been preoccupied with Hitler, although not yet fighting him. The Japanese likewise had been facing away from the Pacific, preoccupied with fighting China. Both the United States and Japan had to engage each other directly across the great ocean and therefore had to try to shrink that space to manageable proportions. New aerial transport technologies and new weapons of naval warfare—the aircraft carrier and its accompanying vessels— offered that possibility.

World War II was a genuine global conflict involving the Pacific rim as much as the Atlantic. Although the Allied grand strategy dictated that Hitler be defeated first, for most Americans the Japan war seemed as important as that in Europe, and perhaps even more so. The United States was more vulnerable in the Pacific, in Alaska as well as in Hawaii, than it was in the Atlantic. The Germans could not attack or even threaten the United States as the Japanese had done. And whereas in the European conflict the United States joined a coalition of powers to fight a war that had already been underway for two years, in the Pacific, all the powers except China went to war at the same time, and the Allies played a role very much subordinate to the United States.

Americans fought much of their war against Japan in Southeast Asia and the South Pacific. Japan had already occupied and consolidated its position in all of the Asian North Pacific rimlands except Siberia, which was part of the neutral Soviet Union. Until Japan began to lose, the Japanese dominated much of the North Pacific oceanic space and, by seizing two Aleutian islands, even held a toehold in the American North Pacific rimlands for a time.

The prewar U.S. policy of attempting to dissuade the Japanese from attempting to absorb China had utterly failed. Americans found their commercial objectives in China increasingly elusive; they may have reached the Orient but had failed to grasp it. And unreality had gripped American strategic planners who had set their goals of defending the western Pacific without having the means to achieve them. Now the nation had to pay the penalty for this folly.

The U.S. Army and Navy lacked the power to protect Guam, the Philippines, or a U.S. presence anywhere in the western Pacific. The Pearl Harbor attack drastically altered the balance of power in the Pacific within a few hours, putting Americans on the strategic defensive and ushering in months of defeat and disaster for the arms of the United States throughout the far western Pacific. Southeast Asia, both insular and peninsular, rapidly fell under Japanese control. Australia, even India, trembled.

The United States had to recruit, train, and equip a huge armed force and then transport and supply it around the globe. The war created unprecedented demands for mass transport and stimulated global international air services. Among the Allies, chiefly Britain and the United States, the common cause temporarily submerged old national rivalries, fusing everyone together in the spirit of alliance for victory. Strategic necessities swallowed commercial controversies.

Pearl Harbor thrust Pan American Airways into a new vulnerability; its planes and its bases became military targets. At Wake Island, Japanese planes destroyed the hotel and the radio station minutes after beginning an attack. Nine employees lay dead. Waves of Japanese aircraft bombed and machine-gunned Guam repeatedly, and company employees who escaped death were later captured, spending the rest of the war languishing in prison camps in Japan. The *Hong Kong Clipper*, moored at the pier in Hong Kong and scheduled to return to Manila that day, never took off again. Set afire by a Japanese bomb, the aircraft burned to the waterline.

At Midway, shells from Japanese warships began to fall shortly before 10:00 P.M. on that momentous December 7. All Pan American's people survived the attack, and they were later safely withdrawn by ship. The *Philippine Clipper*, landing for fuel an hour after the shelling, had no trouble finding its destination because of the tower of flames roaring above the island. No clippers lay at Manila, but the resident Pan American staff there would experience the same fate as those stationed on Guam: Japanese prison camp.

The war thus wiped out Pan American's central Pacific route; flights now stopped at Honolulu. But California-Hawaii traffic would swell enormously, binding the islands far more tightly to the mainland than ever before. This and other new wartime activities saved Pan American from heavy financial losses.

The U.S. Navy assumed direction over what was left of Pan American's Pacific Division, and much of the first wartime traffic carried eastbound from Honolulu consisted of women, children, and the wounded being pulled out of Pearl Harbor. Westbound, the planes carried people with special skills requisite to the Pearl Harbor emergency, as well as cargoes of vaccines, blood plasma, and other badly needed medical supplies.[1] Pearl Harbor Day found *Pacific Clipper* (a Boeing 314) in New Zealand, its normal route homeward across the South Pacific cut off by the hostilities. To get home, the great seaplane took off heading west, flying through Australia on to Java, Ceylon, India, Bahrain, across the waist of Africa to Brazil and north to Trinidad and New York City. This thirty-one-thousand mile trip was the first circumnavigation by a commercial airplane and provided a suitably dramatic end to Pan American's prewar trans-Pacific service.

The global trip was also a sign of the shape of things to come. The war gave hitherto peripheral areas new significance as alternate air transportation routes. Japanese conquest of the western Pacific and Southeast Asia and the Axis domination of most of Europe made it necessary to open new pathways around the edges of these huge areas.

While fighting raged in the South Pacific, the China front lapsed into virtual inactivity. There the Chinese, both Communists and Nationalists, jostled to improve their respective positions and watched the greater conflict beyond. CNAC, largely flying in skies dominated by Japanese military aircraft, dodged attack as best it could and was probably the only airline in the world that cancelled flights because of good weather.

The U.S. Navy and Marine Corps hopped in bloody conflict from island to island across the Pacific, with the aim of bringing American air power within striking range of Japan's industrial heartland. The army under Douglas MacArthur fought its way northward through New Guinea and the Solomons back into the Philippines.

With the exception of the Aleutian campaign, the North Pacific figured only indirectly until the ring of fire closed on Japan in the last terrible months of the conflict. In bloody struggle, Americans then occupied Okinawa and pummelled the home islands. The Japanese strategy had been to consolidate their newly conquered empire, hold out, and force the United States into a negotiated peace. The U.S. strategy was to regain control of the western Pacific in order to crush Japan, liberate the Philippines, and affirm the independence and integrity of China.

At the outbreak of war, the United States had only twenty-seven four-engine air transports, of which Pan American's clippers were a big part.[2] In May 1940 Franklin Roosevelt had called for the nation to turn out fifty thousand planes a year, about the same number as the United States had built during the entire time since Kitty Hawk.[3] For manufacturers the growing complexity of aeronautical technology made these orders a huge challenge. Building airplanes was not like building automobiles. Airplanes demanded a high degree of precision, and did not lend themselves easily to mass production. They were not simply replicas of an initial design. Each plane had its own personality. The commonly used collective term *copy* is therefore something of a misnomer. Yet the president's program was a striking success. Not only fighters and bombers but also transports rolled out of the factories in unprecedented numbers. New models sprang from the drafting board.

As important as changing sizes and shapes of airplanes or even their performances were new devices enabling them to operate with greater safety. Radar proved of prime importance in guiding the airplane through bad weather, and a new de-icing device using engine exhaust to warm wing surfaces removed one of the greatest dangers to flight, particularly in far northern regions.

The army and the navy each created its own "airline"; the Air Transport Command and the Naval Air Transport Service both worked with the civil airlines. Pan American became particularly close to the navy, its longtime unofficial partner in the Pacific. ATC established a Pacific Division in January 1942, and by the acme of its activity in 1945, its routes alone covered forty-two thousand miles and used more than five hundred airplanes, more than had existed in the entire prewar scheduled commercial air fleet of the United States.[4] The intensified use of air transport in the Pacific region would greatly accelerate the postwar development of commercial aviation there. Weather stations, aids to navigation like radar and the new Loran (long-range radio beams), and airfields sprang up in large networks and, although some were abandoned at war's end, many remained for peacetime use.

Surface transport posed as great a challenge as the air did. In World War I the United States had to move its army across only one ocean, the North Atlantic. This time, massive sealifts were required on both the Atlantic and the Pacific. Their success provided an essential ingredient in the Allied victory. Again the United States faced the prospect of war with ships that were too old and too few. Those in service mostly dated from the great shipbuilding boom of War War I.[5] Under the immensely capable leadership of Vice Admiral Emory S. Land, who was appointed chairman of the U.S. Maritime Commission in February 1938, an ambitious and highly successful shipbuilding program was got underway well before the United States began to fight. Admiral Land was fully aware of the mistakes made in the previous war and determined to avoid them. This time the government paid shipbuilders their costs plus a minimum fee but with a bonus awarded for efficient use of resources.

Soaring demand forced production targets constantly to increase. During 1940 and early 1941 the Germans were sinking Allied ships at an accelerating rate, faster than replacements could be built. But the Americans did not set new goals without careful planning. Probably the most important decision was to build ships with a standardized design lending itself to rapid production. The first and major ship type was the Liberty; more than twenty-five hundred of these would slide down the ways before the war was over.

The enormous demand also caused the character of American shipbuilding to change from artisanship to mass production. Prefabricating and arc welding and the assignment of workers to only a few basic tasks sped the construction process. Workers quickly achieved proficiency. This meant that it was easier to recruit people, and it took far less time to train them. In June 1939, some eighty thousand people worked in private American shipyards; that number swelled at its peak in November 1943 to more than 1.4 million.[6] Many of them, like Rosie the Riveter, were women. Total construction time required for a Liberty, from keel-laying to commissioning, shrank from nine months to one. The speed of shipbuilding was so great that steel mills found themselves hard pressed to meet the demand for plate. A combination of prodigious production and the cutting of losses from enemy action meant that at war's end the inventory of merchant shipping, U.S. and British combined, was twice what it had been when the war started.[7] The United States in 1945 was well equipped to dominate the shipping lanes, not simply of the Pacific but of the entire world. But Americans failed to make it happen.

CHAPTER TWENTY-FIVE

New Routes and New Frontiers

Surface transport, the highway, also comes to figure in North Pacific international history and in America's reach toward the Orient. One of the most dramatic episodes during the war, capturing the imagination and engaging the interest of the public, perhaps because it was an epic constructive act at a time when so much of the news dealt with destructive ones, was the building of the Alaska Highway. The Alcan, as it was called, is surely one of the great engineering works of the first half of the twentieth century and an important internal binder for the American side of the North Pacific region.

Like the first transcontinental railroads, the highway carried a pioneer aura, its building provided an epic of human achievement in a challenging environment. As an engineering challenge, the highway could be compared to the Panama Canal. It is a tale of struggle and suffering to a positive end. Like the railways, the Alcan Highway was crudely and rapidly built and required almost immediate reconstruction. Even today it is not totally paved.

The sixteen-hundred-mile highway was laid out under the pressure of war and the seeming threat of Japanese attack. Its purported aim was to supply and service a string of new airfields that would form an aerial pathway, allowing the United States to send planes to the Soviet Union to bolster the Russian war effort. In the mid-1930s Ottawa had shown some interest in an aerial northwest passage to Asia, to China via the great circle route through Siberia. The Canadians had therefore built in 1939 a network of landing strips, known as the Northwest Staging Route, equipped with rudimentary lighting and radio range stations, linking Edmonton with Fairbanks.

But military reasons provided only an immediate rationale for the Alcan Highway. Before the war, people who favored such a road saw it as a source of employment when jobs were particularly scarce and as a means to open up a potentially rich wilderness to tourism and economic development. Historically, the geographical pull of the Canadian nation had been east-west for political and strategic reasons or to the south for commercial ones.

The Alcan, a thrust to the north, resonated with emotional overtones, with sentiments of national rivalry and age-old Canadian fears of American intrusion. Many Canadians saw an Alaska-Canada highway as a response to the priorities of the south rather than to the needs of the north. Would not any highway to Alaska financed by Americans inevitably be controlled by Americans and built to their best interest, not necessarily those of Canadians? Such a highway might "prevent our being masters in our own house," one newspaper complained.[1] Americans thought little about Canadian sensitivities, and, as usual, the indigenous peoples who would be most immediately affected by such a road were not consulted at all.[2]

Before 1941, the realities of transportation made Alaska in effect a remote "island" with many of its parts themselves so mutually isolated as to be islands. The U.S. military, especially the navy, saw no particular value in a highway to Alaska; the most strategic parts of the territory were coastal, best defended and supplied by sea. Sea routes to Alaska were shorter than any land route could be. And, in any event, they would remain essential to the territory's defense. Air routes still could supplement sea routes of communication only tentatively.

But with the possibility after Hitler's invasion of Russia in June 1941 that the Japanese might attack Siberia and threaten Alaska, U.S. military interest in a highway to Alaska began to quicken. The question was one of allocating scarce resources at a time of feverish demand for them virtually everywhere. Six months later, Japan's attack on Hawaii inflated American expectations of Japanese intentions and capabilities. Since much of the U.S. fleet was destroyed or put out of action at Pearl Harbor, many doubted the navy's ability to guard the North American coast. If the enemy should continue to be successful at sea, Alaska's vulnerability would greatly increase, and a land route to it would take on new validity.

Many people still argued against a highway; the required machinery, materials, and engineering talent, taken inevitably at the expense of other parts of the war effort, the expected length of time to build the road, and the inability of any road to reach such island nerve centers as Dutch Harbor, Kodiak, or Sitka were potent reasons for not doing it.[3] Nonetheless, President Roosevelt approved the project on February 11, 1942, and Canada agreed to it two days later, although more for political and monetary than strategic reasons. The Americans wanted it; the Americans were willing to pay for it; let the Americans do it.

The war also required new sources of fuel available to use in the North Pacific region. In the "Canol" (Canadian oil) project the U.S. government for the first time got involved significantly in extracting oil abroad.[4] Norman Wells, on the Mackenzie River close to the Arctic Circle in the Northwest Territories, was developed as a source of fuel for Alaskan air bases. To get the oil out required a 577-mile pipeline to Whitehorse. But the Canol project could be carried out with no regard for cost because it was a strategic, not a commercial, venture. Since Alaska was fuel dependent, a pipeline would avoid the dangers of shipment by sea.

Even after the Japanese threat faded, the demand for oil remained because of the need to fuel aircraft flying the Arctic route to the Soviet Union. The Canol project ultimately was dismantled but not before provoking American criticism for its cost. "We have just carried on a gigantic W.P.A. [Works Project Administration, a much criticized New Deal program] project for the benefit of the Canadian people, opening up the Canadian wilderness, and Uncle Sam isn't getting anything out of it," one congressman complained.[5]

The large U.S. presence in the Canadian north resulting from the highway and the pipeline alarmed some Canadians about the proprietary interest the United States seemed to be showing about Canada's vast, undeveloped lands. Some Canadians felt that "the Americans are developing our country while we are fighting the war." The British were not reluctant to fan these emotions because of their own fears about U.S. ambitions, specifically for postwar domination of the Canadian aerial route to Asia. In the words of one of them, "The Canadians see perpetually the United States rolling up the Highway or streaming through the air to war along the Aleutians, while neither they themselves nor a single Canadian vehicle nor a single Canadian aircraft are on a similar errand."[6] And another Englishman suggested ominously that because of extensive U.S. aerial reconnaissance of the Canadian Northwest, "the Americans are more awake to the importance of the Canadian North-West than are the Canadian authorities!"[7]

But in the Alcan project Canadians would be very much involved: surveying, mapping, and building too. The American Army Engineers formed less than half of the work party; Canadian construction companies labored alongside the Americans, working with everything from hand tools to twenty-three-ton bulldozers that punched through the forest sometimes moving six abreast. One-third of the American work force were African-American soldiers, assigned over the objections of General Simon Bolivar Buckner, commanding general in Alaska whose father had been a general in the Confederate army. One member of an indigenous community who woke up one morning to the roar of oncoming bulldozers remarked that the first white men he had ever seen were black. Construction was a matter of months, not years, the sixteen hundred miles of cutting, clearing, filling, and grading all done essentially in one working season of mosquitoes and blackflies. The men worked long hours, sometimes twelve-hour shifts seven days a week; the machines were rarely stilled. Little attention was paid to the niceties. Speed was top priority. One local boss was reprimanded, "Your road is too good, too wide, and too short."[8]

The road surface could be dressed with gravel or perhaps a thin coat of asphalt, or it might be simply hard–packed earth or even "corduroy," corrugated logs laid side by side, squeezed in tightly together. The workers strung up bridges as rapidly as possible; sometimes these were merely simple wooden trestles, intended to be replaced as soon as possible by something sturdier. Some steel bridges were brought in pieces from the United States for on-site reassembly.

By late November, nine months after President Roosevelt approved the project, the trucks were rolling into Fairbanks. Soon deep winter set in, and the temperature plummeted to seventy degrees Fahrenheit below zero. Up to six feet of ice piled up in some spots on the roadbed. Much of the original work did not survive the first winter and the rainy summer that followed. The worst problem faced by the builders was not the weather but the climate; permafrost seemed to render all building temporary, and Americans had had little experience coping with this problem of far northern life.

The great highway and the speed with which its initial form was laid down captured the public imagination as an illustration of the power of sheer will mobilized for the war effort. And yet as an artery of transport, the Alaska-Canada highway was not truly significant. At war's end, it proved not a suitable road for tourists; the public was led to excessive expectations. And the Canadians, whose responsibility the highway now became, were left with the problem of having to build and maintain a road of the quality the United States had seemed to promise but had not in fact provided.[9]

The eye of the American public in wartime was also drawn to the Far Northwest because of the Aleutians. This little-known island chain had gained new strategic significance because of its position on the great circle route, closest to Japan on the shortest path between North American and Japan. In June 1942 the Japanese bombed Dutch Harbor and seized Kiska and Attu at the end of the Aleutian chain. Because the United States had not fortified the archipelago west of Dutch Harbor, the Japanese "conquest" might more accurately have been called an occupation. Nonetheless, it was psychologically damaging. The Congress had made no appropriations for Alaskan defense until after the outbreak of war on Europe.

In 1941, Alaska's population (about seventy-two thousand, half of them indigenes) was not growing, and its economy remained undeveloped. Alaska's leading industry would rapidly become defense. Americans had largely forgotten about their great northern territory, but the new air age and the war would remind them of its wealth, promise, and especially its vulnerability. In February 1942, Chief of Naval Operations Admiral Ernest J. King warned Governor Ernest Gruening that the navy was not at all sure that Alaska could even be held against the Japanese.[10]

The Japanese may simply have launched their Aleutian campaign as an attempt to divert the Americans away from the central Pacific, but the foray also served Japan defensively as a means to cut off a potential northern entry route to the home islands. The Aleutians, which form the farthest western extension of the North American continent, provide the shortest path across the Pacific. The successful Japanese invasion was only one of many humiliations suffered by the Americans in the early months of the war with Japan, but it held a peculiar sting because enemy soldiers had not set foot on U.S. soil since the War of 1812.

The Aleutian weather may have been a tougher opponent than the Japanese. Certainly it brought more misery. More casualties were caused by exposure than by enemy fire. The weather was both too cold and too warm. For fliers it was especially bad, particularly the fogs and storms of the coastal areas. The ceiling in the Aleutians, they said, "went up and down like a whore's drawers."[11] Conditions to the far north were more consistent, but that was not where the fighting took place. Freezing drizzle, frequent rain and sleet, high winds, especially the notorious and capricious williwaw whipping up mountainous seas—all these phenomena complicated any attempts to move around by either air or sea. For the thousands of Americans who served in the Aleutians during the war, everything had to be imported, the islands offered nothing to the soldier. This required a huge logistical effort. War is never pleasant; service in the Aleutians seemed to be particularly challenging, and troop morale reflected it. The local joke was that the straitjacket was soon to become regular army issue there.[12]

In May 1943, the Americans took Attu in a bloody struggle. This was leapfrogging, the first instance of a process that would be characteristic of much of the U.S. wartime movement across the Pacific. U.S. forces bypassed the nearer Kiska for Attu in part because they thought the Japanese would not expect them to do so. Only a handful of the defending Japanese allowed themselves to be taken prisoner; all the others died. Inadequate equipment, lack of training for operating in the sub-Arctic, and uncertain command handicapped the U.S. effort. The Japanese had problems too, chiefly uncertain supplies of food, ammunition, and everything else a soldier needs. Japan was poorer than the United States, and Japanese logistics reflected it. The Japanese were building airfields on their captured territory with pick, shovel, and pushcart. The Americans had bulldozers to build theirs.

No survivors, American or Japanese, suffered more than the some 850 Aleut people who were evacuated on twelve hours' notice, made refugees by U.S. government decree, and moved to southeastern Alaska. In addition to the profound shock of deracination, the Aleuts were obliged to live wretchedly in makeshift homes like abandoned fish canneries and gold mines. Their disease rates soared; medical care and sanitation were inadequate and of poor quality. One of ten Aleuts died.[13] When peace came they were allowed to return home, but when they did, they found a landscape scarred and torn by war and occupation. Their villages were plundered and destroyed, their fishing grounds fouled. Once again, Aleut culture had suffered grievously at the hand of whites. Not that the Japanese were any better masters. Half of the Aleuts they took back to Hokkaido for imprisonment did not survive the war.[14]

Losing Attu, the Japanese on Kiska, in Dashiell Hammett's words, were "not surrounded, for with the weather as violent as it is in the Aleutians no island can ever be kept surrounded—but pinched between our bases."[15] The subsequent "invasion" of Kiska on August 15, 1943, turned out to be something of a farce, an "optical Aleutian," as one army man quipped.[16] U.S. forces bombed and shelled the island for three weeks before staging a poorly executed landing, to discover that the only living creatures still on Kiska were a few abandoned dogs. The Japanese, early on during the U.S. attack, had taken advantage of a thick fog to slip away home undetected. One American commented: "We dropped 100,000 propaganda leaflets on Kiska but those dogs couldn't read."[17] The only casualties came from friendly fire, a phenomenon all too frequent in warfare.

Douglas MacArthur had written General H. H. "Hap" Arnold, commanding general of the Army Air Forces, that the Japanese seizure of the Aleutians was "part of the general move into Siberia."[18] Because of the initial triumphs of the Japanese, the tendency was to exaggerate what they might be able to do next. The northern front was not to have any particular significance in the U.S.-Japan war in the long run. The Japanese never moved any farther eastward because they lacked the resources to do so; the Americans never used the Aleutians or the rest of Alaska in a meaningful way in carrying the war to Japan and its end.

But the impact of war and invasion on the overall development of Alaska and of Pacific air transport would be important. Ten percent of the local population joined the armed forces.[19] And the arrival of troops from the "lower 48" and the building of bases to house them set off the biggest economic boom in the history of the territory. With air services and the highway forming new connective tissue, Alaska was united to the continental United States as never before.

Franklin Roosevelt saw Alaska as henceforth an important segment of the great circle route, stretching from Puget Sound to Siberia, and a place to encourage American pioneering. After his death and with the onset of the Cold War, Alaska took on new significance and new vulnerability as America's strategic frontier with the Soviet Union, ending the war with a population growth of 78 percent and with three hundred military bases, large and small, representing a $3 billion investment by the federal government.[20] General Billy Mitchell, the early apostle of air power, had often been quoted as saying that "he who controls Alaska will control the world." Strategic realities gave new credence to his words.

The search for a means of supplying Nationalist China in the war against the Japanese led to the opening of the Hump, an aerial freight line between India and China, made necessary by the closure of all the Pacific routes into China. Like the Alcan Highway it was an attempt to establish new and unconventional routes to the Orient. Although the Hump would be devoid of lasting strategic or commercial importance, this air service was the first strategic airlift in history, and it showed dramatically the remarkable and growing capabilities of air transport.

The Hump, a forerunner of the much bigger Berlin airlift of 1949, opened new strategic opportunities, but no other route posed a greater challenge than flying over the Himalayas. The Hump pushed aeronautical technology to its outer limits. This massive, sustained, and scheduled supply effort started in jungle lowlands and then crossed some of the world's highest and most forbidding mountains, with violent updrafts, sudden thunderstorms, severe icing, hail, and sleet all common. And as if these were not enough, the possibility always lurked of attack by Japanese fighter planes. No help was available on the ground in any emergency, and the northern India home of the operation was situated halfway around the world from the source of all its vital supplies.

The Hump proved as challenging and as costly to the airplane as the Horn was to the sailing ship, with the difference that the accelerated pace of the twentieth century doomed the successful aviator to make his journey many times. Both Horn and Hump were routes that people were glad to give up as soon as alternatives were available.

The service became an American Air Transport Command operation in which Pan American's China affiliate, CNAC, would play an important role under the skillful and sensitive leadership of William L. Bond. CNAC got the project started and remained a part of it after the army air force took over, making the operation a combined military-civil effort.

Some of the route over the Hump had never even been crossed by an airplane until the freight run began. Maps yielded little helpful information. Not much romance was tied to the effort, and many of the best air force pilots chose to fly in combat, not to ferry freight, leaving their less experienced colleagues to do so. During 1943 and early 1944, one airplane was lost in every two hundred flights, and every thousand tons of cargo carried cost three American lives.[21]

These grim statistics improved tremendously under the leadership of General William Tunner, with gratifying results. At its peak under General Tunner, the service carried almost fifteen hundred tons of cargo daily, 60 percent of which was gasoline.[22] Sixty thousand American soldiers in China, and many more Chinese, were supplied solely by this route. It is one reason why China stayed in the war, and 1.5 million Japanese troops remained tied down there, not free to fight elsewhere.

CHAPTER TWENTY-SIX

Flying to Russia

Before World War II, very few American public figures had ever traveled abroad, even when out of office. Time did not permit it. They made policy without direct acquaintance with the people or the landscape of foreign places. Now the new global air routes offered fresh possibilities for the firsthand gathering of information and the exercising of informal diplomacy by important persons, both in office and out. Even the president traveled abroad.

The publicity given by the new global travelers was helpful to the Allied war effort because it demonstrated that the Axis could not compete with the Allied command over intercontinental strategic routes. This handicap was one reason why the German-Italian alliance with Japan could remain only a distant and hollow relationship. The Axis could hold no summit conferences like Tehran, Yalta, or Cairo. Japan had to fight its war in virtual isolation from its partners.

But the airplane also brought new hazards to the practice of diplomacy. The new transportation made possible quick, nonreflective trips more conducive to the illusion of international understanding than to the reality of it. And to the general public, for whom such experiences remained highly exotic, the traveler became an instant expert, whether deserving of such respect or not.

The first prominent American wartime traveler was Wendell Willkie, the defeated Republican presidential candidate (1940). Franklin Roosevelt made Willkie his "personal representative," an unofficial roving ambassador, using him as a way of showing U.S. political unity and a means of cultivating personal relationships with world leaders in which Roosevelt had such a keen interest. A Chinese newspaper reported that Willkie was the first leading U.S. statesman to visit China since former president Ulysses S. Grant in 1879.[1]

During the autumn of 1942, Willkie traveled thirty-one thousand miles in forty-nine days in a converted B-24 Liberator bomber named *Gulliver*. Willkie, born and raised in Indiana, became a highly successful New York lawyer and utilities magnate, but his backers in 1940 tried to portray him as the quintessential midwestern American. Frank, exuberant, and energetic, the ursine Willkie was described by one journalist as "the Four Freedoms taken out of the realm of the abstract and clothed in a rumpled blue suit."[2] Tumbling out of his airplane and calling for an end to European colonialism, Willkie dreamed of a postwar world in which "there shall be an equality of opportunity for every race and every nation."[3] Clare Boothe Luce, whose husband was one of Willkie's most enthusiastic backers, hailed Willkie as "a global Abraham Lincoln."[4]

Although they did not elect him president, the American public developed an immense appetite for Willkie's kind of idealism, inspired by both the emotion of wartime alliances and a contemplation of the peace to follow. They rushed to buy the book Willkie wrote describing his trip. Bookstores found themselves unable to stock sufficient copies of *One World* to satisfy the demand for it, and the critics waxed as enthusiastic as the public. Many Americans were prepared to believe that the rhythm of international politics would change, the nations would no longer fight wars or jockey for power. Many foresaw a huge expansion in the demand for international air travel and in the practice of citizen diplomacy. Speaking to an American radio audience estimated at thirty-six million, Willkie proclaimed that "the myriad millions of human beings of the Far East are as close to us as Los Angeles is to New York by the fastest railroad trains. . . . Our thinking and planning in the future must be global."[5]

Vice President Henry A. Wallace was another prominent American wartime globetrotter. Wallace went to Asia in the early summer of 1944, during his last year in office as vice president. Franklin Roosevelt was much interested in China; the old China trade lay within his genes and had furnished the base of the Delano family fortune. The president was ready to invest China with great power status when Churchill and Stalin were not. Wallace later would write that Roosevelt believed that "the West Coast of the United States had an ever-growing future because of the rapidly expanding population in Soviet Asia and the rapid increase in the standard of living in China."[6]

Roosevelt had a wide vision of the North Pacific future, but it did not include Japan. He was not alone in making this omission. Many other Americans simply thought that a defeated Japan would be a nonexistent Japan, at least in an active international sense. The vision of China alone as the real Orient persisted.

Wallace's mission was vague; he had wanted to go to the Soviet Union only, but Roosevelt was against it, at least initially. In his diary Wallace quotes the president as saying, "I think they are going to be shooting at you during the campaign for being too far to the left. My own feeling is that you had better not go to Russia. . . . I think it would be better for you to go to China by way of Alaska and Siberia. You could stop off and visit some of the towns in Siberia on your way to Chungking."[7] Yet later the president warmed to the idea, adding, "I think you ought to see a lot of Siberia."[8]

Roosevelt was interested in minimizing conflict between China and the Soviet Union and thought that Wallace might come up with some interesting information about the little-known border areas between the two Asian nations. He also wanted Wallace to put pressure on Chiang Kai-shek to make an agreement with the Chinese Communists in order to fight Japan with more vigor.[9] Wallace returned home just in time for the July 1944 Democratic National Convention at which he was dumped from the presidential ticket and replaced by Senator Harry S Truman.

Alice Roosevelt Longworth characteristically dismissed Wallace derisively as "Farmer Wallace."[10] Urbane and sophisticated Washington did not quite know what to make of the enigmatic Iowan. His personal style was simple and unsophisticated, and yet there was more complexity to Wallace's character than many people realized. He knew a lot. Even before serving eight years as secretary of agriculture, Wallace had long experience in agricultural matters, and he possessed a wide-ranging intellectual curiosity and a voracious appetite for reading. But the idealistic notions of international affairs he came up with struck many people as hopelessly naive, and his many critics were quick to dismiss his thinking as woolly. Wallace's chief problems were that his enthusiasm sometimes carried him beyond the limits of his knowledge, and he tended to think other people were as well intentioned as he.

On his trip to the Soviet Union Wallace showed that he knew a lot more about soils than he did about Stalinism. He made careful observations of agricultural conditions and talked extensively to local experts. He remarked constantly on the similarities between the American and the Russian frontier experience, but he seemed to have no idea of the political prison camp system in Siberia, worse than anything under the tsars, nor did he seem to understand the real functions of the NKVD, Soviet secret police and predecessor of the KGB. Wallace described the Far Northern Construction Trust, which built the roads and railroads and ran the gold mines, as "a combination TVA [Tennessee Valley Authority] and Hudson's Bay Company."[11] The comparison would have been more apt if either of those North American organizations had habitually used forced labor or shot recalcitrant workers.[12]

Wallace's Soviet hosts tried hard to preserve their guest's conviction that the Soviet Union was marching toward democracy. While Wallace was in Magadan, notorious for its prison camps, the watch towers were temporarily taken down and the prisoners kept busy and out of sight watching movies for three days. Local inhabitants were delighted to see the shop windows suddenly filled with a wide range of goods.[13] If Wallace had heard of Potemkin villages, he apparently did not think of them in a Siberian context. But Wallace did study international affairs conscientiously; he spoke Spanish fluently, and his trips to Latin America generated a lot of local enthusiasm. Beginning the study of Russian in 1942, he had learned enough phrases to attempt a speech in that language during his Soviet tour.

Importantly Wallace held a vision of a global future transcending the Atlantic centered, arguing that too many Americans still viewed Russia solely through a European prism. European money and European bankers, heavily engaged in the tsarist economy, had made the nation a "semicolony of Europe," Wallace judged. Americans of necessity did their business with Russia via Europe, and often indirectly, losing in the process. But Wallace believed that the postwar development of Siberia would open enormous opportunities to American business, especially that part of it located on the Pacific coast.

Wallace's political idealism pushed aside in his mind any possible difficulties in erecting postwar commercial and aerial networks. He saw U.S. wartime aid programs as laying the foundations for a vastly expanded world trade flowing across the oceans and spanning the continents. The great circle northern polar airways would become, he proclaimed, "the world's peacetime highways."[14]

Like Vilhjalmur Stefansson, Wallace believed that development of northern intercontinental transportation routes would ultimately greatly increase the population and prosperity of Alaska and the whole U.S. Northwest, as well as benefiting neighboring Asia, both China and the Soviet Union. And he would later recall that, mindful of the need to find jobs for the demobilized after the war, he mentioned to Soviet foreign minister Vyacheslav Molotov the need for public works projects to "stir the imagination of all peoples in the world." Wallace suggested building a combined highway and air route linking South America to western Europe by way of Alaska and Siberia. "Molotov's first reaction was: 'No nation can do it by itself.' Then he said: 'You and I will live to see the day.' "[15]

Wallace put the British commonwealth alongside the United States, Soviet Union, and China as a major Pacific power. But the United States was clearly to be the first among equals. "I have faith," Wallace said, "that American economic leadership will confer on the Pacific region a great material benefit and on the world a great blessing."[16]

The Wallace optimism was echoed by Franklin Roosevelt, who also traveled out to the Pacific in August 1944 to confer in Hawaii with his top commanders in the Pacific theater. In a speech afterward to the

American public, Roosevelt said, "It is logical that we should foresee a great interchange of commerce between our shores and those of Siberia and China. And in this commercial development Alaska and the Aleutian Islands become automatic stepping-stones for trade, both by water and by cargo planes."[17] Roosevelt had, of course, taken the first step toward reopening the North Pacific Beringian barrier by his decision ten years earlier to renew diplomatic relations with the Soviet Union.

For his Asian trip, and what would today be called Air Force Two, Wallace used a C-47 Dakota drawn from the Air Transport Command, one of some two thousand transport aircraft then flying all over the world, collectively logging 2 million miles every twenty-four hours. He saw the plane as a "fine spacious ship," its "trim lines" suggesting to him the sailing clippers.[18] At the president's suggestion, Mongolia and Inner Asia expert Owen Lattimore accompanied the vice president, the most high-ranking American yet to visit the Soviet Union and the first vice president ever to travel abroad on an official mission. On this tour via what Lattimore called the "new Road to Asia," the vice presidential party flew seven thousand miles from Washington to Irkutsk in ten days, making eleven stops. The flight caused Wallace to think of the shrinkage of distances air travel was causing, creating what he called our new "sixty-hour world."[19] In travel time, he observed, the whole world was now smaller than the United States of America in George Washington's day; "the rowboat that carried Washington across the Delaware at Valley Forge [*sic*] was on a par with the [airplane] . . . which carried President Roosevelt overseas to Casablanca."[20]

Wallace noted that his path for the most part lay more than a thousand miles north of the great transcontinental railroads. Much of it was the Alaska-Siberia (Alsib) route developed for the ferrying of American aircraft given to the Soviet Union in support of the Russian war effort. Lattimore opined that this new route, which Pan American had so long coveted, might offer a landplane alternative to the mid-Pacific flying boats. Each pathway, he suggested, held "its own advantages for American enterprise and America's now vast and diversified resources in planes, flying personnel, and flying know-how."[21] The land-based route would pass to the north of the stormy Aleutians, heading for Yakutsk, which Lattimore points out occupies in eastern Siberia a position analogous to Fairbanks in Alaska, and on into the part of the Soviet Union that is geographically closest to the United States yet least known to Americans. As Lattimore reminds us, the Russian Far East was better known to Americans in the nineteenth century than it came to be in the twentieth.

The artificiality of the Bering barrier intrigued Wallace, and he pointed out the community of problems and commonality of occupations uniting the indigenous peoples of the Far North on both sides of the strait. They are all, he noted, trappers, fishermen, or hunters of the reindeer. And the community of interests extends farther to the south, to the peoples of European origin mining in the Kolyma or the Yukon, or farming in Alberta or Buryat Mongolia.

Wallace remarked that "technology and war have destroyed Western Europe as the center of world power. In a geopolitical sense, the center of world power is shifting toward the Pacific; its primary foci of industrial strength being midcontinental North America and the heartland of Eurasia, now linked together by air across the north, by water across the Pacific. This will be the axis of strategic power in the coming era of the Pacific."[22] The Wallace vision of the Pacific was therefore more of the periphery than of the center; he looked to the continental cores, not their coastlines or the ocean uniting them. And he looked to American initiatives to spin the whole together.

The challenge, he said, would be to ensure that the Pacific would be an area of cooperation, not of conflict, both in commerce and in politics. If Asian agriculture should improve and raise local living standards, Wallace saw Asian peoples as new customers for American goods and investments, and he wanted international commercial exchanges on the basis of equality. He worried that "the range of industry and trade was enormously expanded in the steamship age of the nineteenth century, but the steamship was also the vehicle of nineteenth-century colonial exploitation. It is to our interest that the power and speed of the airplane should be made to serve the century of the common man and should not be perverted to the uses of any new age of airborne colonialism."[23]

International aviation, Wallace speculated, could become either a source of international discord or an integrator of economic regions and political groups. Wallace was captivated by the phrase *freedom of the air* and smitten with the idea of an international air authority that would open all skies equally to all peace-loving nations. The loftiness of Wallace's thinking about the benefits of air travel for world peace provoked Clare Boothe Luce, now a congresswoman from Connecticut, to deliver a speech on the floor of the House of Representatives. "Mr. Wallace's article . . . [she said] is on a very high plane indeed. In it he does a great deal of global thinking. But much of what Mr. Wallace calls his global thinking is, no matter how you slice it, still 'globaloney.' Mr. Wallace's warp of sense and woof of nonsense is very tricky cloth out of which to cut the pattern of the post-war world."[24]

No "open skies" for Clare Boothe Luce. Few other maiden congressional speeches have created such a stir. Oddly enough, Wallace's ideas were not totally dissimilar to those of Wendell Willkie or Henry Luce, but Luce's world was a capitalist one, and he talked of the "American Century." Wallace talked of the "Century of the Common Man." For Mrs. Luce, Willkie's idealism was one thing; Wallace's was another. And,

like her husband, she was both increasingly skeptical about the possibilities for postwar cooperation with the Soviet Union and a strong advocate of American domination of the air.[25]

Neither the United States nor Great Britain yet fully realized that the
span of Britain's imperial glory was about to be over and that the game
was finished. Both anticipated a postwar commercial competition, with
a struggle for supremacy in air transport. Each side held advantages.
The United States had the airplanes, Britain the air bases. Although some
were held on ninety-nine-year lease (Newfoundland, Bermuda, the Ba-
hamas, among them), many of the bases the Americans were now using
in the worldwide air networks were to revert to British control after the
war was over. Writing in *Life Magazine*, Joseph Kastner asserted that "the
fight for top place in the postwar air is much more desperate for the
British than for the Americans. Britain's economy leans far more heavily
on foreign trade than America's does."[26] He then quoted Lord London-
derry as telling Parliament that "our whole existence as a great Empire
Commonwealth depends on the position which we shall occupy in relation to the air in the postwar world."

Geography favored the British; only in the eastern Pacific did the
United States hold an advantage with the Hawaiian islands. As far as
other nations were concerned, Kastner suggests, "the U.S. itself is an
aerial end-of-the line. Only planes plying between Canada, the Caribbean
and Latin America will want to cross it."[27] If the United States could
make a deal with the Portuguese and the French, the base problem might
be solved, but the British might pressure the others not to yield to the
Americans.

Kastner's pessimism was unwarranted. Americans would enter the
postwar competition with more knowledge of international air transport
than any other country because of the experience of global war and the
prewar activity of Pan American. The United States would also have
enormous material resources to use if necessary as bargaining chips in
acquiring landing rights. And Americans would be by far the greatest
customers for air transport of all kinds.

The exclusionism of the Soviet Union and Japan had long closed the
North Pacific to geographically rational patterns of international aviation. China also refused to allow foreign nations flyover or landing
rights, but the Soviet Union formed the most important barrier because
of its size and location. With the success of industrialization and the
achievement of victory in war, the Soviet Union would join the United
States as one of the world's two leading powers. But since Stalin remained stubbornly suspicious of the outside world and of foreign long-
range aircraft, all the wartime maps showing networks of putative future
polar air routes taking advantage of the shortest distances were doomed

to remain mere hypothetical projections. So much for the hopes of Henry Wallace.

The Chicago International Aviation Conference held in 1944 reached agreement that aircraft of signatory nations could fly over and also make stops in other signatory nations, although these stops would not allow cabotage (the pickup and discharge of passengers at these stops). The conference also agreed that an airline could carry passengers and freight from its home nation to any other. The Soviet Union did not attend the conference, and the United States ultimately repudiated it and returned to a regime of bilateral agreements. One of these, with Great Britain, granted for the first time in American history the right to a foreign air carrier (British Overseas Airways Corporation) to cross the United States and continue on into the Pacific.[28]

During the war and the flush of enthusiasm engendered by alliance with the Soviet Union, many Americans were ready to accept a rosy view of long-term prospects for cooperation with that country. The passage of the Lend-Lease Act by the Congress on March 11, 1941, had done much to throw the United States and the Soviet Union together, and Henry Wallace saw much evidence of its impact in his grand tour of Siberia. President Roosevelt put high priority on keeping the Russians in the war and, with an eye on the postwar world, tried hard to build a good working relationship with the Soviet Union. After Pearl Harbor, sea communications across the Pacific were impossible for Americans because the Japanese ruled the whole of the western Pacific. But Japan made little attempt to prevent the neutral Soviets from exploiting the Pacific as a means of moving desperately needed cargo from the United States, huge amounts now being made available under Lend-Lease.

During the last two years of the war alone, nearly a thousand Soviet and Soviet-chartered sailings moved more than 7 million tons of grain, dehydrated foodstuffs, manufactured goods, and war materiel of every description from U.S. west coast ports across the North Pacific to Vladivostok.[29] From Vladivostok this immense cargo was shipped west on a long journey by rail on the Trans-Siberian. Some fifty-three freighters and six tankers were transferred from U.S. to Soviet registry to beef up the Soviet inventory. The disadvantage was, as Robert Sherwood put it, that "any bullet sent by that route had to travel halfway around the world before it could be fired at a German."[30]

The northern aerial route to Asia, from Alaska to Siberia—the Alsib, as it was known—would take on major importance as a way to get airplanes to the Soviet armies. As early as 1927, the Russians had illustrated that the quickest way from European Russia to the United States lay over the Pole. The United States could take an active part in Beringian air communications because the area was shielded by distance from any possibility of Japanese penetration. Japanese air power could not begin to reach that far, although Americans were cautious about making that presumption. The Alsib also seemed to hold great potential in the war against Japan, if the Soviets were to allow Americans to use Siberian bases from which to attack the Japanese home islands.

Secretary of State Cordell Hull asked Foreign Minister Maxim Litvinov for permission to establish U.S. airfields in two specific locations in the Soviet Far East: Vladivostok and the Kamchatka peninsula. Litvinov replied reasonably that the Soviet Union could not afford to antagonize Japan while fighting for its life against the Germans.[31] The Soviet strategy was to remain neutral in the Pacific in order to concentrate all resources (including as much as possible obtained from the United States) in the European theater. Of course, the Soviets were glad to have the Americans fighting the Japanese since it meant that they were less likely to be attacked by them.

Later in the war, as the vise began to close around Japan, heavy bombers, like the B-29, could have operated effectively against Japan if the Russians had allowed them to refuel in Pacific Siberia. One of James Doolittle's sixteen B-25 Mitchell bombers, after its "thirty seconds over Tokyo" on April 18, 1942, was forced to land in Siberia because the plane ran out of gas. Its crew of five were interned, but subsequently they "escaped" to Iran.

This was the first of several such episodes. But the Soviets would not permit the Americans to schedule any Siberian landings. Thus, before serious bombing of Japan could be carried out, the United States had to seize Pacific islands, like the Marianas, as bases. Because the Russians so wished, the Alsib proved useful only in the war against Hitler.

The Russians preferred to be supplied via Europe, closest to the front where many of the materials would be used. But Archangel was not ice free, and Murmansk was subject to German air bombardment. The Allied Arctic convoys were also highly vulnerable to submarine attack or from German planes based in Norway, and they suffered heavy losses at sea. Supplying the Soviet Union by sea put large demands on an Allied transportation system already at strain.

The Alsib air route, secure from enemy attack, proved to be the best means for the United States to supply the Soviet Union with aircraft, the most important item on the list of what the Russians wanted. Roosevelt wanted to give them as many as possible. He was anxious to furnish the weaponry in order to keep the Soviet Union in the war. Supplying war materiel made the United States and the Soviet Union allies months before the former actually entered the conflict.

The British, and the Chinese too, also wanted U.S. combat aircraft. The problem was too few planes to give away, and not enough even for American needs. On the eve of the Pearl Harbor attack, in the words of

"Hap" Arnold, the United States was well equipped "with plans but not with planes."[32] And he later said that "there never would be a United States Air Force except on paper" if the line were not drawn between domestic needs and foreign desires.[33]

But Roosevelt had promised, and the War Department had to deliver. The Soviets all the while were singing a threnody of too little and too slow, constantly invoking the name of the president in order to try to pressure the War Department. They also irked the Americans with their criticism of what they did get. Some of the fighter aircraft (P-40s) sent indeed proved to be defective, yet the Soviets did not want American technicians to come along with the planes in order to correct the deficiencies, and Soviet incompetence sometimes handicapped effective use of what was sent.

The fighters had such a short range as to need intermediate stops before they could reach western Siberia from North America. The Americans anticipated that they would be delivering the planes, if not to the front, at least well into Siberia. Roosevelt proposed to Stalin (June 23, 1942) that the United States deliver aircraft to Lake Baikal.[34] But Stalin wanted to accept the planes in Alaska and Stalin got his way.

The Soviets had no intention of allowing entry to their territory to any more Americans than they could avoid, and they adamantly refused to furnish any specific information about Siberian routes. Soviet secretiveness and Soviet suspicions were based on the not-unwarranted belief that the capitalist world could only wish and work for ultimate destruction of the Soviet system.

Fairbanks would be the site of the transfer of airplanes. There, after some vacillation on the part of the Soviets, the first group of Soviet pilots arrived in early September 1942, leaving for Nome and home at the end of that month.[35] The Soviets might have chosen Nome over Fairbanks; Nome was five hundred miles closer to the Soviet Union than Fairbanks was, but its weather was worse and the town was thought to be more exposed to possible Japanese attack.[36] Merchants in Fairbanks were delighted by the choice; the Soviets spent all they had in the local shops buying whatever was available, particularly luxury underwear for their ladies.

Notwithstanding bad weather, shortages of mechanics and tools, and the need to prepare the aircraft specially for the rigors of Arctic winter, by the end of June 1943, a thousand American-made planes had flown to the Soviet Union. Despite clouds of mistrust on both sides, the Alaska-Siberia route would become the major artery for the transfer of aircraft to the Soviet Union, and 7,925 planes were ultimately accepted by it over this route.[37] Alsib also provided a means to ship priority cargo and a few special passengers back and forth. The U.S. ambassador to the Soviet

Union, Joseph Davies, chose the Alaska route for a return journey from Moscow in June 1943.[38]

Americans assumed that the Japanese might eventually attack Siberia or that the Soviet Union would enter the war anyway, when the time might seem propitious. Late in 1944, Stalin began to tease the Americans with talk of allowing them bases in Pacific Siberia in return for equipping and training a Soviet strategic air force. But by the spring of 1945, the Americans no longer needed such bases; Pacific islands had sufficed for that purpose. U.S. bombs had virtually devastated nearly all of Japan's major cities, and as that nation faced its last agony, the Americans had more need of targets than of bases.

But Americans were thinking of the postwar world, and they wanted to establish regular transport routes to Siberia, comparable to those being flown in so many other parts of the globe by the aircraft of the Air Transport Command. They hoped to entice the Russians into permitting them to fly into the Soviet Union, perhaps as far as Chita or Irkutsk, in return for allowing the Russians to fly to Seattle. These hopes, perhaps even expectations, of 1945 would become realities only in the early 1990s.

PART SEVEN

AMERICA, THE NEW GLOBAL HUB?

CHAPTER TWENTY-SEVEN

The Collapse of the American Merchant Marine

In 1945, all possible competitors to the United States, commercial or political, lay crushed by defeat, exhausted by victory, or convulsed by revolution. The Great Republic finally stood triumphantly at the center of the international system, and to many Americans this appeared to be a realization of the natural order. History had stopped with the achievement of American preeminence. Few reflected on the abnormality of the international situation or its possible impermanence.

The United States now formed the natural hub of the global transportation and communications network, emerging also as the creative and productive center of aviation and maritime technology. No other nation could challenge the formidable combination of U.S. strategic and commercial power thrust across the Pacific. In international air transport, the United States was the only nation with the experience, the money, and the planes to fly the oceans globally. And in 1945 it floated a merchant marine larger than those of all other nations combined. More than half of the world's merchant fleet flew the Stars and Stripes.

The southern edge of the Asian segment of the North Pacific, principally China and Japan, continued to be one of the world's major concentrations of population, but war had disrupted or destroyed its commercial patterns. Although Japan's prospects for reemergence as a major power appeared bleak and John Foster Dulles worried publicly that Japan might be a permanent economic dependency of the United States, China remained a potent image for Americans.

The old dream of the dazzling wealth of the Orient and its potentialities for American enrichment lingered in the American imagination. Trends in world trade before the war buttressed that perception, indicating a rising global commercial importance for the Pacific basin. But much of the statistical record had simply reflected the industrial and commercial success of Japan as that nation girded for war. The Japanese had aggressively and skillfully capitalized on their proximity to the Asian continent to capture and develop much of that market.

Now the devastation of Japanese factories and workshops and the removal of Japan from the continent seemed to open great new opportunities in Asia to American businessmen. And whereas heretofore distance had always been a problem, now it appeared less so. Before the war, trans-Pacific airfares were beyond the budget of the average businessman, the fastest steamship had taken two weeks, and the cable service was both expensive and inefficient. East Asia remained remote from American mainstream commercial and information networks.

The war much improved the means and speed of travel and communication, with notable impact on the Pacific. A pressurized landplane like the DC-4 Skymaster, which reached a ceiling of thirty thousand feet, could at war's end in 1945 cross the Pacific in three days instead of the five the flying boats had required with their nightly stopovers. This meant forty hours of flying time instead of sixty.

But the immediate postwar international situation imposed its own peculiarities to challenge the American businessman, with Japan occupied and internationally isolated by U.S. forces and China preoccupied by a civil war of increasing intensity. The Soviet Union had withdrawn into even tighter seclusion with the growing tensions of the Cold War. Newly liberated Korea, struggling for economic survival amid political turmoil, was of no international commercial significance. The Communist triumph in China in 1949 and the outbreak of war in Korea shortly after further closed off most of the East Asian mainland from trans-Pacific life. Therefore, although the United States enjoyed unchallenged domination of the Pacific oceanic spaces and an unprecedented ability to reach for the Orient, international politics and the detritus of war clouded prospects for building major new American trade networks across the Pacific.

The overpowering American lead in world merchant shipping would not last long. Under the Merchant Sales Act of 1946 the U.S. government sold off many ships to foreigners at bargain prices, and American shipping companies began to buy more ships built abroad than from yards at home. Despite government subsidies for routes deemed essential and exemption from antitrust laws, despite the guarantee of a share of military and other government cargo, as well as the protection offered by cabotage, American shipping continued to decline.

Again American shippers could not meet the competition of nationally subsidized foreign lines or foreign private operators who operated with lower costs. Many American shipowners thereupon fled the flag for open registry, low-cost foreign registrations that furnished the means to avoid high taxes, high wages, and stringent safety (and, later, environmental protection) requirements. The flags of Panama, Liberia, and Cyprus began to flutter around the globe in every major seaport. These flags of convenience, or as the owners preferred to call them, "flags of necessity," flew over an "internationalized" American fleet, shipping goods of American origin, managed from offices located in American cities, and, theoretically at any rate, available to the nation in the event of a defense emergency. The American business community and general public, if they thought of it at all, blithely chose to assume that the nation maintained a merchant marine adequate for the requirements of national security.

The liner *United States* (1952) was perhaps the finest immediate postwar accomplishment of American merchant marine construction and an example of what Americans might have sailed across the Pacific. The *United States* benefited from some of the skills and knowledge that had gone into the building of aircraft carriers. A thirty-five-knot speed pushed her fifty-two-thousand tons across the North Atlantic in record-smashing five-day voyages. And for a time, it seemed that the great years of surface oceanic travel there were to revive after wartime suspension.

After the war, world shipping tonnage began to increase explosively, supporting and reflecting the growth of international oceanic trade. The North Pacific countries began to contribute one-quarter to one-third of the total flow, a revived Japan being the leader.[1] Paradoxically, as the American presence on the oceans faded, Americans proved to be the chief innovators in technologies of oceanic transport.

Sometimes these were unsuccessful. An early romance with nuclear power led to the cargo ship *Savannah*, first of her type. Her career was unhappy, and the Japanese too, through their own subsequent experience, would find the nuclear-powered merchant ship to be "an evolutionary dead end," uneconomical to operate and perhaps environmentally unsafe.[2] But, in general, innovations in the maritime industries stimulated trade growth by bringing down costs, to the enormous benefit of trading states like Japan. Sea transport remains the cheapest way to move anything, and technological changes in the last forty years or so have revolutionized the industry, making it even cheaper. Merchant ships came to be more and more specialized in order to speed loading and unloading, lowering costs in time and therefore money.

As early as 1956, an American shipper began to experiment with containerization of cargo sent between New York and the Gulf of Mexico. The box trade, as it would be called, proved hugely successful and would soon sweep the transportation industry. Aluminum boxes of standard size, either twenty feet by eight by eight, or forty feet by eight by eight (the size of a railroad car), made trucks, trains, and ships interchangeable host units for a seamless and swift system. Containers are handled by giant cranes pierside that can load or unload a ship in twenty-four hours while preserving cargo from damage or pilferage. The use of containers revived interest in land bridges, the transcontinental railroad systems across North America and Eurasia. And they tended to concentrate shipments; larger ports began to grow at the expense of smaller ones.[3]

Automation of ship handling and the introduction of new ship types for special cargoes reflected both the electronic age and the growth of oceanic trade. Demand for more and more ships encouraged larger and larger sizes, and the bulk carrier was born. Iron and other ores, steel and other materials, grain, and above all oil, all needed in increasing quantities, swelled the demand for cheap bulk carriage. Nowhere would this be more important than in the North Pacific.

Bulk carrier is as imprecise a term as is *clipper ship*. It would be difficult to say who was first with the concept of the modern bulk carrier or indeed how large a ship must be to bear that designation. Certainly the American entrepreneur Daniel K. Ludwig was one of its pioneers. Ludwig established his own shipyard at Norfolk, Virginia, in the 1930s, where he designed and built ships distinguished for their efficiency and unconventionality.

Early on, Ludwig was sensitive to the economies of scale and he began to build bigger and bigger ships until he reached the thirty-thousand-ton level in 1947 or 1948. Ludwig was more daring than the oil companies. He had on paper a ship of eighty-thousand tons, but the oil companies were not yet interested in anything that big. Ludwig's Norfolk yard became too cramped, with no room for expansion and without the capacity to build the size ship he wanted. After scouting out possible alternative locations for a yard in Scotland, Germany, and Spain, he settled on Japan, an imaginative choice that proved to be highly fruitful, for him and the Japanese.

Elmer L. Hann was the gifted man who put it all together for Ludwig in Japan. Hann sprang from middle management into the post of general superintendent of production at the Kaiser shipyard on Swan Island, Oregon, during World War II. He trained unskilled men and women to master a simplified method of welding in a course that took ten days instead of the former two or three months. Acceleration was characteristic of Hann's style. Once he oversaw the assembly of a Liberty ship in an astounding four days.[4]

When war's end closed the Kaiser yard, Hann had taken a job with Ludwig's National Bulk Carriers. That company had negotiated a lease of the giant former imperial navy yard at Kure near Hiroshima, still, after severe wartime bombing, simply a twisted mass of burned and broken metal and masonry. At Kure, the Japanese had built some of the world's largest warships including the superbattleship *Yamato*, which startled the world with its unprecedented seventy-two thousand tons. People at Kure were therefore familiar with large-scale construction and ideally qualified for what Ludwig had in mind. More important than the material remains of the shipyard and the spaces it offered was the pool of unemployed and experienced people of talent there: highly skilled, docile (nonunion) workers and cheap engineers and managers. NBC leased the Japanese yard at a very low figure, subleasing part of it to the Japanese shipbuilder Harima. Little happened until Hann arrived in 1951 to manage the yard.

Hann imported American machinery, rebuilt the yard, taught the Japanese the construction methods he had exploited so well during the war years in Oregon, and after his first launch in 1953 began to turn out, at an increasingly rapid rate, dry cargo ships and tankers of increasing size. A handful of Americans supervised a large number of Japanese. The labor was Japanese, the materials and shipbuilding equipment increasingly so. By 1958, when Japan had already displaced Great Britain as the world's leading shipbuilder and was supplying more than one-quarter of the world's new tonnage, National Bulk Carriers was completing large ships at Kure in only five months' time.[5]

Ludwig was concerned not just with size and speed of construction but with raising quality and lowering costs. He accomplished a high standard. The Brooklyn Navy Yard built a merchant ship of 220,000 tons and boasted that it took less than four million man-hours to do so. NBC built a ship at Kure of the same size and was chagrined because it took 760,000 man-hours.[6]

Ludwig operated ships as well as building them. He built ships only for his own use or for charter. He was one of the first people to see the advantages of large vessels for bulk shipments in trans-Pacific commerce because he needed large capacity and low operating costs for his own trade. Ludwig began by selling salt to the Japanese that he had processed in Baja California. He aimed at becoming chief provider to the Japanese chemical industry. But he looked beyond this; Ludwig seems to have foreseen that the North Pacific would become the world's biggest-volume oceanic trade route.

Ludwig was a man with only an eighth-grade education, but with a thirsty intellect and possessed with that enormous appetite for information characteristic of brilliant entrepreneurs like James Jerome Hill and Edward H. Harriman. Ludwig was known to read while talking on the telephone, and he held the reputation for never forgetting anything, even the most technical details of a subject.[7] Usually described as reclusive, Ludwig shunned publicity and invariably declined to be interviewed. A biographer called him "the most secretive man alive," and for years he was one of the world's richest, which may explain why.[8]

Ludwig built the world's first bulk carriers in Kure. The tanker *Universe Leader*, eighty-four thousand tons, the world's largest at the time, slipped down the ways in 1955, just one year before the closing of the Suez Canal and a resulting oil shortage caused by the added distance required for shipments. Eleven years later, the first megacarrier, *Cedrus*, at 170,000 tons, was designed to carry salt across the Pacific. This ship broke all tradition by its size, but in the planning stage Ludwig's only question had been, "Tell me why I can't do it."[9] Ludwig demonstrated the merits of these ships. Other builders were quick to follow. Demand and sizes both grew. Suez had put limits on the size of ships; the closing of the canal (1957–75) accelerated the demand for enormous ones. Ludwig's timing was brilliant.

Ludwig helped make shipbuilding Japan's first spectacular international postwar economic success, the first instance in which Japanese manufacturing seemed to be not only cheaper but also better than American. The Americans who worked for Ludwig in Japan developed a profound appreciation for the technical talents of the Japanese.[10] The modernization pattern then was like that of the late nineteenth-century Meiji era. At first the Japanese had to use imported steel plates and imported machinery. Later they began to make their own. The legacy of this evolution is that Japanese shipbuilding companies are also heavily engaged in the business of engineering and machinery manufacturing, products consumed in the building of ships. But the huge variety of parts required (a ship of fair size is said to need 100,000 different parts) encouraged and demanded a nearby range of manufacturing industries, thereby contributing heavily to Japan's overall industrial expansion. By 1965, Japan was building more ships every year than the rest of the world put together. In 1991 that tonnage amounted to 7.7 million. The United States may have boasted the world's largest navy, but in that same year American shipyards launched only twenty-two merchant vessels, totaling 21,980 gross tons.[11]

New techniques of automated welding, block construction, and the use of huge cranes accelerated the building process. Subsequently, computer-aided design and computer-aided manufacture, just-in-time inventory management, and rigorous quality control came to promote continued Japanese success in this as well as in many other industries.

World demand for new ships peaked in 1974, falling sharply with the first of the oil shocks. After a short recovery in the early 1980s, the industry again slumped, but leadership remained in the North Pacific region. The Japanese now had to worry about competition nearby. The Koreans, using advanced Japanese machinery and their own cheap labor, were able to put a ship in the water for less money than any Japanese yard could. The rise of the yen after 1986 also made it tough for the Japanese to compete. Perhaps the pioneering of new maritime technologies can now help the Japanese. But such things as superconductors and screwless propulsion, "intelligent" ships and robot vessels, reducing costly manpower dramatically, or computer-directed sail-assisted ships all still appear to lie on the very far horizon.[12]

The world trades by ship. In the 1850s a ship of 3,500 tons was very large. In the 1950s a ship of 35,000 tons was good size. In the 1970s, the equivalent was 350,000 tons. Oil is the leading commodity carried by large ships today and comprises nearly half of all cargo tonnage. Ores and grain come next as the staple cargoes. Unfortunately, the leading commodity is also the greatest polluter. Supertankers are the biggest-moving objects yet created by people, and the accident of the *Valdez* would painfully demonstrate their danger, in another episode of damage to the fragile North Pacific environment.[13]

By the mid-1980s, no other nation was contributing more to world trade than the United States, although exports and imports accounted for only about 8 percent of American gross national product (as opposed to 37 percent for Japan and even more for Germany and South Korea).[14] American exports and imports annually totaled more than 640 million tons by weight and some $600 billion by value.[15] But U.S.-flagged ships carried only about 4 percent of this trade. The United States maintained more oceangoing warships than oceangoing merchant ships; the American commitment to strategic power at sea was greater than the American commitment to commercial power at sea.

The first newspapers published in the United States concentrated on shipping and trade, matters of prime interest to their readers. By the 1980s the general press carried little shipping news, and the *Journal of Commerce* remained the only daily publication providing shipping information in detail.[16] The decaying urban waterfronts of the United States, once the pulse of commercial energy and entrepreneurship, were becoming parks, luxury dwellings, and specialty shops to which the water simply provided a pleasant but largely empty background of sight and smell. The shrill of whistles and the roar of horns had disappeared. The box trade moved shipping out of sight to areas where cheap land was available. Los Angeles, not even a maritime city, replaced New York as the leading seaport of the United States.

Christopher Koch, chairman of the Federal Maritime Commission, asked a Seattle audience in May 1991, "We're no longer a major commercial power. The question is do we care? The United States merchant marine continues to decline. Should we have one at all?"[17]

CHAPTER TWENTY-EIGHT

A New Northwest Passage

The war had coincided with the commercial demise of the flying boat. On war's eve, Pan American had been about to shift from flying boats to landplanes, for several reasons. The first was a rising recognition on the part of local communities that they had the responsibility to build airports and a resulting new availability of fields that could handle large landplanes, with ranges equal to those of seaplanes.

Major cities where Pan American flew were now building or had completed airports: New York, Miami, San Francisco. Therefore, the airline no longer needed to look to what nature might have provided in the form of unlimited water takeoff and landing spaces. The new airports provided stable surfaces, easy to illuminate for night flying. Tides, debris, and moving ice did not affect them. Furthermore, Pan American believed public confidence was now sufficient that a landplane would be acceptable for long overwater flights.

The company argued that it made little difference except at takeoff and landing whether the plane was a flying boat or a land transport.[1] Air is the natural operating medium for a plane, and its flight characteristics are the most significant aeronautical factor. And in the event of an emergency landing in the water, the landplanes' sealed cabins gave them a flotation as good as or better than that of the hulled seaplane. Furthermore, landplanes cost much less than seaplanes.

In 1940, Boeing put its B-307 Stratoliner into American domestic service. These were the first planes with pressurized cabins, enabling them to fly above the clouds and avoid bad weather. In 1943, the enormously successful Lockheed Constellation began to fly for the military, and, after 1945, for civilians.

The Allied (U.S.) occupation under the command of General Douglas MacArthur closed Japan to normal patterns of international interaction, a stricture reflected in postwar patterns of trans-Pacific transportation. Although the occupying troops and far-flung U.S. base network in East Asia promised military traffic for American commercial air carriers, no one in the aftermath of war anticipated that Tokyo might become a hub for air traffic.

The primary route to the Orient was still that pioneered by Pan American, across the central Pacific from Honolulu to Manila and on to Hong Kong and the China coast. Americans still hoped for a peaceful resolution of the Chinese civil war and for a thriving commerce with China. The usual American terminus for trans-Pacific flight was San Francisco. Only later, when the range of aircraft greatly increased, did Los Angeles assume importance as a gateway to the Orient.

The great accomplishments of Pan American—the contributions it had made to national defense and to the war effort, the prestige it had won for the United States abroad—faded in the public memory. What surfaced after the war in the mind of the public was the fact that the company enjoyed a monopoly on overseas routes and had bitterly fought off all competition.

For once, Trippe's consummate political skills failed him, and Pan American's opponents argued successfully that the international market would be too large for any one company to handle and that competition would lower costs, to the benefit of the consumer. Perhaps if Trippe had been more amenable to compromise and able to satisfy himself with operating in one or two regions only, the North Atlantic, say, or Latin America and the Pacific, he might have been more successful in the long run. But Trippe would not have been satisfied with any one region or even two. He had, after all, pioneered so many. Trippe's ambitions were manifested by the establishing of an around-the-world passenger service in 1947, another first for Pan American. It would not be a monopoly for very long. Northwest, in cooperation with TWA—those two American systems met in Manila—eventually was able to offer a competitive route.

In Washington, Trippe played on the theme that direct competition between airlines of the same country is damaging to the national interest. There would not be enough business, he argued, and large subsidies would be demanded of the government. He proposed a consortium with shares allotted by the government to the various airline operators. Pan American's share would initially be the largest, rewarding its contribution to the national interest and reflecting the value of its experience, its people, its planes, and its routes. With time, Pan American's share would presumably decrease as other airlines grew. Trippe failed to perceive that American domestic routes would be essential to feed Pan American's overseas services; the company did not own any until it was too late.[2] Trippe did not think of this need because he did not contemplate any real competition from other U.S. flag carriers.[3]

From the industry Trippe got little support for his holding action; only

United Airlines was on his side. United estimated that trans-Atlantic demand in 1948 would be satisfied by some four dozen one hundred–passenger planes.[4] No one could estimate what the air cargo market might be. The Air Transport Command had shown what the technology could do by carrying a substantial volume of cargo at high speed around the globe, but cost was not a factor for them.

American would-be competitors to Pan American were not the only ones chafing under the old aviation order, shaken by the war and its aftermath. British shipping interests disliked the "chosen instrument" air transport policy whereby the only British international airline, British Overseas Airways Corporation, was a government-controlled, privately owned monopoly. They, too, wanted the opportunity to enter the airline business. The aircraft industry in both the United States and abroad also wanted the field opened up in order to enliven the market.

At the end of the war the U.S. military had begun probing the possibilities of long-distance flight by landplanes across the Pacific. The ATC pioneered a twenty-four-hour Seattle-Tokyo run, using Skymaster to carry mail and cargo on a course set through Adak. This cut nearly three thousand miles from the Pan American dogleg via Hawaii and Wake. At the end of October 1945, three Boeing B-29s made a nonstop flight via the great circle route from Hokkaido, Japan, to Washington, D.C., in twenty-seven hours, thirty minutes. The press talked about the spectacular prospects for commercial air travel. But this flight was stretching the current technology to its outer limits; without favorable winds, it would not have succeeded.

A journalist aboard one of these planes during the long and uncomfortable hours aloft thought of all that would be necessary before commercial passengers could fly the great circle route. He speculated that the plane would need to be big enough to contain sleeping, dining, and "recreation facilities." The B-29s had no amenities, not even a heating system adequate for the Arctic skies.[5] But more important than comfort was safety; the industry needed more information about weather patterns. Meteorology remained a highly inexact science. And commercial airlines would need to have access to radio direction-finding systems and to an air-sea rescue system below. But the first requisite would be reliable engines powering a plane capable of carrying a generous fuel supply.

The American government, under the provisions of the Civil Aeronautics Act of 1938, had begun to supervise and regulate airline routes, rates, and technical operations. The Civil Aeronautics Board made the formal decision in January 1946, subsequently approved by President Truman, that for a seven-year trial period, air traffic across the Pacific should be split between two major routes, the great circle and the central Pacific, and two companies, Pan American and Northwest. The argument went that traffic would be sufficiently great to generate profits for both.

No one seems to have contemplated the entry of Japanese and other Asians into the airline business. When in fact they did, they attempted to assuage the apprehensions of the traveler by advertising that they used American pilots, reinforcing the notion that the medium somehow belonged to Americans.

Northwest, the oldest U.S. airline with continuous identification, had been founded in 1926, a year before Pan American, to provide service between the Twin Cities and Chicago. In the early 1930s it began to extend its routes into Canada and across the American West toward Seattle. It grew by extension rather than by merger and achieved an enviable safety record.

During the war, Northwest operated a military cargo route to Alaska and a sixteen-hundred-mile service along the Aleutians, from Anchorage to Attu. The company thus had already acquired useful experience in flying much of the route to Japan; only the last leg would be new. Victory brought landing rights for American planes in Japan. Northwest could draw on its considerable wartime experience of cold weather flying to operate its new service to Japan. The CAB designated New York, Chicago, and Seattle as the U.S. gateways for the great circle route and Manila as its Asian terminus. Northwest's home port, Minneapolis–St. Paul, offered a natural hub for serving the rest of the Midwest.

Northwest's routes would eventually stretch from New York to Tokyo and beyond, by way of Minneapolis, Seattle, and Anchorage. The passenger could, theoretically at least, ride the same aircraft from the northeastern United States all the way to East Asia and travel fewer miles than flying via the Pan American Pacific island route. Northwest secured exclusive rights to serve Korea, Okinawa, and Formosa (Taiwan). The airline also was permitted by the CAB to fly to Peking via the Manchurian cities of Harbin and Mukden (Shenyang), a zigzag route that reflected the old American commercial interest in and hopes for Manchuria. Shanghai was also on the list, as long as the Chinese allowed it, and Manila too, which would be the company's ultimate western terminus. In order to protect Northwest, a newcomer to overseas service, from the veteran Pan American, President Truman required that Pan American on all trans-Pacific flights picking up or discharging traffic at Tokyo include a mandatory stop at Honolulu or Midway Island.

For the airlines Tokyo took on more and more importance with the demands of the U.S. occupation forces in Japan and with the closing of China in 1949. Tokyo's location directly on the way to Manila and Southeast Asia made it a natural Asian gateway for Americans. Northwest's first Japan flight took off from the Twin Cities on July 15, 1947, a fifty-passenger DC-4 making a thirty-six and a half-hour journey from the Twin Cities to Tokyo. Northwest had to convince its Mercator-minded customers that traveling to Asia by way of Alaska was actually the short-est route. Even Manila was closer to the United States via the great circle than by the central Pacific.[6] Northwest also had to combat imagery of frostbite and snow, fog and ice. Soon, with the rapid improvement of equipment, passengers would realize that the weather was largely irrel-evant to flying except for takeoff and landing. Once airborne they would hardly be aware of it, except perhaps for a certain amount of turbulence.

Like Pan American earlier across the central Pacific, Northwest had to set up an elaborate support structure along its new and lengthy flight corridor even though the number of stops was few. The route offered the advantage of being largely overland or near it, making emergency landings possible. Spare parts, radio beacons, electricity generators, and skilled people all had to be in place. The company shipped thousands of precooked frozen meals to Asia to offer passengers returning to the United States a taste of the familiar American cuisine; few then would choose any other.[7] Unlike Pan American, Northwest was able to begin its trans-Pacific schedule with three flights a week instead of one.

The route to Asia from Minneapolis represents a realization of the dream of James Jerome Hill, elevated into a new dimension. Northwest Airlines, which for some years (1964–86) would call itself Northwest Ori-ent, had made the old vision of a Northwest Passage a reality, and the route would ultimately become a conduit for the flow of Asian luxury goods to avid American consumers. But the goods would be cameras and videotape recorders, not teas and silks, and the trade would enrich Asia, not the United States.

In the early 1950s Trans World Airlines also expressed some hope of developing routes in the North Pacific, but entering it from the Asian side—the west, not the east and tying India to Japan in a Bombay-Tokyo service. With China now cut off from the capitalist world, India suddenly took on new interest to Americans as a possible exporter of raw materials and the products of light industry; for Japan, India could perhaps serve as a commercial substitute for China. Tokyo began to seem "an ideal junction point," TWA arguing that it was now "the industrial, military and cultural hub of the Orient."[8] TWA anticipated that "50% of the travel in the foreseeable future on the Bombay-Tokyo route would be Ameri-cans, so expanded have our overseas interests become."[9]

The CAB did not allow Northwest to tap California traffic, but in June 1945 the company had gained authority to extend its service within the United States sufficiently to become the nation's fourth transcontinental airline.[10] Northwest thereby acquired east coast gateways to the Pacific that Pan American lacked. This was important because New York banks were the only American banks to maintain offices in East Asia; most American business firms doing business in East Asia had their headquarters in New York, and the Atlantic seaboard still generated most of American passenger traffic for East Asia.

Seattle feared being circumvented by Northwest on its flight to Asia because the CAB proposed that the airline fly there via Edmonton instead, making a shorter overall distance from any midwestern or Atlantic coast city. Seattle groups put their case in terms of both national security and successful commerce. They argued that an "all-American" route would avoid any possible embarrassment in the event of Canadian neutrality in some international crisis and that economically what was needed en route to Asia was the sort of water, rail, and highway connections that Seattle offered. In other words, intermediate points were significant to the viability of transportation routes.[11]

Seattle need not have feared. The Pacific coast offered more alluring traffic possibilities than the Canadian Midwest. Once Northwest had in the early 1950s acquired Super Constellations with wing-tip tanks permitting a five-thousand-mile range, Seattle became "the only practical take-off point to the Orient."[12] San Francisco or Los Angeles lay too far to the south, beyond the practical nonstop range of any civil equipment then available or even planned for the future, including the new long-range jets.[13]

Pan American was left with its old flying boat route across the central Pacific. This may have been sunnier, and perhaps some passengers were lured to it because of the possibility of a stopover in Honolulu. But the distance from New York to Tokyo is over two thousand miles longer via San Francisco and Hawaii than through Alaska, and cargo and the mails were quite indifferent to the attractions of warm sunshine and beaches.[14] Furthermore, Pan American suffered from not having domestic traffic to feed its international flights, all originating on the coast. Pan American never did become a truly global airline. The United States still does not have a single global airline any more than it ever had a single transcontinental railroad.[15]

For nearly two years of their seven-year trial authorization, both Northwest and Pan American used the same type of planes to Tokyo, unpressurized DC-4s. Northwest attracted twice the volume of traffic that Pan American did. Boeing then converted its B-29 Superfortress into the B-377 Stratocruiser making more than half its sales to Pan American. Trippe liked the aircraft, particularly its bar lounge on the lower deck, which provided the kind of amenity he always sought. As one Pan Am employee reminisced, "More deals were cooked down there than you can imagine."[16]

Airline companies, following Trippe's lead, were still very much concerned with the comfort of their passengers, and all air travel was still first class. Early in 1949, Pan American began to use Stratocruisers to capture the bulk of the passenger traffic to Tokyo. Pan American boasted,

"The public preferred . . . [our] pressurized cabins, the nearly 100 miles an hour higher cruising speed, the reclining chairs and comfortable berths [of the Stratocruisers] to Northwest's DC-4s, despite the longer mileage."[17] During the last four years of the temporary seven-year certificate, Pan American outcarried Northwest between the United States and Japan almost three to one.[18]

Steamships offered no competition to any Pacific airline. Nothing like the great luxury liners of the North Atlantic had ever dominated the North Pacific. Only the Matson line ships sailing from California to Hawaii could compare to the highest standards of the North Atlantic, and they did not cross the Pacific. Trans-Pacific passenger ships like those of the Dollar Line, although lodged fondly in the memory of those who took them, remained relatively few, and they were small. The only competition they could really offer to the airlines was cost, although some passengers would always choose the greater comfort of surface travel, even a freighter, if they had the time.[19]

Juan Trippe, his eye on the market, became a public advocate of cheap mass air travel as early as 1944, declaring that civil aviation could continue catering to the rich, or it could be opened to a new mass clientele. In 1952, Pan American became the first airline to offer economy-class travel across the ocean.[20] And once again, as Charles Lindbergh had long ago observed, what Pan Am did usually determined what others would do.

In the 1950s, pleasure travel by air began to become popular, stimulated by the economy-class fares. Rising popularity was perhaps inevitably accompanied by declining comfort. Anthony Sampson points out that "air travel . . . has become the most constrained form of mass transport since the slave-ships," although the slavers did not have the same obsession with seat dimensions and configurations.[21]

Sampson says nothing about the food. Whereas it is true that orange juice is usually available aboard an airplane and would be a useful antiscorbutic, one can wonder about the long-term effects of a diet of airline food. The airlines claim that quality of food and drink has not been high on the list of passenger concerns, and doubtless an airplane is a difficult environment in which to prepare and serve food, although some manage to do rather well. By the late 1980s, for first- and business-class passengers, the airlines were spending a lot of money on ingredients and the attempt to provide excellent service. The attention that the staff give to the preparing and presentation of the food can, according to the experts, make a lot of difference in how it tastes.[22]

Most trans-Pacific passengers, traveling economy class, ate mediocre food from small rectangular casseroles the trade called "dog dishes."[23] Despite the assertion of George Keck, the president of United Airlines, that the industry had shifted from a technical orientation to a marketing one, service did not show it and the amenities of air travel perceptibly declined.[24] The chief concern of the industry seemed to be to maximize the number of passengers aboard. The paradigm had shifted to the bus, not the river steamer, ocean liner, or even the railroad train. "Getting there is half the fun," the old slogan of the Cunard Lines, could scarcely be applied to trans-Pacific air travel, at least in economy class.

CHAPTER TWENTY-NINE

The Jet Revolution and American Leadership

The American aircraft industry had grown hugely during the war, dwarfing even the automobile industry, the nation's hitherto biggest manufacturer. It primarily served one customer, the U.S. government. At war's end, airplane manufacturers worried about what they might do next, remembering the catastrophic slump the industry suffered after 1918. The outbreak of the Korean War in 1950 and the continuing U.S. emphasis on armaments thereafter prevented any collapse; as the demand for warplanes lessened, the industry survived, although the market remained volatile. Moving into rockets and missiles, airplane manufacturers began to call themselves aerospace companies.

The commercial sector benefited from the enormous sums the government was prepared to invest in research and development for the military. Engines and airplanes for commercial use were often adaptations of military types, although the criteria differed. Military aircraft are rated on performance over the short term, commercial aircraft on the basis of reliability over the long term. In both airframe and aircraft engine markets, a very few large, fiercely competitive companies came to dominate the field. By 1960, 80 percent of the world's airliners were made in the United States, and aerospace had become the largest employer among American manufacturers.[1]

Geographical patterns of American production remained those laid down in the early years of the aviation industry: New England and the Midwest built the engines; airframe manufacture was heavily concentrated in Washington and southern California. The rise of the aviation industry had much to do with the boom of population and growth of the overall economy of the American Pacific, characteristic of the war years and after.

In the postwar period, the Europeans tried to compete with American aeronautics, and the British hoped to take advantage of having pioneered the jet engine by seizing leadership of the world commercial airplane market. If Britain could no longer rule the waves, the skies offered a realm for continuing imperial fantasies. But the highly touted Comet, Britain's first commercial jet, proved to be a costly and embarrassing failure. It was too small to carry a profitable passenger load. More important, its frame was not worthy of its engines; metal fatigue caused several Comets to disintegrate in midair. The consensus of American manufacturers had been that the time was not yet ripe for the commercial jet, but the British pushed them reluctantly into the jet age, American operators joining in the push.[2]

In the summer of 1951, Canadian Pacific talked of soon establishing ten-hour jet service across the Pacific from Vancouver to Tokyo, stopping at Anchorage and one of the Aleutian chain.[3] For competing American airlines like Northwest or Pan American, such a prospect was alarming. A foreign company would be using a traditionally American route to Asia.

Using Soviet-made aircraft, Aeroflot began what would be the world's first long-distance jet flights to the Asian Pacific in 1956, but this remains a historical footnote. These planes did not enter competitive international routes, and Soviet aircraft were never able to crack the international market. They enjoyed no custom outside the iron curtain.

The Boeing 707 was the successful American reply to the British commercial jet. Delivered in late 1958, the 707 was a passenger jet modeled after an air force prototype. The 707 put Boeing triumphantly back into the commercial aircraft business, and the 707 would be followed by a whole family of other Boeing jets.

Characteristically, Pan American was the first or "launch" customer for the plane. And Trippe had insisted that it have sufficient range for non-stop trans-Atlantic flights. The North Atlantic was very much still the world's premier transoceanic air market, but the impact of jet speeds was even more dramatic in the Pacific. The Boeing jet reduced travel time from San Francisco to Tokyo from twenty-five hours via the then fastest propeller-driven plane to less than thirteen. The 707 was joined a year later by the equally fast DC-8, Douglas's attempt to recapture its leadership in passenger planes. But Boeing moved into a commanding lead, and Seattle, its North Pacific global headquarters, became the world's largest civil aviation city. Douglas had dominated the commercial market in the propeller-driven era; in the jet era, it never caught up with Boeing.

Since the jet aircraft cut travel time in half, it scored an immediate success and provided the major reason for an explosive growth of air travel, which, between 1950 and 1974, increased by a factor of sixteen.[4] Seat-mile costs dropped by half in the first decade of the commercial jet era. Jets may require more maintenance than piston-engine aircraft, but they are considerably more reliable and increasingly so highly automated as to cut down the possibility of human error. Air travel became safer and cheaper as well as faster than ever before. The Americans had taken the automobile, a European invention, and democratized it. They did the same with the jet aircraft.

After the airlines began to fly jet-propelled aircraft the next big step in transportation appeared to be the commercial supersonic transport (SST). Again, it was the British, joined this time by the French, who by their competitive example, Concorde, prodded the Americans into action.

Concorde, an aluminum-based aircraft carrying one hundred passengers, cruising at 1,350 miles per hour, nearly twice the speed of sound, at an altitude of fifty thousand feet, and with a range of thirty-six hundred nautical miles, entered regular passenger service on January 21, 1976. Concorde's range was far too short to be practical for the plane to fly the Pacific, and its manufacturers were not interested in doing so. Concorde may have been a triumph for technology—no other airplane can yet fly such a length of time with such a payload at such a speed—but the plane was a commercial disaster. Only sixteen of these aircraft were ever built, and at present writing only eleven were still in service.[5]

President John F. Kennedy formally announced at the Air Force Academy on June 5, 1963, the beginning of a program to build an American supersonic transport. At a floodtide of American self-confidence and optimism, Kennedy declared that a commitment to a supersonic transport was "essential to a strong and forward-looking nation."[6] Uncharacteristic of the pattern of American transportation history, the SST did not arise from the desires of individual enterpreneurs but remained the government's self-conscious attempt to organize, shape, and force technological advance.

The president made it clear that he expected the manufacturers and the airlines to stump up a good part of the development costs. But almost from the start, concern for the costs and commercial feasibility of the SST throughout the aircraft manufacturing industry trimmed some of the enthusiasm for it. "We think we know how to build them," one engineer ventured to say, "but we haven't the faintest idea about seat-mile cost."[7]

The Pacific did not figure in any market analyses. Plans for delivery, drafted in 1963, established priorities as follows: "American-flag carriers, Atlantic; foreign-flag carriers, Atlantic; American-flag carriers, Pacific; foreign-flag carriers, Pacific; and American domestic carriers," the objections of Northwest and American Airlines notwithstanding.[8] In air traffic the Atlantic still reigned supreme.

The airlines too were ambivalent and privately lukewarm, preoccupied with the subsonic jumbo jets just coming on line and the vexatious question of how to pay for them. The question of international cooperation never seriously arose, in spite of European expressions of interest in exploring it. The Americans scorned Europe's Concorde and showed only disdain for its Soviet equivalent.

Yet early on, these programs did provoke an American response; the United States could not tolerate the success of a rival in a sphere regarded as properly American. The head of the Federal Aeronautics Administration (FAA), Najeeb Halaby, warned that if the United States failed to build an SST, it would be at the cost of "relinquish[ing] our position as the world leader of the aviation industry," arguing that "history teaches us that the stifling of innovation has been the death-knell of great societies."[9] The foreign threat kept SST alive through the 1960s.

Commercial uncertainties, technological challenges, and bureaucratic conflict bedeviled the project. More than that, the SST became the focus of a general concern about the social implications of rapid technological advance. The SST injected a new popular opposition to the airplane, something that hitherto had not existed.

Unlike the railroad, or even the bicycle, the airplane had not before been perceived as a threat to the environment or to public morals.[10] Also heretofore in transportation, speed had always been regarded as the yardstick for achievement. The SST ended that. As Najeeb Halaby puts it, "To the airman, progress and speed had been synonymous; growth and compressed time, identical. The airman saw progress and growth as inevitable [and desirable]; the economist and the politician did not."[11]

Government, industry, and the public all voiced their opinions. The debate over whether to go ahead with the SST became wide and unrestricted, the argument not simply a matter for specialists. No longer did the public automatically identify technology with progress. And the association of the aircraft industry with weaponry tended further to estrange it from the large and increasingly vocal part of the public who were unhappy about spending so much money for armaments.

For environmentalists, politically stronger and more articulate than ever before in history, the SST emerged as a key target, "as symbol of all that was wrong with technology."[12] The famous British historian Arnold Toynbee wrote an essay deploring the impact of fast travel on the negotiator. "It lands him in the conference room in a state of physical and psychological disorientation in which he is not fit to make decisions."[13] The Federation of American Scientists came out against the SST. Perhaps the most telling criticism came from a man identified strongly with pioneering aviation, Charles A. Lindbergh, who described the SST as "simply . . . another step upward on the exponential curve of tempo, mechanization, and distraction followed by our western civilization. . . . Without a basic appreciation of nature, I believe an over-emphasis on science will destroy us."[14]

The practical problem of sonic boom loomed large in the dissatisfaction of much of the public. The supersonic plane creates not just one loud bang when it first breaks the barrier but leaves in its wake a conical carpet of sound spreading over the ground. The critical hazard is not so much physical damage to property as it is psychological damage to humans. SST opponents painted lurid pictures of "screaming children, frightened dogs, old people falling downstairs from the shock."[15] But the "killing blow," in the words of Senator William Proxmire, one of the principal assailants, was the real possibility—no odds could be supplied—that a large fleet of SSTs could with engine emissions deplete the stratospheric ozone that wraps the earth with a protective filter against ultraviolet radiation. By doing so, the SST would increase radioactivity and the incidence of skin cancer.[16]

The North Pacific, with its great distances, where the plane would have been most desirable, was not yet a major transoceanic route. The SST therefore generated no specific constituency, and the idea suffered from the temper of the times. The rebelliousness of the 1960s made people quicker to see the nefarious hand of big business and big government at work, ignoring the needs and desires of the ordinary citizen. The Vietnam War had fanned public cynicism. Hearings in the Congress reflected a widespread distrust for the "notoriously powerful and influential" aerospace industry.[17]

The SST never captured the glamour enjoyed by the space program, and in the public eye it increasingly fell more into the dubious category of projects like nuclear-generated electrical power. The plan to build an American SST finally came a cropper in 1971 when the U.S. Senate voted down the essential initial funding.

For Americans, and for most passengers everywhere, including those crossing the Pacific, instead of supersonic aircraft it would be wide-bodied jets. Boeing introduced the "jumbo" jet, 747. Trippe pushed Boeing into it, and contracts were signed in April 1966 when both companies were flush with success. Trippe always wanted to be the first with a new airplane, and Pan Am was probably the only air carrier wanting anything so large. Boeing did not even have a factory big enough to assemble the plane and had to build for the purpose the largest enclosed space in the world.

The airlines ordering the 747 gambled because of the plane's enormous size (with so many seats to be filled). Boeing gambled because no adequate engine had yet been developed for the airframe. The engine finally used was two and a half times the size of anything used before on a commercial airplane. At first the engine gave many problems, and passengers dreaded the unpredictability of the aircraft. Gradual improvement established the 747 as efficient, reliable, and safe, and passengers came to appreciate its space—if the plane were not full. Wide-bodied aircraft were a means of increasing productivity, but the airlines were overly optimistic about the growth of air traffic, and no one anticipated the dramatic rise in the cost of fuel beginning in 1973.

Pan American retained its vigor as long as Trippe was at the helm. He retired in 1968, and the company began to die in a sad chronicle of rising debts and shrinking routes, of mortgaging and selling of assets, of self-dismemberment. In 1985, Pan Am yielded its Pacific Division to United Airlines. The sale gained special poignance because Pan American had been the world pioneer there and because, as the *New York Times* put it, "The Far East is almost universally looked upon as the world's most dynamic growth area, with the greatest potential for generating new waves of international air traffic."[18]

As the company continued to sink, in the late 1980s some people in the aviation industry mused that the United States had "lost sight of the intangible benefits, in prestige and influence, that have accrued from the omnipresence of the Pan Am logotype at the world's major capitals."[19] But, of course, several American airlines began to sport the Stars and Stripes around the world, and the Boeing Company could be said to have replaced Pan American as the symbol abroad of American aeronautical prowess. The 747 became an important status symbol, its massive size and conspicuous profile ensuring its prominence on any airfield. National airlines everywhere wanted to own at least one 747.

The 747 and other wide-bodied aircraft to follow were designed in response to the anticipated demand for more passenger capacity, using fewer airplanes in order to relieve airport crowding. Put succinctly, air transport had become a matter of too much metal and too little concrete. Aircraft size displaced aircraft speed as a criterion of progress, prompted in part by a new interest in conserving energy because of environmental and monetary costs.

Aircraft designed and built in the 1970s and 1980s tended to be quieter and less polluting than earlier ones. Engines burned fuel more efficiently, and wings were more skillfully designed. During those two decades the American aircraft manufacturer did not face the degree of foreign competition that the steel or automobile industries did.

American airframe makers and American engine makers competed with each other in an elaborate international negotiation process, involving both foreign companies and foreign governments. Joint ventures, offshore production, and licensing arrangements effectively made Boeing an international enterprise in manufacture as well as in sales. The company found that it needed to build abroad in order to sell abroad.[20]

Secor Brown, chairman of the Civil Aeronautics Board, underlined the commercial importance of American aeronautics by asserting that "exports of civil aircraft have been the *only* consistently positive contributor to our international export balance."[21] Boeing became America's greatest manufacturing exporter, a huge national asset, the only major advanced high technology (aside from supercomputers) in which, by the end of the Reagan era, the United States still stood as the world leader.

CHAPTER THIRTY

Splendid Fantasies

President Ronald Reagan in his State of the Union speech on February 4, 1986, announced, "We are going forward with research on a new Orient Express that could, by the end of the next decade, take off from Dulles Airport [Washington], accelerate up to 25 times the speed of sound, attaining low-earth orbit or flying to Tokyo within 2 hours."[1] The name "Orient Express" and the intended route of Reagan's aircraft were matters of some significance because during the preceding ten years the economic dynamism of much of the North Pacific rim stretching from San Diego to Shanghai made it increasingly seem likely to become the world's single most productive area.

The old myth of the wealth of the Orient had become reality, even if China were not—yet, at any rate—its center. The vitality of the Asian side of the North Pacific has much to do with countries in Southeast Asia like Malaysia or Thailand achieving the fastest rates of economic growth in the world. The American side of the North Pacific has not—yet, at any rate—had the explosive impact on its southern neighbors that Northeast Asia has had on its south.

During the Reagan years, the share of U.S. gross national product attributable to trade continued to grew exponentially, and American trade across the North Pacific more than doubled, achieving a total value half again as much as trade flows across the North Atlantic. When Reagan spoke of the Orient Express, the North Pacific market, more than any other in the world, called for high-speed transportation to shrink its huge distances to more tolerable travel times.

The president's phrase "Orient Express" artfully wove the concept of a space plane into all the ready imagery of romance and riches attached to the famous European luxury train and the exotic opulence of its destination. And at a time when Americans increasingly talked apprehen-

President Ronald Reagan and the Orient Express (Jose R. Lopez/New York Times Pictures)

sively of Japan's high-tech accomplishments and fretted about their own failures, here was a proud reassertion of what Americans thought they could do. One of the proponents of this high-speed aircraft project, Brigadier General Kenneth E. Staten, described it as "very much in the American personality. It's the kind of thing we've done before. It stimulates the pioneer in all of us."[2]

The characteristically ebullient American optimism expressed in President Reagan's remarks epitomized a longstanding popular readiness to believe that technology makes anything possible, so long as willpower and resources are applied to the problem in sufficient amounts. Certainly this positive spirit helped make the Manhattan Project successful, and it put a human on the moon. Like the lunar walk, Orient Express appealed to policymakers as something that could be flaunted; it did not need to be shrouded by the demands of military secrecy but could instead show the world the staggering technological prowess of the United States at a time when Americans desperately needed to believe in the leadership of their manufacturing.

What the president proposed was the most complex vehicle in history. Orient Express would require the most extreme technological advances, including hydrogen-fueled engines; new materials for the skin, bones, and musculature of the machine; and a highly integrated electrical and electronic design. A space plane would require a quantum leap from existing technologies, both of propulsion and materials, a transition in transportation technology analogous to (but far more abrupt than) the nineteenth-century shift from wind and wood to steam and iron.

What Reagan had in mind was a dual-purpose aircraft that could drop off satellites in space as well as carry passengers across the Pacific. It was an exciting but unrealistic fusion of objectives. Shortly after the speech, the Orient Express split into two separate projects: the hypersonic space plane, or national aerospace plane (NASP), and the high-speed commercial transport (HSCT), in effect, a super Concorde.

The NASP could not be a suitable airliner; the globe is not big enough for a plane that fast.[3] And as the *Wall Street Journal* pointed out, its passengers would scarcely be reassured by the sight of wings flaming in the intense heat generated by the aircraft's speed.[4] But the NASP could provide access to space one hundred times cheaper than any means currently available,[5] and building the NASP would presumably lead to the developing of core technologies relevant to the high-speed commercial transport.

George Keyworth, science adviser to President Reagan, had articulated even before the president's 1986 speech the need for the United States to preserve its preeminence in aeronautics, a field he defined as integral to the national interest in defense, transportation, and international trade.[6] During the 1980s American exports of aerospace products averaged $16 billion yearly. One analyst pointed out that "preserving this strong position may depend on our ability in the mid to late 1990s to take the lead in commercial air transport in an increasingly important market—the countries of the Pacific rim."[7]

Keyworth asserted that "satellite communications and fiber-optic ocean cables are tremendous advances in our ability to transmit information back and forth, but advances in telecommunications have increased demand for transportation, not replaced it,"[8] and according to statistics kept by the International Civil Aviation Organization (ICAO) in Quebec, the Pacific market for air travel was growing at 10 to 12 percent a year compared to total world air traffic growth of 7 to 8 percent annually.[9] Projections were that the overall air market early in the next century would be more than two and a half times that of the late 1980s and that the North Pacific would become the world's busiest international air traffic corridor.

The opportunities promised by travel, even at a comparatively modest

MACH 3 speed across the Pacific, were dazzling to the traveler inured to thirteen-hour nonstop flights. Leaving New York after dinner on a Monday evening, one could fly across the international dateline to Tokyo for Tuesday's lunch, an afternoon of meetings, and early dinner, flying back to New York for a repeat of Tuesday's lunch and dinner. For the New York businessman, a trip to Tokyo by HSCT would consume little more time than the 1990s trip to Tulsa.

But despite these glittering prospects, at the time President Reagan spoke, the world was a long way from the actuality of such travel. Aside from the challenges of the technology, whether the United States could alone undertake such a project was politically debatable. A commercial vehicle like the HSCT would depend on international acceptance. Furthermore, despite the American SST fiasco, the president said nothing about environmental security and how the HSCT might avoid arousing the same fears the SST had. But Reagan's omission fit smoothly into the historical pattern of ecological insensitivity so characteristic of the American reach across the Pacific. Orient Express was simply a reaffirmation of the American bid for leadership in the Pacific era, but it was more theater than reality.

The air is not the only dimension in which the creative entrepreneurial imagination still moves. Some argue that the age of the railroad in world history is yet to come and remind us that rail remains the most economical and environmentally friendly overland transport for large quantities of bulk freight. Recently a small American engineering group has revived the idea of an intercontinental North Pacific railway, a line running under the Bering Strait that could link the railways of all the continents except Australia and would open up now-remote mineral treasures of Canada, Alaska, and especially Siberia to year-round direct access. The new international political climate encourages the project.

The big advantage to this rail system would be the lack of need to break bulk. Through rail service would save two transfers, from land to water and from water to land. Using the great circle route would cut distances considerably for long-range traffic, say from Kansas City to Nanjing or Bombay to Denver. And trains are much faster than ships. The interhemispheric railroad could create a better service for moving bulk cargo around the Pacific Rim than has ever existed before.

The project is not unprecedented; it would require no special new technology. Railways already function satisfactorily in the Far North. This line would run to the south of the Arctic Circle and thus even in the depth of winter never be totally without daylight. At an estimated cost of $30–40 billion, forty-five hundred miles of track would link the northwesternmost Canadian railhead with the Trans-Siberian system by means of a tunnel bored beneath the Bering Strait.[10] Even the tunnel presents no extraordinary technological challenge. Its length would be alleviated by the fortuitous location of two islands, the Diomedes, in the channel of the strait; the longest tube (twenty-two miles) would therefore be shorter than Japan's Seikan Tunnel linking Hokkaido with Honshu.

The proponents of this great project acknowledge the challenges of building on environmentally sensitive tundra and satisfying the wishes of indigenous peoples whose lands would be necessarily impinged upon. They have constituencies to satisfy that nineteenth-century entrepreneurs could ignore or crush. But probably their biggest problem is to persuade enough potential investors that the traffic volume of this mammoth railroad would suffice to pay not only the construction but also the operating costs.

Another intercontinental linkage has appeared again with the Russian reopening to outsiders of the Arctic Sea route across the top of Eurasia, the old Northeast Passage, in 1987. This northern route would cut fifteen days off shipping time between Japan and Europe, compared with current southern routes using the Panama or Suez canals. The savings between western North America and Europe would be about ten days. If this route were found to be commercially feasible, Americans could benefit too. Dutch Harbor might emerge as a maritime analogue to Anchorage as a strategic transfer point for freight.

But ships working the Arctic trade are expensive to build, consume a lot of fuel, move slowly, and demand more insurance than those plying more conventional pathways. For long-haul intercontinental shipping, Panama and Suez still remain more cost-effective than the far northern routes—either the Russian route or the Canadian Northwest Passage. Yet international competition over intercontinental trade routes will undoubtedly continue as it has for the past five centuries.

Conclusion

The rise of Atlantic Europe, beginning in the fifteenth century, illustrates how wealth can derive from efficient and advanced communications and transportation systems.[1] Such systems make trade easier, thereby promoting technological interchanges, stimulating increases in output, and expanding a sense of economic well-being.

In the North Pacific during the late nineteenth and early twentieth centuries, the new steam transport technology opened small, insular Japan to global international life and made it possible for the Japanese to lay the foundations of an industrial economy that would in the late twentieth century make Japan the world's most successful manufacturer. A simultaneous explosive growth of the wealth of the United States occurred because of American skills in projecting flows of people, goods, and information within the large continental limits of the United States. Japan got rich because of the outside world; America got rich without it.

At mid-nineteenth century the United States became a territorial state instead of a trading state; a continental power, not a maritime one. Americans therefore were ill prepared to take full advantage of the huge increases in international trade and investment characteristic of the world economy in the late twentieth century, an economic activity in which no major nation can now afford not to participate. Through much of American history, despite all the rhetoric, overseas trade, especially in the Pacific, remained inconsequential to the U.S. economy, and American attempts at building transport networks across the Pacific, heroic though they often were, enjoyed only spasmodic success and marginal importance to American economic life overall. Despite these cold realities, a myth of the wealth to be had just over the far western horizon remained an American obsession.

Shipping and shipbuilding were the first great American industries to fail in world competition, doing so at the dawn of the American industrial age. Shipping became the first industry in which Japan competed successfully with the United States. Japan began to emerge as a maritime trading state at the same time as the United States faded out of the role, but neither Japan nor China ever really figured in the continuing American talk of the coming Pacific era. Americans had traditionally assumed that the role of leader would unquestionably be theirs. Victory in the Pacific War seemed to bear out the assumption of American leadership in commerce as well as politics. Americans continued to think of Asia as passive and plastic, willing to yield up its wealth to American advantage, and eager to accept and adapt to American ways and the American will.

The emergence of Japan to commanding international economic importance in the 1980s provoked new American interest in the idea of the Pacific era. It brought new reality to the old myth of the wealth of the Orient. Yet for Americans it carried as much apprehension as exhilaration. Since they were not the prime generators of the new wealth, Americans did not perceive this Asian accomplishment as benefiting them too. Moreover, Japan's success made it evident that the United States would not exercise the scope or character of economic dominance within the new Pacific age that Americans had long assumed would be the case. The resulting frustration added embitterment to the complexity of American feelings toward Japan.

Despite the wealth and dynamism of California, now the richest and most populous U.S. state, will the economic center of gravity in the Pacific during the twenty-first century be more likely to rest in Asia than in the United States? In the new world of the North Pacific, the Japanese economy may be momentarily faltering but its underlying strengths remain formidable. The Japanese appear likely to nurture the information industries as successfully as any other people anywhere. And to worried Americans, the Japanese variant of capitalism, whether culturally or institutionally different, seems at least as successful as the American and poses for the United States a profound intellectual challenge.

Japan's success is echoed by South Korea, Taiwan, Hong Kong, and much of Southeast Asia, those parts of the world whose people were influenced historically by Confucianism. Furthermore, China, the core of Confucianism, is emerging from five hundred years of the "development of underdevelopment," a time of protracted disorder and decline. If current patterns of economic growth persist, by 2010 China will surpass the United States and possess the world's largest economy. The current economic success of China is as startling as the current economic failure of Russia. But China's political future remains murky, and its social and ecological problems profound. Americans have a persisting tendency for unwarranted optimism about China, and to ignore its present for its presumed future.

Should Asian economic growth continue to accelerate and the United States fall behind, what then can be the American role in the Pacific era? The United States has embraced Asia to an extent no one anticipated. Historically a proselytizing urge formed a major force behind the American commercial and strategic thrust across the Pacific; Americans were more interested in teaching Asians than in learning from them. Yet American civilization has always been a composite of borrowed cultures. The nation draws deeply from its immigrants who, as the century is ending, are flowing in greater numbers across the Pacific than across the Atlantic. In the last generation, fresh waves of immigrants and a new interest in ethnicity have made American tastes more cosmopolitan. And Americans, long attracted to the arts and religions of East Asia, have begun to go beyond simply admiring the aesthetics of Asian civilizations to studying their social and economic institutions, moving from the "exotic" to the practical. Contemporary East Asia, especially Japan, takes on new interest and commands fresh respect. Americans are asking what they might learn from Japanese schools and Japanese factories.

Americans still have a propensity to reach for leadership in global affairs, and with good reason. The essential attributes for such leadership are military power, national wealth, a set of ideas attractive to others, and a sense of mission. The United States possesses all four in greater measure than any other nation, and no competitor lies on the horizon.

In the North Pacific the United States in the mid-1990s provides the essential military balance, preventing a security vacuum and relieving other nations of the need—or opportunity—to establish regional hegemony. The United States is still the world's richest nation with the largest intellectual capital base as well. As the twentieth century draws to its close, the United States remains the world's prime generator of ideas; its leading universities, libraries, and laboratories set the world standard, drawing from all over the world many of the most talented people to enjoy them. The American language has become the common international tongue. American ideas of freedom and democracy exercise wide appeal. The character of the American nation, that which Walt Whitman called its "unrhymed poetry," derives from its generous size, its political stability, its open society, and above all, its being a demographic microcosm of the world. The human electricity of the United States, its massive collective social energies, continue to invest American civilization with immense attractiveness and excitement.

Although Americans failed to grasp the Orient as they hoped, the power of the myth that pushed them there enabled them to do something bigger, something real. More than any other people, Americans pulled the North Pacific region together and created the essential framework for the long-anticipated Pacific era, with immense incalculable consequences.

Notes

Chapter 1

1. O. H. K. Spate, "The Pacific as Artefact," in Niel Gunson, ed., *The Changing Pacific, Essays in Honour of H. E. Maude* (Melbourne: Oxford University Press, 1978). For further background, see Herman R. Friis, ed., *The Pacific Basin: A History of Its Geographical Exploration* (New York: American Geographical Society, 1967), which offers a comprehensive collection of essays with superb bibliographies.

2. Philip Curtin, *Cross-Cultural Trade in World History* (Cambridge: Cambridge University Press, 1984).

3. Christopher Lloyd and Jack L. S. Coulter, *Medicine and the Navy, 1200–1900*, volume 3, *1714–1815* (Edinburgh: E.& S. Livingstone, 1961), 294.

4. Ibid., 962. The precise statistics of mortality seem impossible to determine.

5. The phrase is John Masefield's, quoted by Roderick Cameron, *The Golden Haze, with Captain Cook in the South Pacific* (Cleveland: World Publishing Company, 1964), 37.

6. Captain David Porter, *Journal of a Cruise Made to the Pacific Ocean, by Captain David Porter in the United States Frigate Essex in the Years 1812, 1813, and 1814,* 2d edition (New York: Wiley and Halsted, 1822), 2:66. Porter reports smoking out 1,200 to 1,500 rats; his ship carried 310 officers and men.

7. Adrien Carré, "Eighteenth Century French Voyages of Exploration: General Problems of Nutrition with Special Reference to the Voyages of Bougainville and D'Entrecasteaux," in J. Watt, E. J. Freeman, and W. F. Bynum, eds., *Starving Sailors: The Influence of Nutrition upon Naval and Maritime History* (Greenwich: National Maritime Museum, 1981), 82. Hereafter cited as *Starving Sailors*.

8. Julian DeZulueta and Lola Higueras, "Health and Navigation in the South Seas: The Spanish Experience," in *Starving Sailors*, 87. Magellan's men suffered from scurvy, but some survived. Ibid., 88. Walter tells us that the Spaniards used earthen jars for drinking water instead of the wooden casks favored by the British, and they also collected rainwater during the voyage. Richard Walter, *Anson's Voyage Round the World* (London: Martin Hopkinson, 1928), 228.

9. See, for example, the case of Captain Cook described below.
Alcohol served as anodyne for the sailor. Admiral Edward Vernon, commanding the British West Indies fleet, was, we are told, distressed by "the swinish vice of drunkenness" prevalent in the fleet and he therefore caused the daily half pint rum ration to be diluted in a quart of water (one to four). The proportions subsequently came to vary; many ships

issued it at one to three. The mixture was called grog because of the admiral's nickname, "Old Grogram," after the peculiar waterproof boatcloak of that material he liked to wear. Vernon's invention inspired a popular song:

> A mighty bowl on deck he drew
> And filled it to the brink;
> Such drank the *Burford's* gallant crew
> And such the Gods shall drink;
> The sacred robe which Vernon wore
> Was drenched with the same;
> And hence its virtues guard our shore
> And Grog derives its name.

The ration, diluted though it may have been, was enough to make a man half drunk or groggy most of the time.

Lawrence Washington, older brother of George, fought under Vernon, returned to Virginia, and named his plantation Mount Vernon to honor his commander. A. J. Pack, *Nelson's Blood, The Story of Naval Rum* (Homewell, Havant, Hampshire: Kenneth Mason, 1982), 131.

10. William Lytle Schurz, *The Manila Galleon* (New York: E. P. Dutton & Company, 1959), is a classic account from which I have drawn heavily. For a British view at the time, see Richard Walter, *op. cit.*

11. Charles E. Chapman, *A History of California: The Spanish Period* (New York: Macmillan, 1921), 88.

12. J. H. Parry, *The Spanish Seaborne Empire* (New York: Alfred A. Knopf, 1966), 132.

13. Schurz, 270.

14. Chapman, 91.

15. Ping-ti Ho, *Studies of the Population of China, 1368–1953* (Cambridge: Harvard University Press, 1967), 183. Ho discusses land routes also.

16. Anson captured the galleon *Nostra Signora de Cabadonga* in June 1743. She carried 1,313,843 silver pieces-of-eight and 35,682 ounces of virgin silver. Walter, 358, 363.

17. O. H. K. Spate, *The Pacific Since Magellan*, volume 1, *The Spanish Lake* (Minneapolis: University of Minnesota Press, 1979), 202.

18. Ibid., 1n, quoting Christopher Marlowe, *Tamburlaine the Great* (1590).

19. Ibid., 264.

20. Raymond H. Fisher, *The Voyage of Semen Dezhnev in 1648: Bering's Precursor, with Selected Documents* (London: Hakluyt Society, 1981), 1. See also *The Journals of Captain James Cook on His Voyages of Discovery*, ed. J. C. Beaglehole (London: Hakluyt Society, 1967), volume 3, *The Voyage of the Resolution and Discovery, 1776–1780*, 1vin. Hereafter cited as Beaglehole.

21. Lydia T. Black, "The Story of Russian America," in William W. Fitzhugh and Aron Crowell, eds., *Crossroads of Continents: Cultures of Siberia and Alaska* (Washington: Smithsonian Institution Press, 1988), 75.

22. Warren L. Cook, *Flood Tide of Empire, Spain and the Pacific Northwest, 1543–1819* (New Haven, Connecticut: Yale University Press, 1973), 524–537.

23. Ibid., 534n, quoting Henry Adams, *History of the United States of America during the First Administration of Thomas Jefferson* (New York: Charles Scribner's Sons, 1898), 1: 339–340.

24. James A. Williamson, *Cook and the Opening of the Pacific* (London: Hodder & Stoughton, 1946), provides a succinct introduction to the subject.

Chapter 2

1. Quoted by Christopher C. Lloyd, "Victualling of the Fleet in the Eighteenth and Nineteenth Centuries," in *Starving Sailors*, 9.

2. After Cook's second voyage, he could report to the Admiralty (July 29, 1775) that after three arduous and perilous years, the ship's company of *Resolution*, 112 strong, lost three men in accidents and only one by disease. And that disease was not scurvy. James A. Williamson, *Cook and the Opening of the Pacific* (London: Hodder & Stoughton, 1946), 181.

3. Cook had two of his men flogged for refusing to eat fresh meat. Christopher Lloyd and Jack L. S. Coulter, *Medicine and the Navy, 1200–1900*, Volume 3, *1714–1815* (Edinburgh: E & S Livingstone, 1961), 305.

4. Beaglehole, volume 4, *The Life of Captain James Cook* (London: Hakluyt Society, Extra Series 37, 1974), 705.

5. Ibid., volume 3, part 1, *The Voyage of the Resolution and Discovery, 1776–1780* (London: Hakluyt Society, Extra Series 36, 1967), 480.

6. Cook's men did not develop scurvy, but Cook's "conquest" of that disease is a myth. He took so many measures against scurvy that he could not be sure what was specifically effective. But shortly after his time, in 1795, the Royal Navy began to issue lemon juice in a daily allowance. That solved the problem, and just in time to enable the British to stay at sea long enough to maintain an effective blockade against the French. Thus, we can say that the lemon provided a major contribution to the defeat of Napoleon. Kenneth J. Carpenter, *The History of Scurvy and Vitamin C* (Cambridge: Cambridge University Press, 1986), 83–84, 95–96. Despite increased understanding of the disease, scurvy remained a problem for Pacific travelers even after the mid-nineteenth century. Lieutenant A. W Habersham, USN, complained of it on the homeward voyage in late 1855 of the Ringgold-Rodgers North Pacific Surveying Expedition. A. W. Habersham, *The North Pacific Surveying and Exploring Expedition* (Philadelphia: J. B. Lippincott, 1857), 449–450.

7. *Starving Sailors*, 65.

8. Alan Frost, "New Geographical Perspectives and the Emergence of the Romantic Imagination," in Robin Fisher and Hugh Johnston, eds., *Captain James Cook and His Times* (Seattle: University of Washington Press, 1979), 18. See also Sir James Watt, "Medical Aspects and Consequences of Cook's Voyages," in Fisher and Johnston, 154–155.

9. Glyndwr Williams, "Myth and Reality: James Cook and His Theoretical Geography of Northwest America," in Fisher and Johnson, 59–60.

10. Stephen D. Watrous, ed., *John Ledyard's Journey through Russia and Siberia, 1787–1788: The Journal and Selected Letters* (Madison: University of Wisconsin Press, 1966), 3.

11. Jared Sparks, *The Life of John Ledyard, the American Traveller; Comprising Selections from His Journals and Correspondence* (Cambridge: Hilliard & Brown, 1828), 5.

12. Ibid., 13.

13. James Wheelock, Hanover, New Hampshire, November 12, 1821, to Richard Bartlett, no. 112, Miscellaneous Papers Relating to John Ledyard, the American Traveller, used in writing his life, 1827, by Jared Sparks. AMs, Sparks Papers, Houghton Library, Harvard University. Wheelock, son of Eleazar, was a fellow member of the class of 1776.

14. James Wheelock, n.p., January 29, 1822, to Jared Sparks. AMs, Sparks Papers.

15. John Ledyard, *Journal of Captain Cook's Last Voyage*, ed. James Kenneth Munford, intro. Sinclair H. Hitchings (Corvallis: University of Oregon Press, 1963), xxiii. Hereafter cited as *Ledyard Journal*.

16. Sparks, 35–36. I find no evidence that Ledyard made any particular impression on Cook during the time of their association.

17. William Woodruff, *Impact of Western Man: A Study of Europe's Role in the World Economy, 1750–1960* (Washington: University Press of America, 1982), 237.

18. Quoted by Roderick Cameron, *The Golden Haze, with Captain Cook in the South Pacific*, (Cleveland: World Publishing Company, 1964), 254. Cook's last diary entry is dated January 17, 1779.

19. Lloyd and Coulter, 72.

20. No one seems to have been tempted to jump ship as they were so often in Hawaii or Tahiti, for instance, and relations with the local women in Nootka seem to have been

slight. For comments by an early American visitor, see Richard J. Cleveland, *Narrative of Voyages and Commercial Enterprises*, 3d edition (Boston: Charles H. Peirce, 1850), 110.

21. *Ledyard Journal*, 71.

22. Beaglehole, 3: 297–298.

23. *Ledyard Journal*, 70.

24. Eufrosina Dvoichenko-Markov, "John Ledyard and the Russians," *Russian Review*, 11, 4, October 1952, 213.

25. Beaglehole, 3: 208–209. Beaglehole points out that Ledyard leaves in "the silly stories . . . adding a few of his own." And that "the pages from 170 to 208 (the end of the book) are an exact transcript of Rickman."

26. Beaglehole, 4: 692.

27. *Ledyard Journal*, xiv.

28. For a discussion of this voyage, see Philip Chadwick Foster Smith, *The Empress of China* (Philadelphia: Philadelphia Maritime Museum, 1984).

29. Quoted by Clarence L. Ver Steeg, "Financing and Outfitting the First United States Ship to China," *Pacific Historical Review* 22, 1, February 1953: 6.

30. *Ledyard Journal*, xlvii.

31. John Ledyard, London, November 25, 1786, to Thomas Jefferson, in Julian P. Boyd, ed., *The Papers of Thomas Jefferson* (Princeton, New Jersey: Princeton University Press, 1954), 10: 548.

32. The quotation is from Jefferson's *Autobiography*, in Boyd, 9: 261.

33. Thomas Jefferson, Paris, August 16, 1786, to John Ledyard, in Boyd, 10:258.

34. *Ledyard Journal*, xxxiii. Ledyard's "walk" across Siberia has crept into legend where it lingers even today. See Frost, 6.

35. Dvoichenko-Markov, 211.

36. "A Report from Ivan V. Iakobii, Governor General of Siberia, to Aleksandr A. Bezborodko, College of Foreign Affairs, Concerning the Travels of John Ledyard," suggests that the American was spying for the English. Basil Dmytryshyn, E. A. P. Crownhart-Vaughan, and Thomas Vaughan, eds. and trans., *To Siberia and Russian America: Three Centuries of Russian Eastward Expansion, 1558–1867*, volume 2, *Russian Penetration of the North Pacific Ocean, 1700–1797: A Documentary Record* (Portland: Oregon Historical Society Press, 1988), 342.

37. Thomas Jefferson, Paris, September 20, 1787, to Charles Thomson, in Boyd, 12:160.

38. At the time of his death, Ledyard attracted favorable comment. An obituary notice in *American Museum, or Repository of Ancient and Modern Fugitive Pieces, Prose and Poetical* (5, 1789), says: "Mr. Ledyard was strong and active, bold as a lion, and gentle as he was bold . . . the miscarriage of his project must be felt as a very general and public loss."

Henry Beaufoy, secretary of the "Association for discovering the inland countries of Africa," who knew Ledyard, wrote that "to those who have never seen Mr. Ledyard, it may not, perhaps, be uninteresting to know, that his person, though scarcely exceeding the middle size, was remarkably expressive of activity and strength; and that his manners, though unpolished, were neither uncivil nor unpleasing. Little attentive to difference of rank, he seemed to consider all men as his equals, and as such he respected them. His genius, though uncultivated and irregular, was original and comprehensive. Ardent in his wishes, yet calm in his deliberations; daring in his purposes, but guarded in his measures; impatient of control, yet capable of strong endurance; adventurous beyond the conception of ordinary men, yet wary and considerate, and attentive to all precautions, he appeared to be formed by Nature for achievements of hardihood and peril." Quoted by Caleb Cushing, review of *Life of Ledyard* by Jared Sparks, *North American Review* (61, October 1828), 371.

39. John M. Maki, "William Smith Clark: A Yankee in Hokkaido," TMs, n.d. (Amherst, Massachusetts: Archives, University of Massachusetts), 2:15.

40. Henry Nash Smith, *Virgin Land: The American West as Symbol and Myth* (Cambridge: Harvard University Press, 1970), 17.

41. Helen Augur, *Passage to Glory: John Ledyard's America* (Garden City, New York: Doubleday, 1946), 180.

Chapter 3

1. The title of Part II is from *Columbia: A Song*, written and set to music by Timothy Dwight, the Elder, printed at the Press of Timothy Dwight College in Yale University, New Haven, Connecticut, 1940. This is a reprint, with brief commentary, of the text printed by Mathew Carey in Philadelphia in 1787, published in the *American Museum*.

2. A Gentleman educated at Yale College [Timothy Dwight], *America, or, A Poem of the Settlement of the British Colonies; Addressed to the Friends of Freedom, and Their Country* (New Haven: Thomas and Samuel Green, 1770), 3.

3. The population of the United States as of August 2, 1790, was 3,929,214 according to *Historical Statistics of the United States* (Washington: United States Department of Commerce, September 1975, Bicentennial Edition).

4. A useful summary account of the maritime history of New England is to be found in Robert G. Albion, William A. Baker, and Benjamin W. Labaree, *New England and the Sea* (Middletown, Connecticut: Wesleyan University Press, 1972).

5. For statistics on both exports and imports, see Gary M. Walton and James F. Shepherd, *The Economic Rise of Early America* (Cambridge: Cambridge University Press, 1979), 80, 82.

6. Adam Smith, *The Wealth of Nations* (New York: Random House, Modern Library Edition, 1937), 71.

7. Tea was still regarded as an "elegant luxury" for Americans according to Samuel Shaw, supercargo, or commercial agent aboard the ship *Empress of China*. Josiah Quincy, *The Journals of Major Samuel Shaw with a Life of the Author* (Boston: Wm. Crosby and H. P. Nichols, 1847), 350. The English began to drink tea in the middle of the seventeenth century, and its popularity increased widely in the eighteenth. By 1800, the yearly rate of consumption was two pounds per person. *Encyclopedia Britannica*, 11th ed., s.v. "Tea." Tea, thought of as quintessentially Chinese, probably originated in northern India and was first carried to China by Buddhist missionaries at about the time of the birth of Christ.

8. Samuel W. Woodhouse, "The Voyage of the *Empress of China*," *Pennsylvania Magazine of History and Biography* 63, 1, January 1939, 24, quoting the *Maryland Journal and Baltimore Advertiser*, March 5, 1784.

9. Quincy, 350.

10. Smith, 33.

11. Quincy, 232.

12. James S. Cox, Philadelphia, May 7, 1810, to John Cox, Cox Papers, Bethlehem, Pennsylvania. Philadelphia, America's leading seaport in foreign commerce in 1790, declined to "a bad third or fourth position by the 1820's." Marion V. Brewington, "Maritime Philadelphia, 1609–1837," *Pennsylvania Magazine of History and Biography* 2, 63, April 1939, 115.

13. Sailing from New York, the brig *Eleanora* may have preceded them. Frederic W. Howay, ed., *Voyages of the Columbia to the Northwest Coast 1787–1790 and 1790–1793* (Boston: Massachusetts Historical Society, 1941), x–xi.

14. Fitch W. Taylor, *A Voyage Round the World and Visits to Various Foreign Countries, in the United States Frigate Columbia, etc.*, 9th edition (New Haven, Connecticut: H. Mansfield, 1850), 322.

15. Quoted in *New Yorker*, March 7, 1988, 59. "A Reporter at Large (Soviet Space Program)," by Henry S. Cooper, Jr.

16. By sea the eastern United Seas is closer even to Japan via the Cape of Good Hope than by the South American route. New York City to Yokohama via the former is 15,200 miles; via the Strait of Magellan, 16,205. United States Department of Commerce and Labor, Bureau of Statistics, *Transportation Routes and Systems of the World, Development of Steam-*

Carrying Power on Land and Sea, 1800 to 1906 (Washington: Government Printing Office, 1907), 24.

17. Harry A. Morton, *The Wind Commands: Sailors and Sailing Ships in the Pacific* (Middletown, Connecticut: Wesleyan University Press, 1975), 276.

18. Melville in *White Jacket* uses it as a metaphor: "Sailor or landsman, there is some sort of Cape Horn for all. Boys! beware of it; prepare for it in time. Greybeards! thank God it is passed." For an excellent comprehensive history of the Horn route, see Raymond A. Rydell, *Cape Horn to the Pacific: The Rise and Decline of an Ocean Highway* (Berkeley: University of California Press, 1952). John Train tells us that to observe correct form in a British naval mess you must "avoid resting elbows on the table for long periods unless you have sailed around the horn." *Harvard Magazine*, November–December 1990, 18.

19. Quincy, 205.

20. Smith, 600, remarks that almost all shipping from Europe to China stops in Batavia, despite "perhaps the most unwholesome climate in the world."

21. Richard H. Dana, Jr., *Two Years before the Mast* (Boston: Houghton Mifflin, 1895), 331.

22. Ibid., 374.

23. Francis Leigh Williams, *Matthew Fontaine Maury, Scientist of the Sea* (New Brunswick, New Jersey: Rutgers University Press, 1963), 66.

24. Howay, 19–20.

25. William Sturgis, "The Northwest Fur Trade, and the Indians of the Oregon Country, 1788–1830" (Boston: Old South Leaflets 219, n.d.), 3.

26. Howay, 145, quoting *Columbian Centinel*, August 11, 1790.

27. D. W. Meinig, *The Shaping of America, A Geographical Perspective on 500 Years of History*, volume 1, *Atlantic America 1492–1800* (New Haven, Connecticut: Yale University Press, 1986), 424, quoting Alexander Mackenzie, *Voyages from Montreal on the River St. Lawrence through the Continent of North America to the Frozen and Pacific Oceans in the Years 1789 and 1793* (Toronto: Radisson Society, 1927), 411.

28. Quoted in "Discovery beyond the Rocky Mountains, Expedition of Mackenzie," *North American Review* 50, 106, January 1840, 89.

29. H. Smith, 20.

30. Derek Pethick, *First Approaches to the Northwest Coast* (Vancouver, British Columbia: J. J. Douglas, 1976), 78.

31. [William Dane Phelps], "Solid Men of Boston," AMs, n.d., Bancroft Library, University of California, Berkeley, 62.

32. Pethick, 102, quotes the great French explorer, La Perouse, embarking on an around-the-world trip, August 1, 1785, a trip he would not survive, who said: "Though the Russians are established in the north and the Spaniards to the south, many centuries will unquestionably elapse before these two nations will meet; and there will long remain between them intermediary points, which might be occupied by other nations." *A Voyage Round the World*, 3:300.

33. Howay, xxvi.

34. Smith, 224–225, quotes the *New York News Dispatch*.

35. Ibid., 69.

36. Robert J. Kerner, *The Urge to the Sea, the Course of Russian History, the Role of Rivers, Portages, Ostrogs, Monasteries, and Furs* (Berkeley: University of California Press, 1942), 88.

37. Dmytryshyn et al., volume 3, *The Russian American Colonies, 1798–1867*, xxivff.

38. Ibid., 105. Letter from Nikolai P. Rezanov to the Directors of the Russian American Company Regarding the Character of the Chief Administrator, Aleksandr A. Baranov, November 6, 1805.

39. Mary E. Wheeler, "Empires in Conflict and Cooperation: The 'Bostonians' and the Russian-American Company, *Pacific Historical Review* 15, 4, November 1971, 422.

40. Quoted by James H. Lanman, "The American Fur Trade," *Hunt's Merchants' Magazine* 3, 3, September 1840, 197.

41. Quoted by James P. Ronda, *Astoria and Empire* (Lincoln: University of Nebraska Press, 1990), xii.

42. The authoritative account is James R. Gibson, *Imperial Russia in Frontier America, the Changing Geography of Supply of Russian America, 1784–1867* (New York: Oxford University Press, 1976).

43. Phelps, 13.

44. Ibid., 15.

45. Quoted by Charles Sumner, "Speech of Hon. Charles Sumner of Massachusetts on the Cession of Russian America to the United States," *Congressional Globe*, 1867, 17. Recently researchers have been studying the *baidarka* for clues to surface vessel hydrodynamics. The skin surface of the *baidarka* may have aided in providing a smooth or laminar flow along the surface, an objective that contemporary ship (and aircraft) designers are still struggling to achieve. We do not yet understand the mathematics of the interacting of waves with hull design. But possibly by intuition and through centuries of experience, the Aleuts knew what the supercomputer has yet to put within grasp. Anthropologists have noted that the upper arms of a mummified Aleut kayaker were remarkably muscular. John Markoff, "Lessons from Ancients Who Plied the Waves, *New York Times*, December 2, 1990, F9.

46. William C. Sturtevant, general editor, and David Damas, volume editor, *Handbook of North American Indians* (Washington: Smithsonian Institution, 1984), volume 5, *Arctic*, 163.

47. Phelps, 20.

48. Sturgis, 6.

Chapter 4

1. *American Museum* 3, 5, May 1788, 440.

2. The standard account is what its author liked in conversation to refer to as his "wooden interpretation of history," Robert Greenhalgh Albion, *Forests and Sea Power: The Timber Problem of the Royal Navy, 1652–1862* (Cambridge: Harvard University Press, 1926). On American shipbuilding, the reader will want to turn to John G. B. Hutchins, *The American Maritime Industries and Public Policy, 1789–1914: An Economic History* (Cambridge: Harvard University Press, 1941). Hereafter cited as Hutchins 1941.

3. For any ship in tropical waters, the destructive power of the worm was awesome. Richard J. Cleveland recalls: "On going into the hold of the ship, when empty, I was astonished at the noise they made; not unlike a multitude of borers with augers," 31.

4. Hutchins 1941, 76.

5. On Magoun's career, see Hollis French, *The Thatcher Magoun: An American Clipper Ship, Her Owners, Captains, and Model* (Cambridge: Houghton Mifflin, 1936).

6. The Middlesex Canal was the second canal to be built in the United States, the first in New England. See Christopher Roberts, "The Middlesex Canal" (Ph.D. dissertation, Harvard University, 1927), 14.

7. James M. Morris, "America's Stepchild," *Wilson Quarterly* 11, no. 3 Summer 1987, 115.

8. Arthur H. Clark, *The Clipper Ship Era* (New York: G. P. Putnam's Sons, 1910), 52.

9. Samuel Eliot Morison, *The Maritime History of Massachusetts, 1783–1860* (Boston: Houghton Mifflin, 1921), 103.

10. Reverend Charles Brooks, *History of Town of Medford* (Boston: James M. Usher, 1855), 363. Also Carl Seaburg and Alan Seaburg, *Medford on the Mystic* (n.p., 1980), 101.

11. Seaburg and Seaburg, 81.

12. *Niles Register*, November 9, 1816, 173.

13. Phelps, 77.

14. William Sturgis took an uncommonly sympathetic view of the indigenous peoples, even studying their languages. Ending a lecture in Boston, he said: "These claimants are powerless, and have neither fleets nor armies to maintain their rights; and 'tis not the practice of *civilized* and *Christian* nations to listen to the claims, or respect the rights of the

Indians, from one extremity of this continent to the other. They have been disregarded, are now disregarded, and will, I fear, continue to be disregarded until the day of retribution comes, when equal justice will be meted out to the Christian destroyer and his heathen victim—and that will be a woful [sic] day for the white man." "The Oregon Question, Substance of a Lecture before the Mercantile Library Association," delivered January 22, 1845 (Boston: Jordan, Swift, and Wiley, 1845), 32. Sturgis writes in his *Journal*, "I believe I am the only man living who has a personal knowledge of those early transactions and I can show *that in each and every case* where a vessel was attacked or a crew killed by them [the local people], it was in direct retaliation for some life taken or for some gross outrage committed against *that tribe.*" S. W. Jackman, ed., *The Journal of William Sturgis* (Victoria, British Columbia: Sono Nis Press, 1978), 15.

15. Quoted by R. H. Dana, "Cleveland's *Voyages*, Voyage to Canton," *North American Review* 55, 116, July 1842, 163.

16. Anon., "Captain Cleveland's Voyage from China to the Northwest Coast of America," *North American Review* 25, 57, October 1827, 459.

17. Cleveland, 76.

18. Dana, "Cleveland's *Voyages*," 163.

19. Phelps, 7. See also Charles G. Loring, "Memoir of the Hon. William Sturgis," *Proceedings of the Massachusetts Historical Society, 1863–1864* (Boston: printed for the Society, 1864), 432.

20. Sturgis, "Northwest," 20.

21. Tyler Dennett, *Americans in Eastern Asia: A Critical Study of United States' Policy in the Far East in the Nineteenth Century*, reprint (New York: Barnes & Noble, 1963), 41.

22. United States Congress, House, 20th Congress, 1st Session, Report 209, March 25, 1828, 7.

23. Harold Whitman Bradley, "Hawaii and the American Penetration of the Northeastern Pacific, 1800–1845," *Pacific Historical Review* 12, 3, September 1943, 278–279.

24. *The United States Magazine and Democratic Review* 13, 61, July 1843, 15, quoting James Jackson Jarves, *History of the Hawaiian or Sandwich Islands* (Boston: Tappan and Dennett, 1843).

25. Hull Gleason, *Old Ships and Ship-building Days of Medford, 1630–1873* (West Medford, Massachusetts: privately printed, 1936), 27.

26. Charles C. Stelle, "American Trade in Opium to China, prior to 1820," *Pacific Historical Review* 9, 4, December 1940, 433.

27. Mira Wilkins, *The Emergence of Multinational Enterprise: American Business Abroad from the Colonial Era to 1914* (Cambridge: Harvard University Press, 1970), 7.

28. Quincy, 341.

29. J. Fenimore Cooper, *History of the Navy of the United States of America*, abridged in one volume (New York: Stringer & Townsend, 1856), 290.

30. *Essex* was the first American warship to enter the Pacific via the Cape of Good Hope (1800) and the first to round the Horn (1813). David F. Long, *Nothing too Daring: A Biography of Commodore David Porter, 1780–1843* (Annapolis, Maryland: United States Naval Institute Press, 1970), 59.

31. Ibid., 81.

32. Thomas Hart Benton, *Thirty Years' View: A History of the Working of the American Government for Thirty Years from 1820 to 1850* (New York: D. Appleton, 1856), 480.

33. D. Porter, 79.

34. Allan B. Cole, ed., "Captain David Porter's Proposed Expedition to the Pacific and Japan, 1815," *Pacific Historical Review* 9, 1, March 1940, 64.

Chapter 5

1. United States Congress, House, 20th Congress, 1st Sess. Report 209, 11.

2. William Stanton, *The Great United States Exploring Expedition of 1838–1842* (Berkeley: University of California Press, 1975), 3. Bryant and Sturgis carried more than half of U.S. trade with China and the American Pacific coast during the period 1810–1840. Loring, 433.

3. Ibid., 6.

4. United States Congress, Report 209, 12.

5. Cole, 63–64.

6. United States Congress, House, 23d Congress, 2d Session, Navy Department, Document 105, 1834–35, Report of J. N. Reynolds to the Secretary of the Navy, September 24, 1828, 28.

7. Magdalen Coughlin, "Commercial Foundations of Political Interest in the Opening Pacific, 1789–1829," *California Historical Society Quarterly* 50, 1, March 1971, 24, citing *Annals of Congress,* 18th Congress, 2d Session, December 21, 1824, 40. *Abridgement of the Debates of Congress,* House of Representatives, "Settlement of the Northwest Coast," December 1824, 213.

8. Captain Edmund Fanning, *Voyages and Discoveries in the South Seas, 1792–1832,* first published in 1833 (Salem, Massachusetts: Marine Research Society, 1924), 80.

9. W. Patrick Strauss, "Preparing the Wilkes Expedition: A Study in Disorganization," *Pacific Historical Review* 28, 3, August 1959, 222.

10. Herman J. Viola and Carolyn Margolis, eds., *Magnificent Voyagers, the U.S. Exploring Expedition, 1838–1842* (Washington: Smithsonian Institution Press, 1985), 12.

11. Cooper, 207.

12. J. R. Poinsett, "Synopsis of the Cruise of the United States Exploring Expedition during the Year 1838, 1839, 1840, and 1841, Delivered before the National Institute, by Its Commander, Charles Wilkes, on the twentieth of June, 1842," *North American Review* 56, 119, April 1843, 257.

13. Viola and Margolis, 25.

14. William H. Goetzmann, *New Lands, New Men: America and the Second Great Age of Discovery* (New York: Viking Penguin, 1986), 278.

15. Charles Erskine, *Twenty Years before the Mast—With the More Thrilling Scenes and Incidents While Circumnavigating the Globe under the Command of the late Admiral Charles Wilkes, 1838–1842* (Boston: published by author, 1890), 195.

16. Goetzmann, 289.

17. In 1822 Russian explorer Thaddeus Bellingshausen had preceded Wilkes.

18. Viola and Margolis, 186–187.

19. H. H. Bancroft, quoted by ibid., 179.

20. Frederick Merk, *Albert Gallatin and the Oregon Problem, A Study in Anglo-American Diplomacy* (Cambridge: Harvard University Press, 1950), 13.

21. George Boutwell, "Oregon: The Claim of Great Britain," *Hunt's Merchants' Magazine* 12, 6, June 1845, 522.

22. Quoted by Norman A. Graebner, *Empire on the Pacific, A Study in American Continental Expansion,* reprint (Santa Barbara, California: ABC-Clio Press, 1983), 71.

23. Dana, 270.

24. See Arthur M. Johnson and Barry E. Supple, *Boston Capitalists and Western Railroads: A Study in the Nineteenth-Century Railroad Investment Process* (Cambridge: Harvard University Press, 1967).

25. Edward Dewey Graham, "American Ideas of a Special Relationship with China, 1784–1900" (Ph.D. dissertation, Harvard University, 1968), 12.

26. Graebner, 127–128, quoting *Congressional Globe,* 29th Congress, 1st Session, Appendix, 212.

27. R. W. van Alstyne, *The Rising American Empire* (New York: Oxford University Press, 1960), 96.

28. Ibid., 100.

29. *North American Review* 68, 142, January 1849, 90–91.

Chapter 6

1. Carl C. Cutler, *Greyhounds of the Sea: The Story of the American Clipper Ship* (New York: G. P. Putnam's Sons, 1930), 302.

2. Edward L. Towle, "Science, Commerce and the Navy of the Seafaring Frontier (1842–1861)—The Role of Lieutenant M. F. Maury and the U.S. Naval Hydrographic Office" (Ph.D. dissertation, University of Rochester, 1966), 42.

3. Ibid., 39.

4. Alexis de Tocqueville, *Democracy in America*, trans. Henry Reeve, with preface and notes by John C. Spencer (New York: Adland and Saunders, 1838), 408.

5. Wilkins, 27.

6. John Haskell Kemble, *The Panama Route 1848–1869* (Berkeley: University of California Press, 1943), 255.

7. Alexander Laing, *Clipper Ship Man* (New York: Duell, Sloan, & Pearce, 1944), 83.

8. J(ohn) N. Reynolds, *Voyage of the United States Frigate Potomac under the Command of Commodore John Downes, during the Circumnavigation of the Globe in the Years 1831, 1832, 1833, and 1834* (New York: Harper & Brothers, 1835), 385.

9. Charles Sellers, *James K. Polk, Continentalist, 1843–1846* (Princeton, New Jersey: Princeton University Press, 1966), 157.

10. Ibid., 213.

11. Merk, 417.

12. Norman A. Graebner, "Maritime Factors in the Oregon Compromise," *Pacific Historical Review* 20, 4, November 1951, 332.

13. Robert G. Cleland, "Asiatic Trade and the American Occupation of the Pacific Coast," American Historical Association, *Annual Report* 1, 1914, 288, citing J. B. Moore, ed., *The Works of James Buchanan* (Philadelphia: Lippincott, 1909), 6:304–306.

14. Ibid., citing Moore, 275–278.

15. Is it of any significance that Seward came from the "Empire State"?

16. Frederic Bancroft, "Seward's Ideas of Territorial Expansion," *North American Review* 167, 500, July 1898, 86.

17. Henry Cabot Lodge, "William H. Seward," *Atlantic Monthly*, May 1884, 690.

18. George B. Baker, ed., *The Works of William H. Seward* (New York: Redfield, 1884), 5: 566.

19. Baker, 3:78.

20. Ibid., 409.

21. Walter G. Sharrow, "William Henry Seward and the Basis for American Empire, 1850–1860," *Pacific Historical Review* 36, 3, April 1967, 339, quoting Seward to the Pacific Railroad Convention, October 1849, Seward Papers.

22. Baker, 3:188.

23. Ernest N. Paolino, *The Foundations of the American Empire: William Henry Seward and U.S. Foreign Policy* (Ithaca, New York: Cornell University Press, 1973), 57.

24. Baker, 1:56.

25. Ibid., 57.

Chapter 7

1. Cutler, xii.

2. Samuel Eliot Morison, *Oxford History of the American People* (New York: Oxford Uni-

versity Press, 1965), 584; Basil Lubbock, *The China Clippers*, reprint (Glasgow: Brown, Son & Ferguson, 1957), 71.

3. *New York Daily Times*, April 30, 1852.

4. Lubbock, 68.

5. Ibid.

6. Hutchins 1941, 318.

7. Matthew Fontaine Maury, *The Physical Geography of the Sea* (New York: Harper & Brothers, 1856) 338.

8. *Rainbow's* bow lines supposedly reflect Asian origin, inspired by the model of a sampan brought back from Singapore by Captain Bob Waterman and turned over to a New York draftsman. Morison, *Maritime*, 329.

9. Laing, 15. It was exceeded only by *Red Jacket*.

10. *Some Ships of the Clipper Ship Era: Their Builders, Owners, and Captains* (Boston: State Street Trust Co., 1913), 16.

11. A Sailor, *Description of the Largest Ship in the World, The New Clipper Great Republic of Boston Designed, Built and Owned by Donald McKay, and Commanded by Capt. L. McKay, with Illustrated Designs of the Construction* (Boston: Eastburn's Press, 1853), 5.

12. Gleason, 33.

13. Cutler, 132.

14. Ibid., 148, quoting *Pacific News*.

15. The Navigation Act of 1817 closed American coastal traffic to foreigners. It also forbade importation of goods that did not come from the carrier's country. George Rogers Taylor, *The Economic History of the United States*, volume 4, *The Transportation Revolution, 1815–1860* (New York: Harper Torchbooks, 1951), 129.

16. Hutchins 1941, 268.

17. Clark, 65.

18. *Flying Cloud's* voyage under sail from New York City to San Francisco in eighty-nine days, eight hours, set in 1854, compares with the 150–200 days required by an ordinary ship. The record was not broken until 1989 when a sixty-foot sloop, *Thursday's Child*, thanks to new materials, like carbon fiber and Kevlar, made the same voyage in eighty days, nineteen hours. *New York Times*, February 11, 1989; *Boston Globe*, February 13, 1989.

19. Richard Henry Dana, Jr., "Cleveland's Voyages, A Narrative of Voyages and Commercial Enterprises," *North American Review* 55, 116, July 1842, 151.

20. Edward E. Bradley, "Before the Mast on the Clipper Ship 'Mary Whitridge' of Baltimore" (Mystic, Connecticut: Marine Historical Association), volume 1, no. 6, August 1, 1932, 94. Richard Henry Dana, *The Seaman's Friend* (Delmar: New York: Scholars' Facsimiles and Reprints, 1979), furnishes a useful guide to the rich culture of seamanship in the age of sail, a vocabulary and an art now largely vanished.

21. Cutler, 187.

22. Morison, *Maritime*, 356.

23. Dana, *Two*, 11.

24. For a good description of this, see Herman Melville's novel, *White Jacket or the World in a Man-of-War* (New York: Library of America, 1983).

25. Lubbock, 41.

26. Dana, *Two*, 308.

27. Ibid., 154.

28. Clark, 122.

29. Maury, viii.

30. Williams, 184.

31. *Hunt's Merchants' Magazine*, May 1854, 631.

32. John Leighly, ed., *The Physical Geography of the Sea and Its Meteorology*, by Matthew Fontaine Maury (Cambridge: Harvard University Press, Belknap Press, 1963), ix.

33. Ibid., xxii, citing *Blackwood's*.

34. Ibid., xiii.

35. Ibid., citing "from *The Economist*," *Littell's Living Age* 45, 577, 1855, 655–658, esp. 657.

36. Ibid., xxi.

37. Nathan Reingold, "Two Views of Maury . . . and a Third," Book reviews, *Isis* 55, 3, 1964, 181.

38. Matthew Fontaine Maury, "Steam Navigation to China," *Hunt's Merchants' Magazine* 18, 4, April 1848, 247.

39. Ibid., 249.

40. Towle, 440.

41. Maury, *Hunt's*, 253.

Chapter 8

1. Towle, 25n.

2. D. A. Farnie, *East and West of Suez: The Suez Canal in History 1854–1956* (Oxford: Oxford University Press, 1969), 179.

3. J. Wade Caruthers, *American Pacific Ocean Trade: Its Impact on Foreign Policy and Continental Expansion, 1784–1860* (New York: Exposition Press, 1973), 115.

4. For a typical contemporary description, see George Francis Train, *An American Merchant in Europe, Asia, and Australia* (New York: G. P. Putnam's Sons, 1857). Train, one of the world's first globetrotters, supposedly inspired Jules Verne's Phileas Fogg.

5. Eldon Griffin, *Clippers and Consuls: American Consular and Commercial Relations with Eastern Asia, 1845–1860* (Ann Arbor, Michigan: Edwards Brothers, 1939), 266, quotes *The Chinese Commercial Guide* (1863) as predicting that "Shanghai will become the greatest emporium of Eastern Asia, the center of the steam navigation throughout the Yangtsz [sic] valley and across the Pacific Ocean; and its commercial influence pervade the whole of China."

6. Kwang-ching Liu, *Anglo-American Steamboat Rivalry in China, 1862–1874* (Cambridge: Harvard University Press, 1962), 10.

7. Ibid., 35.

8. Ibid., 69.

9. Will Lawson, *Pacific Steamers* (Glasgow: Brown, Son & Ferguson, 1927), 2–6.

10. Frederick C. Drake, *The Empire of the Seas: A Biography of Rear Admiral Robert Wilson Shufeldt, USN* (Honolulu: University of Hawaii Press, 1984), 112.

11. Earl Cranston, "Shanghai in the Taiping Period," *Pacific Historical Review* 5, 2, June 1936, 148, cites ms. journal of S. W. Bonney, Canton, August 25, 1858, April 17, 1859.

12. Griffin, 70n.

13. "Opening Trade with Japan," *American Museum* 9, 4, April 1791, 186–187.

14. Ibid., 189.

15. William Adam Borst, "The American Merchant and the Genesis of Japanese-American Commercial Relations, 1790–1858" (Ph.D. dissertation, St. Louis University, 1972), 50–51.

16. The phrase is that of Commodore Perry. Francis L. Hawks, ed., *Narrative of the Expedition of an American Squadron to the China Seas and Japan Performed in the Years 1852, 1853, and 1854 under the Command of Commodore M. C. Perry, United States Navy* (Washington: Government Printing Office, 1856), 1:75.

17. Robert V. Hine, *Edward Kern and American Expansion* (New Haven, Connecticut: Yale University Press, 1962), 95.

18. Peter Booth Wiley, *Yankees in the Land of the Gods: Commodore Perry and the Opening of Japan* (New York: Viking, 1990), 449, citing Henry David Thoreau, February 27, 1853, to Harrison Blake, in F. B. Sanborn, ed., *The Writings of Henry David Thoreau* (New York: Houghton Mifflin, 1906), 6:210.

19. Paul Burton Seguin, "The Deteriorating Strategic Position of Japan: 1853–1945, A Study of the Revolution of Intercontinental Warfare" (Ph.D. dissertation, University of Minnesota, 1972), 21.

20. Helen Mary Humeston, "Origins of America's Japan Policy, 1790–1854" (Ph.D. dissertation, University of Minnesota, 1981), citing *The Writings and Speeches of Daniel Webster* (Boston: Little, Brown, 1903), 14:427–429, letter to Commodore John H. Aulick, June 13, 1851. See also Kenneth E. Shewmaker, "Forging the 'Great Chain': Daniel Webster and the Origins of American Foreign Policy toward East Asia and the Pacific, 1841–1852," *Proceedings of the American Philosophical Society* 129, 3, September 1955.

21. Harold Whitman Bradley, *The American Frontier in Hawaii: The Pioneers, 1789–1843* (Stanford, California: Stanford University Press, 1942), 81.

22. Herman Melville, *Moby Dick* (New York: Library of America, 1983), 911.

23. Humeston, 205.

24. Ibid.

25. William L. Neumann, "Religion, Morality, and Freedom: The Ideological Background of the Perry Expedition," *Pacific Historical Review* 28, 3, August 1954, 249.

26. Hawks, 1:77.

27. Humeston, 193–194.

28. A voyager from Hawaii to Japan might see no land between Diamond Head and Mt. Fuji. Geologist Raphael Pumpelly, traveling under sail in 1861, remembered that his ship nearly ran out of drinking water on the trip. Raphael Pumpelly, *My Reminiscences* (New York: Henry Holt, 1918), 1:268.

29. Commodore M. C. Perry, "The Enlargement of Geographical Science, a Consequence to the Opening of new Avenues to Commercial Enterprise," paper read before the American Geographical and Statistical Society, March 6, 1856 (New York: D. Appleton, 1856), 3, 10. The mail routes Perry envisioned would carry letters from China via the United States to England eleven to fourteen days earlier than if sent via South Asia.

30. Hawks, 2:182.

31. Earl Swisher, "Commodore Perry's Imperialism in Relation to America's Present-Day Position in the Pacific," *Pacific Historical Review* 16, 1, February 1947, 39.

32. Ibid., 34.

33. J. W. Spalding, *Japan and Around the World: An Account of Three Visits to the Japanese Empire* (New York: Redfield, 1855), 129.

34. Perry, 12.

35. Bayard Taylor, *A Visit to India, China, and Japan, in the Year 1853* (New York: G. P. Putnam, 1855), 395.

36. Hawks, 2:178.

37. Ibid., 1:75.

38. Perry, 28.

39. Ibid., 26.

40. Gerald S. Graham, *The Politics of Naval Supremacy: Studies in British Maritime Ascendancy* (Cambridge: Cambridge University Press, 1965), vii.

41. Hawks, 1:45.

42. Perry, 12.

43. Anon., "American Diplomacy in China," *North American Review* 89, 185, October 1859, 517.

44. van Alstyne, 173.

45. Spalding, 152.

46. Ibid., 151.

47. George Francis Train, *Young America Abroad in Europe, Asia, and America* (London: Sampson, Low, Son & Company, 1857), 46.

48. Gordon K. Harrington, "The Ringgold Incident: A Matter of Judgment," in Clayton

R. Barrow, ed., *America Spreads Her Sails: U.S. Seapower in the 19th Century* (Annapolis, Maryland: United States Naval Institute Press, 1973), 105–110.

49. Allan B. Cole, *Yankee Surveyors in Shogunal Seas* (Princeton, New Jersey: Princeton University Press, 1947), 129.

50. Humeston, 166–167.

51. Cole, *Yankee Surveyors*, 161, quoting Rodgers to Dobbin, San Francisco, January 29, 1856.

52. Ibid., 45.

53. Hawks, 1:430.

54. Cole, 57.

55. N. B. Dennys, ed., Wm. Fred Mayers, and N. B. Dennys and Chas. King, *The Treaty Ports of China and Japan, A Complete Guide* (London: Trubner & Company, 1867), 613.

56. Griffin, 315.

57. George Alexander Lensen, ed., *Trading under Sail Off Japan, 1860 to 1899: The Recollections of Captain John Baxter Will, Sailing-Master and Pilot* (Tokyo: Sophia University Press, in cooperation with the Diplomatic Press, Tallahassee, Florida, 1968), 30.

58. Ibid., 25.

59. Kenneth J. Bertrand, "Geographical Exploration by the United States," in Friis, 285.

60. George M. Brooke, Jr., ed., *John M. Brooke's Pacific Cruise and Japanese Adventure, 1858–1860* (Honolulu: University of Hawaii Press, 1986), 317.

61. Towle, 429, quoting Maury to King, House Committee on Naval Affairs, February 11, 1848.

62. Ibid., 457.

Chapter 9

1. "H. B.," "Our Navy: Scraps from the Lucky Bag," *Southern Literary Messenger* 6, 4, April 1840, 238.

2. William H. Seward in *Congressional Globe*, July 29, 1852, 1974.

3. Ibid.

4. Ibid.

5. Melville, 122.

6. Howard I. Kushner, *Conflict on the Northwest Coast: American-Russian Rivalry in the Pacific Northwest, 1790–1867* (Westport, Connecticut: Greenwood Press, 1975), 82. Walter S. Tower, *A History of the American Whale Fishery* (Philadelphia: Publications of the University of Pennsylvania, Series in Political Economy and Public Law 20, 1907), 53, says that in 1847 more than six-sevenths of American whaleships were in the Pacific.

7. Griffin, 333.

8. Stanton Garner, ed., *The Captain's Best Mate, the Journal of Mary Chipman Lawrence on the Whaler Addison, 1856–1860* (Providence, Rhode Island: Brown University Press, 1966), 98.

9. Advice from Konstantin Pobedonostsev quoted by Albert Parry, "Yankee Whalers in Siberia," *Russian Review* 5, 2, Spring, 1946, 36.

10. Melville, 910.

11. Richard C. Kugler, "The Penetration of the Pacific by American Whalemen in the 19th Century," in *The Opening of the Pacific—Image and Reality*, Maritime Monographs and Reports 2 (Greenwich: National Maritime Museum, 1971), 20.

12. Seward, *Congressional Globe*, 1852, 1975.

13. Rydell, 58, quoting Melville.

14. "H. B.," 239.

15. Jean-Loup Rousselot, William W. Fitzhugh, and Aron Crowell, "Maritime Economies of the North Pacific Rim," in William W. Fitzhugh and Aron Crowell, eds., *Crossroads of*

Continents, Cultures of Siberia and Alaska (Washington: Smithsonian Institution Press, 1988), 168.

16. Garner, 275.

17. Hine, 131.

18. Gaddis Smith, "Agricultural Roots of Maritime History," *American Neptune* 44, 1, January 1984, 8.

19. Bat and seal guano is not only intrinsically less rich than what the birds produce but the deposits are smaller and more scattered.

20. Gaddis Smith, 9. The price of guano in the United States rose from forty-five dollars per ton in the 1840s to nearly seventy dollars at the end of the 1850s. Hine, 131. Tui DeRoy Moore says the price peaked at ninety dollars a ton. "Guano," *Oceans* 14, 1, January–February 1981, 46.

21. United States Congress, Senate, 34th Congress, 1st Session, Misc. Doc. 60, George Wood, New York, May 20, 1856, "Memorial of the American Guano Company."

22. Guano would spawn a great American company, W. R. Grace, pioneer in creating a diversified commercial and manufacturing enterprise, now the world's leading specialty chemical manufacturer. Handling chemicals grew naturally, it would seem, from knowledge of agriculture derived from the guano trade. W. R. Grace & Co. was founded in Peru in 1854 by William Russell Grace, a refugee from the Irish potato famine, who ran away to seek his fortune at sea at the age of thirteen. Grace worked first as a ship chandler, then became involved in hauling guano. Later he emigrated to New York, opening in 1865 an office in Hanover Square from which he carried on a lucrative three-way trade between South America, North America, and Europe. W. R. Grace died in 1904, but his son, Joseph, led the company to new heights of success. He established the first U.S.-flag scheduled steamship service to the west coast of South America and would send the first vessel through the new Panama Canal in 1914. In 1928, he would form, with Pan American Airways, a joint airline company operating in Latin America. For a brief history of these events, see J. Peter Grace, Jr., *W. R. Grace (1832–1904) and the Enterprises He Created* (New York: Newcomen Society in North America, 1953).

Chapter 10

1. Norman E. Saul, "An American's Siberian Dream," *Russian Review* 37, 4, October 1978, 408.

2. Albert Parry, in ibid., 43, quoting Peter Kropotkin, *Memoirs of a Revolutionist* (Boston: Houghton Mifflin, 1930), 169.

3. Constance Garnett, trans., revised by Humphrey Higgens, *My Past and Thoughts: The Memoirs of Alexander Herzen* (New York: Alfred Knopf, 1968), 1:242–243. This book was written some time between 1861 and 1866.

4. Griffin, 336.

5. James M. Crane, *The Past, the Present, the Future of the Pacific* (San Francisco: Sterett & Co.. 1856), 54.

6. *Hunt's Merchants' Magazine* 39, 4, August 1858, 176.

7. United States Congress, House, 35th Congress, 1st Session, Executive Document 98, 1858, correspondence between P. McDonough Collins, Commercial Agent of the United States for the Amoor River, and State Department; Perry McDonough Collins, Moscow, November 30, 1856, to Secretary of State W. L. Marcy.

8. Ibid., Irkutsk, January 31, 1857.

9. Ibid.

10. Charles Vevier, "The Collins Overland Line and American Continentalism," *Pacific Historical Review* 28, 4, August 1959, 237–253.

11. Robert Luther Thompson, *Wiring a Continent: The History of the Telegraph Industry in the United States, 1832–1866* (Princeton, New Jersey: Princeton University Press, 1947), 240.

12. Jorma Ahvenainen, *The Far Eastern Telegraphs: The History of Telegraphic Communications between the Far East, Europe and America before the First World War* (Helsinki: Suomalainen Tiedeakatemia, 1981), 13.

13. Ibid., 26.

14. *Communication of Hon. William H. Seward, Secretary of State, upon the Subject of an Intercontinental Telegraph Connecting the Eastern and Western Hemispheres by way of Behring's Strait, etc* (Washington: Government Printing Office, 1864), 44.

15. Ibid., 17.

16. Ibid., 21.

17. On Kennan, see Frederick Francis Travis, "George Kennan and Russia, 1865–1905" (Ph.D. dissertation, Emory University, 1974), subsequently published as *George Kennan and the American-Russian Relationship, 1865–1924* (Athens, Ohio: Ohio University Press, 1990). Kennan in his unpublished autobiography wrote of the importance of the telegraph to his career:

> The web of environment . . . in which I was caught, in my earliest childhood, was spun out of telegraph wire. I made many strenuous efforts to escape from it, but I never wholly succeeded in doing so. It was the telegraph that made me an assistant breadwinner for my father's family, before I was twelve years of age; it was mainly the telegraph that prevented me from getting a university training; it was the telegraph that first sent me to Siberia, made me a traveler and an explorer, and gave me an interest in Russia; and to the telegraph I am indebted for my introduction to journalism, literature and the lecture field. I have sometimes wandered far, but by a telegraph line or the influence of a telegraph line, I have always and everywhere been bound.

Travis dissertation, 13.

18. George Kennan, *Tent Life in Siberia* (New York: G. P. Putnam & Sons, 1870), iii.

19. Ibid., 70.

20. Ibid., 370.

21. Ibid., 400.

22. Travis, 35.

23. Thompson, viii.

24. Ahvenainen, 30.

25. Benjamin Franklin Gilbert, "The Alaska Purchase," *Journal of the West* 3, 2, April 1964, 168.

26. Baker, *Works*, 5:591.

27. Hallie McPherson, "The Interest of William McKendree Gwin in the Purchase of Alaska, 1854–1860," *Pacific Historical Review* 3, 1, March 1934, 30.

28. Ibid.

29. Ibid., 36.

30. Nikolay N. Bolkhovitinov, "The Crimean War and the Emergence of Proposals for the Sale of Russian America, 1853–1861," *Pacific Historical Review* 59, 1, February 1990, 37.

31. Thomas A. Bailey, "Why the United States Purchased Alaska," *Pacific Historical Review* 3, 1, March 1934, 44.

32. Virginia Hancock Reid, *The Purchase of Alaska, Contemporary Opinion* (Long Beach, California: Press Telegram Printers, 1939), 32, quoting *Harper's Weekly*, April 27, 1867, 11: 263.

33. Ibid., quoting the *New York Times*, April 1, 1867, 5.

34. Ibid., 30.

35. Bailey, 47.

36. *Congressional Globe*, 1869, 6.

37. Ibid.

38. Reid, 16, citing Edward L. Pierce, *Memoir and Letters of Charles Sumner* (Boston: Roberts Brothers, 1893), 4:319.

39. David Herbert Donald, *Charles Sumner and the Coming of the Civil War* (New York: Alfred Knopf, 1960), 214.

40. "Speech of Hon. Charles Sumner of Massachusetts on the Cession of Russian America to the United States," *Congressional Globe*, 1867, 12.

41. Ibid., 13.

42. Ibid.

43. David E. Shi, "Seward's Attempt to Annex British Columbia, 1865–1869," *Pacific Historical Review* 47, 2, May 1978, 226.

44. Reid, 38, citing the *British Colonist* (Victoria), May 16, 1867.

45. Baker, *Works*, 5:574.

46. Joseph Whelan, "William Henry Seward, Expansionist" (Ph.D. dissertation, University of Rochester, 1959), 215.

47. Baker, *Works*, 3:333.

48. Caleb Cushing Papers, Library of Congress, Speech, Article & Book File, Box 208, "Reception & Entertainment of the Chinese Embassy, Boston," pamphlet printed by Alfred Mudge.

49. Ibid.

50. Banks, 4, 8.

51. John Dryden Kazar, Jr., "The United States Navy and Scientific Exploration, 1837–1860" (Ph.D. dissertation, University of Massachusetts, 1973), 216.

Chapter 11

1. Andre Siegfried, *Suez and Panama*, trans. H. H. and Doris Hemming (New York: Harcourt, Brace, 1940), 60.

2. Ibid., 119.

3. Ahvenainen, 7.

4. Morison, *Oxford History*, 584.

5. *New York Times*, January 17, 1852, 4, September 20, 1859, 4.

6. Ibid., November 24, 1858.

7. United States Congress, House, 41st Congress, 2d Session, 869–70, Report of William Lynch on the causes of the reduction of American Tonnage, February 17, 1870, 170, 184. Hereafter cited as Lynch Report.

8. Hans Keiler, *American Shipping: Its History and Economic Conditions* (Jena, Germany: Verlag von Gustav Fischer, 1913), 78.

Chapter 12

1. Leo Marx, "Closely Watched Trains," *New York Review of Books*, March 15, 1984, 28.

2. Asa Briggs, *The Power of Steam: An Illustrated History of the World's Steam Age* (Chicago: University of Chicago Press, 1982), 12.

3. Wolfgang Schivelbusch, *The Railway Journey: The Industrialization of Time and Space in the 19th Century* (Berkeley, California: University of California Press, 1986), 111, quoting Lucius Beebe. *Mr. Pullman's Elegant Palace Car* (New York, 1961), 285.

4. Ibid., 91.

5. John P. Davis, *The Union Pacific Railway: A Study in Railway Politics, History, and Economics*, reprint (New York: Arno Press, 1973), 137.

6. Ibid., 13–14.

7. Margaret L. Brown, "Asa Whitney and his Pacific Railroad Publicity Campaign," *Mississippi Valley Historical Review* 20, 2, September 1933, 209, quoting Nelson H. Loomis,

"Asa Whitney: Father of the Pacific Railroads," *Mississippi Valley Historical Association, Proceedings* 6, 1912–13, 166–175.

8. Brown, 216, quoting *New York Herald*, June 14, 1851.

9. Ibid., 221.

10. "The Proposed Railroad to the Pacific," *Hunt's Merchants' Magazine* 19, 5, November 1848, 528.

11. Brown, 218.

12. "Pacific Railroad," *DeBow's*, 1850, 606. John Lewis Payton, traveler to eastern Siberia with Perry McDonough Collins, maintained that the great prize of a continental railroad was trans-Pacific trade with Asia, for "when the trade and commerce of these numerous Pacific and Indian islands, and of the vast regions of the Chinese Empire, shall be direct to our country, we will become the storehouse as well as the highway of nations." *Suggestions on Railroad Communication with the Pacific and the Trade of China and the Indian Islands* (Chicago: 1853), 22, quoted by Charles Vevier, ed., *Siberian Journey, Down the Amur to the Pacific, 1856–1857*, a new edition of Perry McDonough Collins, *A Voyage Down the Amoor* (Madison: University of Wisconsin Press, 1962), 52n.

13. Davis, 28, quoting *Niles' National Register* 68, 20, May 1845.

14. Asa Whitney, *To the People of the United States* (New York: n.p., 1845), 11.

15. James Knowles Medbery, "Our Pacific Railroads," *Atlantic Monthly*, December 1867, 715.

16. Whitney, 1.

17. Robert S. Cotterill, "Early Agitation for a Pacific Railroad, 1845–1850," *Mississippi Valley Historical Review* 5, 4, March 1919, 414, quoting *Athenaeum*, December 1, 1849.

18. Robert G. Athearn, "British Impressions of Western Railroad Service, 1869–1900," *Pacific Historical Review* 20, 4, November 1951, 365–366, quoting Charles Alston Messiter, *Sport and Adventures among the North-American Indians* (London, 1890), 264.

19. Medbery, 705.

20. Maury Klein, *Union Pacific, Birth of a Railroad, 1862–1893* (New York: Doubleday, 1987), 219.

21. Aaron A. Hayes, "China and the United States," *Atlantic Monthly*, May 1887, 590.

22. Klein, 225.

23. Patricia Nelson Limerick, "The Final Frontier?" *Wilson Quarterly* 14, 3, Summer 1990, 82–83, cites the difficulties of pounding the final spikes as illustrating the vulnerability of transport industry to a gap between "executive planning and hands-on implementation."

24. John Debo Galloway, *The First Transcontinental Railroad* (New York: Arno Press, 1981), 167.

25. Lucius Beebe, "Pandemonium at Promontory," *American Heritage*, February 1958, 21.

26. Limerick, 82–3.

27. *New York Times*, May 10, 1869, 1.

28. Ibid., May 11, 1869, 1.

29. *Harper's Monthly*, "Monthly Record of Current Trends," July 1869, 295.

30. Ibid., 294–295.

31. United States Congress, Senate, 29th Congress, 1st Session, Report 466, July 31, 1846, "Report of the Committee on Public Lands . . . Praying the Construction of a National Railroad from the Mississippi to the Columbia River," 11.

32. Ibid., 12–13.

33. Donald MacKay, *The Asian Dream: The Pacific Rim and Canada's National Railway*, (Vancouver, British Columbia: Douglas & McIntyre, 1986), 18, quoting *New York Tribune*, March 27, 1851.

34. William J. Wilgus, *The Railway Interrelations of the United States and Canada* (New Haven, Connecticut: Yale University Press, 1937), 40.

35. Archie W. Shiels, *The Story of Two Dreams: Historical Observations and Original Source*

Material on Early Plans in England and America for Development of a Trans-Continental Railroad, 2d edition (Bellingham, Washington: Shorey Book Store, 1964), 17.

36. MacKay, 28–29.

37. Ibid., 46.

38. Canada, Parliamentary Debates, 1st Parliament, 4th Session, March 28, 1871, 675. For this reference I am endebted to Fletcher student Linda Nowlan.

39. MacKay, 116.

40. Steven G. Marks, *Road to Power: The Trans-Siberian Railroad and the Colonization of Asian Russia, 1850–1917* (Ithaca, New York: Cornell University Press, 1991), 173.

41. J. N. Westwood, *A History of Russian Railways* (London: George Allen and Unwin, 1964), 121.

42. Ibid., 139.

43. Clarence Cary, *The Trans-Siberian Route or Notes of a Journey from Pekin to New York in 1902* (New York: Evening Post Job Printing House, 1902), 50.

Chapter 13

1. Bernard DeVoto, "Geopolitics with the Dew on It," *Harper's Magazine*, March 1944, 315.

2. United States Congress, Senate, 29th Congress, 1st Session, Senate Executive Doc. 306, April 20, 1846.

3. Ibid., 3–4.

4. Ibid., 26.

5. William Gilpin, *The Central Gold Region and the Grain, Pastoral, and Gold Regions of North America* (Philadelphia: Sower, Barnes, 1860), 98.

6. Ibid.

7. William Gilpin, *Mission of the North American People, Geographical, Social, and Political,* 2d edition (Philadelphia: Lippincott, 1874), 162. Hereafter cited as Gilpin 1874.

8. William Gilpin, *The Cosmopolitan Railway* (San Francisco: History Company, 1890), 119.

9. Ibid., 164.

10. Gilpin 1890, 256.

11. Gilpin 1874, 130.

Chapter 14

1. Keiler, 124–138.

2. United States Congress, House, 43d Congress, 1st Session, Report 598 Part 2, 1873–74. Report of Mr. Stowell on the contract for the China mail service, June 22, 1874, 3.

3. United States Congress, Lynch Report, xviii.

4. Robert Bennet Forbes, "Of the Establishment of a Line of Mail Steamers from the Western Coast of the United States on the Pacific to China," *Hunt's Merchants' Magazine* 29, 5, November 1853, 559.

5. Caruthers, 92.

6. John Niven, *The American President Lines and Its Forebears, 1848–1984* (Newark: University of Delaware Press, 1987), 17.

7. United States Congress, Senate, 44th Congress, 1st Session, 1875–76, Misc. Doc. 127, US Doc. 1665, letter from the Postmaster General, July 25, 1876.

8. Forbes, 554.

9. Ibid., 552.

10. A. Clark, 312.

11. Kemble, 133.

12. Gerald S. Graham, "The Ascendancy of the Sailing Ship, 1850–85," *Economic History Review* 9, 2, August 1956, 77, quoting Joseph Conrad, *The Mirror of the Sea* (New York, 1932), 47–48. Hereafter cited as Graham 1956.

13. Charles Carleton Coffin, *Our New Way Round the World* (Boston: Fields, Osgood, 1869), 466.

14. John Haskell Kemble, "Side-Wheelers Across the Pacific," *American Neptune*, 2, 1, January 1942, 11.

15. United States Congress, Doc. 1665.

16. J. F. Campbell, *My Circular Notes, [Extracts for Journals, etc. Written While Travelling Westwards] Round the World, July 6, 1874–July 6, 1875* (London: Macmillan, 1876), 153–154.

17. *China*, originally named *Celestial Empire*, was constructed by William Henry Webb at his East River yards in New York. She would in June 1879 make the last trans-Pacific crossing by a side-wheeler. Kemble, "Side-Wheelers," 38.

18. Olive Risley Seward, ed., *William H. Seward's Travels Around the World* (New York: D. Appleton & Company, 1873), 29.

19. Ibid., 33.

20. Campbell, 153, 155.

21. Seward, 30.

22. W. S. Caine, *A Trip Round the World in 1887–8* (London: George Routledge and Sons, n.d.), xi.

23. Reverend William McMahon, *A Journey with the Sun around the World* (Cleveland: Catholic Universe Publishing Company, 1907), 50.

24. Horace Capron "Memoirs," July 4, 1871, TMs, Capron Papers, Library of Congress. He traveled to Japan aboard *America*, sister to *China*.

25. United States Congress, Senate, 58th Congress, 3d Session, Senate Reports, Report 2755, 1904–5. Report of Merchant Marine Commission, 1344.

26. Capron.

27. Ibid., August 7, 1871.

28. Ibid., August 22, 1871.

29. Farnie, 191, offers some comparative figures.

30. Caine, xi.

31. Niven, 32.

32. Paul Maxwell Zeis, *American Shipping Policy* (Princeton, New Jersey: Princeton University Press, 1938), 25.

33. John Haskell Kemble, "The Transpacific Railroads, 1869–1915," *Pacific Historical Review* 18, 3, August 1949, 333.

34. John Haskell Kemble, "The Big Four at Sea: The History of the Occidental and Oriental Steamship Company," *Huntington Library Quarterly* 3, 3, April 1940, 340.

Chapter 15

1. Julius Grodinsky, *Transcontinental Railway Strategy, 1869–1893: A Study of Businessmen* (Philadelphia: University of Pennsylvania Press, 1962), 429, quoting *Railroad Gazette*, August 8, 1884, 587.

2. Ibid., 423.

3. John Foster Carr, "Creative Americans: A Great Railway Builder," *Outlook*, October 26, 1907, 395.

4. C. M. Keys, "The Contest for Pacific Traffic," *World's Work* 10, 4, August 1905, 6507.

5. Ibid., 6508.

6. L. Girard, "Transport," in H. J. Habakkuk and M. Postan, eds., *The Industrial Revolutions and After: Incomes, Population and Technological Change*, volume 6, *The Cambridge Economic History of Europe* (Cambridge: Cambridge University Press, 1965), 253.

7. The Northern Pacific certainly had an eye on the Orient. The railroad had chosen for its logo the ancient Chinese symbol of yin and yang, signifying in Chinese cosmology the ceaseless interplay of complementary opposites. But the reason that the Northern Pacific chose this would seem to have been purely aesthetic. E. H. McHenry, chief engineer, was attracted to the design when he saw it on a Korean flag displayed at the Columbian Exposition in Chicago, 1893. Little Falls, Minnesota, *Daily Transcript*, August 2, 1968, Northern Pacific Railroad Papers, Minnesota Historical Society, St. Paul, Minnesota.

8. Ralph H. Hidy, Muriel E. Hidy, and Roy V. Scott, with Don L. Hofsommer, *The Great Northern Railway: A History* (Boston: Harvard Business School Press, 1988), 121, 310. The train would bear its name until 1951 when it became the *Western Star*. But long before then, the *Oriental Limited* had yielded pride of place to the *Empire Builder*, honoring the founder. Just a decade earlier, in 1883, the diplomats concluded negotiations necessary to running a through train from France to the Ottoman Empire. The passenger could ride in the same carriage from Calais to Constantinople; from Paris the train was called the *Orient Express*, bearing an imagery forever enriching the romance and excitement of international travel.

9. Nylon was first used to make hosiery in 1938 when, coincidentally, American relations with Japan were rapidly worsening.

10. Hidy et al., 179.

11. Carr, 397.

12. James J. Hill, "The Future of Our Oriental Trade," *World's Work* 10, 4, August 1905, 6467. Hereafter cited as Hill 1905.

13. John W. Oliver, *History of American Technology* (New York: Ronald Press, 1956), 427.

14. F. N. Stacy, "Giant Ships for Our Oriental Trade," *American Monthly Review of Reviews* 27, 5, May 1903, 565.

15. W. Kaye Lamb, "The Trans-Pacific Venture of James J. Hill, A History of the Great Northern Steamship Company," *American Neptune* 3, 3, July 1943, 191.

16. Ibid., 192.

17. Howard B. Schonberger, *Transportation to the Seaboard: The "Communications Revolution" and American Foreign Policy, 1850–1900* (Westport, Connecticut: Greenwood, 1971), 214.

18. Gary Dean Best, "James J. Hill's 'Lost Opportunity on the Pacific,' " *Pacific Northwest Quarterly* 64, 1, January 1973, 9.

19. Ibid., 10.

20. Ibid.

21. James J. Hill, "History of Agriculture in Minnesota," speech given January 18, 1897, at Annual Meeting of the Minnesota Historical Society, *Minnesota Historical Society Collections* 8, 1895–98, 289. Hereafter cited as Hill 1897.

22. Schonberger, 228, citing George F. Parker, *Recollections of Grover Cleveland* (New York: Century, 1909), 326.

23. Hill 1897, 290.

24. Carr, 397.

25. On the eating of rice or wheat, Professor Yasuhiko Yuize of Chiba University suggested that a way out of Japan's rice dilemma—a huge surplus production supported by massive government subsidy dictated by political concerns—would be to convert Americans from bread to rice. Because of growing American concerns about healthy diet and American interest in nutritious low-fat Japanese cuisine, American palates might be ready for this change, Professor Yuize suggested. Not that white rice itself is that nutritious but "a meal rich in variety, taste and nutrients requires something light and bland, filling but non-fattening, to refresh the palate and guard against excessive intake of animal protein and fat. With its high water content and unobtrusive flavor, rice fills the bill." "Rice or Wheat?" *Tokyo Shimbun*, Asia Foundation, Translation Service Center: TSC 1238, October 16, 1989.

26. Hill 1910, 160, 179.

27. Ibid., 167.

28. Ibid., 178; Hill 1905, 6467.

29. Hill 1910, 182.

30. Ibid., 158.

31. Albro Martin, *James J. Hill and the Opening of the Northwest* (New York: Oxford University Press, 1976), 471. Hill in a speech at a reception for U.S. senator from Minnesota Cushman K. Davis, September 1898.

32. Ibid., 546.

33. Ibid.

34. In 1898 San Francisco held more than 70 percent of trans-Pacific business; in 1904 that figure dropped to 56 percent. Keys, 6505.

35. Terrence Cole, "The Bridge to Tomorrow: Visions of the Bering Strait Bridge," *Alaska History* 5, 2, Fall 1990, 6. A Chinese-American San Francisco civil engineer, T. Y. Lin, is now proposing an intercontinental Peace Bridge, linked with an "Arctic corridor" stretching from British Columbia to Siberia, with a super-high-speed (300 mph) magnetic levitation train (MAGLEV) similar to that with which the Japanese are now experimenting. The Arctic corridor would not simply serve passenger and freight transport but would also form a conduit for oil, gas, and electric power. New York art dealer Glen Weiss, who sponsored a Beringian bridge design contest, believed that such a bridge would serve as an antithesis to the Berlin Wall. Ibid., 11–12.

36. United States Congress, Senate, 49th Congress, 1st Session, Senate Misc. Doc. 84, Petition of John Arthur Lynch to Committee on Foreign Relations, March 17, 1886.

37. United States Congress, Senate, 43d Congress, 2d Session, letter from the Secretary of the interior transmitting Report of the Director of the U.S. Geological Survey on the merits of bill S 1907 "to facilitate the settlement and develop the resources of the Territory of Alaska, and open an overland and commercial route between the United States, Asiatic Russia, and Japan," and the feasibility of the construction of the railroad proposed. December 21, 1886, 10.

38. *New York Times*, November 15, 1890, 2.

39. *St. Paul (Minnesota) Pioneer Press*, August 4, 1901.

40. *New York Times*, August 4 1901, 2, September 20, 1901, 9.

41. Harry DeWindt, "A Land Journey from Paris to New York," *Harper's Monthly*, April 1902, 765.

42. Ibid. Later he discards this notion of the determining importance of seasickness.

43. Herman Rosenthal, "From New York to Paris by Rail," *Review of Reviews* 33, 5, May 1906, 592–593.

44. Alexander Hume Ford, "A Railway across Five Continents," *Independent*, February 1, 1906, 269.

45. *Engineering News*, June 7, 1906, 634.

46. Charles Vevier, *The United States and China, 1906–1913: A Study of Finance and Diplomacy* (New Brunswick, New Jersey: Rutgers University Press, 1955), 18, quoting Alice Roosevelt Longworth, *Crowded Hours* (New York: Charles Scribner's Sons, 1933), 106.

47. Lloyd C. Griscom, *Diplomatically Speaking* (Boston: Little, Brown, 1940), 223.

48. Robert A. Lovett, *Forty Years After: An Appreciation of the Genius of Edward Henry Harriman (1848–1909)* (New York: Newcomen Society in North America, 1949), 21.

49. Ibid., 14.

50. Ibid., 24.

51. Otto H. Kahn, *Reflections of a Financier: A Study of Economic and Other Problems* (London: Hodder & Stoughton, 1921), 406.

52. Lovett, 19.

53. William H. Goetzmann and Kay Sloan, *Looking Far North: The Harriman Expedition to Alaska, 1899* (New York: Viking Press, 1982), xv.

54. Shiels, 10.

55. Richard T. Chang, "The Failure of the Katsura-Harriman Agreement," *Journal of Asian Studies* 21, 1, November 1961, 66–67.

56. Michael H. Hunt, *Frontier Defense and the Open Door: Manchuria in Chinese-American Relations, 1895–1911* (New Haven, Connecticut: Yale University Press, 1973), 157.

57. George Kennan, *E. H. Harriman's Far Eastern Plans* (New York: Country Life Press, 1917), 4. Hereafter cited as Kennan 1917.

58. Hunt, 156.

59. Ibid., 22–23.

60. Albert J. Beveridge, *The Russian Advance* (New York: Harper & Brothers, 1904), 9.

61. Ibid., 81.

62. Griscom, 263.

63. Chang, 68.

64. Ibid., 71.

65. Hunt, 155–156.

66. Charles Vevier, "The Open Door: An Idea in Action, 1906–1913," *Pacific Historical Review* 1, February 1955, 56.

67. Kennan 1917, 47–48.

68. Ford, 207.

69. Sir Halford J. Mackinder, "The Geographical Pivot of History," *Geographical Journal* 23, 4, April 1904, 434.

70. Ibid.

71. Ibid., 441.

Chapter 16

1. Chandler was able to prune the officer corps, close down two unneeded navy yards, and retire some of the old wooden ships. "I think that I did my best work in destroying the old Navy," he would later judge. Justus D. Doencke, *The Presidencies of James A. Garfield and Chester A. Arthur* (Lawrence, Kansas: Regents Press of Kansas, 1981), 149.

2. Drake, 100.

3. Ibid., 116, 145.

4. Guam's garrison was ignorant of the war and when a U.S. warship entered the harbor at Fort Santa Cruz, its firing was interpreted by the Spaniards as a salute. The Spanish commander sent out a boat to offer apologies for not returning the "courtesy." He lacked the guns to do so, he said. The event was not a strong advertisement for the quality of American marksmanship. Pan American Airways Archives, New York (hereafter cited as PAA), Harold M. Bixby, "Top Side Rickshaw," TMs, 1938, 303. Cf. Frank Freidel, *The Splendid Little War* (Boston: Little, Brown, 1958), 283.

5. Alfred Thayer Mahan, *The Problem of Asia and Its Effect upon International Policies* (Boston: Little, Brown, 1900), 131.

6. Ibid., 192.

7. Josiah Strong, *Expansion under New World-Conditions* (New York: Baker and Taylor, 1900), 198.

8. Leslie Bennett Tribolet, *The International Aspects of Electrical Communications in the Pacific Area* (Baltimore: Johns Hopkins Press, 1929), 167.

9. Charles H. Cramp, *Commercial Supremacy and Other Papers* (Philadelphia: privately printed, 1894), 15.

10. Brooks Adams, *America's Economic Supremacy* (New York: Harper & Brothers, 1947, first published 1900), 98.

11. Ibid., 194.

12. Ibid., 105.

13. *San Francisco Examiner*, September 22, 1899.

14. Seymour Broadbridge, "Shipbuilding and the State in Japan since the 1850s," *Modern Asian Studies* 2, 4, October 1977, 604–605.

15. William D. Wray, *Mitsubishi and the N.Y.K. 1870–1914: Business Strategy in the Japanese Shipping Industry* (Cambridge: Harvard University Press, 1984), 408–409.

Chapter 17

1. Howard K. Beale, *Theodore Roosevelt and the Rise of America to World Power* (New York: Collier, 1962), remains an extremely valuable book.

2. *California Addresses by President Roosevelt* (San Francisco: California Promotion Committee, 1903), 96.

3. Morgan B. Sherwood, *Exploration of Alaska, 1865–1900* (New Haven, Connecticut: Yale University Press, 1965), 10.

4. George Sinkler, *The Racial Attitudes of American Presidents from Abraham Lincoln to Theodore Roosevelt* (Garden City, New York: Doubleday, 1971), 323–324, quoting letter from Roosevelt to John Hay, July 28, 1904.

5. Beale, 234.

6. *Congressional Record*, December 4, 1906.

7. Eugene P. Trani, *The Treaty of Portsmouth: An Adventure in American Diplomacy* (Lexington: University of Kentucky Press, 1969), 80, quoting a letter from Roosevelt to Cecil Spring Rice, June 16, 1905.

8. Bernard S. Schlessinger and June H. Schlessinger, eds., *The Who's Who of Nobel Prize Winners* (Phoenix: Oryx Press, 1986), 128.

9. Tyler Dennett, *Roosevelt and the Russo-Japanese War* (New York: Doubleday, Page, 1925), 3.

10. Mark J. Davidson, "Power and Civilization: Theodore Roosevelt, Portsmouth and the Balance in Asia" (M.A.L.D. thesis, Fletcher School of Law and Diplomacy, 1986), 31.

11. David H. Burton, *Theodore Roosevelt: Confident Imperialist* (Philadelphia: University of Pennsylvania Press, 1968), 34.

12. Peter Karsten, "The Nature of 'Influence': Roosevelt, Mahan and the Concept of Sea Power," *American Quarterly* 23, 4, October 1971, 589.

13. Stead, 371.

14. Karsten, 598.

15. Thomas A. Bailey, "The World Cruise of the American Battleship Fleet, 1907–1909," *Pacific Historical Review* 1, 4, December 1932, 418, quoting letter from Roosevelt to Sydney Brooks, December 28, 1908.

16. Ibid, 389.

17. Ibid., 396, quoting Theodore Roosevelt, *An Autobiography*, 564–565.

18. Ibid., 411–12, quoting *Melbourne Age*, February 25, 1909.

19. Ibid., 420, quoting *New York Times*, February 23, 1909.

20. Quoted in David McCullough, *The Path between the Seas: The Creation of the Panama Canal, 1870–1914* (New York: Simon & Schuster, 1977), 249.

21. Paul B. Ryan, *The Panama Canal Controversy: U.S. Diplomacy and Defense Interests* (Stanford, California: Hoover Institution Press, 1977), 80.

22. Graham 1956 has an excellent discussion of this.

23. Siegfried, 308–309.

24. Mahan 1900, 84.

25. Barry Lopez, *Arctic Dreams: Imagination and Desire in a Northern Landscape* (New York: Charles Scribner's Sons, 1986), 371n.

26. Wilkins 1970, 201, 203.

27. Kemble 1949, 332.

28. Fred A. McKenzie, *The American Invaders: Their Plans, Tactics and Progress* (New York: Street and Smith, 1901), 9–10.

29. Correlli Barnett, *The Pride and the Fall: The Dream and Illusion of Britain as a Great Nation* (New York: Free Press, 1987), 107.

30. McKenzie, 37.

31. United States Congress, Report 2755, 1904–5, 845.

32. "Private Diary of Robert Dollar on His Recent Visits to China" (Robert Dollar Company, 1912), 64.

33. Walter LaFeber, "A Note on the 'Mercantilistic Imperialism' of Alfred Thayer Mahan," *Mississippi Valley Historical Review* 48, 4, March 1962, 680.

34. James A. Field, Jr., "Transnationalism and the New Tribe," *International Organization* 25, 3, Summer 1971, 365.

Chapter 18

1. Abraham Berglund, "The War and Trans-Pacific Shipping," *American Economic Review* 7, 3, September 1917, 557.

2. For a firsthand account, see William S. Graves, *America's Siberian Adventure, 1918–1920* (New York: Peter Smith, 1941), and for a later analysis, George F. Kennan, *Russia and the West under Lenin and Stalin* (Boston: Atlantic Monthly Press, 1961), 91–104.

3. The law also found it necessary explicitly to forbid flogging or any other corporal punishment aboard ship and to specify that every seaman was entitled to a daily allowance of five quarts of water and two ounces of butter. United States Congress, *An Act to Promote the Welfare of American Seamen in the Merchant Marine of the United States*, 63d Congress, 3d sess., Chapter 153, 1915, 1167, 1169.

4. Berglund, 563; Noel H. Pugach, "American Shipping Promoters and the Shipping Crisis of 1914–1916: The Pacific & Eastern Steamship Company," *American Neptune* 35, 3, July 1975, 168.

5. Ibid., 170–171.

6. Zeis, 89. Fred L. Israel, ed., *The State of the Union Messages of the Presidents, 1790–1966* (New York: Chelsea House-Robert Hector, 1966), 3:2566–2567.

7. Zeis, 97, 99.

8. Ibid., 108.

9. Jeffrey J. Safford, "World War I Maritime Policy and the National Security: 1914–1919," in Robert A. Kilmarx, ed., *America's Maritime Legacy: A History of the U.S. Merchant Marine and Shipbuilding Industry since Colonial Times* (Boulder, Colorado: Westview Press, 1979), 126.

10. No one asked why American business would not profit from using subsidized shipping. Paul Zeis, a scholar looking at these questions in the late 1930s, suggested that the artificial creation of a merchant fleet hindered rather than helped American foreign trade, that American shipping companies exhibited no particular interest in encouraging the sale of American commodities overseas, and that their sole interest, rightfully, was to make as much money as possible, and this meant charging the maximum rates. See Zeis, 213–236, for a discussion of these issues.

11. "Crossroads of the Pacific Are Located at Honolulu," *New York Times*, January 30, 1927, sec. VIII, 16.

12. Ronald Spector, *Professors of War: The Naval War College and the Development of the Naval Profession* (Newport, Rhode Island: Naval War College Press, 1977), 96.

13. For a good history of this see Louis Morton, "War Plan *Orange*, Evolution of a Strategy," *World Politics* 11, 2, January 1959, 221–250.

14. *New York Times*, October 7, 1929, 24.

15. In 1937, Radius tells us, 38,805 passengers traveled between the American Pacific coast and China, Japan, the Philippines, Dutch East Indies, and the Straits Settlements; 659,077 traveled across the North Atlantic the same year. Walter A. Radius, *United States Shipping in Transpacific Trade 1922–1938* (Stanford: Stanford University Press, 1944), 12.

16. Ibid., 7, citing Ellsworth Huntington, *Principles of Economic Geography* (New York: John Wiley, 1940), 638.

Chapter 19

1. The *New York Times*, for example, ran a small article on December 26, 1903, reporting that "the inventors of a North Carolina box kite machine" were eager to sell their device to the government. Not until January 7, 1906, did the newspaper credit the Wright Brothers by name with the invention of a self-propelled "flying machine," moving by its own power, developed in secret.

2. The authoritative account is Eileen F. Lebow, *Cal Rodgers and the Vin Fiz, the First Transcontinental Flight* (Washington, D.C.: Smithsonian Institution Press, 1989).

3. Ibid., 250–251.

4. Roger E. Bilstein, *Flight in America, 1900–1983: From the Wright Brothers to the Astronauts* (Baltimore: Johns Hopkins Press, 1984), 31–32.

5. Harold M. Bixby, "Topside Rickshaw," 1938, TMs, 3.

6. Frederick C. Thayer, Jr., *Air Transport Policy and National Security, A Political, Economic, and Military Analysis* (Chapel Hill: University of North Carolina Press, 1965), 3.

7. Bilstein, 50.

8. John Bell Rae, *Climb to Greatness: The American Aircraft Industry, 1920–1960* (Cambridge: MIT Press, 1968), 35. The best account of Lindbergh's flight is John William Ward, "The Meaning of Lindbergh's Flight," *American Quarterly*, 10, 1, Spring 1958, 3–16.

9. Rae, 49.

10. Thayer, 10.

Chapter 20

1. Henry Beaubois, *Airships, Yesterday, Today and Tomorrow* (New York: Two Continents Publishing Group, 1976), 165. Literature on the airship is extensive. Some of the most interesting information is to be found in the Pan American Archives (PAA), in correspondence from historian Henry Cord Meyer.

2. PAA 40.20.00.

3. Cedric A. Larson, "Giant Airships of the Future," *Science Digest* 29, 5, May 1951, 4.

4. Carson C. Hathaway, "The Map of the World Takes on New Meanings," *New York Times*, September 11, 1927.

5. Hugo Eckener, "The First Airship Flight around the World," *National Geographic Magazine* 57, 6, June 1930, 661.

6. Douglas H. Robinson, *Giants in the Sky: A History of the Rigid Airship* (Seattle: University of Washington Press, 1973), 270.

7. Ibid., 271.

8. Eckener, 687.

9. Ibid., 675.

10. "Germany's New Laurels," *New York Times*, August 20, 1929, 26.

11. "Earth's New Satellite," *New York Times*, August 27, 1929, 26.

12. "Zeppelin Again in Flight Heading for Lakehurst; Touring Nation on Way," *New York Times*, August 27, 1929, 16.

13. PAA 40.20.00, The Performance Record of the *Graf Zeppelin* by Dr. Hugo Eckener, March 10, 1931.

14. PAA 40.20.00, Paul W. Littlefield, Chairman, Pacific Zeppelin Transport Co., to Juan T. Trippe, July 1, 1931.

15. PAA 40.20.00, "Address before Society of Automotive Engineers," by J. C. Hunsaker, Vice President and General Manager, International Zeppelin Transport Corporation, Detroit, Michigan, April 16, 1931.

16. PAA 50.13.11, Charles A. Lindbergh to Henry Cord Meyer, March 26, 1974.

17. "Lindbergh Urges Use of Dirigibles," *New York Times*, August 27, 1929, 16.

18. PAA 10.10.00. The *New York Herald Tribune*, April 18, 1937, had commented just the month before that "the airship, despite the disasters that have befallen it in military and naval service, is the world's only form of commercial transportation that has never suffered a fatal accident."

19. The British had lamented that they had neither the means nor the talent to enter the airship race. Their record with these craft was poor, checkered by death and disaster. Yet as late as 1935 British newspapers were arguing that airships were desirable because of their endurance; unlike airplanes they could ride around storms. And they thought perhaps they could persuade Hugo Eckener, not a narrow nationalist, to take on some British apprentices and enable Britain to catch up. PAA 40.20.00.

20. Interview with John Swihart, Medford, Massachusetts, November 3, 1987.

21. "The whole system of railroad traveling is addressed to people who, being a hurry, are therefore, for the time being, miserable. No one would travel in that manner who could help it—who had the time to go leisurely over hills and between hedges instead of through tunnels and between banks: or at least, those who would, have no sense of beauty so acute as that we need consult it at the station. The railroad is in all its relations a matter of earnest business, to be got through as soon as possible. It transmutes a man from a traveller into a living parcel." Schivelbusch, 121n, from John Ruskin, *The Complete Works*, 8: 159.

22. Ibid., 58.

Chapter 21

1. At the end of his career Trippe was preoccupied with showing, by means of an authorized history of the company, that Pan American had been a private enterprise, sometimes only narrowly escaping government ownership or control. Trippe wanted his story to inspire younger people to preserve the "private capital system" that had made Pan American possible. PAA 50.20.02. John C. Leslie, Confidential Memorandum for the files, October 5, 1970, lunch with J. T. Trippe.

2. *New York Times*, September 6, 1931, sec. 3, 1.

3. Ibid., September 11, 1927.

4. Papers of Juan Terry Trippe, New York City (hereafter cited as JTT), speech, May 2, 1940, U.S. Chamber of Commerce, Washington, D.C.

5. Diary of Betty Stettinius Trippe, (hereafter cited as BST), 14.

6. PAA 50.13.01, Archibald MacLeish to J. T. Trippe, Mill Reef, Antigua, n.d.

7. PAA 50.20.02.

8. PAA 10.10.00, Notes for the Files by John C. Leslie, 11 November 1973.

9. PAA 50.22.01.

10. Interview, Donald Usher, Annisquam, Massachusetts, September 1, 1987.

11. For observations on the Trippe personality, see PAA 50.12.02.

12. Carried on the masthead of the company's house organ, *Pan American Airways*.

13. Thomas Prescott Bartow, "Early Transpacific Aviation, 1930–1941" (M.A. thesis, University of Hawaii, 1958), 58.

14. Robin Higham, *Britain's Imperial Air Routes 1918 to 1939: The Story of Britain's Overseas Airlines* (Hamden, Connecticut: Shoe String Press, 1961), 40, describes the British case.

15. Cable policy adumbrated air landing rights. In 1875 President Grant decided that the United States would refuse to allow cable landing rights to any foreign company exercising a monopoly in any country excluding American cables. Oliver J. Lissitzyn, "The Diplomacy of Air Transport," *Foreign Affairs* 19, 1, October 1940, 165.

16. Joseph Kastner, "The Postwar Air," *Life Magazine*, November 1, 1943, 101.

17. Horace Brock, *Flying the Oceans: A Pilot's Story of Pan Am, 1935–1955* (Lunenburg, Vermont: Stinehour Press, 1978), 72. Brock served in Pan Am's Pacific Division from April 1937 to February 1939.

18. JTT, speech at luncheon in honor of the visiting Chiefs of Staff of the Navies of Latin America, New York, May 13, 1941.

19. PAA 50.22.01, letter of William van Dusen to John C. Leslie, October 11, 1972.

20. PAA 50.20.02.

21. JTT, Annual Meeting, National Association of State Aviation Officials, Miami, Florida, December 3, 1937, 8.

22. *New York Times*, March 18, 1935, 16.

Chapter 22

1. PAA, Lindbergh Survey Flight ORIENT, July 1931.

2. Ibid., press release, October 28, 1937.

3. Anne Morrow Lindbergh, *North to the Orient* (New York: Harcourt, Brace, 1935), 20, 22.

4. "Lindbergh Drafting Route East over Arctic to China via Greenland and Siberia," *New York Times*, June 6, 1931, 1.

5. PAA, Lindbergh Survey Flight, ORIENT, July 1931. Memorandum from Mary Market, Historian, Lockheed Aircraft Corporation, ND.

6. A. Lindbergh, 28. Charles Lindbergh says sixteen pounds. Charles A. Lindbergh, *Autobiography of Values* (New York: Harcourt Brace Jovanovich, 1977), 110.

7. *New York Times*, June 6, 1931.

8. PAA 50.12.06.

9. A. Lindbergh, 19.

10. PAA 50.12.05, Charles A. Lindbergh to Wolfgang Langewische, November 19, 1967.

11. PAA 50.20.02.

12. PAA 50.12.05. Lindbergh to Langewische, November 19, 1967.

13. "Lindbergh Visions Pacific Air Route," *New York Times*, August 25, 1931.

14. The *Sirius* was displayed at the Osaka World's Fair, EXPO 70, as the centerpiece of an exhibit entitled "Wings across the Pacific." It is on permanent display at the National Air and Space Museum.

15. Lindbergh, *Autobiography*, 110.

16. United States Civil Aeronautics Board, CAB Docket 547. Exhibit PA-113, 4–5. Hereafter cited as PA-113.

17. Matthew Josephson, *Empire of the Air: Juan Trippe and the Struggle for World Airways* (New York: Harcourt, Brace, 1944), 197–198.

18. JTT, letter to Federal Aviation Commission, 1934.

19. JTT, John C. Leslie Memorandum to Mr. J. T. Trippe, June 28, 1935.

20. Vilhjalmur Stefansson, "By Air to the Ends of the Earth," *Natural History* 28, 5, September–October 1928, 453, and "The Arctic as an Air Route of the Future," *National Geographic Magazine* 42, 2, August 1922, 205.

21. Stefansson 1928, 455.

22. For a suggestive article on looking at the map, see the article of my colleague, Alan K. Henrikson, "Mental Maps," in Michael J. Hogan and Thomas G. Patterson, eds., *Explaining the History of American Foreign Relations* (Cambridge: Cambridge University Press, 1991), 177–192.

23. PAA 10.03.00, Alaska, 1932, "Intercontinental Trans-Bering Airways."

24. Ibid.

25. Ibid.

26. Bartow, 167.

Chapter 23

1. William M. Leary, Jr., *The Dragon's Wings: The China National Aviation Corporation and the Development of Commercial Aviation in China* (Athens: University of Georgia Press, 1976), 16.

2. Ibid., 68.

3. Ibid., 74.

4. United States Civil Aeronautics Board, CAB Docket Nos. 851 et al. Exhibit PA2. "History of the Transpacific Air Services to and through Hawaii," 9. Hereafter cited as PA-2.

5. Bixby, 62–63.

6. Ibid., 263.

7. JTT 1934: Federal Aviation Commission, 19.

8. Rae, 71. Within two years of its introduction to service, the DC-3 was carrying 95 percent of American air traffic.

9. Leary, 108.

10. "D," "Pacific Airways," *Foreign Affairs* 18, 1, October 1939, 61.

11. BST, 53.

12. Ibid., 109.

13. Bartow, 17.

14. Lieutenants Lester J. Maitland and Albert F. Hegenberger, "Real Story of the Army Flight to Hawaii," *New York Times*, July 8, 1927, 21.

15. PAA 10.10.00

16. Igor Sikorsky, "Sixty Years in Flying," *Aeronautical Journal* 75, 731, November 1971, 761.

17. Dorothy Cochrane, Von Hardesty, and Russell Lee, *The Aviation Careers of Igor Sikorsky* (Seattle: University of Washington Press, published for the National Air and Space Museum, 1989), has a good account.

18. Frank J. Delear, *Igor Sikorsky: His Three Careers in Aviation* (New York: Dodd, Mead, 1969), 135.

19. Lindbergh, *Autobiography*, 112.

20. PAA 50.12.05, Lindbergh to Langewische, November 19, 1967.

21. Ibid.

22. Russell Owen, *New York Times*, "Flight of China Clipper Opens a New Travel Era," December 1, 1935, and Russell Owen, "Wings over the Oceans, A New Flying Era Opens," *New York Times Magazine*, September 27, 1936.

23. Martin gave up the civilian market entirely for the military. Industry-wide, 70 percent of the value of aircraft and engine production was for the military. Rae, 92–93. Martin did not give up making flying boats. For the U.S. Navy, the company would produce the largest one every built, the PBM Mars, a seventy-ton patrol plane with a wing span of two hundred feet.

24. PAA 50.12.05, Lindbergh to Langewische, November 19, 1967.

25. Stan Cohen, *Pan American Clipper Planes 1935 to 1945, Wings to the Orient, A Pictorial History* (Missoula, Montana: Pictorial Histories Publishing Company, 1985), 34, 38.

26. William M. Masland, *Through the Back Doors of the World in a Ship That Had Wings*, (New York: Vantage, 1984), 258.

27. Rae, 91.

28. For comments, see Lindbergh, *Autobiography*, 116.

29. JTT, Charles A. Lindbergh to Juan T. Trippe, Long Barn Weald, Seven Oaks, England, October 28, 1936.

30. PAA 30.10.04.

31. Bartow, 88.

32. "Pan American Airways," *Fortune* 21, 4, April 1936.

33. "D," 66.

34. Tribolet, 85.

35. Francis X. Holbrook, "United States National Defense and Trans-Pacific Commercial Air Routes, 1933–1941" (Ph.D. dissertation, Fordham University, 1969), 254, quoting Memorandum from the President to Secretary of State Hull, July 30, 1937.

36. Werner Levi, "American Attitudes toward Pacific Islands, 1914–1919," *Pacific Historical Review* 17, 1, February 1948, 60.

37. Holbrook, 325–327.

38. Harold Bixby remembers that Admiral Marquart in the Philippines was willing to remove two wrecked Spanish gunboats, victims of Dewey's victory, from the floor of Manila Bay. The sunken ships endangered Pan American's flying boats. But the Admiral reminded Bixby that "my job is sinking ships, not raising them." Bixby, 271.

39. PAA 30.10.04. William Van Dusen, "Log of the China Clipper."

40. William Stephen Grooch, *Skyway to Asia* (New York: Longmans, Green, 1939), 25.

41. Holbrook, 107.

42. Bartow, 74.

43. PAA, "Fast Boat to Manila, Recollections of the First Transpacific Flight," by Captain Victor Wright. Hereafter cited as PAA, Victor Wright.

44. PAA 10.10.00.

45. Robert Daley, *An American Saga: Juan Trippe and His Pan Am Empire* (New York: Random House, 1980), 108.

46. PAA 10.10.00.

47. Ibid.

48. Grooch, 119.

49. PAA, Miscellaneous Notes, John C. Leslie, on reading Holbrook dissertation.

50. Holbrook, 113.

51. PAA, Victor Wright.

52. PAA: 10.10.00.

53. Ibid.

54. Grooch, 189.

55. PAA, Victor Wright.

56. PAA, 10.10.00.

57. Brock, 74.

58. PAA, 10.10.00.

59. Clare Boothe, "Destiny Crosses the Dateline, Report on a Flight across the Pacific." *Life Magazine*, November 3, 1941, 98–109.

60. PAA, Victor Wright.

61. Brock, 97.

62. R. E. G. Davies, *Airlines of the United States since 1914* (Washington, D.C.: Smithsonian Institution Press, 1982), 255.

63. PAA 10.10.00, Note from Harvey L. Katz to J. C. Leslie reporting that Trippe had said in a meeting August 26, 1970, that "in 1937 [sic] one of our M-130 Flying Boats disappeared between Guam and Manila . . . and that after the war he was told by the Navy Department that Japanese hid in the aircraft and commandeered it in mid-flight. The aircraft was then flown to a Japanese base where the engines were studied and . . . copied in detail for Japanese fighter aircraft. He said passengers and crew were killed." If this were

true, it would have been history's first skyjacking. See also PAA 30:20.02 for report of Civil Aeronautics Authority, November 18, 1938. BST writes in her *Diary* of two instances of attempted sabotage: Two Japanese were arrested for trying to tamper with aircraft navigation equipment in Alameda. And also at Alameda some steel rods were found mysteriously anchored in the aircraft takeoff path. These unlikely episodes were typical stories of the time. The public talked much more about the mysterious disappearance of Amelia Earhart, a pioneer in the development of long-distance air routes. In July 1937 she and her co-pilot disappeared on the leg of a trans-Pacific journey, somewhere between New Guinea and Howland Island. Rumor had it that Earhart was on a secret U.S. government mission and intercepted by the Japanese. This rumor is yet to be substantiated.

64. Bilstein, 49–50.

Chapter 24

1. PAA, "Twenty Years of Progress, History of the Pacific-Alaska Division," Public Relations Department, November 1955.

2. Rae, 144.

3. Ibid., 114–115.

4. Weldon B. Gibson, *Skyways of the Pacific*, IPR Pamphlet 27 (New York: American Institute of Pacific Affairs, 1947).

5. Ninety-two percent of U.S. merchant ships over two thousand gross tons were twenty years or older. Daniel Levine and Sara Ann Platt, "The Contribution of U.S. Shipbuilding and the Merchant Marine to the Second World War," in Robert A. Kilmarx, ed., *America's Maritime Legacy: A History of the U.S. Merchant Marine and Shipbuilding Industry Since Colonial Times* (Boulder, Colorado: Westview Press, 1979), 175.

6. Ibid., 181.

7. Ibid., 192.

Chapter 25

1. David Remley, "The Latent Fear: Canadian-American Relations and Early Proposals for a Highway to Alaska," in Kenneth Coates, ed., *The Alaska Highway, Papers of the 40th Anniversary Symposium* (Vancouver, British Columbia: University of British Columbia Press, 1985), 7, quoting *Daily Province* (Vancouver), May 12, 1938.

2. Lack of American interest in Canada has been outstanding. *Canada, Our Northern Neighbor* was once overwhelmingly voted by a group of American publishers to be the most boring book title imaginable.

3. M. V. Bezeau, "The Realities of Strategic Planning: The Decision to Build the Alaska Highway," in Coates, 29.

4. Mira Wilkins, *The Maturing of Multinational Enterprise: American Business Abroad from 1914 to 1970* (Cambridge: Harvard University Press, 1974), 273, quoting Under Secretary of War Robert P. Patterson, in an address to the Senate, November 23, 1943.

5. Ibid., 275.

6. Curtis R. Nordman, "The Army of Occupation: Malcolm MacDonald and U.S. Military Involvement in the Canadian Northwest," in Coates, 91.

7. Ibid., 90.

8. John T. Greenwood, "General Bill Hoge and the Alaska Highway," in Coates, 46, quoting *Bulletin* (Edmonton), June 5, 1943.

9. Richard J. Diubaldo, "The Alaska Highway in Canada–United States Relations," in Coates, 113.

10. Jonathan M. Nielson, *Armed Forces on a Northern Frontier: The Military in Alaska's History, 1867–1987* (Westport, Connecticut: Greenwood Press, 1988), 102. For a rousing

account, see also Brian Garfield, *The Thousand-Mile War: World War II in Alaska and the Aleutians* (New York: Doubleday, 1975).

11. Nielson, 145, quoting Garfield, 190–191.

12. Ibid., 146.

13. Ibid., 112–113.

14. *Personal Justice Denied*, Report of the Commission on Wartime Relocation and Internment of Civilians, Washington, D.C., December 1982, 337.

15. Cpl. Dashiell Hammett and Cpl. Robert Colodny, "The Battle of the Aleutians, 1942–1943," in Terrence Cole, ed., *The Capture of Attu: Tales of World War II in Alaska as Told by the Men Who Fought There* (Anchorage, Alaska: Alaska Northwest Publishing Company, 1984), 12. Hammett is better known for *The Maltese Falcon* and *The Thin Man* than he is for his part in writing an official history of the Aleutians campaign. Prominently identified with left-wing causes, Hammett had enlisted in the army in 1942 at the age of forty-eight. He had not been a productive writer for ten years. But he is the man who, said Raymond Chandler, "took murder out of the parlor and put it in the alley where it belongs." Quoted by Andrew Hoyem, "Gumshoe! Detectives Real and Imagined," Bohemian Club Library Notes, 68, Fall 1991, 5.

16. Nielson, 164.

17. Cole, 6.

18. Nielson, 165.

19. Ibid., 168.

20. Nielson, 179.

21. William H. Tunner, *Over the Hump* (Washington: Office of Air Force History, United States Air Force, 1985), 55.

22. Ibid; Thayer, 248.

Chapter 26

1. Steve Neal, *Dark Horse, A Biography of Wendell Willkie* (Garden City, New York: Doubleday, 1984), 253.

2. Ibid., 244, quoting *Christian Science Monitor* correspondent Edmund Stevens.

3. Wendell L. Willkie, *One World* (New York: Simon and Schuster, 1943), 202.

4. Neal, 261.

5. Ibid., 260–261.

6. Henry A. Wallace, with the collaboration of Andrew J. Steiger, *Soviet Asia Mission* (New York: Reynal & Hitchcock, 1946), 18.

7. John Morton Blum, ed., *The Price of Vision: The Diary of Henry A. Wallace, 1942–1946* (Boston: Houghton Mifflin, 1973), 308–309.

8. Ibid., 315.

9. Ibid., 332n.

10. Ibid., 10.

11. Ibid., 337n.

12. Paul Hollander, *Political Pilgrims: Travels of Western Intellectuals to the Soviet Union, China, and Cuba, 1928–1978* (New York: Oxford University Press, 1981), 158.

13. J. Samuel Walker, *Henry A. Wallace and American Foreign Policy* (Westport, Connecticut: Greenwood Press, 1976), 107.

14. Wallace, 22.

15. Ibid., 30.

16. Ibid., 194.

17. Ibid., 196–197.

18. Ibid., 26.

19. Ibid., 160.

20. Ibid., 244.

21. Owen Lattimore, "New Road to Asia," *National Geographic* 86, 6, December 1944, 641.

22. Wallace, 211.

23. Henry A. Wallace, *Our Job in the Pacific*, IPR Pamphlet 12 (New York: American Institute of Pacific Affairs, 1944), 42.

24. *Congressional Record*, volume 89, point 1, 78th Congress, 1st Sess., January 6, 1943 to March 1, 1943, 761.

25. Henry Ladd Smith, *Airways Abroad, The Story of American World Air Routes* (Madison, Wisconsin: University of Wisconsin Press, 1950), 131, citing *Congressional Record*, Volume 89, Part 1, February 9, 1943, 759–764. Later Henry Luce at least would take a more generous view of Wallace. They were friends. "A good man," Luce wrote in 1966, "an American idealist, and unvainglorious, Henry Wallace went with good cheer from limelight into obscurity." Patricia Neils, *China Images in the Life and Times of Henry Luce* (Savage, Maryland: Rowman & Littlefield, 1990), 70–71.

26. Kastner, 101.

27. Ibid., 102.

28. Gibson, 32.

29. Robert Huhn Jones, *The Roads to Russia: United States Lend-Lease to the Soviet Union* (Norman: University of Oklahoma Press, 1969), 210. The information is from U.S. Department of State, *Report on War Aid Furnished by the United States to the U.S.S.R.*, June 22, 1941–September 20, 1945, Washington, 1945, 14–15.

30. Ibid., 113, quoting Robert E. Sherwood, *Roosevelt and Hopkins: An Intimate History* (New York: Harper & Brothers, 1948), 545.

31. Robert C. Lukas, *Eagles East: The Army Air Forces and the Soviet Union, 1941–1945* (Tallahassee: Florida State University Press, 1970), 98–99.

32. Ibid., 5.

33. Ibid., 39, quoting Henry H. Arnold, *Global Mission* (New York: Harper and Brothers, 1949), 184.

34. Ibid., 106–107.

35. Jones, 158.

36. Nielson, 135.

37. Lukas, 219.

38. Jones, 160.

Chapter 27

1. Edward Miles et al., *Atlas of Marine Use in the North Pacific Region* (Berkeley: University of California Press, 1982), 57.

2. Clark G. Reynolds, "American Maritime Power since World War II," in Kilmarx, 222.

3. Miles, 57.

4. Interview with Frank Joyce, New York City, June 17, 1988.

5. *New York Times*, March 16, 1990, B7, obituary of Elmer L. Hann by Glenn Fowler.

6. Joyce interview.

7. Ibid.

8. Jerry Shields, *The Invisible Billionaire Daniel Ludwig* (Boston: Houghton Mifflin, 1986), xi.

9. Joyce interview.

10. Ibid.

11. Hideo Kubota, "Japan as Top Shipbuilder," *Inside/Outside Japan* 2, 5, June 1993, 3.

12. Bob Johnstone, "The Shipbuilders Get That Sinking Feeling," *Far Eastern Economic Review*, October 20, 1988, 72–76.

13. Reynolds, 252n, quoting Noel Mostert, *Supership* (New York: Knopf, 1974), 130.

14. Morris, 132.
15. Ibid., 113.
16. Ibid., 129.
17. *Seattle Times*, May 23, 1991, E3.

Chapter 28

1. *New Horizons*, December 1940, 26.
2. Usher interview.
3. PAA, letter by Charles E. Maher to the *Miami Herald*, September 25, 1974. When Pan Am sold its Pacific Division, one of the reasons offered by chairman C. Edward Acker was that the company could not develop the major California hubs necessary to nourish its trans-Pacific traffic.
4. Kastner, 105.
5. George E. Akerson, ed. Frederick R. Neely, "Wing Talk," *Collier's*, January 5, 1946, 8.
6. *Time Magazine*, September 10, 1945, 81, informed its readers that the difference is 1,051 miles.
7. Robert J. Gibbons, "Across the Pacific for 40 Years," *Northwest*, July 1987, 95.
8. Scott H. Reiniger, "TWA Pacific Bid," *Aviation Week*, July 20, 1953, 75.
9. Ibid., January 5, 1953, 95.
10. "Pacific Competitor for PAA?" *Business Week*, September 8, 1945, 22.
11. Ibid., "Seattle Air Battle," October 27, 1945, 44.
12. PAA 10.10.00. "The U.S.-Orient Air Route," n.d., 7.
13. Ibid.
14. Ladd Smith, 282.
15. As a popular advertisement in the late 1940s put it: "A hog can cross the United States without changing trains, but you can't."
16. Usher interview.
17. PAA 10.10.10, "Transpacific American Flag Air Service, Tokyo and the Orient," Confidential, n.d., 1957.
18. Ibid.
19. *Aviation Week*, November 10, 1947, 49.
20. Ann Crittenden, "Juan Trippe's Pan Am," *New York Times*, July 3, 1977.
21. Anthony Sampson, *Empires of the Sky: The Politics, Contests and Cartels of World Airlines* (New York: Random House, 1984), 226.
22. Eric Weiner, "Airlines Trying to Make Food Fly at 35,000 Feet," *New York Times*, May 6, 1990, C6.
23. Monci Jo Williams, "Why Is Airline Food So Terrible," *Fortune*, December 19, 1988, 172.
24. John Newhouse, "A Sporty Game," *New Yorker*, June 21, 1982, 80.

Chapter 29

1. Rae, 214.
2. PAA 50.12.05, Wolfgang Langewische conversation with Charles A. Lindbergh, September 1957.
3. "Jet Transport Schedule: 10 Hours, Canada to Tokyo," *Science News Letter*, June 23, 1951, 392.
4. From 10.2 billion revenue passenger miles to 162.4 billion. United States Congress, Senate, Committee on Commerce, Oversight Hearings on the SST, February 20, 1976.
5. S. J. Swadling, Executive Director, Technical British Aerospace, PLC Filton, Bristol,

England, "Commercial Supersonic Operation—Ten Years of Experience with Concorde," Society of Automotive Engineers, 1986, 1.

6. Mel Horwitch, *Clipped Wings: The American SST Conflict* (Cambridge: MIT Press, 1982), 54.

7. Ibid., 33.

8. Ibid., 64.

9. Ibid., 97.

10. Joseph J. Corn, *The Winged Gospel: America's Romance with Aviation, 1900–1950* (New York: Oxford University Press, 1983), 42.

11. Najeeb E. Halaby, *Crosswinds: An Airman's Memoir* (Garden City, New York: Doubleday, 1978), 182.

12. Horwitch, 2.

13. Ibid., 296.

14. Ibid., 145–146.

15. Ibid., 232.

16. United States Congress, Hearings, 1972, Joint Economic Committee, Subcommittee on Priorities and Economy in Government, "The Supersonic Transport," December 27 and 28, 1972, 99. Hereafter cited as Hearings, 1972.

17. Ibid., 78.

18. Richard Witkin, "Shock for Airline Industry," *New York Times*, April 23, 1985, D19.

19. Ibid.

20. Barry Bluestone, Peter Jordan, and Mark Sullivan, *Aircraft Industry Dynamics: An Analysis of Competition, Capital, and Labor* (Boston: Auburn House, 1981), 12.

21. Hearings, 1972, 3.

Chapter 30

1. *New York Times*, February 5, 1986, A20. The space shuttle *Challenger* was lost on January 28, 1986.

2. Gene Bylinski, "The 10,000-MPH Airliner," *Fortune*, December 8, 1986, 60.

3. MACH is the term named for the Austrian physicist Ernst Mach and refers to the ratio of the relative speed of a body to the speed of sound at the same point. MACH 1 is about 760 miles per hour at sea level. Supersonic speeds are in excess of MACH 1. The term *hypersonic* is imprecise but generally refers to speeds greater than about five times the speed of sound.

4. *Wall Street Journal*, June 27, 1989.

5. United States Congress, Hearings, House of Representatives, Committee on Science and Technology, Subcommittee on Transportation, Aviation, and Materials, "High Speed Aeronautics," July 24, 1985, 20. Hereafter cited as Hearings, 1985.

6. Ibid., 11–12.

7. Jerry Grey, "The Aerospace Plane, The Timing Is Right," *Issues in Science and Technology* 3, 3, Spring 1987, 17.

8. Hearings, 1985, 13.

9. Bylinski, 60.

10. For an enthusiastic discussion of this see George Koumal, ed., *Proceedings of the Interhemispheric Bering Strait Tunnel & Railway Group Conference*, Washington, D.C., June 22–23, 1992. Cost figures are cited by C. E. Burroughs, 41.

CONCLUSION

1. Nathan Rosenberg and L. E. Birdzell, Jr., *How the West Grew Rich, The Economic Transformation of the Industrial World* (New York: Basic Books, 1986), contains a stimulating discussion of this subject.

Bibliography

UNPUBLISHED

Archival

Horace Capron Papers, Library of Congress.
Caleb Cushing Papers, Library of Congress.
Cox Family Papers, Bethlehem, Pennsylvania.
Northern Pacific Railroad Papers, Minnesota Historical Society.
Pan American Archives, New York City.
Jared Sparks Papers, Houghton Library, Harvard University.
Juan Terry Trippe Papers, New York City.

Theses

Bartow, Thomas Prescott. "Early Transpacific Aviation, 1930–1941." M.A. thesis, University of Hawaii, 1958.

Borst, William Adam. "The American Merchant and the Genesis of Japanese-American Commercial Relation, 1790–1858." Ph.D. dissertation, St. Louis University, 1972.

Davidson, Mark J. "Power and Civilization: Theodore Roosevelt, Portsmouth and the Balance in Asia." M.A.L.D. thesis, Fletcher School of Law and Diplomacy, 1986.

Graham, Edward Dewey. "American Ideas of a Special Relationship with China: 1784–1900." Ph.D. dissertation, Harvard University, 1968.

Holbrook, Francis Xavier. "United States National Defense and Trans-Pacific Commercial Air Routes, 1933–1941." Ph.D. dissertation, Fordham University, 1969.

Humeston, Helen Mary. "Origins of America's Japan Policy, 1790–1854." Ph.D. dissertation, University of Minnesota, 1981.

Kazar, Jr., John Dryden. "The United States Navy and Scientific Exploration 1837–1860." Ph.D. dissertation, University of Massachusetts, 1973.

Roberts, Christopher. "The Middlesex Canal." Ph.D. dissertation, Harvard University, 1927.

Seguin, Paul Burton. "The Deteriorating Strategic Position of Japan: 1853–1945. A Study of the Revolution of Intercontinental Warfare." Ph.D. dissertation, University of Minnesota, 1972.

Towle, Edward L. "Science, Commerce and the Navy on the Seafaring Frontier (1842–1861)—The Role of Lieutenant M. F. Maury and the U.S. Naval Hydrographic Office." Ph.D. dissertation, University of Rochester, 1966.

Travis, Frederick Francis. "George Kennan and Russia, 1865–1905." Ph.D. dissertation, Emory University, 1974.
Whelan, Joseph. "William Henry Seward, Expansionist." Ph.D. dissertation, University of Rochester, 1959.

Conference Proceedings

Koumal, George, ed. *Proceedings of the Interhemispheric Bering Strait Tunnel & Railway Group Conference.* Washington, D.C., June 22–23, 1992.

Manuscripts

Bixby, Harold M. "Top Side Ricksha." Unpublished memoir, 1938, Pan American Archives, New York City.
Dollar, Robert. *Private Diary of Robert Dollar on his Visits to China,* copyrighted 1912 by the Robert Dollar Company.
Maki, John M. "William Smith Clark: A Yankee in Hokkaido." 2 volumes. Amherst, Massachusetts: Archives, University of Massachusetts, n.d.
[Phelps, William Dane] "Solid Men of Boston." Unpublished ms, n.d., Bancroft Library, University of California, Berkeley.
Trippe, Betty. Diary and letters of Betty Stettinius Trippe, 1925–1968. New York City.

Interviews

Joyce, Frank. Universe Tankships, New York City, June 17, 1988.
Swihart, John M. Boeing Corporation, Medford, Massachusetts, November 3, 1987.
Usher, Donald. Pan American Corporation, Annisquam, Massachusetts, September 1, 1987.

PUBLISHED

Government Documents

Canada. Parliamentary Debates. 1st Parliament, 4th Session, March 18, 1871.
United States Civil Aeronautics Board. CAB Docket 547, Exhibit PA-113.
———. CAB Docket 851, Exhibit PA-2.
United States Congress. *An Act to Promote the Welfare of American Seamen in the Merchant Marine of the United States.* 63d Congress, 3d Session, Chapter 153, 1915.
United States Congress. House. Abridgement of the Debates of Congress. "Settlement of the Northwest Coast." December 1824.
———. 20th Congress, 1st Session, Report 209, March 25, 1828.
———. 23d Congress, 2d Session, Navy Department, Document 105, 1834–35, Report of J. N. Reynolds to the Secretary of the Navy, September 24, 1828.
———. 35th Congress, 1st Session, Executive Document 98, 1858.
———. 41st Congress, 2d Session, 28, 1869–70, February 17, 1870.
———. 99th Congress, 1st Session, 21, July 24, 1985.
United States Congress. Joint Economic Committee, Hearings, 1972.
United States Congress. Senate. Abridgement of the Debates of Congress, "Occupation of the Oregon River," Volume 8, March 1825.
———. 29th Congress, 1st Session, Senate Executive Document 306, April 20, 1846.
———. 29th Congress, 1st Session, 466, July 31, 1846.
———. 34th Congress, 1st Session, Misc. Doc. 60, May 20, 1856.
———. 40th Congress, 2d Session, Executive Document 79, 1867–68.

————. 40th Congress, 3d Session, Report 194, November 18, 1866.

————. 43d Congress, 2d Session, December 21, 1873–74.

————. 44th Congress, 1st Session, Misc. Document 127, 1875–76, July 25, 1876.

————. 49th Congress, 1st Session, Senate Misc. Document 84, March 1886.

————. 58th Congress, 3d Session, Senate Reports, Report 2755, 1904–5.

United States Congress. Senate. Committee on Commerce. February 20, 1976.

United States Department of Commerce and Labor. Bureau of Statistics. *Transportation Routes and Systems of the World, Development of Steam-Carrying Power on Land and Sea, 1800–1906.* Washington, D.C.: Government Printing Office, 1907.

Books

A Gentleman educated at Yale College [Timothy Dwight], *America, or, A Poem on the Settlement of the British Colonies; Addressed to the Friends of Freedom, and Their Country.* New Haven: Thomas and Samuel Green, 1770.

A Sailor. *Description of the Largest Ship in the World, the New Clipper Great Republic of Boston, Designed, Built and Owned by Donald McKay, and Commanded by Capt. L. McKay, with Illustrated Designs of the Construction.* Boston Eastburn's Press, 1853.

Adams, Brooks. *America's Economic Supremacy* (first published 1900). New York: Harper & Bros., 1947.

Ahvenainen, Jorma. *The Far Eastern Telegraphs: The History of Telegraphic Communications between the Far East, Europe and America before the First World War.* Helsinki: Suomalainen Tiedeakatemia, 1981.

Albion, Robert Greenhalgh. *Forests and Sea Power: The Timber Problem of the Royal Navy, 1652–1862.* Cambridge: Harvard University Press, 1926.

Albion, Robert G., William A. Baker, and Benjamin W. Labaree. *New England and the Sea.* Middletown, Connecticut: Wesleyan University Press, 1972.

Augur, Helen. *Passage to Glory, John Ledyard's America.* Garden City, New York: Doubleday, 1946.

Baker, George B., ed. *The Works of William H. Seward.* 5 volumes. New York: Redfield, 1884.

Barnett, Correlli. *The Pride and the Fall: The Dream and Illusion of Britain as a Great Nation.* New York: Free Press, 1987.

Barrow, Clayton R., ed. *America Spreads Her Sails: U.S. Seapower in the 19th Century.* Annapolis, Maryland: United States Naval Institute Press, 1973.

Beaubois, Henry. *Airships, Yesterday, Today and Tomorrow.* New York: Two Continents Publishing Group, 1976.

Beaglehole, J. C., ed. *The Journals of Captain James Cook on His Voyages of Discovery.* Volumes 3 and 4. London: Hakluyt Society, 1967, 1974.

Beale, Howard K. *Theodore Roosevelt and the Rise of America to World Power.* New York: Collier, 1962.

Benton, Thomas Hart. *Thirty Years' View: A History of the Working of the American Government for Thirty Years from 1820 to 1850.* New York: D. Appleton, 1858.

Beveridge, Albert J. *The Russian Advance.* New York: Harper & Brothers, 1904.

Bilstein, Roger E. *Flight in America 1900–1983, from the Wright Brothers to the Astronauts.* Baltimore: Johns Hopkins Press, 1984.

Bluestone, Barry, Peter Jordan, and Mark Sullivan. *Aircraft Industry Dynamics: An Analysis of Competition, Capital, and Labor.* Boston: Auburn House, 1981.

Blum, John Morton, ed. *The Price of Vision: The Diary of Henry A. Wallace, 1942–1946.* Boston: Houghton Mifflin, 1973.

Boyd, Julian P., ed. *The Papers of Thomas Jefferson.* Princeton, New Jersey: Princeton University Press, 1954.

Bradley, Harold Whitman. *The American Frontier in Hawaii: The Pioneers, 1789–1843.* Stanford, California: Stanford University Press, 1942.

Briggs, Asa. *The Power of Steam: An Illustrated History of the World's Steam Age.* Chicago: University of Chicago Press, 1982.

Brock, Horace. *Flying the Oceans: A Pilot's Story of Pan Am 1935–1955.* Lunenburg, Vermont: Stinehour Press, 1978.

Brooke, George M., Jr., ed. *John M. Brooke's Pacific Cruise and Japanese Adventure, 1858–1860.* Honolulu: University of Hawaii Press, 1986.

Brooks, Charles. *History of Town of Medford.* Boston: James M. Usher, 1855.

Burton, David H. *Theodore Roosevelt: Confident Imperialist.* Philadelphia: University of Pennsylvania Press, 1968.

Caine, W. S. *A Trip Round the World in 1887–8.* London: George Routledge and Sons, n.d.

Cameron, Roderick. *The Golden Haze, with Captain Cook in the South Pacific.* Cleveland: World Publishing Company, 1964.

Campbell, J. F. *My Circular Notes [Extracts from Journals, etc.] Written While Travelling Westwards Round the World, July 6, 1874–July 6, 1875.* London: Macmillan, 1876.

Carpenter, Kenneth J. *The History of Scurvy and Vitamin C.* Cambridge: Cambridge University Press, 1986.

Caruthers, J. Wade. *American Pacific Ocean Trade: Its Impact on Foreign Policy and Continental Expansion, 1784–1860.* New York: Exposition Press, 1973.

Cary, Clarence. *The Trans-Siberian Route or Notes of a Journey from Pekin to New York in 1902.* New York: Evening Post Job Printing House, 1902.

Chapman, Charles E. *A History of California: The Spanish Period.* New York: Macmillan, 1921.

Clark, Arthur H. *The Clipper Ship Era.* New York: G. P. Putnam's Sons, 1910.

Cleveland, Richard J. *Narrative of Voyages and Commercial Enterprises.* 3d ed. Boston: Charles H. Peirce, 1850.

Coates, Kenneth, ed. *The Alaska Highway: Papers of the 40th Anniversary Symposium.* Vancouver: University of British Columbia Press, 1985.

Cochrane, Dorothy, Von Hardesty, and Russell Lee. *The Aviation Careers of Igor Sikorsky.* Seattle: University of Washington Press published for the National Air and Space Museum, 1989.

Coffin, Charles Carleton. *Our New Way Round the World.* Boston: Fields, Osgood, 1869.

Cohen, Stan. *Pan American Clipper Planes 1935 to 1945, Wings to the Orient, A Pictorial History.* Missoula, Montana: Pictorial Histories Publishing Co., 1985.

Cole, Allan B. *Yankee Surveyors in Shogunal Seas.* Princeton, New Jersey: Princeton University Press, 1947.

Cole, Terrence, ed. *The Capture of Attu, Tales of World War II in Alaska as Told by the Men Who Fought There.* Anchorage: Alaska Northwest Publishing Company, 1984.

Cook, Warren L. *Flood Tide of Empire: Spain and the Pacific Northwest, 1543–1819.* New Haven, Connecticut: Yale University Press, 1973.

Cooper, J. Fenimore. *History of the Navy of the United States of America.* New York: Stringer & Townsend, 1856.

Corn, Joseph J. *The Winged Gospel, America's Romance with Aviation, 1900–1950.* New York: Oxford University Press, 1983.

Craig, Albert M. *Choshu in the Meiji Restoration.* Cambridge: Harvard University Press, 1961.

Cramp, Charles H. *Commercial Supremacy and Other Papers.* Philadelphia: privately printed, 1894.

Crane, James M. *The Past, the Present, and the Future of the Pacific.* San Francisco: Sterett & Co., 1856.

Curtin, Philip. *Cross-Cultural Trade in World History.* Cambridge: Cambridge University Press, 1984.

Cutler, Carl C. *Greyhounds of the Sea: The Story of the American Clipper Ship.* New York: G. P. Putnam's Sons, 1930.

Daley, Robert. *An American Saga: Juan Trippe and His Pan Am Empire.* New York: Random House, 1980.

Dana, Jr., Richard H. *The Seaman's Friend.* Delmar, New York: Scholars' Facsimiles and Reprints, 1979.

————. *Two Years before the Mast.* Boston: Houghton Mifflin, 1895.

Davies, R. E. G. *Airlines of the United States since 1914.* Washington, D.C.: Smithsonian Institution Press, 1972.

Davis, John P. *The Union Pacific Railway: A Study in Railway Politics, History, and Economics.* Reprint. New York: Arno Press, 1973.

Delear, Frank J. *Igor Sikorsky: His Three Careers in Aviation.* New York: Dodd, Mead, 1969.

Dennett, Tyler. *Americans in Eastern Asia: A Critical Study of United States' Policy in the Far East in the Nineteenth Century.* Reprint. New York: Barnes & Noble, 1963.

————. *Roosevelt and the Russo-Japanese War.* New York: Doubleday, Page, 1925.

Dennys, N. B., Wm. Fred. Mayers, and Chas. King. *The Treaty Ports of China and Japan, A Complete Guide.* London: Trubner & Company, 1867.

Dixon, Joe C., ed. *The American Military and the Far East: Proceedings of the Ninth Military History Symposium.* United States Air Force Academy, October 1–3, 1980. Washington, D.C.: Government Printing Office, 1980.

Dmytryshyn, Basil, E. A. P. Crownhart-Vaughan, and Thomas Vaughan, eds. and trans. *To Siberia and Russian America: Three Centuries of Russian Eastward Expansion, 1558–1867,* volume 1, *Russia's Conquest of Siberia, 1558–1700: A Documentary Record,* volume 2, *Russian Penetration of the North Pacific Ocean, 1700–1797: A Documentary Record,* volume 3, *The Russian American Colonies, 1798–1867, A Documentary Record.* Portland: Oregon Historical Society, 1985, 1988, 1989.

Donald, David Herbert. *Charles Sumner and the Coming of the Civil War.* New York: Alfred Knopf, 1960.

Drake, Frederick C. *The Empire of the Seas: A Biography of Rear Admiral Robert Wilson Shufeldt, USN.* Honolulu: University of Hawaii Press, 1984.

Erskine, Charles. *Twenty Years before the Mast—With the More Thrilling Scenes and Incidents While Circumnavigating the Globe under the Command of the Late Admiral Charles Wilkes, 1838–1842.* Boston: published by the author, 1890.

Fanning, Edmund. *Voyages and Discoveries in the South Seas, 1792–1832.* Salem, Massachusetts: Marine Research Society, 1924.

Farnie, D. A. *East and West of Suez: The Suez Canal in History 1854–1956.* Oxford: Clarendon Press, 1969.

Fisher, Raymond H. *The Voyage of Semen Dezhnev in 1648: Bering's Precursor with Selected Documents.* London: Hakluyt Society, 1981.

Fisher, Robin, and Hugh Johnson, eds. *Captain James Cook and His Times.* Seattle: University of Washington Press, 1979.

Fitzhugh, William W., and Aron Crowell, eds. *Crossroads of Continents: Cultures of Siberia and Alaska.* Washington, D.C.: Smithsonian Institution Press, 1988.

French, Hollis. *The Thatcher Magoun: An American Clipper Ship, Her Owners, Captains, and Model.* Cambridge: Houghton Mifflin, 1936.

Friis, Herman R., ed., *The Pacific Basin, A History of Its Geographical Exploration.* New York: American Geographical Society, 1967.

Galloway, John Debo. *The First Transcontinental Railroad.* Reprint. New York: Arno Press, 1981.

Garfield, Brian. *The Thousand-Mile War: World War II in Alaska and the Aleutians*. Toronto: Bantam, 1988.

Garner, Stanton, ed. *The Captain's Best Mate: The Journal of Mary Chipman Lawrence on the Whaler Addison 1856–1860*. Providence, Rhode Island: Brown University Press, 1966.

Garnett, Constance, trans., revised by Humphrey Higgens. *My Past and Thoughts, The Memoirs of Alexander Herzen*. New York: Alfred Knopf, 1968.

Gibson, James R., *Imperial Russia in Frontier America, the Changing Geography of Supply of Russian America, 1784–1867*. New York: Oxford University Press, 1976.

Gibson, Weldon B. *Skyways of the Pacific*, Pamphlet 27. New York: American Institute of Pacific Affairs, 1947.

Gilpin, William. *The Central Gold Region and the Grain, Pastoral, and Gold Regions of North America*. Philadelphia: Sower, Barnes, 1860.

————. *The Cosmopolitan Railway*. San Francisco: History Company, 1890.

————. *Mission of the North American People, Geographical, Social, and Political*. 2d edition. Philadelphia: Lippincott, 1874.

Gleason, Hull. *Old Ships and Ship-building Days of Medford, 1630–1873*. West Medford, Massachusetts: privately printed, 1936.

Goetzmann, William H. *New Lands, New Men: America and the Second Great Age of Discovery*. New York: Viking Penguin, 1986.

Goetzmann, William H., and Kay Sloan. *Looking Far North: The Harriman Expedition to Alaska, 1899*. New York: Viking Press, 1982.

Graebner, Norman A. *Empire on the Pacific: A Study in American Continental Expansion*. Santa Barbara: California: ABC-Clio Press, 1983.

Graham, Gerald S. *The Politics of Naval Supremacy: Studies in British Maritime Ascendancy*. Cambridge: Cambridge University Press, 1965.

Griffin, Eldon. *Clippers and Consuls: American Consular and Commercial Relations with Eastern Asia, 1845–1860*. Ann Arbor, Michigan: Edwards Brothers, 1939.

Griscom, Lloyd. *Diplomatically Speaking*. Boston: Little, Brown, 1940.

Grodinsky, Julius. *Transcontinental Railway Strategy, 1869–1893: A Study of Businessmen*. Philadelphia: University of Pennsylvania Press, 1962.

Grooch, William Stephen. *Skyway to Asia*. New York: Longmans, Green, 1939.

Habakkuk, H. J., and M. Postan, eds. *The Cambridge Economic History of Europe*, volume 6, *The Industrial Revolutions and After: Incomes, Population and Technological Change*. Cambridge: Cambridge University Press, 1965.

Habersham, A. W. *The North Pacific Surveying and Exploring Expedition*. Philadelphia: Lippincott, 1857.

Halaby, Najeeb E. *Crosswinds: An Airman's Memoir*. Garden City, New York: Doubleday, 1978.

Hawks, Francis L., ed. *Narrative of the Expedition of an American Squadron to the China Seas and Japan Performed in the Years 1852, 1853, and 1854 under the Command of Commodore M. C. Perry, United States Navy*. 4 volumes. Washington, D.C.: Government Printing Office, 1856.

Hidy, Ralph W., Muriel E. Hidy, and Roy V. Scott, with Don L. Hofsommer. *The Great Northern Railway: A History*. Boston: Harvard Business School Press, 1988.

Higham, Robin. *Britain's Imperial Air Routes 1918 to 1939: The Story of Britain's Overseas Airlines*. Hamden, Connecticut: Shoe String Press, 1961.

Hill, James J. *Highways of Progress*. New York: Doubleday, Page & Company, 1910.

Hine, Robert V. *Edward Kern and American Expansion*. New Haven: Connecticut, Yale University Press, 1962.

Ho, Ping-ti. *Studies on the Population of China, 1368–1963*. Cambridge: Harvard University Press, 1967.

Hogan, Michael J., and Thomas G. Patterson, eds. *Explaining the History of American Foreign Relations.* Cambridge: Cambridge University Press, 1991.

Hollander, Paul. *Political Pilgrims: Travels of Western Intellectuals to the Soviet Union, China, and Cuba 1928–1978.* New York: Oxford University Press, 1981.

Horwitch, Mel. *Clipped Wings: The American SST Conflict.* Cambridge: MIT Press, 1982.

Howay, Frederic W., ed. *Voyages of the Columbia to the Northwest Coast, 1787–1790 and 1790–1793.* Boston: Massachusetts Historical Society, 1941.

Hunt, Michael H. *Frontier Defense and the Open Door: Manchuria in Chinese-American Relations.* New Haven, Connecticut: Yale University Press, 1973.

Hutchins, John G. B. *The American Maritime Industries and Public Policy, 1789–1914: An Economic History.* Cambridge: Harvard University Press, 1941.

Israel, Fred L., ed. *The State of the Union Messages of the Presidents, 1790–1966*, Volume 3, *1905–1966.* New York: Chelsea House-Robert Hector, 1966.

Jackman, S. W., ed. *The Journal of William Sturgis.* Victoria, British Columbia: Sono Nis Press, 1978.

Johnson, Arthur M., and Barry E. Supple. *Boston Capitalists and Western Railroads: A Study in the Nineteenth-Century Railroad Investment Process.* Cambridge: Harvard University Press, 1967.

Jones, Robert Huhn. *The Roads to Russia: United States Lend-Lease to the Soviet Union.* Norman: University of Oklahoma Press, 1969.

Josephson, Matthew. *Empire of the Air: Juan Trippe and the Struggle for World Airways.* New York: Harcourt, Brace, 1944.

Kahn, Otto H. *Reflections of a Financier: A Study of Economic and Other Problems.* London: Hodder & Stoughton, 1921.

Keiler, Hans. *American Shipping: Its History and Economic Conditions.* Jena: Verlag von Gustav Fischer, 1913.

Kemble, John Haskell. *The Panama Route, 1848–1869.* University of California Publications in History. Berkeley: University of California Press, 1943.

Kennan, George. *E. H. Harriman's Far Eastern Plans.* New York: Country Life Press, 1917.

———. *Tent Life in Siberia.* New York: G. P. Putnam & Sons, 1870.

Kennan, George F. *Russia and the West under Lenin and Stalin.* Boston: Atlantic Monthly Press, 1961.

Kerner, Robert J. *The Urge to the Sea, the Course of Russian History, the Role of Rivers, Portages, Ostrogs, Monasteries, and Furs.* Berkeley: University of California Press, 1942.

Kilmarx, Robert A., ed. *America's Maritime Legacy: A History of the U.S. Merchant Marine and Shipbuilding Industry Since Colonial Times.* Boulder, Colorado: Westview Press, 1979.

Klein, Maury. *Union Pacific, Birth of a Railroad, 1862–1893.* New York: Doubleday, 1987.

Kushner, Howard I. *Conflict on the Northwest Coast, American-Russian Rivalry in the Pacific Northwest, 1790–1867.* Westport, Connecticut: Greenwood Press, 1975.

Laing, Alexander. *Clipper Ship Men.* New York: Duell, Sloan & Pearce, 1944.

Lawson, Will. *Pacific Steamers.* Glasgow: Brown, Son and Ferguson, 1927.

Leary, Jr., William M. *The Dragon's Wings, The China National Aviation Corporation and the Development of Commercial Aviation in China.* Athens: University of Georgia Press, 1976.

Lebow, Eileen F. *Cal Rodgers and the Vin Fiz, the First Transcontinental Flight.* Washington, D.C.: Smithsonian Institution Press, 1989.

Leighly, John, ed. *The Physical Geography of the Sea and Its Meteorology*, by Matthew Fontaine Maury. Cambridge: Harvard University Press, Belknap Press, 1963.

Lensen, George Alexander, ed., *Trading under Sail Off Japan, 1860 to 1899: The Recollections of Captain John Baxter Will, Sailing-Master and Pilot.* Tokyo: Sophia University Press in cooperation with the Diplomatic Press, Tallahassee, Florida, 1968.

Lindbergh, Anne Morrow. *North to the Orient.* New York: Harcourt Brace, 1935.

Lindbergh, Charles A. *Autobiography of Values.* New York: Harcourt Brace Jovanovich, 1977.

Liu, Kwang-ching. *Anglo-American Steamship Rivalry in China, 1862–1874.* Cambridge: Harvard University Press, 1962.

Lloyd, Christopher, and Jack L. S. Coulter, *Medicine and the Navy, 1200–1900,* volume 3, *1714–1815.* Edinburgh: E & S Livingston, 1961.

Long, David F. *Nothing Too Daring: A Biography of Commodore David Porter, 1780–1843* Annapolis, Maryland: United States Naval Institute Press, 1970.

Lopez, Barry. *Arctic Dreams, Imagination and Desire in a Northern Landscape.* New York: Charles Scribner's Sons, 1986.

Lukas, Richard C. *Eagles East: The Army Air Forces and the Soviet Union, 1941–1945.* Tallahassee: Florida State University Press, 1970.

MacKay, Donald. *The Asian Dream: The Pacific Rim and Canada's National Railway.* Vancouver, British Columbia: Douglas & McIntyre, 1986.

McCullough, David. *The Path between the Seas: The Creation of the Panama Canal 1870–1914.* New York: Simon & Schuster, 1977.

McKenzie, Fred A. *The American Invaders: Their Plans, Tactics and Progress.* New York: Street and Smith, 1901.

McMahon, William. *A Journey with the Sun around the World.* Cleveland, Ohio: Catholic Universe Publishing Company, 1907.

Mahan, Alfred Thayer. *The Problem of Asia and Its Effects upon International Policies.* Boston: Little, Brown, 1900.

Marks, Steven G. *Road to Power: The Trans-Siberian Railroad and the Colonization of Asian Russia, 1850–1917.* Ithaca, New York: Cornell University Press, 1991.

Martin, Albro. *James J. Hill and the Opening of the Northwest.* New York: Oxford University Press, 1976.

Masland, William M. *Through the Back Doors of the World in a Ship That Had Wings.* New York: Vantage, 1984.

Maury, Matthew Fontaine. *The Physical Geography of the Sea.* New York: Harper & Brothers, 1856.

Meinig, D. W. *The Shaping of America: A Geographical Perspective on 500 Years of History.* Volume 1, *Atlantic America, 1492–1800.* New Haven, Connecticut: Yale University Press, 1986.

Melville, Herman. *White Jacket or the World in a Man-of-War.* New York: Library of America, 1983.

Merk, Frederick. *Albert Gallatin and the Oregon Question: A Study in Anglo-American Diplomacy.* Cambridge: Harvard University Press, 1950.

Morison, Samuel Eliot. *The Maritime History of Massachusetts, 1783–1860.* Boston: Houghton Mifflin, 1921.

———. *Oxford History of the American People.* New York: Oxford University Press, 1965.

Morris, Keith, *The Story of the Canadian Pacific Railway.* London: William Stevens, 1916.

Morton, Harry A. *The Wind Commands: Sailors and Sailing Ships in the Pacific.* Middletown, Connecticut: Wesleyan University Press, 1975.

Munford, James Kenneth, ed., with an introduction by Sinclair H. Hitchings. *Journal of Captain Cook's Last Voyage,* by John Ledyard. Corvallis: University of Oregon Press, 1963.

Neal, Steve. *Dark Horse: A Biography of Wendell Willkie.* Garden City, New York: Doubleday, 1984.

Neils, Patricia. *China Images in the Life and Times of Henry Luce.* Savage, Maryland: Rowman & Littlefield, 1990.

Nielson, Jonathan M. *Armed Forces on a Northern Frontier: The Military in Alaska's History, 1867–1987.* Westport, Connecticut: Greenwood Press, 1988.

Niven, John *The American President Lines and Its Forebears, 1848–1984.* Newark: University of Delaware Press, 1987.

Oliver, John W. *History of American Technology.* New York: Ronald Press, 1956.

Pack, A. J. *Nelson's Blood: The Story of Naval Rum.* Homewell, Havant, Hampshire: Kenneth Mason, 1982.

Paolino, Ernest N. *The Foundations of the American Empire: William Henry Seward and U.S. Foreign Policy.* Ithaca, New York: Cornell University Press, 1973.

Parry, J. H. *The Spanish Seaborne Empire.* New York: Alfred A. Knopf, 1966.

Pethick, Derek. *First Approaches to the Northwest Coast.* Vancouver, British Columbia: J. J. Douglas, 1976.

Porter, David. *Journal of a Cruise Made to the Pacific Ocean, by Captain David Porter in the United States Frigate Essex in the Years 1812, 1813, and 1814.* 2d edition. 2 volumes. New York: Wiley and Halsted, 1822.

Pumpelly, Raphael. *My Reminiscences.* Volume 1. New York: Henry Holt, 1918.

Quincy, Josiah. *The Journals of Major Samuel Shaw with a Life of the Author.* Boston: Wm. Crosby and H. P. Nichols, 1847.

Rae, John Bell. *Climb to Greatness: The American Aircraft Industry, 1920–1960.* Cambridge: MIT Press, 1968.

Reid, Virginia Hancock. *The Purchase of Alaska, Contemporary Opinion.* Long Beach, California: Press Telegram Printers, 1939.

Reynolds, J(ohn) N. *Voyage of the United States Frigate Potomac under the Command of Commodore John Downes, during the Circumnavigation of the Globe in the Years 1831, 1832, 1833, and 1834.* New York: Harper & Brothers, 1835.

Robinson, Douglas H. *Giants in the Sky: A History of the Rigid Airship.* Seattle, Washington: University of Washington Press, 1973.

Ronda, James P. *Astoria and Empire.* Lincoln: University of Nebraska Press, 1990.

Rosenberg, Nathan, and L. E. Birdzell, Jr. *How the West Grew Rich: The Economic Transformation of the Industrial World.* New York: Basic Books, 1986.

Ryan, Paul B. *The Panama Canal Controversy: U.S. Diplomacy and Defense Interests.* Stanford: Hoover Institution Press, 1977.

Rydell, Raymond A. *Cape Horn to the Pacific: The Rise and Decline of an Ocean Highway.* Berkeley: University of California Press, 1952.

Sampson, Anthony. *Empires of the Sky: The Politics, Contests and Cartels of World Airlines.* New York: Random House, 1984.

Schivelbusch, Wolfgang. *The Railway Journey: The Industrialization of Time and Space in the 19th Century.* Berkeley: University of California Press, 1986.

Schonberger, Howard B. *Transportation to the Seaboard: The "Communications Revolution" and American Foreign Policy, 1850–1900.* Westport, Connecticut: Greenwood Press, 1971.

Schurz, William Lytle. *The Manila Galleon.* New York: E. P. Dutton & Company, 1959.

Seaburg, Carl, and Alan Seaburg. *Medford on the Mystic.* N.p., 1980.

Sellers, Charles. *James K. Polk Continentalist, 1843–1846.* Princeton, New Jersey: Princeton University Press, 1966.

Seward, Olive Risley, ed. *William H. Seward's Travels Around the World.* New York: D. Appleton & Company, 1873.

Sherwood, Morgan B. *Exploration of Alaska, 1865–1900.* New Haven, Connecticut: Yale University Press, 1965.

Shields, Jerry. *The Invisible Billionaire Daniel Ludwig.* Boston: Houghton Mifflin, 1986.

Siegfried, André. *Suez and Panama.* Translated from the French by H. H. and Doris Hemming. New York: Harcourt, Brace, 1940.

Sinkler, George. *The Racial Attitudes of American Presidents from Abraham Lincoln to Theodore Roosevelt.* Garden City, New York: Doubleday, 1971.

Smith, Adam. *The Wealth of Nations*. New York: Random House, Modern Library Edition, 1937.

Smith, Henry Ladd. *Airways Abroad: The Story of American World Air Routes*. Madison: University of Wisconsin Press, 1950.

Smith, Henry Nash. *Virgin Land: The American West as Symbol and Myth*. Cambridge: Harvard University Press, 1970.

Smith, Philip Chadwick Foster. *The Empress of China*. Philadelphia: Philadelphia Maritime Museum, 1984.

Spalding, J. W. *Japan and Around the World: An Account of Three Visits to the Japanese Empire*. New York: Redfield, 1855.

Sparks, Jared. *The Life of John Ledyard, the American Traveller: Comprising Selections from His Journals and Correspondence*. Cambridge: Hilliard & Brown, 1828.

Spate, O. H. K. *The Pacific Since Magellan*. Volume 1, *The Spanish Lake*. Minneapolis: University of Minnesota Press, 1979.

Spector, Ronald. *Professors of War: The Naval War College and the Development of the Naval Profession*. Newport, Rhode Island: Naval War College Press, 1977.

Stanton, William. *The Great United States Exploring Expedition of 1838–1842*. Berkeley: University of California Press, 1975.

Stead, W. T. *The Americanization of the World*. New York: Horace Markley, 1901.

Strong, Josiah. *Expansion under New World Conditions*. New York: Baker and Taylor, 1900.

Sturtevant, William C., General Editor, David Damas, Volume Editor. *Handbook of North American Indians*. Volume 5, *Arctic*. Washington, D.C.: Smithsonian Institution, 1984.

Taylor, Bayard. *A Visit to India, China, and Japan, in the Year 1853*. New York: G. P. Putnam, 1855.

Taylor, Fitch W. *A Voyage Round the World and, Visits to Various Foreign Countries, in the United States Frigate Columbia, etc.* 9th edition. New Haven, Connecticut: H. Mansfield, 1850.

Taylor, George Rogers. *The Economic History of the United States*. Volume 4, *The Transportation Revolution, 1815–1860*. New York: Harper Torchbooks, 1951.

Thayer, Jr., Frederick C. *Air Transport Policy and National Security: A Political, Economic and Military Analysis*. Chapel Hill: University of North Carolina Press, 1965.

Thompson, Robert Luther. *Wiring a Continent: The History of the Telegraph Industry in the United States, 1832–1866*. Princeton, New Jersey: Princeton University Press, 1947.

Tocqueville, Alexis de. *Democracy in America*. Trans. Henry Reeve, with preface and notes by John C. Spencer. New York: Adland and Saunders, 1838.

Tower, Walter S. *A History of the American Whale Fishery*. Series in Political Economy and Public Law 20. Philadelphia: University of Pennsylvania Press, 1907.

Train, George Francis. *An American Merchant in Europe, Asia and Australia*. New York: G. P. Putnam's Sons, 1857.

———. *Young America Abroad in Europe, Asia and America*. London: Sampson, Low Son & Company, 1857.

Trani, Eugene P. *The Treaty of Portsmouth: An Adventure in American Diplomacy*. Lexington: University of Kentucky Press, 1969.

Travis, Frederick Francis. *George Kennan and the American-Russian Relationship, 1865–1924*. Athens: Ohio University Press, 1990.

Tribolet, Leslie Bennett. *The International Aspects of Electrical Communications in the Pacific Area*. Baltimore, Maryland: Johns Hopkins Press, 1929.

Tunner, William H., *Over the Hump*. Washington, D.C.: Office of Air Force History, United States Air Force, 1985.

van Alstyne, R. W. *The Rising American Empire*. New York: Oxford University Press, 1960.

Vevier, Charles. *The United States and China, 1906–1913: A Study of Finance and Diplomacy*. New Brunswick, New Jersey: Rutgers University Press, 1955.

Vevier, Charles, ed. *Siberian Journey: Down the Amur to the Pacific, 1856–1857*, a new edition of *A Voyage down the Amoor* by Perry McDonough Collins. Madison: University of Wisconsin Press, 1962.

Viola, Herman J., and Carolyn Margolis, eds. *Magnificent Voyagers: The U.S. Exploring Expedition, 1838–1842*. Washington, D.C.: Smithsonian Institution Press, 1985.

Walker, J. Samuel. *Henry A. Wallace and American Foreign Policy*. Westport, Connecticut: Greenwood Press, 1976.

Wallace, Henry A., with the collaboration of Andrew J. Steiger. *Soviet Asia Mission*. New York: Reynal & Hitchcock, 1946.

Walter, Richard. *Anson's Voyage Round the World*. Ed. G. S. Laird Clowes. London: Martin Hopkinson, 1928.

Walton, Gary M., and James F. Shepherd. *The Economic Rise of Early America*. Cambridge: Cambridge University Press, 1979.

Watrous, Stephen D., ed. *John Ledyard's Journey through Russia and Siberia 1787–1788: The Journal and Selected Letters*. Madison: University of Wisconsin Press, 1966.

Watt, J., E. J. Freeman, and W. F. Bynum, eds. *Starving Sailors: The Influence of Nutrition upon Naval and Maritime History*. Greenwich: National Maritime Museum, 1981.

Weber, David J., *The Spanish Frontier in North America*. New Haven: Yale University Press, 1992.

Westwood, J. N. *A History of Russian Railways*. London: George Allen and Unwin, 1964.

Wiley, Peter Booth. *Yankees in the Land of the Gods: Commodore Perry and the Opening of Japan*. New York: Viking Press, 1990.

Wilgus, William J. *The Railway Interrelations of the United States and Canada*. New Haven, Connecticut: Yale University Press, 1937.

Wilkins, Mira. *The Emergence of Multinational Enterprise: American Business Abroad from the Colonial Era to 1914*. Cambridge: Harvard University Press, 1970.

———. *The Maturing of Multinational Enterprise: American Business Abroad from 1914 to 1970*. Cambridge: Harvard University Press, 1974.

Williams, Francis Leigh. *Matthew Fontaine Maury: Scientist of the Sea*. New Brunswick, New Jersey: Rutgers University Press, 1963.

Williamson, James A. *Cook and the Opening of the Pacific*. London: Hodder & Stoughton, 1946.

Willkie, Wendell L. *One World*. New York: Simon and Schuster, 1943.

Woodruff, William. *Impact of Western Man: A Study of Europe's Role in the World Economy, 1750–1960*. Washington, D.C.: University Press of America, 1982.

Wray, William D. *Mitsubishi and the N.Y.K. 1870–1914: Business Strategy in the Japanese Shipping Industry*. Cambridge: Harvard University Press, 1984.

Zeis, Paul Maxwell. *American Shipping Policy*. Princeton, New Jersey: Princeton University Press, 1938.

Pamphlets

California Addresses by President Roosevelt. San Francisco: California Promotion Committee, 1903.

Dwight, Timothy. *Columbia, A Song*. New Haven, Connecticut: Press of Timothy Dwight College, Yale University, 1940.

Forbes, R. B. *Remarks on China and the China Trade*. Boston: n.p., 1844.

Grace, J. Peter. "W. R. Grace (1832–1904) and the Enterprises He Created." Newcomen Lecture, November 19, 1953. New York: Newcomen Society in North America, 1953.

Lovett, Robert A. "Forty Years After: An Appreciation of the Genius of Edward Henry Harriman (1848–1909)." Newcomen Lecture, November 17, 1949. New York: Newcomen Society in North America, 1949.

Perry, M. C. "The Enlargement of Geographical Science, a Consequence to the Opening of new Avenues to Commercial Enterprise." Paper read before the American Geographical and Statistical Society, March 6, 1856. New York D. Appleton & Co., 1856.

"Personal Justice Denied." Report of the Commission on Wartime Relocation and Internment of Civilians. Washington, D.C.: December 1982.

Shiels, Archie W. "The Story of Two Dreams. Historical Observations and Original Source Material on Early Plans in England and America for Development of a Trans-Continental Railroad." 2d edition. Bellingham, Washington: Shorey Book Store, 1964.

"Some Ships of the Clipper Ship Era, Their Builders, Owners, and Captains." Boston: State Street Trust Company, 1913.

Sturgis, William. "The Northwest Fur Trade, and the Indians of the Oregon Country, 1788–1830." Boston: Old South Leaflets 219, n.d.

————. "The Oregon Question, Substance of a Lecture before the Mercantile Library Association." Delivered January 22, 1845. Boston: Jordan, Swift, and Wiley, 1845.

Swadling, S. J. "Commercial Supersonic Operation—Ten Years of Experience with Concorde." Society of Automotive Engineers, Inc., 1986.

"Communication of the Hon. William H. Seward, Secretary of State, upon the Subject of an Intercontinental Telegraph Connecting the Eastern and Western Hemispheres by Way of Behring's Strait, etc., in Reply to Hon. Z. Chandler, Chairman of the Committee on Commerce of the U.S. Senate. To Which Was Referred the Memorial of Perry McDonough Collins." Washington, D.C.: Government Printing Office, 1864.

Wallace, Henry A. with Owen Lattimore and John Carter Vincent. "Our Job in the Pacific." New York: Institute of Pacific Relations, Pamphlet #12, 1944.

Whitney, Asa. "To the People of the United States." New York: n.p., 1845.

Articles

Akerson, George E., ed. Frederick R. Neely. "Wing Talk." Collier's, January 5, 1946.

Anon. "American Diplomacy in China." North American Review 89, 185, October 1859.

Anon. "Captain Cleveland's Voyage from China to the Northwest Coast of America." North American Review 25, 57, October 1827.

Athearn, Robert G. "British Impressions of Western Railroad Service, 1869–1900." Pacific Historical Review 20, 4, November 1951.

Bancroft, Frederic. "Seward's Ideas of Territorial Expansion." North American Review 167, 500, July 1898.

Bailey, Thomas A. "Why the United States Purchased Alaska." Pacific Historical Review 3, 1, March 1934.

————. "The World Cruise of the American Battleship Fleet, 1907–1909." Pacific Historical Review 1, 4, December 1932.

Beebe, Lucius. "Pandemonium at Promontory." American Heritage 4, 2, February 1958.

Berglund, Abraham. "The War and Trans-Pacific Shipping." American Economic Review 7, 3, September 1917.

Best, Gary Dean. "James J. Hill's 'Lost Opportunity on the Pacific.' " Pacific Northwest Quarterly 64, 1, January 1973.

Bolkhovitinov, Nikolay N. "The Crimean War and the Emergence of Proposals for the Sale of Russian America, 1853–1861." Pacific Historical Review 59, 1, February 1990.

Boothe, Clare. "Destiny Crosses the Dateline, Report on a Flight Across the Pacific." Life Magazine, November 3, 1941.

Boutwell, George, ed. "Oregon: The Claim of Great Britain." Hunt's Merchants' Magazine 12, 6, June 1845.

Bradley, Harold Whitman. "Hawaii and the American Penetration of the Northeastern Pacific, 1800–1845." Pacific Historical Review 12, 3, September 1943.

Brewington, Marion V. "Maritime Philadelphia 1609–1837." *Pennsylvania Magazine of History and Biography* 2, 63, April 1939.

Broadbridge, Seymour. "Shipbuilding and the State in Japan since the 1850s." *Modern Asian Studies* 2, October 1977.

Brown, Margaret L. "Asa Whitney and His Pacific Railroad Publicity Campaign." *Mississippi Valley Historical Review* 20, 2, September 1933.

Bylinski, Gene. "The 10,000-MPH Airliner." *Fortune*, December 8, 1986.

Carr, John Foster. "Creative Americans: A Great Railway Builder." *Outlook*, October 26, 1907.

Chang, Richard T. "The Failure of the Katsura-Harriman Agreement." *Journal of Asian Studies* 21, 1, November 1961.

Cole, Allan B., ed. "Captain David Porter's Proposed Expedition to the Pacific and Japan, 1815." *Pacific Historical Review* 9, 1, March 1940.

Cole, Terrence. "The Bridge to Tomorrow: Visions of the Bering Strait Bridge." *Alaska History* 5, 2, Fall 1990.

Cotterill, Robert S. "Early Agitation for a Pacific Railroad, 1845–1850." *Mississippi Valley Historical Review* 5, 4, March 1919.

Coughlin, Magdalen. "Commercial Foundations of Political Interest in the Opening Pacific, 1789–1829." *California Historical Society Quarterly* 50, 1, March 1971.

Cushing, Caleb. Review of *Life of Ledyard* by Jared Sparks. *North American Review* 27, 61, October 1828.

"D." "Pacific Airways." *Foreign Affairs* 18, 1, October 1939.

Dana, Jr., Richard Henry. "Cleveland's *Voyages*, Voyage to Canton." *North American Review* 55, 116, July 1842.

———. "Cleveland's Voyages, A Narrative of Voyages and Commercial Enterprises." *North American Review* 55, 116, July 1842.

DeVoto, Bernard. "Geopolitics with the Dew on it." *Harper's Magazine*, March 1944.

DeWindt, Harry. "A Land Journey from Paris to New York." *Harper's Monthly*, April 1902.

Dvoichenko-Markov, Eufrosina. "John Ledyard and the Russians." *Russian Review* 11, 4, October 1952.

Eckener, Hugo. "The First Airship Flight around the World." *National Geographic Magazine* 57, 6, June 1930.

Field, Jr., James A. "Transnationalism and the New Tribe." *International Organization* 25, 3, Summer 1971.

Forbes, Robert Bennet. "Of the Establishment of a Line of Mail Steamers from the Western Coast of the United States on the Pacific to China." *Hunt's Merchants' Magazine* 29, 5, November 1853.

Ford, Alexander Hume. "A Railway across Five Continents." *Independent*, February 1, 1906.

Gibbons, Robert J. "Across the Pacific for 40 Years." *Northwest*, July 1987.

Gilbert, Benjamin Franklin. "The Alaska Purchase." *Journal of the West* 3, 2, April 1964.

Graebner, Norman A. "Maritime Factors in the Oregon Compromise." *Pacific Historical Review* 20, 4, November 1951.

Grey, Jerry. "The Aerospace Plane: The Timing is Right." *Issues in Science and Technology* 3, 3, Spring 1987.

"H. B." "Our Navy: Scraps from the Lucky Bag." *Southern Literary Messenger* 6, 4, April 1840.

Hayes, Aaron A. "China and the United States." *Atlantic Monthly*, May 1887.

Hill, James J. "The Future of Our Oriental Trade." *World's Work* 10, 4, August 1905.

———. "History of Agriculture in Minnesota." Speech given January 18, 1897, Annual Meeting of the Minnesota Historical Society. *Minnesota Historical Society Collections* 8, 1895–98.

Hoyem, Andrew. "Gumshoe! Detectives Real and Imagined." *Bohemian Club Library Notes*, 68, Fall 1991.

Karsten, Peter. "The Nature of 'Influence': Roosevelt, Mahan and the Concept of Sea Power." *American Quarterly* 23, 4, October 1971.

Kastner, Joseph. "The Postwar Air." *Life Magazine*, November 1, 1943.

Kemble, John Haskell. "The Big Four at Sea: The History of the Occidental and Oriental Steamship Company." *Huntington Library Quarterly* 3, 3, April 1940.

————. "Side-Wheelers across the Pacific." *American Neptune* 2, 1, January 1942.

————. "The Transpacific Railroads, 1869–1915." *Pacific Historical Review* 18, 3, August 1949.

Keys, C. M. "The Contest for Pacific Traffic." *World's Work* 10, 4, August 1905.

Kubota, Hideo. "Japan as Top Shipbuilder." *Inside/Outside Japan* 2, 5, June 1993.

Kugler, Richard C. "The Penetration of the Pacific by American Whalemen in the 19th Century." In *The Opening of the Pacific—Image and Reality*. Maritime Monographs and Reports 2. Greenwich, London: National Maritime Museum, 1971.

LaFeber, Walter. "A Note on the 'Mercantilistic Imperialism' of Alfred Thayer Mahan." *Mississippi Valley Historical Review* 48, 4, March 1962.

Lamb, W. Kaye, "The Trans-Pacific Venture of James J. Hill, A History of the Great Northern Steamship Company." *American Neptune* 3, 3, July 1943.

Lanman, James H. "The American Fur Trade." *Hunt's Merchants' Magazine* 3, 3, September 1840.

Larson, Cedric A. "Giant Airships of the Future." *Science Digest* 29, 5, May 1951.

Lattimore, Owen. "New Road to Asia." *National Geographic* 85, 5, December 1944.

Levi, Werner. "American Attitudes toward Pacific Islands, 1914–1919." *Pacific Historical Review* 17, 1, February 1948.

Limerick, Patricia Nelson. "The Final Frontier?" *Wilson Quarterly* 14, 3, Summer 1990.

Lissitzyn, Oliver J. "The Diplomacy of Air Transport." *Foreign Affairs* 19, 1, October 1940.

Lodge, Henry Cabot. "William H. Seward." *Atlantic Monthly*, May 1884.

Loring, Charles G. "Memoir of the Hon. William Sturgis." *Proceedings*, Massachusetts Historical Society, 1863–1864. Boston: The Society, 1864.

Mackinder, Halford J. "The Geographical Pivot of History." *Geographical Journal* 23, 4, April 1904.

McPherson, Hallie. "The Interest of William McKendree Gwin in the Purchase of Alaska, 1854–1861." *Pacific Historical Review* 3, 1, March 1934.

Marx, Leo. "Closely-Watched Trains." *New York Review of Books*, March 15, 1984.

Medbery, James Knowles. "Our Pacific Railroads." *Atlantic Monthly*, December 1867.

Moore, Tui DeRoy. "Guano." *Oceans* 14, 1, January–February 1981.

Morris, James M. "America's Stepchild." *Wilson Quarterly* 11, 3, Summer 1987.

Morton, Louis. "War Plan *Orange*, Evolution of a Strategy." *World Politics* 11, 2, January 1959.

Neumann, William L. "Religion, Morality, and Freedom: The Ideological Background of the Perry Expedition." *Pacific Historical Review* 28, 3, August 1954.

Newhouse, John. "A Sporty Game." *New Yorker*, June 21, 1982.

Parry, Albert. "Yankee Whalers in Siberia." *Russian Review* 5, 2, Spring 1946.

Poinsett, J. R. "Synopsis of the Cruise of the United States Exploring Expedition during the Year 1838, 1839, 1840, and 1841, Delivered before the National Institute by Its Commander, Charles Wilkes, on the twentieth of June, 1842." *North American Review* 56, 119, April 1843.

Pugach, Noel H. "American Shipping Promoters and the Shipping Crisis of 1914–1916: The Pacific & Eastern Steamship Company." *American Neptune* 35, 3, July 1975.

Reingold, Nathan. "Two Views of Maury . . . and a Third." Book reviews. *Isis* 55, 3, 1964.

Rosenthal, Herman. "From New York to Paris by Rail." *Review of Reviews* 33, 5, May 1906.

Saul, Norman E. "An American's Siberian Dream." *Russian Review* 37, 4, October 1978.
Sharrow, Walter G. "William Henry Seward and the Basis for American Empire, 1850–1860." *Pacific Historical Review*, 36, 3, April 1967.
Shewmaker, Kenneth E. "Forging the 'Great Chain'; Daniel Webster and the Origins of American Foreign Policy toward East Asia and the Pacific, 1841–1852." *Proceedings of the American Philosophical Society* 129, 3, September 1955.
Shi, David E. "Seward's Attempt to Annex British Columbia, 1865–1869." *Pacific Historical Review* 47, 2, May 1978.
Sikorsky, Igor. "Sixty Years in Flying." *Aeronautical Journal* 75, 731, November 1971.
Smith, Gaddis. "Agricultural Roots of Maritime History." *American Neptune* 44, 1, January 1984.
Spate, O. H. K. "The Pacific as Artefact." In Niel Gunson, ed., *The Changing Pacific, Essays in Honour of H. E. Maude*. Melbourne: Oxford University Press, 1978.
Stacy, F. N. "Giant Ships for Our Oriental Trade." *American Monthly Review of Reviews* 27, 5, May 1903.
Stefansson, Vilhjalmur. "The Arctic as an Air Route of the Future." *National Geographic* 42, 2, August 1922.
———. "By Air to the Ends of the Earth." *Natural History* 28, 5, September–October 1928.
Stelle, Charles C. "American Trade in Opium to China, prior to 1820." *Pacific Historical Review* 9, 4, December 1940.
Strauss, W. Patrick. "Preparing the Wilkes Expedition: A Study in Disorganization." *Pacific Historical Review* 28, 4, August 1959.
Swisher, Earl. "Commodore Perry's Imperialism in Relation to America's Present-Day Position in the Pacific." *Pacific Historical Review* 16, 1, February 1947.
Ver Steeg, Clarence L. "Financing and Outfitting the First United States Ship to China." *Pacific Historical Review* 22, 1, February 1953.
Vevier, Charles. "The Collins Overland Line and American Continentalism." *Pacific Historical Review* 28, 4, August 1959.
———. "The Open Door: An Idea in Action, 1906–1913." *Pacific Historical Review* 24, 1, February 1955.
Ward, John William. "The Meaning of Lindbergh's Flight." *American Quarterly* 10, 1, Spring 1958.
Wheeler, Mary E. "Empires in Conflict and Cooperation: The 'Bostonians' and the Russian-American Company." *Pacific Historical Review* 15, 4, November 1971.
Williams, Monci Jo. "Why Is Airline Food So Terrible?" *Fortune*, December 19, 1988.
Woodhouse, Samuel W. "The Voyage of the Empress of China." *Pennsylvania Magazine of History and Biography* 63, 4, January 1939.
Yuize, Yasuhiko. "Rice or Wheat?" from the *Tokyo Shimbun*, Asia Foundation Translation Service Center, TSC 1238, October 16, 1989.

Newspapers and Journals

American Museum or Repository of Ancient and Modern Fugitive Pieces, Prose and Poetical
Aviation Week
Boston Globe
Business Week
Congressional Globe
Congressional Record
Debow's
Engineering News
Far Eastern Economic Review
Harper's Monthly

Harvard Magazine
Hunt's Merchants' Magazine
New Horizon
New Yorker
New York Times
Niles Register
North American Review
Pacific Historical Review
Pan American Airways
San Francisco Examiner
Science News Letter
Seattle Times
St. Paul (Minnesota) Pioneer Press
Time Magazine
The United States Magazine and Democratic Review
The Wall Street Journal

Reference

Encyclopedia Britannica. 11th edition.
Historical Statistics of the United States. Washington, D.C.: United States Department of Com-
    merce, September 1975, Bicentennial Edition.
Kodansha Encyclopedia of Japan.
Miles, Edward, et al. *Atlas of Marine Use in the North Pacific Region.* Berkeley: University of
    California Press, 1982.
Schlessinger, Bernard S., and June H. Schlessinger, eds. *The Who's Who of Nobel Prize Win-
    ners.* Phoenix, Arizona: Oryx Press, 1986.

Index

About the Author

JOHN CURTIS PERRY is Henry Willard Denison Professor of History and Director, North Pacific Program, The Fletcher School of Law and Diplomacy, Tufts University. In 1991 the Japanese government awarded an imperial decoration, the Order of the Sacred Treasure, to Perry for "extraordinary contributions to American-Japanese relations."